ORGANIZATIONAL COMMUNICATION

Arnold E. Schneider, Ph.D.
Dean Emeritus
Distinguished Professor of Business
College of Business
Western Michigan University

William C. Donaghy, Ph.D.
Associate Professor
of Communication
The University of Wyoming

Pamela Jane Newman, Ph.D.
Training Consultant
Peat, Marwick, Mitchell & Co.

McGraw-Hill Book Company
New York   St. Louis   San Francisco   Auckland   Düsseldorf   Johannesburg
Kuala Lumpur   London   Mexico   Montreal   New Delhi   Panama   Paris
São Paulo   Singapore   Sydney   Tokyo   Toronto

Library of Congress Cataloging in Publication Data

Schneider, Arnold Edward, date
   Organizational communication.

   Includes bibliographies.
   1. Communication in management. I. Donaghy,
William C., joint author. II. Newman, Pamela Jane,
joint author. III. Title.
HF5718.S3   658.4'5   74-16491
ISBN 0-07-055465-X

ORGANIZATIONAL COMMUNICATION

1234567890 KPKP 798765

This book was set in Helvetica by Black Dot, Inc. The editors were Thomas H. Kothman and Claudia A. Hepburn; the designer was Hartmuth Bender; the production supervisor was Thomas J. LoPinto. The drawings were done by J & R Services, Inc.
Kingsport Press, Inc., was printer and binder.

CONTENTS

Part 2 ORAL COMMUNICATION

PREFACE

This book is basically concerned with the management aspects of communication. Fundamentally, what we are talking about is the human beings who comprise the organization. All of the telephones, all of the typewriters, all of the "squawk boxes," flashing lights, closed-circuit televisions, and all the rest of the communication gadgetry are only for the purpose of assisting human beings in attaining their communicative goals. The objectives and goals of business communication are rather simple. Management, through the organizational communication processes, necessarily needs to get people to receive a message, to interpret it correctly, and, then, to pass it along accurately or to act on it properly. In actual situations this simple process gets thoroughly fouled up. People get the message wrong or they do not get it at all. People misunderstand, they misinterpret, or, what is even worse, they do not go along with the sender of the message as to the end purposes of what needs to be accomplished. A whole series of problems frequently arises out of lack of understanding, misunderstanding, and, finally, not understanding. This is going on all the time, as the following article will demonstrate. What happens in normal day-to-day business and organizational functioning that brings humans to this sad state of affairs? Why are communications so garbled between sender and receiver as to create countless problems and actual breakdown in proper functioning? These problems are in the province of management, and an understanding of them requires an understanding of the nature of communication in the organizational processes.

TALKINGATORTALKINGWITH?[1]

Successful communications to and among
corporate employees cannot be a duty delegated
to an individual or an organization with a fancy
title and then forgotten. Employee information
is everyone's job, and when it isn't, the consequences can be formidable.

Within the greatest communications organization in the world we are hurt and puzzled by a seeming communications failure—the problem of talking with our employees. By all odds, with the media and money at our command, we of all companies should be *the* case history of successful internal communications. No other business has so much communication paraphernalia, technology, and expertise at its command, and probably no other business spends so much time, thought, and money filling pipelines of corporate communications media.

Yet, as we look around us, as we study the effect of this plethora of information, as we dip our toe into the chilly waters of employee attitudes and morale, the evidence is frighteningly consistent that—as is the case with every other large organization—there is a big difference between *information* and *communication*. Our employee body—at all levels—seems, if we can believe the multitude of research at our disposal, more confused, more misinformed, more distrustful, more alienated than ever. Furthermore, as we have

[1]John A. Howland, "Talking At or Talking With?" *Bell Telephone Magazine* (New York: American Telephone & Telegraph Company, March/April 1971), pp. 4–9.

grown in size, in numbers of people, and in complexity of work, this communications gap has geometrically widened.

The fact that we are, perhaps, no worse off then any other comparable organization (perhaps even better) is small comfort. In a corporation of more than a million population, such a gap can be destructive. We should perhaps replace the omnipresent job safety plaque that says, "No Job Is So Important and No Service Is So Urgent . . ." with one that reads, "Communicate or Perish."

Within the Bell System we collectively spend several millions of dollars for employee information through company magazines, employee newspapers, management and employee bulletins, films, CCTV, booklets, discussions, and other orientation programs.

Tons of paper, miles of film and tape—all magnitudes—all shapes—all sizes—all telling the company story—each giving off its own bit of light. All are edited or produced by competent, knowledgeable and professional information people—all working hard (and not necessarily by divine right) on what each feels best for his company.

But what of the collective impact?

Confusion in Communications

Dr. Napoleon N. Vaughn, president of Urban Market Developers, Inc., Philadelphia, recently researched attitudes of employees—mainly minorities, but with all employees as a bench mark—toward internal information media. This qualitative study indicated that most employees—black or white—derive little from employee information that they feel is useful in their jobs and careers.

Vaughn describes our employee communication problem this way:

> The American Telephone and Telegraph Company is the largest communications system in the world, and yet its internal organization suffers outright confusion in the communications area. The irony of the individual employee isolated within the massive system is everywhere apparent. Workers are saturated with the minutiae of their own jobs, while knowledge of related positions and responsibilities is kept in shrouded secrecy. No direct line is open, so the employee is marooned on an island of limited access. The prevailing situation is characterized by cynical resignation. No personal consideration is really expected in a network that is too powerful to be challenged from within.

Black employees at Bell, says Vaughn, feel they are the last ones to know anything. They are forced to move outside of conventional channels of information and turn to their own communications network, the grapevine, which they recognize as unreliable but better than nothing. According to Vaughn, white employees who were surveyed showed little more love for company publications.

Hardly a Measure of Success

This and other surveys indicate that many employees, especially those in nonmanagement and lower management positions, either ignore or at best scan their company bulletins, newspapers, and magazines. Perhaps this is due to a second problem in the dimension of information versus communication, which employee information people do not discount—the question as to whether formal employee information channels (controlled, not free, media) *can* effectively communicate.

To be sure, after spending this time and money, something must be coming out of all this effort. And of course something is. A lot of material *is* real and *is* helpful to the employee or manager. But sometimes it seems that the best that can be said for most of our employee information activity is that it keeps a lot of people employed, and it doesn't seem to do any harm. Hardly a measure of success.

Yet every study taken reinforces the theory that the employee *wants* to know. If the wind is right and the moon in favorable phase, he just might listen and even believe. But to answer the question as to why we seem to fail in our efforts to communicate, we must first, like Alice, ask, "Would you tell me, please, which way I ought to go from here?" To which the Cheshire Cat replied, "That depends a good deal on where you want to get to."

Why *do* we try to communicate within the employee body in the first place? A recent conference of Bell System employee information managers tried to answer that rather unsettling question this way:

> Through formal, organized programs, we try to communi-
> cate with employees in order to promote the welfare and useful-
> ness of the business as a corporate enterprise and to promote
> the welfare and usefulness of employees in the business.

To Build Support and Understanding

Within this broad, overall objective, what are some specific reasons why we try to communicate with employees? The information managers said it was to build support and understanding for company and System goals of providing good service, staying socially viable, technically innovative, and financially sound. They also agreed, or almost agreed, that we try to communicate in order to make employees effective spokesmen for the business in explaining changes—ANC, DDD, EDDD, etc.—and in defending policy—need for deposits, reasonableness of rates, etc. Another reason is to increase employee effectiveness and performance through improved safety, sales expense control, housekeeping, and productivity. Employee information also should attempt to make the business more aware of and responsive to employee needs and desires by serving as a pipeline *up* to management as well as a pipeline *down* to employees. Information channels should serve to satisfy employee needs and desires to be informed on items of interest; to feel "in" on company activities, and to feel their efforts are worthwhile and appreciated. Finally, the managers agreed, information activities should strive to make implementation of basic business changes acceptable and possible by providing employees with knowledge they must have to effect the changes, e.g., building moves, benefit changes and work situation changes such as new hours, etc.

Whether or not this rationale is adequate, I leave to your own judgment, for I suspect that top, middle and first-level management and the body politic all might have different definitions geared to their own vantage point and needs.

But "purpose" is a tough proposition—one of those words that force thinking through.

Simplistically, the purpose of any communications program is, indeed, in support of the purposes of the business itself.

But purpose is double-edged. What of the employee? What is on his mind? What of *his* purpose?

I'm not sure that we know, or that any of our survey takers yet know, or for that matter that even the employee, himself, knows.

There Is No Average Employee

But we do know this: "Employee" too often connotes one amorphous mass to us. And yet we know there is no average employee. He is a conglomerate, an aggregate—functionally, professionally, ethnically, educationally—a company of individual people. We have failed in reaching these *people* probably because the efforts we exert are spent in a something-for-everyone approach that probably fails to satisfy anybody. The need is to communicate locally, personally, and pertinently to the *person*, not to the impersonal employee.

We know about the faceless "they" who run this company—the shadowy forces that skulk behind all management decisions—the "they" who in their perversity ruin otherwise sound plans. No one can ever, of course, pin "them" down. But as an example of this *they* syndrome, we need only look at a recent management attitude pilot study conducted by researcher Stanley Peterfreund for AT&T:

> There's no evidence that management people have a
> consistent awareness of what company goals are, where the
> company is headed or how they fit into the overall scheme.
> There's a view that top executives and those below them
> speak a different language, that each is tuned in to some-
> thing quite different. Some feel their top executives don't
> have an accurate picture of the field because the information
> being fed to them is often watered down.

Little Contact with Executives

> At a more fundamental level, there are examples of
> information breakdowns that have operational consequences.
> "It's not," said some respondents to the survey, "that (we)
> are resistant to change. It's the *company, top management*
> or the *system* that's slow and ponderous in innovating."
> . . . (They!) "Managers have so little direct contact with
> their top executives that they really don't know what the
> executives are thinking, what their plans are."

Our employee information media are *only one dimension,* and a not too satisfactory dimension at best, in this process of communication—a process that includes such intangibles as climate, trust, credibility, integrity, access, personal relationships, levels and other factors. We must keep in mind that our media in their communications dimensions frequently have little relationship to what the employee wants to know or even needs to know just to do his job.

Information versus Communication

Furthermore, whether anything is put out through formal media or not, communications quite obviously is going on—implicitly. Silence communicates, visual impressions communicate, experiences communicate as do the environment and supervision with which every one of us works.

And this is where you—not I as an employee information practitioner—come in.

Peterfreund, who for more than fifteen years has worked closely with the Bell System, as well as many other large clients in this area of employee communications, has said continuously that communications cannot take place unless every manager supports the maintenance of a positive communications climate. By that he means developing a working environment in which every employee has access to the information he needs and wants—an environment in which, when management had something to say, it would be heard and believed. When employees had something to say, there would be somebody listening—not because the book said management *should* listen, but because what was being said was potentially of value and because the person who was communicating was an important member of the company, with a contribution to make. Peterfreund points out, and I suspect he is right, that because each company has a staff group responsible for employee information—at least theoretically experts in their field, putting out technically fine publications, films, presentations, and the like—the rest of management falls into the trap of assuming that the job of *communications* is being done just because we're there— producing *information,* but not necessarily producing communications.

If It's Propaganda, So Be It

In large part, because there are too many in management who assume employees are opposed to company objectives, we communicate, I fear, accordingly. It is almost inevitable that the prophecy becomes fulfilled in these circumstances.

Communication is important because unless people *know* the company objectives, they can't associate them with their own. If conveying the company viewpoint is "propaganda," so be it. We shouldn't apologize for it. We should just do it well.

Communication is important because it's essential to the management of change. Without facts, understanding, and acceptance, efforts to change are doomed to failure. Without well-directed communication, there isn't a chance.

Communication is important because without a communion, a sharing of ideas with others in a mood of mutuality, the gaps will never be bridged. The polarization that seems to plague the Bell System today will only become more pronounced.

So it boils down to this: Communication is *your*—the individual supervisor's—job more than mine or that of my colleagues.

You are the one who must articulate company objectives and develop communications channels that both satisfy management's desire to have its goals known and fulfill the employee's needs as well as his desires to know.

Job-Related Information

Peterfreund has learned in virtually every study he has been associated with, whether for the Bell System or others:

If people feel well informed, their attitudes on every
score tend to be better. Their interest starts high and is
maintained at a high level until they become demotivated
and frustrated.

Their primary interest is in job-related information
—in a very personal sense. They are concerned with
their job, *their* department, *their* growth and advancement
opportunities, the results of *their* work, how well *they're*
doing.

Peterfreund continues:

And it's here that communications most often break
down—right on the job, itself—where the consequences
are tangible. Where new practices and procedures aren't
adequately explained. Where discipline is substituted for
constructive corrective communication. Where barriers
to productivity—and waste—go uncorrected (and often
undetected). Where the supervisor has no time (and
sometimes no interest) in listening, in getting feedback.
We find plenty of "company information"—social news,
peripheral subjects, etc.—but a neglect of the communication about the guts of the work, itself.

Communication is no more important than in times such as these, when job economies,
rigid cost control and cost reductions are sought. According to Peterfreund,

Yet, it's at times like these that communication is
often curtailed, rather than expanded. Unless there is
a mutuality of objectives, you're not going to get the benefit
of your employees' ability to contribute to these objectives.
They start off wanting to, but wind up frustrated and rejected.

It's Your Payoff

It is your job to foster a climate in which employees at every level feel well informed.

It is your job to know what's going on, what people think is really happening "down
there."

No small order, but it's your payoff.

Some fifteen years ago William H. Whyte wrote a series of articles for *Fortune* magazine
called "Is Anybody Listening?" which dealt with this and other communications problems.
He said:

Only with trust can there be any real communication,
and until that trust is achieved, the techniques and gadgetry
of communication are so much wasted effort. Study after
study has pointed to the same moral: If management does
not enjoy confidence, it has itself to blame. Either its
policies have not been such as to be proof against animadversions
or, more frequently, it does not realize that resentment and
suspicion exist at all. It is easy for management to overlook
this suspicion, for it will feel that company policies do not
warrant any. They may not. But because of an absence of real
communication, the present executives may be unaware of the

fact that a stereotype born of policies long since past is still
haunting their shop.

It may be reassuring to be reminded by that fifteen-year-old article that our predecessors were no wiser than we. But it also indicates we have not learned much in the intervening years.

And I would suspect that by his reference to "management," Whyte did not mean "they."

"If the people around you are spiteful and callous, and will not hear you," wrote Dostoevski in *The Brothers Karamazov,* "fall down before them and beg their forgiveness; for in truth you are to blame for their not wanting to hear you."

Arnold E. Schneider
William C. Donaghy
Pamela Jane Newman

INTRODUCTION

CHAPTER 1

MAN, COMMUNICATION, AND THE ORGANIZATION

Of all the achievements of mankind the communicative art is the most dramatic and the most fundamental. Man has the ability to think in the abstract, and this priceless possession has been translated into the manifold gifts of civilization as we all know it through the transmission of human thought and the application of all facets of the communication processes, oral or written. All aspects of knowledge—the sciences, the arts, history, and geography—as well as organizational relationships and governmental and legal relationships, are gathered, stored, refined, and transmitted through language processes.

It would appear that so vital a factor as the methodology employed in transmission of thought, current and past, would have received man's undivided attention over the centuries. Strange as it may seem, it has been only during the last two or three decades that we have begun to study the very process by which we communicate these thoughts, understand, create and re-create ideas, all to the end of moving forward the vastness of our enterprises which we label with the general term "civilization." Civilization and humanity are reflected through the capacity to communicate, which is one of the chief attributes of the human race. Through the communication arts, unscientifically developed as they are in the world, and with as many difficulties as we encounter in meaning, usage, and interpretation, we have nevertheless been able not only to profit from the past experiences of the human race, but also to move forward as each generation builds upon the contributions of its predecessors. Alfred Korzybski, one of the pioneer semanticists, stated in *Science and Sanity*, "Language is time-binding."[1] What he meant by this is that the communicative processes are a unique ingredient in that they permit man to use and reuse in the present the experiences of others not only in the past but in a broad-range present. Irving Lee has stated this fact in the following words: "Men can draw from the *past*, in and through the *present*, and make ready for the *future*. The experience of the race can be accumulated, worked over, magnified, and transmitted."[2] We are able to do this because we have the capacity to use *symbols*.

COMMUNICATION, THE BEHAVIORAL SCIENCES, AND INDUSTRY

A number of academic disciplines have through the years undertaken the thorough study of man as a dynamic organism and as an instrument acting and interacting with the social forces that surround him. Included in these disciplines are: psychology, biology, physiology, sociology, communication, and group dynamics, as well as the related fields of psychiatry, human anthropology, education, and, finally, cultural and ecological sciences.

These fields of learning, when and as they bear upon man, as a total ongoing, dynamic, functioning entity, have been given the descriptive term "the behavioral sciences." The behavioral sciences are devoted to research and study of people as vital forces in relation to themselves and others within the environment in which they live and work. As the work of the social scientists is interpreted for application in the fields of business, industry, and government, we are discovering that human thought, human action, human aspirations, and human behavior are all catalyzed by the communicative processes of speech, language, and written reports. Human actions, which result from communication input and communication perception, result in behavior that affects productive effort toward reaching the goals of the organization. Communication, then, which in a way is an abstraction or subjective, may be more critical to end results in organizations than many of the so-called concrete or objective factors. Researchers have discovered that how people feel about their work, the information they receive from their coworkers and their supervisors, along with their relationships with their coworkers, may be more important to the final productive efforts than are such obvious concrete factors as materials, light, heat, and ventilation or wage-salary structures, job routines, and work-flow processes.

Several decades ago this nation suffered a catastrophic event which has since been labeled "the Great Depression." A few years before the Depression gripped us in its relentless icy clutches, it was believed that if we could solve the production problems which are inherent in a large-scale, highly diversified type of economic society, we then could solve all the other problems rather handily. Since then we have developed our technological capability and our productive processes to a very sophisticated level, but in so doing management has discovered another very disconcerting fact—one with which management was not prepared to cope. A new ingredient in the productive process of industry was isolated and found to be a fundamental factor. The discovery was that engineering efficiency or marketing efficiency or information-processing efficiency is vitally affected by "human engineering"—or human relations, if one wishes to use a commonly accepted term. Stated simply, this means that human beings working alone or in groups are more than mere cogs in wheels. They are forces in and of themselves who can create or destroy morale, who can be motivated to outstanding effort and loyalty, or who may merely lend their nervous systems to the tasks at hand in a foot-dragging, dispirited, lackadaisical fashion. Human beings make the difference between those organizations that are alive, vital, and dynamic and those that merely get by. The behavioral

4

scientists have discovered that humans as acting and interacting organisms are motivated or debilitated, made loyal or disloyal, interested or alienated, by the kind of communication they receive, understand, and, finally, accept and by their capacity to interpret communications in terms of their own objectives, interests, needs, and desires.

The behavioral sciences in general have given us an insight into a number of intangible yet critical processes of management which are fundamentally related to the communicative processes. Among these are:

1. The nature of morale as a productive force.
2. The grapevine as a communication tool and its effect on work processes and morale.
3. Employee attitudes as an outcome of communication input.
4. Motivation as a managerial responsibility imbedded in organizational communication.
5. The role of communication in employee development and growth.
6. The role of the communicative activities in developing the corporate image internally and externally.
7. Public relations as a total act of communicative processes.
8. Communication as a method for orientation to and indoctrination of organizational goals.
9. The need for continual restructuring and reinforcement of the human relationships within an organization.
10. The continuing need for goals and objectives to be communicated on a planned basis.
11. The need to maintain management's communication channels at all times and at every level.
12. The need at times to circumvent formal organizational communication channels with informal contacts.
13. The need to have people through the communication processes made a recognized part of the organization.
14. The need to reward individual achievement and to give it recognition among many employees.

THE COMMUNICATIVE ASPECTS OF BUSINESS

If you had the capacity to dissect the activities of any large, ongoing service, manufacturing, or financial organization and to hold these activities in suspension for research purposes, you would discover that throughout the day the process of *communication* was the most consistent activity of all the undertakings. This process is intertwined and interwoven throughout the entire web and woof of the organizational activities and touches everyone, from the president, vice president, or general manager down through to the mail messenger. These communication activities run through every department, whether it be line or staff, and flow through all segments of the operation. If you were to stride rapidly through an organization, you would see people communicating in every possible situation with every possible technique and device. People would be talking to one another face to face; people would be visiting via the telephone; people would be dictating messages; and vast numbers of people would be engaged in reading information from printed forms and memoranda. In

5

addition, a whole series of machines would be abstracting information from forms and memos and entering data for permanent recording on IBM cards or magnetic tape. In other rooms one could find groups of people "talking it over." Some would be listening, others would be speaking, and still others might be taking notes on what was being said. In fact, at times business seems to be one vast panorama of individuals and groups communicating with one another through every possible medium and device.

This communication activity is a fundamental characteristic of the business enterprise. It uses up a large portion of management time and effort. Yet it has remained one area which has only recently received recognition and which has slowly yielded itself to study and analysis upon the part of management practitioners in the hopes of refinement and improvement. The need for improvement in this fundamental managerial skill area has been receiving increasing recognition as management diagnosticians have been discovering that ineffective communications cause problems, increase costs, decrease morale, slow down sales, act as a drag upon efficiency, and, finally, create barriers to managerial aspirations. Management consultants in general and communication specialists in particular have been discovering that communication is one of the prime areas for improving the effectiveness of the business organization and of the individuals associated with the organization.

It is well recognized by management theoreticians and practitioners that communication is a fundamentally important factor in effective management. Awareness of communication, per se, as one of the basic management ingredients dates back only to recent decades. There are a number of reasons why this important aspect of management has received increasing recognition. Chief among the reasons may be cited such factors as the increasing complexity of the business structure, depersonalization of the work force, the development of behavioral sciences, the development of the science of communication, including semantics, the increasing role of professionalization of the managerial function, the need for meeting employee aspirations, and, finally, the demands upon the organization to communicate with its customers, the general public, and the vast number of governmental agencies on the local, state, and national levels.

BUSINESS ORGANIZATION AND COMMUNICATION

Shown on page 7 is a "typical" business organization chart. On the surface, this seems to visualize adequately the various functions, responsibilities, and activities of the various segments of the business. In actual practice, however, this organization chart is only an inert, lifeless, schematic attempt to portray how the founders *hope* the business will operate. Someone must put the organization plan into operation, and once this is done, it then becomes an active, ever-changing, ever-reforming type of ceaseless activity. The ingredients that make the business organization alive, effective, and dynamic lie in the realm of communication. *Communication is to the business organization what electrical current is to a wiring system.* Communication is the activating force. The wires in an electrical system are in and of themselves inert objects, their chief function being to carry the current, which in turn operates the electrical appliance at the receiving end of the system. In the same manner the act of communication activates the business organization. What gets done or does not get done or gets done incorrectly stems from the original communication efforts of those

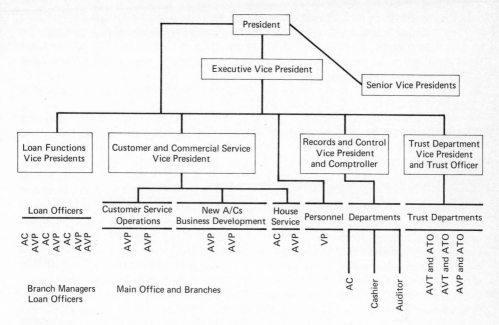

Figure 1-1 **Actual Bank Organization Chart**

who are the communicators to those who are the receivers of the communication and who interpret correctly or incorrectly that which needs to be accomplished.

If one were to attempt to visualize the importance of communication in the business world, one would need only to imagine a world in which communication, as a function of business, were to cease. We then quickly see that in reality all activities of the business world hinge on communication—oral or written, formal or informal, stated or implied.

In reviewing the practice of communication as it relates to the activities of the business firm we can say, among other things, that:

1. The establishment of objectives is the first act of management.
2. The development of an "organization" is the fundamental strategy through which management hopes to achieve its objectives.
3. In reality *people* are the organization and bring to life the various organizational arrangements.
4. The act of communication is the electrical current which generates and sustains all relationships within the business structure.
5. *Management* is in essence the act of communication, for management processes are linked to the receipt of information and its valid interpretation which results in effective decision making. Such decisions are then communicated through the organization so that proper action may be taken at the proper levels.
6. Communication input is a primary function of management.
7. Communication input units require planning, thought, and careful review to the same extent as other basic policy considerations of the organization. They cannot be left to chance factors.
8. Communication activities constitute the prime methodology for "change agent" effects.

7

9. Information and communication are two aspects of what appears to be a similar function, but they are different and must be treated by management as such.
10. Communication is too important a function for management to leave it entirely to amateurs.

COMMUNICATION WITHIN THE ORGANIZATION

Normal Routine Communication Processes

A large part of the activity of information gathering, recording, storing, and transmitting can logically fall under the heading of *routine* information processing. Modern organizations have undertaken analytical studies in the effort to systematize the volume of information that is normally processed through the organization and that has to do with the everyday ordering of the business activities. EDP, or electronic data processing, represents one of the major attempts to systematize large amounts of information and store it for the purposes of use when it is needed by management. In this connection it may be stated that the function of information processing on this level has a threefold objective:

1. Historical
   a. Collection of relevant data
   b. Processing of data
   c. Storing of data
2. Analytical (or interpretative)
3. Decision making
   a. Comparative judgments
   b. Interpretative judgments

Routine information has to do with, for example, sales volume of a particular item, cost of manufacturing a particular part, number of items on hand, number of items that will be needed, the number of orders that have come in, and the number of items covered in each order. Routine information arises out of such forms as:

Sales order
Purchase order
Manufacturing order
Inventory records
Time cards
Cost records
Work in process records
Shipping order
Receiving receipts
Quality control records
Production scheduling records
Maintenance records

When these are all added together, analyzed, related, dissected, and viewed in varying frames of reference, we arrive at the usages of routine information in the managerial processes for decision making.

Management is concerned with the methods employed for processing routine communications because it is aware that information is a prelude to judgment, and judgment is fundamental to decision making. All information processing is predicated upon its:

1. Relevance
2. Timeliness
3. Accuracy

It is apparent that information that is not relevant is worthless; that if information is not received in time for proper analysis, it may be too late to be effective; and, finally, if information is not accurate, it may be worse than no information at all.

Those who are responsible to management for the collecting, processing, storing, and compiling of routine data governing business operations have a responsibility to the organization for assisting in making the following types of information-processing determinations:

1. What types of information might be developed that will best assist management in its critical decision making?
2. How best might this information be communicated?
3. How best might this information be systematized?
4. How best might this information be coordinated?

Normal Oral and Written Communication Processes

In addition to the ongoing *information processing* which is in constant operation throughout the organization, there are the oral and written communication activities such as those listed below:

ORAL COMMUNICATION PROCESSES
1. Conferences
2. Conventions
3. Face-to-face conversations
4. Formal speeches
5. Phone conversations
6. Staff meetings
7. Committees
8. Orientation programs
9. Training courses
10. Radio
11. Blackboard presentations
12. Television

WRITTEN COMMUNICATION PROCESSES
1. Written memoranda
2. Reports
   a. Research reports
   b. Special reports
   c. Monthly reports
   d. Accounting reports
   e. Progress reports
   f. Interim reports

9

3. Telegrams
4. Letters
5. Employee newspaper
6. Plant magazine
7. Bulletins
8. Annual reports
9. Stockholder reports

This list is not all-inclusive. Other processes may be added to the list, such as executive seminars and presentations by marketing or research groups. It is also apparent to the astute communication student that at times combinations of these methods may be employed, as in conferences where a secretary is appointed to take the minutes of the meeting for the purpose of the record and to further inform the members of the committee as to the action which has been agreed upon.

THE STRUCTURE OF COMMUNICATION

Communication as it is related to the business organization may also be classified in terms of its structural arrangements.

Administrative or Formal Communication

Administrative communication deals with all forms of communication, oral and written, actual or implied, that are related to the organizational hierarchy. Most major corporations have policy manuals covering every facet of organization. We may find policy manuals covering:

1. Manufacturing processes
2. Purchasing regulations
3. Personnel relations
4. Travel expense
5. Investments
6. Sales programs
7. Advertising relations
8. Public relations
9. Accounting practices
10. Legal relationships
11. Foreign operations
12. Research activities

Administrative communication is related to the organizational hierarchy and assumes the flow of orders, directives, and control media from higher-level management down to those individuals who will be controlled and guided by these directives in the execution of their responsibilities and their tasks and in their reports back to the hierarchy that the job has been accomplished.

Interpersonal or Informal Communication

In addition to downward and upward communications, all organizations abound with what is called *interpersonal* or *informal* communication. This communication is generally conducted between peer groups, but it may involve levels of higher authority as well as subordinate levels. Communication of this type, usually on the oral plane, may cover work processes, questions, and training interpretation as well as mere human intercourse. That great American institution known as *the coffee break* abounds with the opportunity for individuals to relate to others on a personal level. In general, communication of this type, whether it is work- or social-related, is considered to be carried out on a horizontal plane.

Communication Flow

In general, administrative communication is considered to be downward, and one of the chief criticisms of communicating systems in large or formal organizations is that *all* communications flow downward. In fact, most writers in the field point out that one of the major problems is the distortion or blocking that can occur at each managerial level. Each of us tends to hear that which we wish to hear, and in the repeating of the information we tend to bring to it normal distortions in terms of our ability to understand, comprehend, relate, communicate, visualize, and interpret the message. The phenomenon of loss of meaning or clarity or preciseness of a message during transmission from one human to another or from a group of humans to another group or individual is known as *entropy*. This concept embraces the idea that distortion tendencies are going on not only in the physical conditions of the senders but in the physical, emotional, and psychological receptivity of the receiver. As we shall see in the next chapter, communication is a highly complex activity which involves the whole range of our capacity to relate to all of the phenomena that surround us.

Sophisticated managers are aware that two-way communication is essential to the health of the organization. They are vitally concerned with maintaining an upward flow of communications. Most of the routine information processing which is carried on within the organization does move upward in that it finally does come to rest upon higher management's desk for the crucial task of decision making. It is only in the more abstract areas of morale, feeling, tone, understanding, and interpretation that we find difficulty in creating continuing and stable channels for its upward flow. Many organizations have sought to overcome this handicap through communication training for first-line supervisors, through morale surveys, and through open discussion meetings in which management attempts to meet the questions of employees. In fact, the annual stockholders' meeting is in essence a two-way device permitting management to communicate directly to the stockholders and the stockholders to ask of management those questions which they deem pertinent.

One of the major formal devices instituted by management to encourage creativeness and the upward flow of information governing the work processes is the suggestion system. This is a formalized attempt to give recognition to the fact that employees have sound ideas, and that they need a channel through which they can express these ideas directly to those most concerned without bumping into the normal communication barriers that exist at each managerial level.

COMMUNICATION AS A
COST FACTOR

Certain aspects of communication activities within an organization are measurable in terms of cost. One can tote up the total telephone bills for a period of time and can add up such charges as cables, telegrams, and postage. Shown on page 12 is a 11 statement covering telephone communication cost savings in a national organization. There are other items of expense in relationship to communication which do not lend themselves to cost analysis quite so readily. For example, how much of a junior executive's time, office cost, and secretarial cost can be attributed to any specific phase of his or her communication activities?

REDUCTION OF TELEPHONE COSTS[3]

The communications division recently conducted a thorough study of the various telephone systems in the Home Office. This study revealed several areas where we could save money without eliminating any necessary service. We are passing this information on to you with the thought that your office might benefit from this type of survey.

There are several areas which should not be overlooked when considering ways to reduce telephone costs. One area is telephone company-installed buzzer systems for which a recurring charge is made. In each case where additional charges for buzzer systems are incurred, we recommend that a company-owned buzzer system be installed. A push button, buzzer, and transformer can be purchased for $2.59. Once the initial installation cost has been absorbed, the annual savings would be approximately $7.20 per unit (based on our local telephone company rates). To illustrate the potential savings that can be made, installing 25 company-owned buzzer systems will reduce Home Office telephone costs $180 annually.

A second area which should be carefully considered is multiple-line telephones. In many cases a less expensive model or type can be substituted without affecting the quality of service to any extent. For example, changing 63 telephones in the Home Office will result in an annual savings of over $1,200, yet the quality of service will remain about the same. Most of the telephones involved are General Telephone Company "type 47" and will be replaced by their "type 85D" (Bell Company equivalent HCK-1). For those who are not familiar with General Telephone Company instruments, the "type 47" and the "85D" are both key-type telephones. The "type 47" is capable of picking up two lines and holding both lines. If necessary, a third line or intercom line, without the hold feature can be added. In practically all cases the "type 47" is being used to pick up two lines or one line plus an intercom line. The "type 85D" can pick up two lines but can hold only one; or, if desired, pick up one line, hold this line, and have intercom. The only disadvantage to the "type 85" versus the "type 47" is not being able to hold both lines. We do not anticipate this being any real problem since the employees involved seldom find it necessary to hold both lines. It should be pointed out that one line being in use will in no way interfere with the second line being available for incoming or outgoing calls. The savings per telephone will be $1.65 a month; with intercom, $2 a month. (Again, this is based on local rates.) In some instances a comparable or even greater savings can be made by replacing other key-type telephones.

A third area to consider is nonessential telephones and lines. In addition to removing telephones which are obviously not needed, such as one seldom used, a good look should be taken at areas where extension phones and lines are installed mostly for convenience. An example of this might be extension telephones on secretaries' desks. As you know, the secretary's desk is usually located directly in front of the supervisor and frequently both have a telephone. In many cases, the secretary's telephone can be eliminated without having any appreciable effect in terms of efficiency. This would mean the secretary would simply turn around (in some cases move her chair a foot or so) to answer her supervisor's telephone. We admit this could cause some inconvenience; however, the annual savings will more than justify any slight inconvenience. To illustrate the potential savings that can be made in this area; removing thirteen telephones and three connected lines will reduce Home Office telephone costs over $400 annually.

There may be a question in your mind as to whether installation charges would justify the changes discussed in this article. It is estimated that in most cases the savings realized will offset installation charges in three to four months. For example, the cost of changing the 63 Home Office telephones will be approximately $285. This is based on the standard change rate of $6 for the first telephone and $4.50 for the others. It is probable that the cost would be less if done on telephone company overtime (on overtime, we pay for only the time used, rather than paying a flat rate per instrument).

We realize that many different telephone companies are dealt with throughout our network of regional offices, and as a result, the types of key telephones in use, associated equipment, rates, etc., will vary from one office to another. The point is, there may be an area in your office where a company buzzer system can be installed, a telephone removed, or a less expensive telephone may be available that will do the job just as well. Needless to say, a few dollars saved in each office means many dollars saved companywide.

Assistant Superintendent—Communications

Intangible Communication Costs

What is of even more importance than the obvious costs as illustrated above is the continuing costs which arise from communications which have failed, from inept communication, and, finally, from misunderstood communication. Errors, poor performance, misunderstandings, and many other problems may arise out of ineffective communication. Communication takes place with every action, every word, every statement—oral or written—which management makes. It may sound like a dramatic statement, but, nevertheless, it is accurate to say that communication in all of its forms and aspects is one of the critical activities of the organization. The ability of management to communicate goals, aims, methods, techniques, and objectives, and the ability of the members of the organization to interpret and act upon communication, may frequently spell the difference between average performance and great performance or, in fact, the difference between success and failure. Organizing, planning, directing, controlling, and evaluating, in all of their ramifications, have their lifelines firmly rooted in the organizational heartbeat of communication.

MAN, SYMBOLS, AND SEMANTICS

The function of a course in organizational communication involves teaching those who are to exercise a leadership role to understand the complexities of the task that faces them. The neophyte manager undertakes tasks with a number of competencies at hand, for example, a specific knowledge of the task to be performed, adeptness in learning new tasks, and a learned response to the meaning of the task in relationship to the work that has to be performed. The responsible person, however, is first, foremost, and always a communicator. Paul Pigors, in *Effective Communication in Industry*, stated, "As a key member in modern scientific management, the foreman's chief task is to serve as a communication center."[4] As one moves up each successive step in the organization hierarchy, the need for communication skills becomes increasingly more evident. Perhaps one could generalize to the effect that those who possess unique communication skills are most likely to move up the managerial ladder.

It should be further noted that modern technology has created islands of specialized knowledge with a specialized language to express that knowledge. In your own experience, you possibly have discovered that engineers speak one language, **13** accountants another, lawyers still another, labor negotiators still another, and so on ad infinitum. To get the job done, specialists have to talk to other specialists, engineers to production people, marketing personnel to research test people, and all must understand one another. Above all, general management has to understand the specialists and be able to communicate with every facet of the complex organization in order to achieve organizational goals and objectives.

Symbol Systems

The human nervous system is uniquely adaptable to receiving, analyzing, storing, recalling, and reacting with a programmed or unprogrammed response. It can, in fact, react totally through a verbal, pictorial, or action signal. Our most common communication system is based on words as behavior signals. The words may be verbal or written. This is a word culture, and words can even call up responses to things that do not exist in reality. "Peace" is a word. "Hate" is a word. "Love" is a word. These are abstractions which become real through the responses created by the stimulus of the word symbol.

All of us have been using symbols throughout our entire life. In fact, our life style, our behavior, and the meaning of our lives are all symbol-controlled, symbol-motivated, and symbol-evaluated. Therefore, in a study of communication, we first need to understand the meaning of *symbols*. S. I. Hayakawa defines symbols as "things-that-stand-for-other-things" and says that "the process by means of which human beings can arbitrarily make certain things *stand for* other things may be called the symbolic process."[5] "Semantics," according to John C. Condon, Jr., "is the study of how persons respond to words and other symbols."[6] Technically defined, *semantics* is the science of symbol meanings.

Symbols as Adaptive Behavior

E. T. Hall in *The Silent Language* referred to symbols as a learning mechanism in the following way:

> Warm-blooded animals obviously needed some other adaptive technique because of offspring. They grew to depend more and more on learning as an adaptive device. Learning really came into its own as an adaptive mechanism when it could be *extended in time and space by means of language*. A fawn can learn about men with guns by the reaction of its mother when a man with a gun appears, but there is no possible way, lacking language, for that fawn to be forewarned in the absence of an actual demonstration. Animals have no ways of *symbolically storing* their learning against future needs.[7]

Animals, including man, survive not only because they may have sharper teeth or keener vision or protective coloring or a faster birthrate or quicker feet or larger size, but more because they are able to adapt to a changing environment. A raccoon which at one time had to hunt for its food is able to survive in a mechanized culture because it has learned to raid garbage cans, while the dinosaur died off because it was not able to make crucial life-saving adaptations. If conditions change too much, however, the raccoon will join the dinosaur, because its adaptive potential is limited to a narrow scale. Humans have survived and will probably survive longer than any of the other animals because they are the most adaptive; and this adaptation is a result of what, as we have noted, Korzybski has called "the time-binding effect of language." Humans can think through the use of symbols and language. Thinking requires symbolism and language, and the more highly developed the symbolic capacity of the animal, the more adaptable it becomes. Many animals have ingenious ways of filtering or warning of danger, and some chimps have even learned several dozen different symbols; but linking together possible symbolic responses is far beyond the brightest ape. As we will see in more detail later, this symbolic capacity is a mixed blessing. It has allowed people to walk on the moon and under the sea, but it has also made us afraid to walk in many sections of our own community. It has allowed us to make the biggest technological advances ever imagined in the world, but it has failed us in our attempts to make peace with ourselves and in the world at large.

Symbols, Signs, and Their Development

Nonhuman animals respond to *signs*, that is, something that stands in a one-to-one relationship with something else. For example, if a dog hears the sound "Heel," it will respond in the only way it has been taught. We can interpret that sound in many ways, as something on the bottom of our shoe, or as a reference to someone of low character. Humans are capable of responding to either signs or symbols. Animals respond only to signs. Humans can make a symbol stand for anything they want it to; it can even take the place of reality. We grow up learning to respond to different symbols (and signs). We learn these responses or meanings for symbols through the process of identification. We select certain people in our environment whom we like or identify with, usually our parents at first and later our companions, teachers, bosses, etc., and try to determine their meanings for certain symbols. A parent says the word "milk" and gives the child a bottle of white fluid. The child may also call the bottle, when it is empty, "milk," but through the process of elimination with cups of milk and spilled milk, the child soon learns the proper response or meaning for the term. At each stage of life we need our symbol meanings because they provide us with an anchor or reference point. In one of his text chapters entitled "Meaning Is as Meaning Does," Professor Condon says:

> Language is personal. Learned through imitating sounds that are associated with things, our language is our own, determined by the training, whims, and historical accidents of our culture, community, family. To the extent that each person's associations and experiences are different, each person's language is a little different. Words of one speaker may sound very much like those of another. Object referents may be similar for many persons, but the experiences that determine the meaning (in response) can never be quite the same for any two people. If we recognize the arbitrary manner in which we have learned our language, we should be freer to change those semantic habits that, although they "made sense" to us as children, no longer seem sensible in light of additional experiences and increased understanding. Language is personal, but the "personality" of language should change as we do, and as our knowledge does.[8]

Symbols and Their Referents

What, in essence, we have been saying about symbols is that they allow us to think and communicate about things, people, events, etc., without having to carry the actual object of discussion around with us. S. I. Hayakawa developed the often cited analogy to a map and territory, saying that symbols are like maps which represent 15

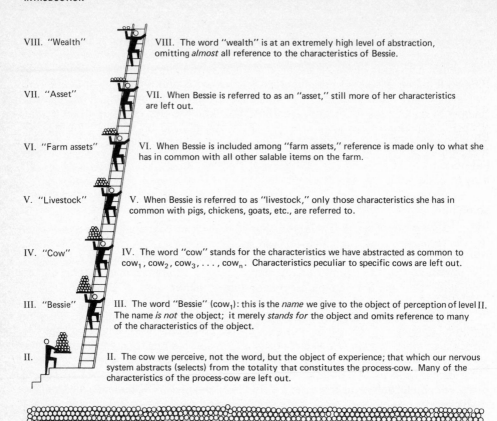

VIII. "Wealth"   VIII. The word "wealth" is at an extremely high level of abstraction, omitting *almost* all reference to the characteristics of Bessie.

VII. "Asset"   VII. When Bessie is referred to as an "asset," still more of her characteristics are left out.

VI. "Farm assets"   VI. When Bessie is included among "farm assets," reference is made only to what she has in common with all other salable items on the farm.

V. "Livestock"   V. When Bessie is referred to as "livestock," only those characteristics she has in common with pigs, chickens, goats, etc., are referred to.

IV. "Cow"   IV. The word "cow" stands for the characteristics we have abstracted as common to cow_1, cow_2, cow_3, ..., cow_n. Characteristics peculiar to specific cows are left out.

III. "Bessie"   III. The word "Bessie" (cow_1): this is the *name* we give to the object of perception of level II. The name *is not* the object; it merely *stands for* the object and omits reference to many of the characteristics of the object.

II.   II. The cow we perceive, not the word, but the object of experience; that which our nervous system abstracts (selects) from the totality that constitutes the process-cow. Many of the characteristics of the process-cow are left out.

I. The cow known to science: ultimately consisting of atoms, electrons, etc., according to present-day scientific inference. Characteristics (represented by circles) are infinite at this level and ever changing. This is the *process level*.

Figure 1-2 **Abstraction Ladder**[9]

some actual physical territory but are not themselves the territory. If the map (or symbol) is accurate, it allows us to deal with the territory efficiently, but if it is inaccurate or outdated, it could cause us much confusion and difficulty. We manage to get inaccurate symbols in a number of ways, but the most common seems to be selective misperception or inaccurate abstraction, either of what someone is telling us or of the environment itself.

It certainly would be impossible to encompass all of the myriad diversity of one's actual environment in the symbols used to represent that environment. One must, therefore, abstract or select certain features of the environment upon which to focus and choose to neglect the rest. You might, for example, be working in your office composing a letter when the secretary walks in and says something; at first the message will be unheard because you have been filtering out all extraneous sources of noise which could affect your concentration upon the letter. Although he/she may get a little peeved, the secretary would have to repeat the message before it would actually be communicated, since there is no communication without reception.

One more interesting point must be made here about symbols and the concrete or abstract things they represent. Professor Hayakawa and other general semanticists have, for many years, talked about symbols and things (in the "real" world) as if they were mutually exclusive. With his "ladder" of abstraction, Hayakawa endeavors to make the point that symbols begin at the third level while objects begin at the perception and microscopic levels (II and I, respectively) and exist separate and apart from those who talk about them. Dorothy Lee, the anthropologist, along with Professor John Condon and the authors of this text tend to disagree somewhat with that simplistic distinction. We may get somewhat mixed up in our own language here, but perhaps the disagreement can be made clear. It is of critical importance if one is truly to understand the nature of symbolism.

By giving an object a name, we have, in a sense, "created" that object. No doubt something existed before there was a symbol to represent it, but, to quote Dorothy Lee, "They are interdependent, incapable of existence apart from and without the act of the individual."[10] The symbols we have chosen to represent the "things" of the world actually structure our perception of that world whether we use our eye or a microscope. We cannot "see" what we cannot symbolize. Because of our cultural heritage we have chosen to symbolize some parts of the environment and not others. Lee notes her finding in her work with other cultures that many do not have a symbol for "pencil" but might react to the pencil as a means of pointing; that then a suffix would be added to the verb, "to point," which would indicate pointing with a long, thin instrument, which could be a pencil or any number of other things. In this case, "pencil" would have no special meaning different from other thin objects, would be abstracted out of the perceptual field, and thus would not exist for that individual.

> This attitude cannot be overemphasized, for it is popularly thought that somehow the scientist (or worse, Science) sees the world "as it really is!" Superstitions or misinformed ideas about the scientist in his laboratory portray him as one without bias, without perceptual distortions, characteristics of the rest of us poor souls. But this is not so. The scientist no more sees what is "really there" than does a mystic or poet or taxi driver.[11]

The Abstraction Process

While we have the Hayakawa abstraction ladder before us, and since we have attacked it somewhat, let's discuss some of its valid points regarding symbolism and semantics. Levels III through VIII on the abstraction ladder illustrate how many degrees of specification we have in our complex symbol system. We have symbols that stand for symbols. A company's stock, for example, stands for the money it is worth, which in turn stands for the possible items one could buy with the money. In a very real sense we live in two different worlds, the extensional world of objects, people, and events and a symbolic world of abstractions labeled by words and representations. Many semanticists go so far as to imply that people are either intentionally or extensionally oriented, that is, they operate either from a base of low-level abstraction close to reality or from a high-level conceptualization some distance from reality.

The terms "extensional" and "intentional" can also apply to the meaning of symbols. Hayakawa talks about extensional meaning as the connotative characteristics of the symbol—what it connotes in the "real" world, the kind of meaning one finds in a dictionary. In this sense, then, *intentional meaning* refers to the connotative aspects of a symbol, the individual meanings of that symbol, because of the past   **17** experiences of the individual with that symbol and the things it represents. The term "merger," for example, is defined denotatively as a "statutory combination of two or more corporations by the transfer of the properties to one surviving corporation,"[12] but for an employee whose job is in jeopardy, the word connotes a great deal more: in fact may connote personal disaster due to the machinations of big-business wheeling and dealing.

Stereotyping

It would be impossible for us to communicate with anywhere near the facility we now have if we did not have the capability for symbolizing on many different levels. If this were not so, we would have to have a special name for every possible individual event to which we could possibly react. These same high-level abstractions, however, provide us with the frame of reference which leads to stereotyping. We don't need to know all teenage drivers or all Italians or all corporation presidents to prejudge them. All we need to know is one or two such people, and then we can generalize, that is, go up the ladder of abstraction and have a field day in lumping them all together. "When you've seen one, you've seen them all." The secret in using the abstraction process legitimately is always knowing at what level the communication process is taking place. This, coupled with constant checking at a lower level of abstraction, will assist in preventing the use of stereotyping as a semantic trap.

The second cause of stereotyping, according to Alfred Korzybski, is the subject-predicate structure of our language, which he claims is derived chiefly from the Aristotelian "is of identity."[13] The "is of identity" allows one to make value judgments without qualifying them. Statements like "The boy *is* strong," "Athletes *are* dumb," and "War *is* hell" are all examples of how a subject-predicate language regards objects as static, and the "is of identity" allows one to consider all objects of a certain class as identical. This results in the tendency to stress similarities and ignore differences. Along with the "is of identity," Korzybski also attacked the Aristotelian "law of the excluded middle." According to Korzybski, it says in effect that whatever is, is itself absolutely and there is no middle ground—a thing either is or is not. A thing is either black or white, good or bad, or true or false, and shades of gray, goodness, and falsity are impossible. Obviously, this kind of orientation leads us to rigidity, totalitarianism, and authoritarianism. This kind of thinking leads one to make what the semanticists call *signal reactions*, that is, reacting to a symbol (with many meanings) as if it were a sign (with only one meaning). Thus, when we hear the word "athletic," we might react instinctively, "Dumb." In times of crises we often do react signally, but times of crises occur only occasionally.

Learning to use language intelligently begins by learning not to be used by language.[14]

Semantic Guidelines

When people read general semantics textbooks, they soon discover that most of the books tend to express and define the same ideas and thoughts, but in different ways. We have tried to select the ten most important semantic guidelines which we believe represent the best thoughts from several of the most widely accepted semantics texts as a conclusion to this discussion.[15]

1. *Check the accuracy of symbols by going directly to the reality whenever possible.* This is a must in fact gathering and in pre-decision structuring. Wrong end results may have their causes in incorrect input. Remember, symbols are merely pointers or representations of reality, not the reality itself. We become intentionally oriented when we come to depend too heavily on symbols.

2. *It is not enough to be positive of the denotative meaning of a word or symbol. What may be of more importance and influential is what the denotative and/or contextual meaning of the symbol represents to the user.* Make sure there is agreement on the symbol usage. It is not so much what you think people said that matters as what they think that you heard. Words and symbols may serve many purposes, but it is only when the sender and the receiver are in total agreement on what the meaning is that we have true and agreed-upon communication.

3. *Maintain an awareness of whether you are transmitting and/or receiving the facts or the generalizations, and whether your judgments and conclusions are based on the reality of hard, objective facts.* Facts and inferences may sound very much alike, but they definitely are based on different types of information.

4. *Learn to mentally attach the word "etc." to anything you say, hear, write, or see (i.e., "fact, etc.").* Our perceptions of reality are distorted to a greater or lesser extent by all the events in our lifetime which have shaped our lives; religion, family, education, travel, friends, and a whole host of other conditions all have contributed to our communicative receptors and communicative screening. The word "etc." reminds one that we selectively and unconsciously abstract from reality.

5. *Develop the habit of mentally dating your information (i.e., "fact, 1945").* The world is constantly changing, but our language and thought patterns have a tendency to remain static. Dating information reminds one that reality in truth may have changed as the calendar time passed.

6. *Develop an awareness of the importance of mentally indexing information, that is, numbering the items* (i.e., "fact 1—fact 2—fact 3"). This assists the communicator in differentiating between similarities and differences and protects against overstressing the similarities while stereotyping reality. Indexing prevents us from confusing one piece of information with another simply because they may have common characteristics.

7. *Check to determine if a given situation involves an either/or, polarized contradiction or contrary parameters, where middle-ground possibilities should be included.* Failure to recognize differences and the need for reaction on the basis of degrees of difference can lead to real problems.

8. *Use the verb "to be" correctly.* The word "is" can be used not only as an auxiliary word, but also as a directive ("Business is business"), as a level-of-abstraction confuser ("Mr. Miller is a Jew"), and as a thought freezer ("This is the best company of its kind"). The latter two uses (projection and identity) obviously cause the most problems.

9. *Be careful of situations where affective symbols are being used in place of informative ones.* Many affective words and other symbols have inside-the-skin meanings; they are sometimes called *purr* and *snarl* words. They are bad not in and of themselves, but only when used in place of information.

10. *As a rule, size up the total situation (analyze it, get more data, and look for alternatives) before you react as a communicator.* It is relatively easy to become ensnared in a situation through incorrect analysis of the communication or through improper reception. Give yourself time to analyze all aspects of input or transmission before you commit yourself.

REVIEW
QUESTIONS

1. What is meant by the statement "Language is time-binding"?

2. Why is communication in organizations so important in this technological age?

3. Why is it said in the text that the terms "communication" and "management" are almost synonymous?

4. Why have some kinds of communication been labeled in the text "routine information processing"?

5. What are the three criteria for good information processing, and why are they important?

6. What are some of the normal *oral* communication processes in organizations?

7. What are some of the normal *written* communication processes in organizations?

8. How can one differentiate administrative or formal communication from interpersonal or informal communication in organizations?

9. What is meant by "two-way" communication in organizations?

10. List and elaborate on some of the costs of poor communication within organizations.

11. What is a symbol and how does it differ from a sign?

12. How do we learn our meanings for symbols?

13. What is the relationship between a symbol and its referent?

14. Describe the abstraction process and its potential for helping or hindering communication.

15. What is the difference between extensional and intentional meaning?

16. Describe the causes of stereotyping.

17. List and discuss the purpose of each of the ten semantic guidelines presented in the text.

EXERCISES

1. In April 1962, J. D. Trent and W. C. Redding of Purdue University asked over seventy executives of corporations doing a minimum daily business of $1 million a number of questions regarding communication within their organizations.[16] One of these questions was: "Which of the following factors are the most important *causes* of breakdowns in business and industrial communication?" The answers were summarized as follows:

   a. Fifty (50) executives indicated "lack of communicative ability in management personnel."

   b. Thirty-four (34) executives indicated "inadequate use of communication media."

c. Twenty-four (24) executives indicated "lack of communicative ability in foremen."

d. Twenty-two (22) executives indicated "little opportunity for communication 'up.'"

e. Twenty (20) executives indicated, "Management withholds information from subordinates."

f. Seventeen (17) executives indicated "inadequate training program in techniques of communication."

g. Ten (10) executives indicated "confusion of authority."

h. Nine (9) executives indicated, "Management doesn't listen to subordinates."

i. Four (4) executives indicated "clashing personalities."

j. One (1) executive indicated, "Communicators are not well liked by subordinates."

k. One (1) executive indicated, "Union meddling agitates employees."

Your task is to rearrange the items in the above list in their order of importance as you see them and to add whatever other causes of organizational communication breakdowns you consider important. Your answers for this exercise will be compared with those of the other members of the class.

2. List ten (10) words or other symbols which are currently being widely communicated in your organization or in one with which you are familiar. Note whether the symbols are high-level or low-level abstractions; then list both the denotative and the connotative meanings of the symbols.

EXAMPLE: "Morale"—High-level abstraction
Denotative meaning: Moral or mental condition with respect to cheerfulness, confidence, zeal, etc.
Connotative meaning: Management's explanation for whatever keeps production down besides mechanical failure.

3. The following is an example of inference drawing (i.e., jumping to conclusions) that really happened. You are to think of at least two (2) similar occurrences which you witnessed and discuss (using the text) how these problems could have been prevented.

EXAMPLE: A young mother came to the door of the nursery and saw her husband, a lumber dealer, standing over the baby's crib. Silently, she watched him as he stood looking at the sleeping infant. In his face she read rapture, doubt, admiration, ecstasy, incredulity, wonder. Deeply touched, with eyes glistening, she tiptoed to his side and put her arms around his neck. "A penny for your thoughts, darling," she whispered. Startled into consciousness, he blurted, "For the life of me, I don't see how they can make a crib like that for four bucks."

4. Give two examples each of (a) inferences, (b) generalizations, and (c) stereotypes you have heard floating around your organization (or around one with which you are familiar) which do not square with the facts. Then suggest how using "etc.," dating, or indexing might have prevented the spread of such information.

EXAMPLE: Word had gotten around that our company was going to lay off a number of employees, on the basis that other companies manufacturing similar products were reducing their personnel. If the gossips would have indexed the information, that is, realized that company number 1 is never exactly like company number 2, they could have found out that our company was in fact going to hire more people because of the increased sales that other companies were losing to our superior product.

5. Give one somewhat detailed example of each of (a) an either-or polarized contradiction, (b) a misuse of the verb "to be," and (c) the use of affective symbols. These take place every day all around you. See if you can find some recent ones which might be of interest to the class as a whole.

EXAMPLE (from *Language Habits in Human Affairs*, by Irving J. Lee, p. 101): "The world is divided into people who do things and people who get the credit." (Dwight Morrow) "Life is either a daring adventure or nothing." (Helen Keller) "This war is a fight between two worlds, a world of special privilege in which is included the United States, and a world of real freedom and equality as represented by Germany." (Adolf Hitler)[17]

6. Starting with the one at the lowest level of abstraction, arrange the items of the following two sets of statements in the order of increasing abstraction.

____I like working with my hands better than working at a desk.
____I like repairing automobiles.
____I like repairing American cars better than repairing foreign ones.
____I like to work on my 1973 Ford Pinto.
____I like mechanical work.

Perhaps you will find this second group more difficult.

____Sam keeps our division of the company running smoothly.
____Sam is an administrative genius.
____Sam is a very fine organizer.
____Sam is a 100 percent real American man.
____Sam is an awfully useful person to have around.
____Yesterday Sam solved a problem which had stumped us for months.
____Sam could be president of the company some day.

7. Below you will find a group of words which is used to indicate differing degrees of certainty. Obviously, most of these words have different meanings to different people. Just how different the meanings can be is examined with this exercise. If someone asks whether something will happen or not, and you answer, "It is absolute" or "It is a cinch," what does that mean to you? If it means a 95 percent chance, mark down "95%" next to the word. Then do the same for every word on the list. Your instructor will select some words for comparison within the class.

1. ___ Absolute		12. ___ Favorable
2. ___ Ambiguous		13. ___ Firm
3. ___ Beyond the shadow of a doubt		14. ___ Fishy
		15. ___ Gamble
4. ___ Certain		16. ___ Hopeful
5. ___ Chancy		17. ___ Imaginable
6. ___ Cinch		18. ___ Impossible
7. ___ Conceivable		19. ___ Improbable
8. ___ Conditional		20. ___ Indefinite
9. ___ Definite		21. ___ Irrefutable
10. ___ Doubtful		22. ___ Likely
11. ___ Dubious		23. ___ Official

24. ___ Open to question		37. ___ Shot in the dark	
25. ___ Outlandish		38. ___ Solid	
26. ___ Plausible		39. ___ Speculative	
27. ___ Positive		40. ___ Sure as hell	
28. ___ Possible		41. ___ Sure thing	
		42. ___ Ticklish	
29. ___ Precarious		43. ___ Toss-up	
30. ___ Probable		44. ___ Trustworthy	
31. ___ Promising		45. ___ Uncertain	
32. ___ Questionable		46. ___ Unclear	
33. ___ Risky		47. ___ Undeniable	
34. ___ Secure		48. ___ Unlikely	
35. ___ Settled		49. ___ Unofficial	
36. ___ Shaky		50. ___ Vague	

8. Determine if and/or why each of the following examples are "communication" problems. Once you have done that, explain how these problems could have been prevented.

EXAMPLE 1: The personnel of one of the departments interviewed was moved from one building to another. In the new location, because of lack of space, it was found necessary to seat four people across the aisle from the remainder of the group.

It happened that there were three women in the department who were to be transferred to other work. These women were given desks across the aisle so that their going would not necessitate a rearrangement of desks. The fourth person, a man, was given a desk there simply because there was no other place for him to sit. In choosing the fourth person, the supervisor was undoubtedly influenced by the fact that he was older than the rest of the group and was well acquainted with the three women. But, beyond that, nothing was implied by the fact that he was chosen.

Now see how this employee interpreted the change in his seating position. He felt that his supervisor evaluated him in the same way in which he evaluated the women—two of the women were being returned to jobs in the shop. He felt that he himself might be transferred to the shop; and there was nothing he dreaded more. Having dwelt on speculations like these for a while, the employee recalled with alarm that his name had been omitted from the current issue of the house telephone directory. This omission had been accidental.

He became so preoccupied over what might happen to him that for a time he could scarcely work.[18]

EXAMPLE 2: At X Corporation, a foreman of inspection noticed a mistake in the assembling of transmitter cases. The foreman, a shy man when speaking to his immediate superiors, mentioned this matter to the senior supervisor in a weak, ineffectual manner.

The senior supervisor nodded his head and continued to work on a report that he was writing. Later on, a production slowdown occurred, and it was discovered that this flaw in the transmitter was the cause. The chief of production engineering, upset because this error had passed inspection unnoticed, reproved the senior supervisor in a brusque manner.

The senior supervisor called in the foreman of inspection and asked why this error had not been brought to his attention. The foreman said, "I told you the other day they were missing some of the punch-outs in those transmitter cases." The senior supervisor said, *"Yes, but you didn't pound the desk when you told me!"*[19]

FOOTNOTES

1. Alfred Korzybski, *Science and Sanity: An Introduction to Non-Aristotelian Systems and General Semantics*, 2d ed. (Lakesville, Conn.: Non-Aristotelian Library Publishing Company, 1950), p. 39.

2. Irving Lee, *Language Habits in Human Affairs: An Introduction to General Semantics* (New York: Harper & Brothers, 1941), p. 4.

3. *The Services Synchronizer*, Apr. 29, 1965.

4. Paul Pigors, *Effective Communication in Industry: What Is Its Basis?* Lt. Rush Toland Memorial Study 1, National Association of Manufacturers, New York, 1949.

5. This quotation and some paraphrasing regarding signs, abstraction, identification, symbols, and map-territory analogy were taken from *Language in Thought and Action*, 2d ed., by S. I. Hayakawa, copyright, 1941, 1949, 1963, 1964, by Harcourt Brace Jovanovich, Inc., and reprinted with their permission, pp. 24–25.

6. This quotation and the others appearing below as well as some paraphrasing were taken from *Semantics and Communication*, by John C. Condon, Jr., copyright, 1966, by The Macmillan Company and reprinted with their permission, p. 1.

7. Edward Hall, *The Silent Language* (Garden City, N.Y.: Doubleday & Company, Inc., 1959), p. 53.

8. John C. Condon, Jr., op. cit., p. 47.

9. S. I. Hayakawa, op. cit., p. 169.

10. This quotation and the paraphrasing in this paragraph were taken from an essay entitled "Symbols and Values, an Initial Study," by Dorothy Lee, presented in the Thirteenth Symposium of the Conference on Science, Philosophy and Religion, 1954, and reprinted with the permission of the Conference on Science, Philosophy and Religion. The same essay can also be found in *Freedom and Culture* by Dorothy Lee (Englewood Cliffs, N.J.: Prentice-Hall, Inc., 1959), p. 80.

11. John C. Condon, Jr., op. cit., p. 23.

12. *The American College Dictionary* (New York: Random House, Inc., 1962), p. 762.

13. Alfred Korzybski, op. cit., pp. 194–203.

14. John C. Condon, Jr., op. cit., p. 10.

15. Sources consulted for this section on semantic guidelines were Samuel J. Bois, *Explorations in Awareness* (New York: Harper & Brothers, 1957), Stuart Chase, *The Power of Words* (New York: Harcourt, Brace and Co., 1954), S. I. Hayakawa, *Language in Thought and Action*, 2d ed. (New York: Harcourt, Brace & World, Inc., 1964), Wendell Johnson, *Your Most Enchanted Listener* (New York: Harper & Brothers, 1956), Kenneth S. Keyes, *How to Develop Your Thinking Ability* (New York: McGraw-Hill Book Company, 1950), Irving Lee, *Language Habits in Human Affairs* (New York: Harper & Brothers, 1941), and Harry L. Weinberg, *Levels of Knowing and Existence* (New York: Harper & Row, Publishers, Inc., 1959).

16. Taken from Special Report No. 8, September 1964, of the Communication Research Center, Purdue University, entitled "A Survey of Communication Opinions of Executives in Large Corporations," by J. D. Trent and W. C. Redding and reprinted with their permission.

17. Irving Lee, op. cit., p. 101.

18. Taken from *Management and the Worker*, by F. J. Roethlisberger and W. J. Dickson, copyright, 1939, by the Harvard University Press and used with their permission, pp. 544–545.

19. Taken from *Technically Speaking*, by Harold Weiss and James B. McGrath, Jr., copyright, 1963, by the McGraw-Hill Book Company and used with their permission, p. 3.

RELATED TEXTS

Applbaum, Ronald L., et al.: *Fundamental Concepts in Human Communication*, Canfield Press, San Francisco, 1973.

Argyris, Chris: *Integrating the Individual and the Organization*, John Wiley & Sons, Inc., New York, 1964.

Condon, John C., Jr.: *Semantics and Communication*, The Macmillan Company, New York, 1966.

DeVito, Joseph: *Language: Concepts and Processes*, Prentice-Hall, Inc., Englewood Cliffs, N.J., 1973.

Haney, William V.: *Communication and Organizational Behavior: Text and Cases*, Richard D. Irwin, Inc., Homewood, Ill., 1967.

Hayakawa, S. I.: *Language in Thought and Action*, 2d ed., Harcourt, Brace & World, Inc., New York, 1964.

Huseman, Richard, Cal M. Logue, and Dwight L. Freshley: *Readings in Interpersonal and Organizational Communication*, Holbrook Press, Inc., Boston, 1969.

Johnson, Wendell, and Dorothy Moeller: *Living with Change: The Semantics of Coping*, Harper & Row, Publishers, Inc., New York, 1972.

March, J. G., and H. A. Simon: *Organizations*, John Wiley & Sons, Inc., New York, 1958.

McLaughlin, Ted J., Lawrence P. Blum, and David M. Robinson: *Communication*, Charles E. Merrill Books, Inc., Columbus, Ohio, 1964.

Redding, W. Charles, and George A. Sanborn: *Business and Industrial Communication: A Source Book*, Harper & Row, Publishers, Inc., New York, 1964.

Weinberg, Harry L.: *Levels of Knowing and Existence*, Harper & Row, Publishers, Inc., New York, 1959.

INTRODUCTION TO COMMUNICATION MODELS

In order to have a functioning and realistic grasp of what the processes are when A communicates with B or when a *manager* communicates with a specific segment of the organization, the communicator should have a mental construct of what is really taking place. A number of respected theorists in the field of communication have constructed working models which illustrate what is taking place in the communicative processes. The models of communication which are the most germane to the practitioner of management in understanding and grasping the complexities of management communication are:

1. The Aristotelian persuasion model
2. The Hovland persuasion model
3. The Newcomb interpersonal model
4. The Shannon and Weaver information theory model
5. The Collins and Guetzkow group communication model
6. The Thayer organization model

As we review each of these models in the pages to follow, it will be for the express purpose of showing the relationship the model bears to management communication. Gerald Miller suggests that there are three basic functions for any communication model.[1] The first function is its organization and/or teaching potential. It allows the student or practitioner to isolate certain aspects of the communicative processes in order to demonstrate the relevancy factor in sending or receiving activities. The second function of a communication model is its heuristic or research function. Since a model outlines the relevant variables in a given communication situation, it thus serves as an impetus or sample in generating communication research. The third function of a model is its anticipatory or predictive function. It allows us to make an educated guess concerning the possible factors which determine the level of success or failure in a communication situation.

Miller also discussed the limitations of communication models. The first limitation of any model is one of premature closure.[2] This limitation stresses the tendency for the communication student or analyst to assume that all of the relevant variables are represented in the model. In order to overcome this obvious defect, this chapter presents a number of models which permit the reader to view the communicative processes from different angles and differing perspectives. The reader must have an awareness that any one or all of these models do not reflect the extremely complicated nature of communication as it relates to the exercise of the managerial arts.

A second limitation of a communication model is its static quality. Communication, in whatever form or manner it is encountered, is a dynamic, ever-changing, ongoing process which in a certain sense feeds upon itself for the variables that are created and, therefore, can never be truly represented by a static or still picture. In order to visualize the dynamics of communication, one might think of a movie. Viewing a communication model is like looking at a single frame of a total film. If we look at only the one frame, we have no way of knowing how it fits together with all of the other frames which precede or follow. We are viewing an isolate out of context, and therefore we cannot be sure of its true meaning or the relative importance of that frame with reference to the totality of the imagery which the movie maker had hoped to convey. A model usually represents no particular communication situation, but instead a kind of average of all similar communication events. Finally, the architects of communication models are limited because of the necessity of omitting extraneous details, which leads to the problem of oversimplification. It would be impossible to include all of the relevant factors in any communication model; therefore, the model creators must select those factors which seem most important to a given model construct, or else the model creator must use terms which will be so general as to be meaningless when applied to a specific situation. Even with these obvious limitations, we have deemed it wise and helpful to present communication models. It is felt that these communication models will provide a frame of reference for the rest of the information in this text and, therefore, a valid information and teaching tool.

PERSUASION MODELS OF COMMUNICATION

Probably the oldest communication models were of the persuasive type. The first formal writings on communication, Aristotle's *Rhetoric*, also provide the first basic model. (Although he did not provide a diagram, the figures presented here were taken directly from his work by Professor Kenneth Andersen.[3]) The forms of communication observed by Aristotle were chiefly persuasive in nature: advocacy in the courtrooms, legislative assemblies, and public meetings praising men and events.

Perhaps the greatest fault in Aristotle's theory was his view of persuasion as a one-way process flowing from the speaker through his messages to the listener. He failed to see or at least discuss how the listener can in turn affect or persuade the speaker, principally through nonverbal cues (shuffling feet, troubled or questioning expressions, outright sleeping, etc.).

Figure 2-1 also demonstrates one of the major strengths of the Aristotelian theory, and that is its emphasis on the setting of communication. He recognized that the type of situation in which one speaks has a profound influence on the speaker and

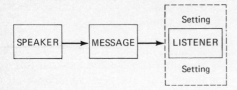

Figure 2-1 **Aristotle's View of the Communication Process**[4]

the message. One could not persuade a listener in a courtroom setting by using the same type of message prepared for a ceremonial address. The speaker must analyze the audience and the setting accurately, to be truly effective. This aspect of Aristotle's theory is further noted in Figure 2-2. The broken line connecting the speaker and the listener-setting demonstrates Aristotle's realization that such factors as age, economic status, and personal goals are primary factors influencing the reception and effect of persuasion. It therefore becomes essential for the speaker to know and use this information in preparing a message. Message preparation, according to Aristotle, involves invention—finding materials to include in the message; arrangement—organizing the materials in some persuasive fashion; style—adding the flourishes which fit the speaker and audience; and delivery—the practice and actual presentation of the persuasive message. Memory was also included in this list at one time, but it no longer really applies to contemporary discourse.

Finally, Aristotle believed that since persuasion effectiveness depended upon probability and doubt, rather than on purely scientific accurate information, one must use "proofs" of both the scientific and the unscientific type. Proofs for Aristotle were of three types: logical (scientific), i.e., statistics, quotations, first-hand reports, etc.; emotional (unscientific), i.e., stories, hypothetical illustrations, and other personal appeals; and ethical (unscientific), i.e., references to the speaker's moral, intellectual, and social attributes, as well as one's expertise. One of Aristotle's most interesting conclusions with regard to proofs has since been confirmed by research: "It is not true, as some writers on the art maintain, that the probity of the speaker contributes nothing to his persuasiveness; on the contrary, we might affirm that his character

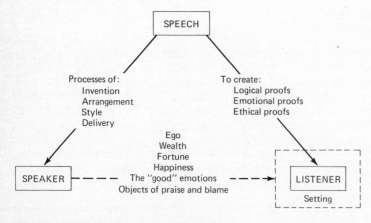

Figure 2-2 **Aristotle's View of the Persuasive Act**[5]

(ethos) is the most potent of all the means of persuasion."[6] Being a scientist himself, Aristotle obviously wanted to see persuasion weighted on the side of logical proof, but he was realistic enough to understand that listeners trust some men more than others and are more often persuaded if first brought into a state of emotional arousal.

The Aristotelian model has had a profound influence on communication theory for many years. It is still widely read in the disciplines of speech and English. We suspect that its application today is much more important to written communication than to oral. We can still see remnants of it in the more modern persuasion models, such as the one by Hovland which follows.

The Hovland model is receiver- or listener-oriented, that is, it deals basically with the area in the Aristotelian model which was called *listener-setting*.[7] In this model, both the speaker *and* the message are seen as "observable communication stimuli." Aristotle generally covered those characteristics which Hovland calls *content*, *communicator*, and *situational*. He did not, however, have much to say about media

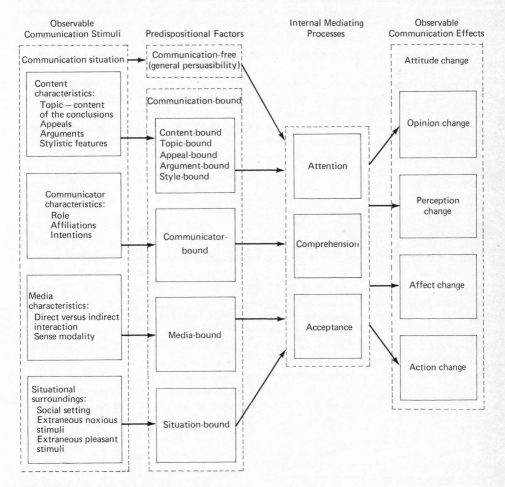

Figure 2-3 **Major Factors in Attitude Change Produced by Means of Social Communication**[8]

characteristics. We have increased the number of potential communication media greatly since the time of ancient Greece, and each of these media presents certain stimulus problems for the receiver.

The predispositional factors enumerated in the Hovland model represent prior opinions, attitudes, values, and beliefs that we bring with us to any communication situation; they represent the result of all our past experiences. In the process of reacting to other message contents, communicator styles, and media types, and under different situational backgrounds, the receiver has formed basic attitudes and value judgments regarding each. These preconceptions cannot help but influence the reception of new communication stimuli. These preferences will in great part determine (either consciously or unconsciously) whether and/or how much attention will be directed toward the stimulus, how well it will be comprehended, and whether it will be accepted.

Attention, comprehension, and acceptance are all tightly interrelated. If a managerial communication fails to elicit the attention of intended receivers, it is highly unlikely that either comprehension or acceptance will follow. There are, however, simple ways of increasing the probabilities that a message will be attended to, comprehended, and even accepted, just as there are ways of decreasing the possible negative effects of predispositional factors. These will be discussed in great detail later in the text.

Even if a message is accepted, there is no guarantee that conformance or performance change will necessarily follow or that the desired type of change will occur. It is entirely possible for one to change one's opinion, perception, action, or feelings (affect) without any of the others changing. It is certainly not an all-or-nothing proposition, as is commonly thought. It is often the case in upper-level management to find people changing their actions on the basis of the perceived feelings of a superior but remaining internally convinced that their personal opinion is correct.

AN INTERPERSONAL
COMMUNICATION MODEL

The Newcomb A-B-X model is one of the simplest communication models developed.[9] It assumes that person A communicates to person B about something X. The heart of the Newcomb theory is that both A's and B's orientation toward X will be determined not only by X itself, but by the relationship of the other person to X as well. In other words, if B (the receiver) has some kind of positive feelings toward A, his or her feeling toward X will be more like A's feelings toward X after a communication act than before it. B's feelings about any X will be modified by his/her feelings with regard to the communicator.

This desire on the part of communicators to perceive outside persons and events in the same way is labeled by Newcomb a "persistent strain toward symmetry." The likelihood of the continued interaction between A and B is dependent upon the

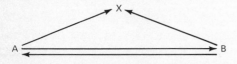

Figure 2-4 . Schematic Illustration of Minimal A-B-X System[10]

perceived symmetry or consensus in the relationship. According to A-B-X theory, it is not necessary for symmetry to exist between A and B toward X for A and B to coordinate their efforts in some task. It is, of course, desirable for them to view X in a similar fashion, but they can do a job and still disagree about X.

According to Newcomb, several situational factors can affect the A-B-X theory. First is the nature of the association, that is, whether it is a constrained (enforced) or voluntary association. In the former, A and B would probably be able to establish symmetry only toward a few essential X's, while in the latter association consensus with regard to a whole range of nonessential X's is quite likely.

A second situational factor involves prescribed role differentiation, in which case symmetry may involve complementarity rather than sameness. For example, in an organization both a first-year employee and a twenty-year man may subscribe to the same norms which prescribe differentiated behavior for the two men with regard to vacation date choice (the seniority system). When it comes time to select vacation dates, there is a demand on both of them for coordination, but the strain toward symmetry regards only the established pattern and does not refer to the vacation date itself. Here the code or the role system becomes the X, not the vacation schedule.

A third situational factor that affects the A-B-X system is the possibility that symmetry may be threatening. This is often the case when multiple-membership groups are involved. For example, a factory worker might want to achieve symmetry with his foreman with regard to, say, production demands; however, his desire for symmetry with the foreman may be outweighed by his strains toward symmetry with his fellow workers, whose orientation toward the production demands is directly contradictory to that of the foreman. In these cases, where A perceives asymmetry with regard to X and a demand for coordination with both B and X, Newcomb sees the possibilities for A as:

1. Achieve, or attempt to achieve, symmetry with regard to X.
   a. By influencing B toward own orientation.
   b. By changing own orientation toward B's.
   c. By cognitively distorting B's orientation.
2. Introduce changes in other parts of the system.
   a. Modify his attraction toward B.
   b. Modify his judgment of own attraction for B.
   c. Modify evaluation of (attraction toward) himself (A).
   d. Modify his judgment of B's evaluation of himself (B).
3. Tolerate the asymmetry, without change.[11]

Newcomb also discusses the value of his theory with regard to groups of individuals. He cites two properties of groups which seem to be predictable from his model. First is the desire for "homogeneity of orientation," that is, group members expect one another to orient themselves toward the group and its problems in certain ways, and they want both verbal and nonverbal indications of this desired orientation. Second, groups value "homogeneity of perceived consensus." Groups intentionally try to convince all members that if they deviate, they will be the only dissenters in the group. Homogeneity of orientation is something that is striven toward, while homogeneity of perceived consensus involves the group member's judgment as to the degree to which this goal has been accomplished. It is a subtle difference, but a very important one. Managers may want all employees to think that their product is the best of its kind, but they are really effective in these efforts only if dissenters can be kept from making their feelings known, i.e., if the managers can keep dissent out of the company newsletter, isolate the dissenter, coerce dissenters into keeping their opinions to themselves, etc.

Finally, Newcomb feels that attraction among members can be explained through his theory. He believes that when coordination is provided by communication acts, there is a corresponding increase in attraction or friendship. This introduces the concept of "social reality." It seems that when group members A and B establish a high degree of attraction, coordination, and symmetry between one another, they often forget about the real-life X and begin to believe that their conception or internalized interpretations of X are all that really matters. As in S. I. Hayakawa's map-territory analogy, they become convinced that the map is such an accurate representation of the territory that no further investigation is necessary. An advertising firm might be a good example; many times their managers become so convinced that they know what people like, want, and need that they act upon this social reality without ever checking the real-life environment. When examining a group, then, it is perhaps more important to check the individuals' perceptions of how another perceives X than it is to check how the individuals perceive X directly. The former seems to have more influence upon behavior.

AN INFORMATION THEORY MODEL

In this section we will be combining the theory of Norbert Wiener[12] and that of Claude E. Shannon and Warren Weaver[13] together to form what we believe can be accurately called *information theory*. Information theory can be distinguished from its broader counterpart, communication theory, in that it deals with information devoid of meaning, that is, the information theorist is not interested in *what* is communicated, but only in the fact that the information is communicated both accurately and correctly. This elimination of the value, judgmental, affective side of human communication, which demands the ability to deal with people as if they were little different from machines, is also the central attribute of cybernetics. It is through this rationale that we have chosen to handle these theories together.

The basic information theory model involves an information source which selects a desired message out of all the possible messages it could select, a transmitter which changes the message into a signal which can be sent over some communication channel to a receiver, a destination to whom the message was originally intended, and finally a noise source which can introduce extraneous information into the signal.

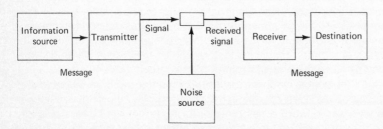

Figure 2-5 **Shannon and Weaver Model**[14]

As viewed by an information theorist, communication problems can arise at any one of three levels: the technical level, where one asks the question, "How accurately can the symbols of communication be transmitted?"; the semantic level, where one asks the question, "How precisely do the transmitted symbols convey the desired meaning?"; and the effectiveness level, where one asks the question, "How effectively does the received meaning affect conduct in the desired way?"[15] As can be seen from the model proposed and the questions asked, information theorists are primarily concerned with the technical level. They feel certain that although problems on the semantic and effectiveness levels are irrelevant to the engineering aspects, the engineering aspects are not necessarily irrelevant to the semantic- and effectiveness-level problems, and they take great pains to support this assertion.

The basic starting point for all information theorists is the concept of "entropy" first introduced by Willard Gibbs[16] in response to Newtonian physics, which described the universe as a highly organized unit where everything follows prescribed laws. Gibbs's theory of entropy held just the reverse—that things tend to become disorganized, deteriorated, and less distinct over time. With regard to the communication model, this means that the tendency is for information to be lost, disorganized, and less meaningful as it travels from the information source to the destination; and the more complex or spread-out the process becomes, the more likelihood there is that entropy will increase.

According to the information theorists, two basic processes work to reduce entropy in the system. The first is *feedback*, which Wiener defines as "a method of controlling a system by reinserting into it the results of its past performance."[17] It is the feedback process which allows both human and machine to become anti-entropic systems. Feedback to a company manager through a suggestion box or interoffice communication allows for heading off confusion and disorganization in much the same way as a thermostat operates to maintain a constant room temperature. According to Wiener, it is our distinctive ability to adapt to our environment and thus avoid disorganization or entropy that gives us mastery over the other animals, and it is our communication ability which makes the feedback possible which makes the adaptation possible, which in turn makes survival possible. In the words of Wiener, "Speech is the greatest interest and most distinctive achievement of man."[18] The importance of feedback and communication to the survival of an organization goes without saying; we must never take them for granted or misuse them to the extent that entropy is allowed to set in, for the tendency of entropy is always to increase.

The second basic process that operates to impede entropy is *redundancy*, that is, predictability. In a message, that part is redundant which could be left out and still leave the message essentially complete. The relative redundancy in the English language is approximately 50 percent, so that approximately half of the words or letters we choose in our spoken or written communications are chosen randomly, while the other half are more or less controlled by the structure of our language. It is this redundancy in our language which allows us to overcome the noise in the communication process from the information source to the destination. This means that the destination need not receive a message word for word to get the main emphasis of the communication. The more redundant a communication code, the less chance there is that entropy will impair information transfer.

There does not seem to be a great deal of information in the Shannon-Weaver model that is currently relevant to the management situation, but as data storage, retrieval, and transmission devices become more and more central to the management process, we are sure that information theory will also become more important in understanding organizational communication.

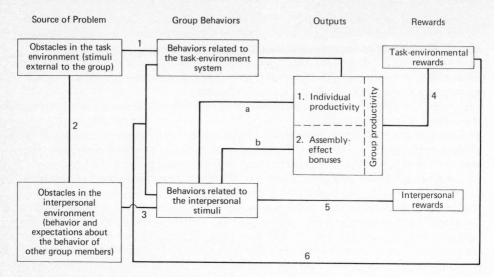

Figure 2-6 **A Simple Working Model of Decision-Making Groups**[20]

A GROUP
COMMUNICATION MODEL

There are not a great many group communication models, and only one really adds any substantial new information to the other models discussed in this section. Like the Hovland persuasion model, the Barry E. Collins and Harold Guetzkow group communication model reflects a great deal of the area's research.[19] It is especially valuable because it makes the crucial distinction between task and interpersonal behaviors or communications in groups. As can be seen in Figure 2-6, the lower three boxes represent the sources, behaviors, and rewards associated with the *interpersonal* aspect of a group's operation, while the top three boxes represent the sources, behaviors, and rewards associated with the *task* aspect of group operation. Perhaps the most interesting portion of the model is the outputs box. This we will discuss later, but first we should expand somewhat on the six parts of the model mentioned previously.

Obstacles in both the task environment and the interpersonal environment affect the group's internal communication behaviors and the final group product. It is interesting, however, that when asked about the sources of problems in their group relationships, executives rarely mention the interpersonal aspects, concerning themselves only with the task.[21] Also, those executives and researchers who do recognize both aspects of group behavior often act as if these were two distinctly different phenomena with little or no relationship to one another. This is one of the real values of the Collins and Guetzkow model: it stresses the relationships between task and interpersonal behavior.

Task obstacles are normally things external to the group. A company manager, for example, might recognize a problem with regard to sales in a certain area. The task obstacles standing in the way of a solution might be fairly obvious to the sales staff (of that area) when they are called together to discuss the problem: too many salesmen are quitting and taking other jobs, management cannot find qualified personnel to replace them, training new people takes too long and costs the unit both time and money, the salary scale cannot be increased until the total group's sales are up, and so on down the line. Thus far, most of the obstacles viewed by the group exist because of conditions in the world beyond the group (external to the group). Many times these are the only obstacles to a problem solution that business groups and individuals are willing to recognize. As is often the case, in this situation the group as a whole is being affected by the task environment; no single group member is being hit much harder than the rest.

Because the company manager called the group together in his or her office rather than contacting each of the members of the sales staff individually or bringing in an outside "expert" to solve the problem, the group will have to overcome some interpersonal obstacles before it can get down to working out a problem solution. When an individual works alone on a problem, or when a number of people work in isolation on the same problem, they can devote their full energies to accomplishing the task; but when they choose or are forced to work together, they must learn to work together efficiently before they can ever hope to effectively accomplish the task. For many business people the added time, effort, and problems associated with working as a group are not worth the possible benefits, even though, as we will point out later in this section, the benefits can be quite substantial.

In discussing task and interpersonal rewards, Collins and Guetzkow say:

> Task environmental rewards are events external to the group; they constitute feedback from the environment to the group. Task rewards may be delayed for long periods of time after group action. In contrast, interpersonal rewards are events in the behavior of group members and, therefore, internal to the group. Group members will have much more control over their own behavior than they will over task-environmental feedback. For this reason, the group members can mold, maintain, and motivate behaviors through the use of interpersonal rewards which would not be supported if task-environmental rewards were the only motivating stimuli. . . . Furthermore, the unitary nature of task-environmental rewards makes it difficult to allocate extra rewards to deserving group members. Interpersonal rewards, however, can be tied to the success and failure of individual group members, can follow the behavior immediately, and extra rewards can be allocated to competent members.[22]

We can demonstrate the applied meaning of the preceding statements by turning again to our sales group. It is obvious that any solution to the task problems facing that group is going to take a great deal of time. New personnel must be hired, trained, and start producing before the cycle of lower profits due to low sales volume and fewer sales due to lower profits can be broken. In the meantime, what is going to happen to the next member of the sales group when a good offer is received from another company? If all that has been offered to the group is a hope of distant future success in the task environment, the company will probably lose another employee and the already large problem will be further complicated. If, however, some immediate interpersonal rewards have been received, he/she might just remain. Remember, people tend to prefer the status quo; they like the security of familiar surroundings and associates. Suppose, for example, that the district manager or even the company manager had come over after the meeting and said, "Listen, I liked your ideas in there; with ideas and motivation like yours, I think you have a real future with us once we get over this difficult period!" Employees remember that kind of statement for a long time after most of the rest of the meeting is forgotten. They also remember such things as the fact that the company manager was concerned enough to call them together; that the ideas and suggestions of the sales personnel were asked for, listened to, and incorporated in the final decision; and that the whole group seemed to pull together as a team. In other words, feeling wanted and needed is a major interpersonal reward in and of itself. We would venture to say that for the majority of people, psychic income is worth at least as much as and in some cases more than material rewards.

Before we finish discussing the Collins and Guetzkow group communication model, we need to talk some about that all-important outputs box. As can be seen in Figure 2-6, Collins and Guetzkow have divided group productivity into two parts: (1) individual productivity, and (2) assembly-effect bonuses. The single line going from task behaviors to individual productivity represents the proposition that when a group concentrates its efforts solely on the task obstacles, they are acting merely as a collection of individuals. They will probably not produce an outcome which exceeds what could have resulted from having each of the participants work on the problem alone.

Researchers feel, however, that it is possible in groups to have results which exceed a simple combination of individual results; this is an *assembly effect*. According to the Collins and Guetzkow definition, "An assembly effect occurs when the group is able to achieve collectively something which could not have been achieved by any member working alone or by a combination of individual efforts."[23] The assembly effect is not something that comes automatically because people decide to sit down together. It merely represents a *potential* which individuals can only develop when they interact together. They must, however, build an interpersonal relationship which allows them to exceed their individual efforts. As we mentioned before, this takes time and effort, and, to be worthwhile, the result must offset the costs. Once an effective interpersonal relationship has been established, it can continue to function profitably for a long period of time and for a variety of problems.

Collins and Guetzkow call the problems a group faces in switching from a totally task-oriented structure to one generating assembly-effect bonuses the *costs of conversion*. Some of these costs involve establishing full and open channels of communication, reducing the inhibiting effect of authoritarian leadership, promoting a warm and friendly group climate in which none of the members fears sanctions for unpopular remarks, and maintaining a high level of motivation regardless of the nature of the task. How one goes about converting a group or organization so as to elicit assembly bonuses and the risks a group takes in doing this will be discussed fully later in this text. For now, let us simply say that it is the feedback, represented by line six (6) and discussed more fully with regard to some of the other models presented in this section, which provides the key to promoting assembly-effect bonuses. It is very similar to telling a joke: the first triggers a follow-up in someone else, who in turn triggers a third, and so on, until the result is far more impressive than any or all of the jokesters could have produced working individually. Even at the level of joke-telling, the experience is an exciting and enjoyable one which leaves the participants extremely proud of themselves.

AN ORGANIZATION COMMUNICATION MODEL

The organizational communication model we have chosen to include in this text is that of Lee Thayer, primarily because he talks about "levels of communication."[24] For Lee Thayer, the levels are organizational, interpersonal, intrapersonal, and technical, which he says are derived for his purposes from the four basic sources or determinants of human communication behavior: physiological, psychological, sociological, and technological.

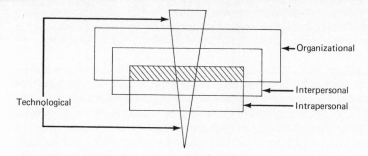

Figure 2-7 **A Scheme of the Levels of De-terminants of Human Communication in Organizations**[25]

At the intrapersonal level one must distinguish between that which actually exists in reality (data) and what is perceived or assumed to exist in reality by the human observer (information). It is the perceived reality upon which people base their behavior, so for the purposes of this theory actual data are unimportant. At the intrapersonal level, all communication is within us; we originate the messages and also receive them. Because the whole process is internal, correction of errors is nearly impossible. Communication reception at this level involves both messages regarding the state of the organism and messages regarding the relations between the organism and the external environment. We have different internal channels for each of these types of messages. The central functions of coordination, interpretation, and storage of the received information are really possible only if the information from these two sources is complementary. When a piece of information is received from the environment which is not consistent with the existing internal information, it is usually rejected or perhaps distorted to fit. In other words, we are programmed or socialized to the extent that we will not convert data to information unless it will fit with previous information.

This proposition is tenable at least in part because one's concept of something "outside" himself can be meaningful only in relation to his concept of himself—or in relation to some other concept that is related to one's concept of himself. Thus, the world with which one deals (other than through sheer motor activity) is his own "model" of the world constituted by his psychological system and its functions. "Reality" is a social process, and "facts" are whatever we agree they are. Yet we must behave "as if" our own models of the world were good and true for all time. It is only our inter-subjectivity that permits us to affect each other in more or less intended ways. The manifold implications of this view for the many interpersonal functions of thinking, problem-solving, decisioning, and so on, are only beginning to be explored.[26]

At the interpersonal level, Thayer makes the point that individuals follow certain rules of communicative behavior. For the most part these rules are programmed into us from the time when we first begin to communicate. For example, our vocal pitch rises at the end of a question; we begin an interaction by first testing to see if the lines of communication are open ("Hi, how are you?" "I haven't seen you around lately!"); and we tend to attribute different degrees of credibility to certain individuals because of their status. If we do not follow the rules or "play the game" correctly, we must suffer the prescribed sanctions.

The actual mechanics of interaction at the interpersonal level have already been discussed elsewhere in this chapter, so we will not go into them further, except to point out that since more than one person is engaged in the communication situation, **37** correction of information is much more possible than at the intrapersonal level. Whereas it is possible for one individual to carry around inaccurate information in his head for years, it is less possible to share misinformation with another person without having the mistake corrected.

If we become observers of communication, as this text proposes, we must realize that we are part of the system we are observing. We will be subject to the problem of prejudging the situations we are examining because of the pictures we carry around in our own heads of how things should be. We must continually strive for objectivity and be receptive to new ways of looking at management communication.

The Thayer model stresses the fact that although we can talk about communication at all of these different levels, one must realize that at any point in time "the ultimate conceptual-theoretical problems are those that exist at the interfaces or the overlapping zones of the various levels and their combinations."[27] Obviously the most difficult problems arise, then, in that crosshatched central zone where all of the various communication levels overlap. We like to have the reader picture the triangular figure in the center of Thayer's model as one person. This conception allows one to visualize the fact that all of the various levels affect a single individual just as any one individual affects all of the various communication levels. This is all part of what Thayer calls the "communication-organization interface."

Lee Thayer pictures the organizational level as a complex, open, information-decision system when he points out that "a plant does not operate on the basis of the existence of certain raw materials, but on the basis of certain *information* about the condition, place, price, utility, and so on, of those raw materials."[28] He prefers to disregard such traditional notions as upward and downward communication and management-employee communication in favor of one which considers three basic information systems within an organization—the operational system, the regulatory system, and the maintenance-development system. In each case these are part of the information flow system of a corporation which exist to supply information for "conversion centers" where the information is processed and decisions are made.

    a. The *operational information system* is that system which maps the flow of the set of all messages relevant to the enterprise's daily work on its basic tasks (short- or long-range) from their origination to their destination.

    b. The *regulatory information system* is that system which maps the flow of the set of all messages relevant to the goal-setting, task-defining, rule-setting, and decision-framing functions of the enterprise from their origination to their destination.

    c. The *maintenance and development information system* is that system which maps the flow of the set of all messages pertaining to the maintenance and support of all conversion centers, channels, and action centers—in their material, non-material, and human aspects—from their origin to their destination.[29]

In effect what Thayer has done is try to divide an organization according to the kinds of messages that are within each information system. In the first system order, production, inventory, and invoice messages are handled. In the second system policy statement and directive messages are handled. And in the third system, payroll, suggestion, grievances, training, performance, evaluation, and personnel messages flow. This way of looking at the organization allows us to cut across departments and executive levels to look at the organization as basically an information processing system similar in nature to the one the information theorists propose and using many of their methods to study the system.

In this text we will not be looking at organizations in exactly this way, but it will be valuable to you to keep this perspective in mind when studying management communication. Much of what we will have to say in the remainder of this text can fit neatly into this model.

Summary—Part I

In the preceding introductory section we have discussed a number of things relevant to communication.

1.   We have pointed out that the primary objective of business communication is to get people to receive a message, interpret it correctly, and then pass it along accurately or act on it properly.

2.   We have also pointed out, however, that this seemingly simple objective, when put into practice, becomes extremely difficult.

3.   Mr. John A. Howard pointed out in his article that even in the most advanced communications organization in the world, Bell Telephone, communication difficulties are still very evident.

4.   We have tried to point out in limited detail the importance and types of communication in a business organization.

5.   We have discussed in some detail the importance and problems associated with the primary building block of communication, the symbol.

6.   The basic problems we saw associated with symbol usage were (a) its referent, (b) its abstraction nature, and (c) its ability to breed stereotypes.

7.   Finally, we have presented a number of communication models because no single model is able to deal with all the communication variables relevant to organizational communications. The various models and their primary value in understanding the rest of this text are as follows:

a.   The persuasive models are concerned primarily with the one-to-many situation which is represented in business by organizational directives, announcements, and formal presentations of various sorts.

b.   The interpersonal model is concerned primarily with the one-to-many and many-to-one situation represented in business by intraorganizational newsletters, magazines, and filmstrips, as well as basic interpersonal relations within the organization and the companies' public relations activities with the larger public.

c.   The information theory model attempts to deal with the preceding two types of situations from an engineering point of view and is very relevant to our newly developing electronic communications explosion.

d.   The group communication model deals with communications in the decision-making groups, both large and small, which often occur as a basic part of organizational communications.

e.   Finally, the organizational model attempts to place the individual's communication efforts within the large organizational communication setting which influences him/her.

REVIEW QUESTIONS

1.   What are the three basic functions of any communication model?

2.   What are some of the major limitations of communication models?

3. What is the greatest fault of the Aristotelian persuasion model?

4. What are some of the main points that the Aristotelian persuasion model emphasizes?

5. Why does the text emphasize the point that the Hovland model is "receiver- or listener-oriented?"

6. What is the importance of understanding what Hovland calls "predispositional factors"?

7. Differentiate between opinion, perception, affect, and action change.

8. What are some of the situational factors which Newcomb says affect interpersonal "symmetry"?

9. How can one increase symmetry?

10. Explain Newcomb's concept of social reality.

11. What is meant by the term "entropy," and what are its implications for communication within an organization?

12. How do feedback and redundancy reduce entropy?

13. What is the difference between task and interpersonal behaviors in groups?

14. What are the links between the task and interpersonal behaviors in groups?

15. What are assembly-effect bonuses in groups, and when do they occur?

16. What are the four levels of communication in organizations, and how do they differ from one another?

17. Differentiate between the three basic information systems in organizations.

18. Several of the models mention "social reality" or reality as a social process. What does this mean, and why is it important in understanding organizational communication?

EXERCISES

1. Think of a persuasive situation in which you have recently been involved or which you witnessed personally. Copy the model below and fill in the names or titles of the persuader and receiver involved as well as a brief description of the message content and setting.

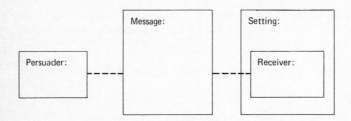

2. In your opinion, what were some of the communication stimuli, predispositional factors, and internal mediating processes which produced the observable com-

munication effects in the situation you presented for Exercise 1? Make a list of these, and the class will try to discover others which you may not have even been aware of at the time.

3. Now, using the same situation as described above (or another if your instructor prefers), try casting the information in terms of the A-B-X model and discussing the interpersonal factors involved as Professor Newcomb might. The following diagram will help you with this exercise.

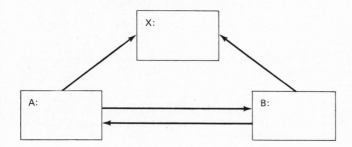

4. Explain how the information theory concepts of entropy, noise, feedback, and redundancy might help explain the results of the preceding communication encounter (i.e., in Exercises 1–3). If you do not find them useful, try to explain why and in what kind of communication situations they might be more useful.

5. Think of another recent *group* communication situation in which you were involved or which you witnessed personally. State the primary purpose of the meeting and the people involved. Then outline the source of the problem (task or interpersonal), group behaviors (task or interpersonal), outputs, and rewards (task or interpersonal) which developed in this meeting. The following outline should be useful in writing this exercise.
    PURPOSE OF THE MEETING:_____

    PEOPLE INVOLVED:_____

    Source of Problem:
        Task:
        Interpersonal:
    Group Behaviors:
        Task:
        Interpersonal:
    Outputs:
    Rewards:
        Task:
        Interpersonal:

6. Lee Thayer discusses three types of information systems which operate in any organization: the operational information system, the regulatory information system, and the maintenance and development information system. You are to list some of the most important types of communication breakdowns which occur in each information system and attempt to discuss why these breakdowns occur. **41**

7. Choose one of the case studies presented in the Appendix and determine how each of the models presented in this chapter might be useful in understanding the situation. Perhaps your instructor will choose one specific case and the whole class can compare their findings for this exercise.

8. Attempt to create a communication model which seems to reflect the specific factors involved in your particular communication situation at work, in class, at home, in recreation, etc. You will then be asked to describe it to the other class members and answer any questions they have about it.

FOOTNOTES

1. Much of the material on functions and limitations of communication models was paraphrased from *Speech Communication: A Behavioral Approach*, by Gerald R. Miller, copyright 1966, by The Bobbs-Merrill Company, Inc., and used by permission of the publisher.

2. Ibid.

3. Much of this discussion on the Aristotelian persuasion model was paraphrased from *Speech Communication: Analysis and Readings*, by Howard H. Martin and Kenneth E. Andersen, copyright 1968, by Allyn and Bacon, Inc., and used by permission of the publisher.

4. Ibid., p. 9.

5. Ibid., p. 10.

6. Aristotle, "From THE RHETORIC," in Howard H. Martin and Kenneth E. Andersen, *Speech Communication: Analysis and Readings* (Boston: Allyn and Bacon, Inc., 1968), p. 28.

7. Much of this discussion on the Hovland persuasion model was paraphrased from *Personality and Persuasibility*, by Carl I. Hovland and Irving L. Janis (eds.), copyright 1959, by the Yale University Press and used by permission of the publisher.

8. Ibid.

9. Much of this discussion on the Newcomb A-B-X model was paraphrased from "An Approach to the Study of Communicative Acts," by Theodore H. Newcomb, in *Psychological Review*, no. 60, copyright 1959 by the American Psychological Association and used by permission of the publisher, pp. 393–404.

10. Ibid.

11. Ibid.

12. Norbert Wiener, *The Human Use of Human Beings* (Garden City, N.Y.: Doubleday & Company, Inc., Anchor Books, 1954).

13. Much of this discussion on the information theory model was paraphrased from *The Mathematical Theory of Communication*, by Claude E. Shannon and Warren Weaver, copyright 1949 by the Board of Trustees of the University of Illinois and used by permission of the publisher.

14. Ibid., p. 7

15. Ibid., p. 4.

16. See discussion of Willard Gibbs's contribution in Norbert Wiener, op. cit., pp. 7–12.

17. Norbert Wiener, op. cit., p. 61.

18. Norbert Wiener, op. cit., p. 85.

19. Much of this discussion on the group communication model was paraphrased from *The Social Psychology of Group Processes for Decision-Making*, by Barry E. Collins and Harold Guetzkow, copyright 1964, by John Wiley & Sons, Inc., and used by permission of the publisher.

20. Ibid., p. 81.

21. M. Kriesberg, "Executives Evaluate Administrative Conferences," *Advanced Management*, vol. 15 (1950), pp. 15–18.

22. Collins and Guetzkow, op. cit., pp. 85–86.

23. Collins and Guetzkow, op. cit., p. 58.

24. Much of this discussion on the organizational communication model was paraphrased from "Communication and Organization Theory," by Lee Thayer, in *Human Communication Theory: Original Essays*, by Frank E. X. Dance (ed.), copyright 1967 by Holt, Rinehart and Winston, Inc., and used by permission of the publisher.

25. Ibid., p. 87.
26. Ibid., p. 90.
27. Ibid., p. 87.
28. Ibid., p. 92.
29. Ibid., pp. 94–95.

RELATED TEXTS

Berlo, David K.: *The Process of Communication*, Holt, Rinehart and Winston, Inc., New York, 1960.

Borden, George A.: *Human Communication Theory*, Wm. C. Brown Company Publishers, Dubuque, Iowa, 1971.

Boulding, Kenneth: *The Image*, University of Michigan Press, Ann Arbor, Mich., 1956.

Cherry, Colin: *On Human Communication*, Science Editions, New York, 1961.

Collins, B. E., and H. Guetzkow: *A Social Psychology of Group Processes for Decision-Making*, John Wiley & Sons, Inc., New York, 1964.

Dance, Frank E. X. (ed.): *Human Communication Theory: Original Essays*, Holt, Rinehart and Winston, Inc., New York, 1967.

Martin, Howard, and Kenneth E. Andersen: *Speech Communication: Analysis and Readings*, Allyn & Bacon, Inc., Boston, 1968.

Miller, Gerald: *Speech Communication: A Behavioral Approach*, The Bobbs-Merrill Company, Inc., Indianapolis, Ind., 1966.

Sereno, Kenneth K., and David C. Mortensen: *Foundations of Communication Theory*, Harper & Row, Publishers, Inc., New York, 1970.

Shannon, Claude E., and Warren Weaver: *The Mathematical Theory of Communication*, The University of Illinois Press, Urbana, Ill., 1964.

Smith, Raymond G.: *Speech-Communication: Theory and Models*, Harper & Row, Publishers, Inc., New York, 1970.

Thayer, Lee: *Administrative Communication*, Richard D. Irwin, Inc., Homewood, Ill., 1961.

ORAL
COMMUNICATION

COMMUNICATION TRANSMISSION

Those of you who have served in the military or in R.O.T.C. are familiar with the experience of hearing an officer bark: "Company, halt!" Down the ranks this command was reverberated by the first lieutenant, then the second lieutenant, the company sergeant, and finally the platoon corporal, each in turn repeating the shouted command, "Company, halt!"

This is communication transmission in its simplest form—a plain statement repeated throughout the entire organization by each level of subordinate management in exactly the same manner as the order was issued. No opportunity here for misinterpretation, or for someone to ask, "I wonder what they mean by that?" The command was simple, straightforward, direct, and almost impossible to misconstrue. And yet, even direct orders can be misunderstood. Again, if you happen to have had experience in football or in a dance revue, you may recall how difficult those early exercises were when you were learning how to execute simple maneuvers. One may hear the directive and one may hear it correctly, but it is another thing to interpret and execute maneuvers promptly and accurately. In fact, to your sorrow and to the other people's amusement, you may have found yourself dancing or playing football all by yourself.

THE BASIC PRINCIPLES
OF COMMUNICATION
TRANSMISSION

Communication transmission refers to that part of the communication process involving the sender of the message. In the chapter on communication models it was noted that the sender of a message could be a single speaker, a group of speakers, a nonhuman information source such as a computer, a newspaper, or even an entire culture or organization. Regardless of who the sender of the message is, the basic principles remain the same. When one understands the basic principles of communication transmission, he/she can evaluate all types of communication, whether it is the president of the company talking to a vice president, the production manager discussing a problem with the plant supervisor, a company newsletter explaining the different types of medical insurance available, a customer asking a question of one of the company's salespeople, or even two machine operators discussing the upcoming football game. The basic principles remain the same.

Perhaps one can approach these basic principles by charting the cycle of sequential actions and reactions that takes place when we speak.

> An idea forms in the speaker's mind where it is translated into language symbols; reacting to impulses from the nervous system, the muscles used in speech convert these language symbols into audible speech; the sounds are carried as wave patterns in the air until they strike the eardrums of the listener; as nerve impulses, they travel to the brain, where they again become language symbols which convey meaning to the listener's mind; the listener reacts to what he heard; the speaker observes this reaction and responds to it.[1]

You will notice the similarity between Monroe's description of the communication cycle and the earlier models of communication—the key parts being the sender, with his/her mind, nervous system, muscular system, and language capacity; the message, with its various structures, arrangements, styles, and potential channels; and the receiver, with his/her mind, nervous system, muscular system, and language capacity. These, then, break down the various areas where we can expect to find the basic principles which determine good and poor communication transmission: the sender, the message, the channel, and the receiver.

As was mentioned earlier in this text, until recently the sending or transmission of messages was considered the primary problem area. We thought that by simply teaching people how to speak, write, and organize their thoughts and messages in a better fashion, we would reduce or eliminate problems of communication. Our business communication textbooks reflected this orientation—most of them were constructed to resemble basic English grammar or public speaking texts. In the last decade or so we have discovered that improving one or more of the basic skills involved in the communication process—such as writing, speaking, reading, or listening—could make a significant improvement in the entire communication process only when and if the basic principles of communication were understood. It is the purpose of this chapter on communication transmission and the chapter that follows on communication reception to present in detail these basic principles.

Purposes of Communication

According to most communication theorists, speaking is one of the primary means of manipulating, controlling, and understanding one's environment. Each of us would like to maintain a kind of equilibrium within our own particular environment; that is, we would like to keep our spouse and children happy without sacrificing our own pleasure. We would like to maintain a friendly relationship with our fellow workers and superiors and still reach our own goals. We would like to be an active and worthwhile member of the community, but without having these activities dominate our life. We can do this, however, only if we first understand our family, job, friends, and community, and then have some ability to manipulate and control those environments. To put it in its simplest terms, the spoken and written word provide a means by which we can obtain the maximum rewards from our environment and minimize the difficulties.

If we can obtain what we consider to be the maximum rewards available with a minimum of punishment, we have no real need to communicate. In most cases people will initiate communication only when they feel that their equilibrium state has been disturbed. This same principle holds true for the organization as a whole. Business organizations tend to have a minimum or low level of communication within and outside of themselves when things are running smoothly. When business is slumping or production has decreased or costs are up or any number of other problems occur, communication transmission increases in an effort to bring all of the functions back into balance.

Individual Incentives and Impediments to Communication

People within organizations communicate or fail to communicate for the same basic reasons they behave in other ways—they have needs which are satisfied or need satisfaction. If they believe that asking a question, answering a question, volunteering information, expressing an emotion, or making any other type of communication will help them fulfill one of their needs or prevent a need from arising, they will then communicate. On the other hand, if they feel that transmitting a communication will only serve to increase an already current need or create a new need, they may choose to remain silent.

In today's modern society most of our basic physical needs—hunger, thirst, warmth, rest, etc.—have been fulfilled. It is the secondary or social needs, however, that occupy our time, concern, and attention. The following three basic needs are the most prevalant in organizations—as well as in other environments. First is the desire for some minimum level of acceptance, recognition, and security. *Acceptance* involves a desire to be part of the organization—in the mainstream, so to speak—and not an isolate to be excluded from the relevant information and contacts. Second is the need for *recognition*. This involves the desire to be given praise or reward—in one of its many forms, such as salary increase, promotion, or verbal or written statements for work well done, etc. Third is *security*, which involves a desire to be confident of one's position within the organization and free from doubt as to possible negative or disturbing changes.

Depending upon the organizational situation and personality characteristics of the individual involved, any one of the three basic needs—acceptance, recognition, and security—can be an incentive either to communicate or not. An example will illustrate this point:

Tom Newcomer recently joined the Lowcost Insurance Company as a salesman and in his first year has made a record number of "rookie" sales. At lunch one afternoon some of his fellow salesmen ask him for his "secret." It would be impossible to predict whether Tom would transmit this information unless we first knew something about Tom's perception of his current state of acceptance, recognition, and security. It does not matter much how he actually stands with regard to these three needs in the eyes of the Lowcost Insurance Company. The only thing that really matters is how he perceives himself with regard to his basic needs, and how he feels his communication would affect his needs. Under normal circumstances, one would predict that a person who is confident and satisfied with his level of acceptance, recognition, and security would be willing to share his secret with his fellow salesmen in order to increase his acceptance with them and perhaps gain some further recognition if, for example, his technique is incorporated into future training manuals for salesmen. It might decrease his security somewhat because he would no longer have his advantage, but he would certainly rationalize this with consideration of the probable increase in acceptance and recognition. Perhaps he is single and security is not too important to him anyway.

On the other hand, suppose his secret involves some kind of deception which is frowned upon by the company. Tom would then probably decline to tell the other salesmen his secret for fear of losing the acceptance, recognition, and security which he has already achieved. Another possible reason for his not communicating might be his desire to gain further acceptance and recognition from his superiors, not his fellow salesmen. He might then decide that, if he is going to tell anyone his secret, it will be his superior, and thus he will decline to tell his friends at lunch. We could go on and on, predicting possible outcomes given varied situations, but perhaps it would be better to dissect this example and examine it carefully.

First of all there are Tom and his current feelings with regard to his basic social needs. For each need—acceptance, recognition, and security—the possible range is all the way from very satisfied to very unsatisfied. We should also know which needs are most important to him. Such things as marital status, current rank in the company, and outcomes of previous similar communication situations, as well as many, many other factors, will affect the relative importance of each need.

Second, we should know something about Tom's reference group for each of his needs. That is, Tom may feel very satisfied with his acceptance by the other salesmen, but he is not sure or is unsatisfied with his acceptance by his superiors (in the case of middle managers, the feelings of subordinates may also play a role here). Recognition and security are also related to superior, coworker, and subordinate reference groups.

Third, the message itself is important. All messages do not automatically increase one's acceptance, recognition, or security. Some messages can increase one need while reducing others. The selection of the wrong message or a statement at the wrong time can sometimes get one into more trouble than the act of remaining silent. How often have we said, "I could have bitten off my tongue after I said that," or, "I wish I had kept my big mouth shut." Humans have a predilection for "talking first and thinking afterward." That is why it is so very important to understand the nature of the receptor of the message prior to the transmission. Obviously no one wants to or intends to increase his needs by communicating, and normally one will attempt to control statements which possibly would decrease his/her acceptance, recognition, or security. Regrettably, however, many times a communication transmission which is designed for one purpose actually performs another. In Tom Newcomer's case, it might be that his secret is merely that he begins making calls at seven in the morning and doesn't quit until nine at night. He might tell his friends this anticipating that it will increase his acceptance and recognition. After he has told them his secret, they look at one another as if to say, "This man is crazy!" Instead of gaining acceptance from his friends and recognition for his work, his accomplishments have lost much of their need-satisfying value, at least with his peers.

Organizational Incentives and Impediments to Communication

The preceding incentives and impediments to communication are those over which the organization has little or no control. There are, however, other factors in this complicated formula which can be consciously controlled by the organization, and one is the working conditions within the organization. In Tom's case the working conditions in the Lowcost Insurance Company might be a key factor in determining his reaction to the question concerning his secret of increased selling.

COMMUNICATION CLIMATE

If the communication climate at Lowcost is friendly, and if a good espirit de corps has been built up by stressing the mutual benefits of teamwork, then Tom would probably be unable to see any real benefit in withholding his information. He would also feel free to ask questions and express his feelings and opinions in such an organizational atmosphere. If, on the other hand, the climate at Lowcost is authoritarian, competitive, or "cutthroat," he would probably not say anything or would dismiss the question by saying that he was just lucky.

Jack R. Gibb calls these two types of climates *defensive* and *supportive* and develops the following six subcategories and counterparts under each type of climate:[2]

Defensive Climates	*Supportive Climates*
1. Evaluation _____	Description
2. Control _____	Problem Orientation
3. Strategy _____	Spontaneity
4. Neutrality _____	Empathy
5. Superiority _____	Equality
6. Certainty _____	Provisionalism

Supportive climates, according to Gibb, provide incentives to communication transmission while defensive climates provide impediments to communication.

In defensive climates the individuals get the continual feeling that they are being evaluated or judged; they receive a great deal of criticism without an equal amount of praise. This situation, of course, reduces their feelings of acceptance, recognition, and security. In organizations with a supportive climate the same kinds of information are transmitted, but in a descriptive manner. The workers get the feeling that such comments are not meant to degrade them, but to improve their performance and thus make them more valuable employees. In such climates workers are more willing to express their feelings because they feel everyone is working together to get the job done and not evaluating and judging one another constantly. Criticism is not perceived as threatening to one's basic needs.

This leads directly to the matter of control. Organizations with a defensive climate tend to give the employee the impression that all important matters are controlled some place higher up in the organization; employees are seldom, if ever, asked their opinions concerning matters relevant to them. It is a sad commentary on our contemporary industrial society that a climate of control from above has become the norm to such an extent that persons with a genuine problem orientation must first convince those to whom they are communicating that they have no hidden motivation. Disagreement and the suggestion of possible alternatives are encouraged in situations where there is a problem orientation, but all one hears in the highly controlled climate, if anything, is the same old "party line."

A direct result of control such as described in the preceding paragraph is the strategy which carries the label "manipulation." Employees of such organizations tend to imagine that there is a grand plan behind each occurrence in the organization. They will not transmit any communication until they have determined for themselves what the plan actually is and until they are certain that they will not be entrapped. A company in which events seem to occur too spontaneously can obviously be **51** defensive as well, but some degree of spontaneity is supportive to the transmission of honest communication.

Neutrality, which at first glance seems to be more supportive than defensive, is interpreted in most companies as apathy, boredom, and lack of concern. An organizational atmosphere which has the capacity to convey concern for the feelings and respect for the worth of its employees is much more supportive and provides more incentive to communication transmission. The term "empathy" implies that the individuals within the organization see others as understanding their problems. There is a great deal of difference between empathy and sympathy; the former implies understanding another while the latter implies feeling sorry for another. Most people want their problems to be understood by others in the organization, but they don't want others to feel sorry for them.

In companies where organizational hierarchy is stressed and superiors maintain a "distance" between themselves and their subordinates, a defensive climate generally is created. Human beings tend to prefer communication with others whom they perceive as somewhat similar to themselves. In many organizations, as we have noted, the differences are stressed rather than the similarities. Complete equality is an ideal which is impossible to attain in most business organizations. However, an attitude of equality, mutual trust, and respect reduces the number of artificial impediments to communication.

Finally, a climate of certainty in an organization conveys the impression that the last word on any matter has already been said. Provisionalism, on the other hand, implies that all decisions are temporary and other opinions are encouraged. In some companies even the most important decisions are open to change. This creates a very supportive communication climate. It also allows for creative change and does not commit the organization to live with its mistakes. These general rules were employed by Mr. Osborne in developing brainstorming. In general, he stressed that acceptance, openness, support, provisionalism, and absence of negative attitudes, looks, and feeling tones contribute to a freewheeling creative climate.

The communication climate in an organization is a crucial factor in determining the quantity and quality of communication which can be achieved. Picture for a moment the behavior of a person like Tom Newcomer in a defensive organizational climate and then in a supportive climate. Regardless of the kind of person Tom is, the nature of his reference groups, and the kind of message he has to convey, his whole approach would be different merely because of the fact that he works in one type of organizational climate as opposed to the other. Now that we have introduced the concept of communication climate at this point, we will be referring to it throughout the following chapters. This is an area where good organizational planning and enlightened leadership can make significant morale and communication improvements within an organization. As ideas are presented on how to put positive communication principles into practice, practical suggestions will be made concerning ways to create a supportive communication climate—a climate which helps to satisfy the basic social needs of acceptance, recognition, and security for all of the organization's members.

COMMUNICATION STRUCTURE

The hierarchical structure, in addition to the communication climate, is another factor within the organization which generally serves as a potential incentive or impediment to communication. All organizations need some kind of structure for efficient information processing and decision making. The nature of that structure, however,

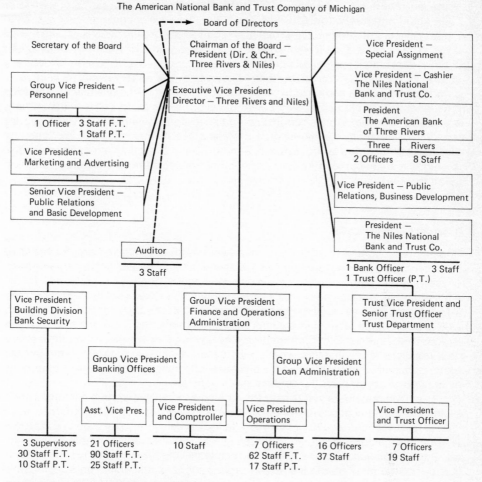

Figure 3-1 **Basic Organization Chart**

can have negative effects on communication within the organization. A typical organizational chart looks something like Figure 3-1.[3]

In the organization as illustrated above, communication is basically of three types: (1) downward—from the vice president, president, board of directors, etc., level to the lower level of supervisors, officers, staff, and so on; (2) sideways—between various staff, officers, vice presidents, supervisors, etc.; and (3) upward—from the staff, supervisors, etc., level to the upper level of vice president, president, board of directors, and so on. Each of these possible directions of communication in the structure accounts for a number of potential communication channels. In a company of sixty people, for example, the number of potential interactions of all types would be 1,770. Obviously, if all of these channels were available for use, the result for the organization would be chaos. The organization must, then, impose restrictions and constraints in order to limit communication to those channels necessary to accomplish the organizational objectives.

It would be extremely difficult for any organization to anticipate all of its present and future communication needs. In most organizations a basic internal responsi- **53** bility and reporting relationship is established, generally based on the organization chart and normal work flow activities, and other channels of communication, such as the grapevine, are developed informally. As long as the organization is getting the job done, relationships are allowed to remain as they develop. However, when problems in the organizational communication system occur, such as a strike, a slowdown, or a failure at the production level, then all aspects are reviewed and evaluated to determine why goals and objectives are not being met. It is obvious that organization personnel cannot plan all of their communication needs or demands ahead of time, but it is also obvious that responsible administrators should be constantly on the lookout for potential communication problems before they occur. In the following three sections on downward, upward, and horizontal communication, we would like to point out some of the more serious potential problems for which managers should be on the alert.

Downward Communication

Communications that normally flow downward in an organization are, for the most part, generated by the formal written statements with regard to the organization. These may encompass such well-known managerial tools as a statement of the philosophy of the business, the organizational objectives, position descriptions, standard procedures, quality control procedures, accounting manuals, and other written information relating to the importance, rationale, and interrelationships of the various departments. Other information may cover general organization procedures and practices and changes when they occur, feedback regarding the current performance of individuals in various positions, and material designed to motivate the employees to accomplish the goals of the organization.

As can be readily seen, it is easy for problems to develop in such communication systems. Communication network breakdowns may occur from many sources, such as failure of the message to get through, failure to deliver the message at the proper time or place, improper coding of message—i.e., the message is simple to management but complicated and unclear to recipients, the work force. It is commonly stated that the most fragile link in the organizational communication system is the managers themselves who fail to, or cannot, communicate properly. It has been said that the most important function of a manager is that of communicating. In some organizations, for example, people are told what to do but not why they are doing it. This reduces the worker's feeling of acceptance. When we are told why our job is important and how well we are doing in our position, our need for recognition and security is decreased. This is an important aspect of communication activity which is often neglected, and the result is lower productivity due to increased absenteeism and turnover. Goals are often not reached because employees are not aware of the standards. One type of feedback mechanism is performance evaluation forms. See Figure 3-2.

The way in which this information is collected and fed back to the employee is vitally important to the success of the organization. In an organization with a defensive climate, this kind of evaluation form might well be considered a threat and thus reduce one's feeling of security.

We have presented only two of the various types of downward communication methodologies. The reader must keep in mind, however, that there are many types of downward communication which may be necessary and important to the efficient functioning of the organization. When, for example, any of these basic types of

54

WEST COAST LIFE
Insurance Company
HOME OFFICE · SAN FRANCISCO

NAME	SIGNATURE
JOB TITLE	APPRAISED BY
ANNIVERSARY DATE INTERVIEW DATE	REVIEWED BY

OBJECTIVE:

JOB DUTIES AND RESPONSIBILITIES:

Alternate Duties and Responsibilities with Comments on Performance Relating to Those Objectives, Duties, and Responsibilities

USE ADDITIONAL SHEETS IF NECESSARY

P—1123

Figure 3-2 **Performance Evaluation Form**[4]

WEST COAST LIFE *Insurance Company*
Employee Progress Review and Development
General Scale

> This portion of the form is to be retained in the employee's department.

Employee _____ Date of hire _____
Classification _____ Date review is due _____
Dept. and Sect. _____ Date of review with employee _____

CAREFULLY READ INSTRUCTIONS BEFORE RATING THE EMPLOYEE

If particular words or phrases in an item selected as most descriptive of the individual do not specifically apply, line or cross them out.

If there are other items not selected as most descriptive of the individual but which contain words or phrases which apply, circle the appropriate parts of the item.

I. QUALITY OF PERFORMANCE: Consider how the employee's work measures up to departmental standards of accuracy, neatness, and thoroughness. Disregard volume of work.
   A. Work is only marginal, requires close checking. Is often careless. Takes little pride in his work.
   B. Quality is above minimum requirements but below the group average. Work must be critized frequently.
   C. Regularly meets recognized standards of accuracy and neatness. Errors are average in number. Work requires occasional checking.
   D. Work quality exceeds group standards. Is thorough, neat, and accurate. Mistakes are uncommon or insignificant.
   E. Output is consistently of outstanding quality. Work seldom or never requires checking. Results are always neat and accurate.

II. VOLUME OF WORK: Consider speed and quantity of satisfactory work regularly produced, allowing for departmental work load and opportunity to produce.
   A. Volume is only marginal. Seldom gets job done in the required time.
   B. Output is limited, usually below the average of the group.
   C. Production meets the average for the section. Works steadily, usually on schedule.
   D. Production exceeds average for the section. Work is often ahead of schedule.
   E. Volume is exceptionally high. Unusually industrious in turning out work.

III. COOPERATION: Consider willingness and ability to work with and for others; include outside contacts when such are important to the job.
   A. Frequently uncooperative, occasionally antagonistic. Has little interest in associates and in their work.
   B. Usually will help others but grudgingly. Is tolerant, but not friendly.
   C. Cooperates satisfactorily with others. Shows average amount of respect and consideration for others' rights and problems.
   D. Is very cooperative, likes to work with others. Considerate of others' problems.
   E. An outstanding teamworker. Shows considerable tact and diplomacy.

IV. INITIATIVE: Consider the extent to which the employee is a "self-starter" in attaining the objectives of the job.
   A. A routine worker; usually waits to be told what to do.
   B. Sometimes needs to be prodded along.
   C. Does regular work without waiting for directions.
   D. Resourceful; alert to opportunities for improvement of work.
   E. Seeks and sets for himself additional tasks; highly ingenious.

V. JOB KNOWLEDGE: Consider the extent to which the employee possesses information and understanding of his job.
   A. Comprehension of work details inadequate. Needs continuous assistance.
   B. Insufficient knowledge of some phases of the job.
   C. Adequate knowledge; knows job sufficiently well to give average performance.
   D. Thorough knowledge of practically all phases of his work.
   E. Has remarkable mastery of all phases of his work.

P-1130   DETACH AND RETAIN IN EMPLOYEE'S DEPARTMENT

Figure 3-2 **Performance Evaluation Form (Cont'd)**

Employee Development

VI. In comparing the employee's skills, attitudes, and knowledges to those required by the job, what are his strong points? Be specific. _____

_____

_____

_____

_____

_____

VII. In what important respects does the employee need to improve in terms of skills, attitudes, and knowledge required by the job? _____

_____

_____

_____

VIII. What specifically has the employee done to improve in his present job since the last progress review and development interview? Were recommendations in the last interview followed? If not, why? _____

_____

_____

_____

_____

IX. What kind or type of training should the employee undertake to improve in his present job? When should it be undertaken? Specify. _____

_____

_____

_____

_____

X. What other comments and pertinent facts should be known concerning this employee? (If additional space is needed, attach extra sheets of paper to this form.)_____

_____

_____

_____

_____

_____

Supervisor _____ Div. or Dept. Mgr. _____
             signature and date   signature and date

Assisted by _____ Employee _____
             signature and date   signature and date

WEST COAST LIFE *Insurance Company*

Employee Progress Review
In-Training Scale

Complete and retain this form in the Dept. with the employee's Personnel Records.

Employee _____ Date of hire _____

Classification _____ Date review is due _____

Dept. and Sect. _____ Date of review with employee _____

CAREFULLY READ INSTRUCTIONS BEFORE RATING THE EMPLOYEE

(Leadership Guide)

I. <u>LEARNING PROGRESS</u>: Consider the individual's ability to learn the assigned tasks.
   A. Has continual difficulty in learning the job.
   B. Sometimes has difficulty in learning the job.
   C. Learns as well as the average trainee.
   D. Learns at a moderately fast rate.
   E. Learns very rapidly.

II. <u>ATTITUDE</u>: Consider the individual's interest in the job and his willingness to respond.
   A. Goes about his work half-heartedly.
   B. Sometimes appears indifferent.
   C. Shows normal interest; all that is ordinarily expected.
   D. Shows above average interest in his work.
   E. Very enthusiastic about his work.

III. <u>INITIATIVE</u>: Consider the extent to which the individual is a "self-starter" in accomplishing the tasks of the job.
   A. Work output and quality unsatisfactory. Work is generally late.
   B. Productivity and quality poor. Often fails to get work done on time.
   C. Generally productive both as to quality and quantity. Usually gets work done on time.
   D. Does a very good job both as to quality and quantity. Rarely fails to get work done on time.
   E. Quality and quantity of work outstanding. Always gets work done on time.

IV. <u>POTENTIALITY</u>: Consider the individual's capacity to assume full responsibility for his own work.
   A. Works in spurts, often needs a push to get started.
   B. Usually maintains a steady pace. Occasionally goes off on tangents.
   C. Maintains a steady pace. Efforts usually well directed.
   D. Maintains a strong pace with little or no direction from supervision.
   E. Sets and maintains a strong pace which inspires co-workers to do likewise.

P-1126

Figure 3-2 **Performance Evaluation Form (Cont'd)**

Employee Development

V. In comparing the employee's skills, attitudes, and knowledges to those required by the job, what are his strong points? _____

_____

_____

_____

_____

_____

VI. In what important respects does the employee need to improve in terms of skills, attitudes, and knowledge required by the job? _____

_____

_____

_____

_____

VII. What are the steps which should be taken to improve the employee in his present job? When should they be undertaken? How will they be accomplished? _____

_____

_____

_____

_____

VIII. What other comments and pertinent facts should be known concerning this employee? (If additional space is needed, add extra sheets of paper to this form.)

_____

_____

_____

_____

_____

Supervisor_____   Div. or Dept. Mgr._____
          <small>signature and date</small>   <small>signature and date</small>

Assisted by_____   Employee_____
          <small>signature and date</small>   <small>signature and date</small>

These ratings of the employee's progress and the summary will be referred to when considering salary adjustments, promotions, transfers, terminations, etc.

downward communication are missing or poorly handled, the result is a reduction in the employees' sense of acceptance, recognition, or security and a corresponding reduction in organizational efficiency.

Before we leave this area of downward communication, it would be well to focus on the importance of the language that should be used in downward communications. Employees on different levels in any organization normally perceive things differently; this differentiated viewpoint creates at each organization level not only specialized language, but also a different semantic perception. To use an extreme, machine operators do not tend to see and talk about the organization, its purpose, profit, and projections as would vice presidents. Workers in the normal course of events may take a narrow and self-centered view of major policy decisions, whereas a vice president talks about events in broad, long-range terms such as "modernization," "marketing stance," and "five-year plan." Machine operators employ terminology and shorthand names for various machines they use and the people they come in contact with during a working day. This special terminology may not be understandable to a vice president. Middle managers play a translator's role between those people in upper management and the rank-and-file employee.

For this reason, communication in the downward flow pattern from top management should go through the normal channels, and whatever communication is transmitted directly from a high level to a low level in the organization should be edited very carefully. Newsletters, bulletin board notices, loudspeaker announcements, and so on, are examples of direct downward communication. Management needs to be constantly aware that because of the hierarchical structure of the organization, employees are conditioned to expect that most of their important communications come to them from their immediate superior. By having important messages communicated down the normal chain of command, an added advantage is also achieved. The workers at various levels have a chance to express their opinions about the matter, and middle managers feel obliged to get familiar enough with the contents of the communication to answer whatever questions are raised. In the theory of catharsis, merely expressing gripes, even though nothing comes of it, is therapeutic. Encouraging such gripes helps promote a supportive climate within structured organizations. It assists greatly in reducing the impersonality of the establishment.

Upward Communication

The types of communication that normally flow upward in an organization are based on the communication demand system as designed by management in conformance to various organizational practices, policies, and decisions. Standard reporting items generally revolve around the activities of the organizations. These are, for example:

1. Production reports
2. Quality control reports
3. Shipping reports
4. Inventory control
5. Absenteeism
6. Profit
7. Costs
8. Orders
9. Projections—long- and short-range
10. Programs
11. Production schedules

12. Sales
13. Finished inventory
14. Customer complaints
15. Engineering—research and development

If there is any area of communication in business which seems to concern management most, it is probably the variation between the formal upward reporting system and the true nature of activities on the working level. This leads to inaccurate and low-quality upward communication. One of the most startling examples of faulty communication came to light in the Penn Central bankruptcy fiasco.

Many company presidents will readily admit that they know little or nothing about what is going on several levels below them. It is only in recent years, as behavioral scientists have shown the relationship between communication and performance, that senior management has become concerned about what is going on at the lower levels. Many fairly new techniques, such as an open-door policy, an example of which is shown below, are being tried, as well as some old standbys such as the suggestion box. We do not have any new or revolutionary methods to offer, but we would like to again stress the importance of upward communication and analyze some of the impediments to upward communication in hierarchies.

It is a simple matter of fact that superiors are generally better talkers and writers than subordinates are. They have usually gone to school longer and are often selected for their position partly on the basis of their demonstrated communication skills. Managers have an innate awareness of and confidence in their need to communicate downward. A second factor here, which shows up in all of the research, is that employees are very cautious about the kinds of information they communicate to their superiors. Researchers have found that a careful screening or filtering of information from low-status to high-status persons is characteristic of communication in industrial hierarchies,[5] and have demonstrated that the mere introduction of status differentiation "produces restraining forces against communicating criticisms of persons to the other level,"[6] in experimentally created hierarchies. One of the authors, Dr. Donaghy, found in a study of General Dynamics Corporation that the mere presence of a high-status individual increases a subordinate's emotional level even when he did nothing but sit quietly.[7] If honest, legitimate upward communication is one of the organization's goals, it is obvious that a great deal of effort must be expended to secure it. Only under very exceptional circumstances will lower-level employees volunteer the type of information that is truly necessary for senior management to make decisions, particularly with regard to morale, feeling, tone, and communication climate.

It is not enough to simply provide channels for upward communication; the organization must also provide the supportive climate and reward system necessary to encourage such communication. Many organizations have what is called the *open-door* policy to help improve upward communication. This plan normally involves informing employees that their superiors are always available for discussion of problems. Although this concept is sound theoretically, in actual practice it seldom works out in the way it is intended. In the first place, employees will hesitate to discuss negative things and seldom have the nerve to approach some higher-status individual directly. Secondly, when they do "walk in," what they have to say is usually not what the superior wants to hear. Further, the superior may have poorly developed listening skills, making it impossible to create a good communication climate which will maximize the opportunity for both management and the employee to benefit from the interchange. Relatively few organizations have devoted the time and effort necessary to achieve competence on the part of first-line and middle managers to use positive listening skills for the benefit of management, the employee, and the organization.

Many organizations have attempted to redesign their communication programs to the end that management takes the initiative in a positive way through a program that permits management to communicate more or less directly with employees. This can be accomplished in many ways. One of the easiest ways is for the manager simply to get out of the office and walk in the work areas, have a cup of coffee or lunch in the employee lunchroom, or merely stop and visit with some of the employees during slack periods. Other methods might be to hire an outside agency to interview and discuss important questions with employees in an anonymous fashion, or to send out periodic questionnaires regarding various pertinent issues, such as is done in a morale survey, or, finally, to devise a method of tapping the employee grapevine. Not enough really creative thought has been given to the problem of improving upward communication.

Horizontal Communication

Horizontal communication is generally considered to be unproductive in many organizations. It can, however, be one of the most productive forms of communication in the entire plant. Most of you have been employees in various companies. You will recall that you exchanged information with your fellow employees on all aspects of the company: whether it was a good place to work, what the easy jobs were, how the bosses acted, the various aspects of their personality and their peculiarities, and, finally, pay and gossip. No organization can stop peer-group interchange. It can only hope to supply an input which will assist in producing accurate and meaningful information. People increase their feelings of security, acceptance, and recognition by comparing themselves with others on their same level. Just as Tom Newcomer's friends wanted to discover why he was doing so well, all employees want to see how they are doing compared with others in similar positions and to make the changes necessary to become important functioning members of the corporation.

The only type of organization in which horizontal communication is discouraged is the extremely autocratic one. Autocratic management subconsciously tries to "divide and conquer." It does not want the subordinates to get information in any other way than through the front office. The result of this kind of impediment to horizontal communication is usually uncertainty, apathy, and discouragement, which eventually lead to reduced efficiency. Horizontal communication is one of the important checks employees have on authoritarian leadership. Positive horizontal communication is absolutely necessary in promoting a supportive organizational communication climate.

Finally, horizontal communication benefits the organization by providing increased coordination. Supervisors, for example, who have coffee together can many times organize their activities in such a way that all, as well as the company, benefit. There is, of course, a danger here, and that is that employees might overdepend on horizontal communication when they should be going down or up the communication ladder.

Summary—Part 1

At this point in this chapter we have in the main presented the theory governing organizational communication. The basic principles of communication transmission have been presented. In the portion of the chapter that follows ways will be suggested as to how these principles may be put into practice. It has been shown that transmission is that part of the communication process which involves the sender. We also presented information on the message and various channels. More will be discussed with regard to these elements in a following chapter on reception. The division of the chapters into transmission and reception has been made simply for the ease of the reader; it should be quite obvious after reading this first section that this arbitrary division is purely artificial and that in actual communication situations it is nearly impossible to separate the sender, message, channel, and receiver.

The purposes of communication as we have defined them are to allow one to understand, manipulate, and control the environment. This is done in order to maintain an internally balanced state for individuals as well as groups and larger organizations. Communication occurs either to maintain that balance or to correct it when the internal state is out of balance.

Two types of incentives and impediments to communication have been discussed: individual and organizational. Individuals initiate communication when one or more of their basic needs are unfulfilled. The basic social needs that are most important in our current society are acceptance, recognition, and security. The state of these needs in any individual, and thus his/her potential for communication transmission, is dependent upon personal feelings based upon background and current status, the reference groups relevant to each of these needs, and finally the nature of the potential messages that could be transmitted.

Organizational incentives and impediments to communication revolve primarily around the climate and structure of the organization. Gibb denominated the two extremes of organizational climate as *defensive* and *supportive,* and developed several subcategories under each. In general, defensive climates impede communication transmission while supportive climates provide incentives to communication transmission. With regard to organizational structure we pointed out that all organizations need some kind of structure, but that the structure itself can provide impediments to communication. When there is an organizational structure, the three types of communication that can occur are upward, downward, and horizontal. The basic problem that occurs in downward communication is that information which needs to be communicated is neglected or poorly transmitted. We also pointed out that people on different structural levels have different viewpoints and specialized languages. The basic problem with upward communication is simply increasing both the quantity and the quality of communication transmitted. Finally, with regard to horizontal communication, we discussed its importance in determining feelings of acceptance, recognition, and security and its contributions to democratic leadership and increased coordination.

PUTTING THE BASIC PRINCIPLES INTO PRACTICE

In this section effective and ineffective communication practices in face-to-face communication situations will be presented. Although other types of communication situations—one person to a group, one group to another group, etc.—involve many of the same practices present in the face-to-face situation, they will be discussed in more detail in later chapters. This section will consist of a basic discussion of the voice and expression, some do's and don'ts of all face-to-face communication, and a detailed discussion of what we consider to be the two most difficult and important types of face-to-face communication situations which occur in business: the improvement interview and the problem interview. We have chosen these two interviews because we feel that the most salient practices with regard to these face-to-face situations parallel the most important practices in all organizational face-to-face communication transmission situations.

How to Say What You Mean

In many communication transmission situations, it isn't what we say, it is *how we say it* that really makes the difference. Actually, there are two important parts to this "sounding like what you mean." First of all, we are concerned with making those to whom we are speaking believe, understand, and appreciate what it is that we are attempting to get across. The second important part deals with the fact that people consciously or unconsciously judge us by the expression and voice tone that we use in speaking to them.

In our modern business world the importance of dress, neatness, physical appearance, manners, and other outward aspects of the pleasing personality is continually stressed. As for our speaking voices, very little has been said. Yet, we are judged every time we begin to speak. Our personalities show through our speech. If you were to judge solely on the basis of a telephone conversation, what picture would you conjure of the various people with whom you have spoken? On the basis of incorrect pronunciation you would visualize, perhaps, crudely dressed individuals. The person might, however, be very well dressed. You might imagine some woman to be young and attractive. In fact, though her voice may be youthful, she actually may be quite old and plain, We do judge personalities by various voice and expression qualities of the speaker.

Have you ever had the opportunity to listen to a playback of your voice? Perhaps it was recorded on one of the electronic recording devices. If so, you had the opportunity of judging your voice in all of its shades of delivery. Perhaps you said, "Is that my voice?" If you said that, you were thinking to yourself that certainly you did not sound as you thought you sounded. Therein lies the danger. Too frequently—all too frequently—we do not sound as we think we sound. We fire from the hip, we give a command, make a comment, or do one of a thousand little duties we have to do during the course of the day, and we do not realize how the sound effects we make register on others.

Ever notice a youngster when he is being remonstrated with by his parents? He watches the eyes of his dad or mother. It is from the additional judgment area that one can determine if the tone of voice means what the voice is saying. A child is smart enough, or, shall we say, aware enough, to learn to judge from some base wider than just the tonal inflection that ears bring. He/She is, in reality, saying, "Is the voice I'm listening to actually saying what it means?"

FIVE ASPECTS OF THE VOICE

Tone

Vocal tone refers to the coloring or hue in the voice, just as in art *tone* is a quality of color or shade. We are all familiar with the situation where someone may say, "Yes, I'll do that," but how they say it implies, "Well, I'll do it, but I certainly don't want to." We can all remember a movie in which the leading character used the term, "Yeah!" It was a derisive term. It was a term calculated to say, "That's what you think, bud." It was a case where *yes* meant absolutely *no*.

The tone of voice is an instrument for conveying various shades of emotion. We portray anger, love, hate, fear, and a whole host of other emotions through the inflections of our speaking instrument. Who among us can forget Shaw's Professor Henry Higgins, in which he espoused the concept that the only difference between a lady and an urchin was in the ability to speak in a cultured voice? Who among us can forget the smooth voices of Charles Boyer, Omar Shariff, Sophia Loren, Marcello Mastrioni, and Catherine Deneuve, as they portrayed the lover? Who among us can forget Charles Laughton as Captain Bligh, when he vented his calm wrath on the mutineers, or George C. Scott as General Patton instructing his troops? Each of these individuals possessed the outstanding ability for using the voice to portray a specific emotion.

Quality

An acceptable voice quality has a commercial and cultural value. For example, on almost all recommendation blanks for positions there is a space for remarks about the voice. The quality of one's voice is dependent on both the physical and the emotional makeup of the individual. Physically, one's vocal quality is dependent on the structure of the vocal mechanism. We can train our own ear to appreciate pleasing vocal quality. To a trained interviewer and, to a lesser degree, to almost all individuals, emotional stability is easily determined through the quality of one's voice. Joy tenses the vocal muscles and animates our voice, while grief relaxes our throat and causes a duller speech. In the same ways, contempt, cynicism, fear, eagerness, and many, many other emotions display themselves in vocal quality. A speaker who would like to develop a pleasing vocal quality must first develop emotional control.

Pitch

The pitch of one's voice is determined at birth; we are all sopranos, contraltos, tenors, baritones, or basses. We can do little to change our basic pitch, but we can learn to control our pitch within nature's limits. One of the prime pitch problems is called *vocal monotony*—that is, using either little pitch variation or an endless repetition of the same pitch pattern. A lullaby is a repetition of the same pitch pattern, and it is designed to produce sleep. Vocal monotony is most likely to occur in formal speaking situations. In normal everyday speaking we all use a great deal of pitch variation, but the formal interview, speech, or similar situation causes us to fall into a monotonous pitch pattern. Finally, some speakers tend to gravitate to the higher pitches for emphasis in speaking. The problem here is that the speaker has no place to go when he/she wants to emphasize certain points. In most cases it is better for a speaker to stay with a low enough pitch to be heard and to leave enough room for vocal variation.

Rate

Besides changing our pitch in speaking, we can also change our pace. Most speakers without training or practice tend to speak at a very rapid rate. Again, this is more often

65

true in a formal situation than in everyday conversation. Variation in vocal rate promotes interest on the part of the listener while monotony quickly loses the receiver's attention.

One of the major differences between writing and speaking is the ability to use the pause. The pause is the speaker's form of punctuation; however, the pause is a much more effective tool in speaking than punctuation in writing. The pause has a number of uses: it allows time to secure the consent of the receiver; it allows time for one to mentally rehearse what he/she is going to say next; and it emphasizes the most important points in the message. If there is any one major difference between an excellent speaker and an average one, it would probably be a highly developed ability to use the vocal pause!

Force

Vocal force is often defined as the intensity of the tone. It involves the loudness or quietness with which the message is expressed. For many speakers vocal force is synonymous with loudness, but skilled speakers can make a quiet statement as forceful as a loud one. Vocal force can come in one of many ways: long-term sustained force; short, quick applications of force; or an explosive display of force used primarily in times of deep emotion. Stress is also a form of force which is used with particular words or phrases. It can come at the beginning, middle, or end of a word or phrase and often can entirely change the meaning of the sentence. A favored illustration of this change is in the reading of the sentence, "What's that in the road ahead?" which with a pause gives: "What's that in the road—a head?"

Perhaps the best way to summarize this section is to simply suggest what we believe to be the things one should keep in mind with regard to how we say what we mean and then suggest some possible ways of improving voice and expression. In face-to-face communication transmission, as well as all other types, one should keep the following rules in mind:

1. Be calm and collected at all times.
2. Be loud enough to be heard easily.
3. Express words you are using with accurate diction and correct pronunciation.
4. Speak slowly and make use of the pause to stress main ideas.
5. Use a confident tone that carries the calm pitch of certainty and expresses the fact that you know what you are doing and requiring.
6. Make use of *both* the quiet and the loud forms of force.
7. Be free from any expression of worry, anxiety, or uncertainty as to what you are requesting.
8. Be vibrant and enthusiastic and avoid the dull, monotonous voice that does not inspire people to believe in what they are doing.
9. Express sincerity; remember that your honesty and integrity will show through in your voice.
10. Know what you are talking about and don't bluff.

As we mentioned earlier, there are many aspects of one's voice which cannot be changed, but such things as resonance, flexibility, pace, variety, and quality can be improved with a minimal amount of training and practice. We have listed some of the things that we feel will help one improve his/her oral expression most quickly.

1. Join a toastmasters' club.
2. Enroll in a public school speech course.
3. Read a good self-help book on vocal improvement.
4. Practice reading out loud from newspapers or books.
5. Think before you speak. Attempt to say, "Just what is it that I am trying to get across here?"
6. Practice in front of a mirror, watching the movement of your lips.
7. Practice being alive and interested in all that is going on around about you. Express this interest in your voice. Learn to become enthusiastic about something.
8. Work with a close friend on improving your voice. Practice reading and speaking aloud with him/her.
9. Begin listening for vocal qualities in others that you feel are good or bad and thus improve your own ear for voice and expression differences.

UNDERSTANDING YOUR COMMUNICATION ROLE

Many writers have tried to classify the various purposes of communication that go on in face-to-face settings. Perhaps the most accepted, however, in terms of research and textbook writing, is that of Robert Bales. In Bales's system of classifying interaction, both verbal and nonverbal communication are classified into four main areas with twelve subcategories:

1. Positive reactions
   a. *Shows solidarity,* raises other's status, gives help, reward.
   b. *Shows tension release,* jokes, laughs, shows satisfaction.
   c. *Agrees,* shows passive acceptance, understands, concurs, complies.
2. Attempted answers
   d. *Gives suggestions,* direction, implying autonomy for other.
   e. *Gives opinion,* evaluation, analysis; expresses feeling, wish.
   f. *Gives orientation,* information; repeats, clarifies, confirms.
3. Questions
   g. *Asks for orientation,* information, repetition, confirmation.
   h. *Asks for opinion,* evaluation, analysis, expression of feeling.
   i. *Asks for suggestion,* direction, possible ways of action.
4. Negative reactions
   j. *Disagrees;* shows passive rejection, formality; withholds help.
   k. *Shows tension,* asks for help, withdraws from field.
   l. *Shows antagonism,* deflates other's status, defends or asserts self.[8]

It is not important at this point what the purpose of one's communication transmission is, but the sender should be aware of the purposes of his/her communication effort. Whether one's purpose is merely to show solidarity by recognizing and greeting another person warmly and understandingly and making the person feel wanted and important as an individual and human being, or to give a suggestion which must be carried out quickly and efficiently, the nature of the end purpose determines to a great extent the proper technique for transmitting the communication. We do not have the space in this text to go into all of the various means of transmission which are appropriate to each communication purpose; what we will try to do instead is discuss those communication practices which we feel are relevant to most organizational communication purposes.

In the preceding section on voice and expression, it was pointed out that we communicate with our tone, quality, pitch, rate, and force. However, there are other important factors that go into communication transmission, such as words, gestures, sounds, ideas, and meaning. Perhaps we can discuss the first and last of these factors together. *Words* are simply symbols which we either write or speak in certain culturally prescribed ways. They do not have meaning in and of themselves. If you are over thirty years of age, the phrase "cut down" to you probably refers to something you do to a tree or bush, but to someone under thirty it can also mean an insulting remark made to another person. One must constantly remember that the meaning for words is found in the heads of the sender and receivers, not in a dictionary. We can go to a dictionary to get some idea of what a word means, but we can make some serious mistakes if we take a dictionary meaning as the final authority. Words mean different things to different people at different times, as do gestures, sounds, ideas, and even vocal variations.

We communicate also through gestures. Our bodily postures, our faces, our arm movements, and the movements of many other parts of our body, all are part of our communication equipment. This text is not designed to teach you how to gesture or how to make more efficient use of your gestures, but merely to point out the importance of bodily language in communication transmission. The effective oral communicator must be alert to the gestures which accompany his/her other communication tools. Listeners tend to believe what is said nonverbally more than what is said with words. It is fairly easy for a communicator to lie with the tongue, but much more difficult to lie with one's whole body. We register acceptance, rejection, hurt, indignation, and happiness all through bodily and facial movements and gestures. This is called *kinesics,* and the practice of proper kinesics is important to the communication transmitter.

Many times we communicate with sounds other than words. Many sounds, such as "You don't say," "Well, I'll be darned," "Hi, nice weather we're having," and even "Rumph," can and do have very definite and different meanings in different circumstances. A grunt many times can have as much meaning to a subordinate as an entire statement, and many times we are not even aware that we have transmitted a communication. Like gestures and vocal expression, sounds carry much more meaning than we normally give them credit for. To prove this point to yourself, someday just stand back in the lunchroom or at a board meeting or anyplace else you choose, and listen very carefully to what is being said. You will find that sentences are interrupted and still carry their meaning, that incoherent sounds are uttered and everyone knows what was meant, and that word omissions and substitutions occur which are not even noticed. When people are close to one another and friendly, they tend to speak in "short-tongue," which is, of course, the spoken equivalent of shorthand.

Finally, we communicate by means of ideas. These ideas are formed into groups of words with which we attempt to get the other person to do as we do, accept our thinking, and change their behavior patterns to fit what we think is the correct action in a particular case. Ideas are the lifeblood of communication. Without new ideas, communication transmission would soon disintegrate to the level of a broken record. Ideas transcend words, gestures, sounds, etc.; they are our conception of what reality is or how it should be which we carry around in our heads. Words are truly incapable of accurately expressing ideas. We would have no communication problems if we could read each other's minds and transmit ideas directly rather than first translating them into words. When we are initiating communication, we must constantly be aware that any time we attempt to transmit an idea to other human beings, we are going to create a distorted picture of our idea in their mind. To paraphrase an old expression, "Ideas are worth a thousand words or gestures or sounds."

This leads directly to what we consider to be the fundamentals of good face-to-face communication. This does not involve speaking style or organization of material or depth of preparation—we will discuss many of those things later because they are important—but the basic fundamentals of communication revolve around a sense of humanity toward one's fellow human beings. And what does humanity stand for in communication transmission?

H — Honesty with other people.
U — Understanding of their problems.
M — Mutual respect,
A — Awareness of their limitations,
N — Negotiability,
 I — Identification with their feelings,
T — Trust, and finally a
Y — "You" orientation, not "I."

WHY PEOPLE DON'T COMMUNICATE WELL

There are any number of reasons why people do not communicate well; we have pointed to many of them in the earlier part of this book and in other chapters, but we would like to point out four major impediments to good communication which we think cause many problems. These four problem areas relate primarily to the transmission of communication; problems directly related to communication reception will be discussed in the following chapter.

First, people do not communicate well because they often have emotional blocks. They are more concerned with things like, "Does this person like me?" "Does this person think I know what I'm doing?" "Do I appear qualified to do the job I am doing?" "Do they believe me?" "He/She makes me unsure of myself"; "This person doesn't seem to know what I am talking about"; or "These people are stubborn because they can't see my viewpoint," than they are about getting their message across. Emotional blocks come from all kinds of sources: anger, fear, nervousness, defensiveness, uncertainty, and so on. They may be due to the fact that the individual has had unsatisfactory experiences in previous interaction encounters or that he/she got up on the wrong side of the bed that morning or that he/she is just a normally oversensitive person. Regardless of the source of the emotional block or its type, it must be removed before good communication can take place. When we are emotionally aroused, we are neither a good communicator nor a good receptor. Like a football quarterback, we must keep our cool if we are to do our best.

Second, people do not communicate well if they come from different environments or have different frames of reference. This means, for example, that an agent and an underwriting person do not have on the surface a common purpose and a common goal. Just as in hockey, some people are trying to drive the puck into the cage and the goalkeeper is trying to keep them from so doing; however, in this instance they are *not* on the same team. As was mentioned above, actions and symbols mean different things to different individuals. For any two individuals to

Frame of reference for person A	Frame of reference for person B

Figure 3-3 Persons A and B have no common ground on which to base meaningful communication

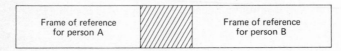

Figure 3-4 Persons A and B can communicate meaningfully because they have a common ground in the hatched area

communicate well, they must find some common ground in order to get acceptance and agreement. Compare the frames of reference for persons A and B in Figure 3-3 with the frames of reference for persons A and B in Figure 3-4. In Figure 3-4 they can at least begin to communicate because their frames of reference overlap in the hatched region, but persons A and B in Figure 3-3 might just as well live on different planets.

Third, some people cannot communicate well because they are incapable of expressing themselves through the use of the spoken and/or written word. In order to communicate, one must have the capacity to use words, since words are the medium through which we express thoughts, ideas, and feelings. Some people have a limited inventory of words with which to express themselves, or their recall in a given situation is limited. An individual might think that he or she is saying the right thing, but it always seems to come out wrong. Words are building blocks, and the correct use of the building blocks creates the structure—or the ideas, feelings, and attitudes toward which we are driving. Other people have the basic words necessary to express their ideas, but they have one of the many different types of speech impediments. In either case the individual must work very hard to overcome these handicaps through education and training, development, and experience.

Finally, some people cannot communicate effectively because they are unable to use their personality effectively. Communication depends in a large measure on the vibrations one sends out in the process of communicating. One's outward appearance, gestures, smile, animation, eyes, bodily posture, vitality, and voice quality all express one's personality. These factors are particularly important in face-to-face communication where individuals are constantly looking for the "meaning of meaning"[9] and are aware of the goodness of intent or the soundness of what the individual is attempting to communicate.

Summary on Applied Aspects of Communication

In summarizing this section on how to say what you mean, it would be beneficial to present some do's and don'ts of face-to-face communication transmission. Obviously, we cannot list all of the ideas that have been elaborated in this section, so we have picked out those which we feel are most important for people involved in organizational communication.

THE DO'S OF FACE-TO-FACE COMMUNICATION

1. *Do learn to express yourself.* What you understand and what you know might not be effective unless you communicate it to others. We learn by doing. We learn to walk by walking, to think by thinking, and to speak by speaking. It would be well for all managers to obtain experience in expressing themselves through speech classes, toastmasters' groups, and role playing.

2. *Do learn to use your personality.* As was mentioned in the preceding section, your personality affects others. Smile! Be pleasant! Use your personality to win over those with whom you are working.

3. *Do learn to think through your problems.* Know why a decision was made and what the basis was for a particular decision—the sound logic governing it.

4. *Do learn to think in terms of how an employee might view a particular decision,* since you will be faced with the problem of explaining it sooner or later.

5. *Do learn to stick to your decisions once you have made them* upon a basis of sound judgment and logical follow-through on company policy.

6. *Do learn to make your voice confident, quiet, and cordial.* Negative decisions need not be made in a negative tone of voice. It can be done understandingly and with patience.

7. *Do learn to give people room to express themselves, to retreat, to be different from you, and to honestly and reasonably differ in their opinions.* Even though others may not agree with you, nevertheless, they have the right to an opinion; so let them retain that right, even though it may not square with the facts as you see them.

8. *Do learn to put forth your ideas even though others may not accept them and will not be converted by you.* State your case and let it be done without feeling the necessity for hammering it home with a full agreement or acceptance from the other party.

9. *Do learn to accept differences of opinions without getting angry, upset, or negative toward another.* Try to understand the other individual and, through this understanding, have an appreciation for his/her viewpoint, although you may have to decide in the opposite manner.

10. *Do learn to accept the fact that not everyone is going to agree with your decisions,* and that as good a case can sometimes be made for a decision opposite to the one which you thought correct at the time you made it.

11. *Do learn to live with your decisions,* good or bad, and to go on from where you are.

THE DON'TS OF FACE-TO-FACE COMMUNICATION

1. Don't be bossy.
2. Don't use sarcasm.
3. Don't threaten.
4. Don't act angry.
5. Don't swear.
6. Don't take it personally or make it personal.
7. Don't lose your poise or act frightened.
8. Don't take a position from which you cannot deviate.
9. Don't lose your patience.

Superior-Subordinate Communication

Of all the kinds of face-to-face communication that go on in an organization, perhaps the most important and at the same time the most difficult is the interaction between a superior and a subordinate. Nearly every course of action a supervisor takes to improve or better utilize employees involves "talking things over" with them. This is entirely normal. Discussions with individual employees occur in normal day-to-day relationships. When a new employee reports for work, job induction involves communication with the superior. When work is assigned, it is necessary for the superior to talk with employees about the work to be done, the quantity and quality expected, and any time limitations involved. When a worker's performance is appraised, this should usually involve a discussion as well as a performance rating. Many times subordinates come to their superior for information regarding policies, rules, and regulations which affect them. Employees also go to their employers many times with their problems which might have arisen either within the company or outside of the company. Of all these types of superior-subordinate communications, the two that seem to be the most troublesome are the improvement interview and the problem interview. These, then, are the two types of interviews which we will deal with in detail later in this section.

Employer-employee relations are sometimes impaired because the superior fails to talk things over with employees. Many superiors avoid holding planned discussions with employees, but for several different reasons. Some would like to hold interviews: they know what they would like to achieve, but don't know how to begin, and having begun, they can't seem to carry through to the desired objective. They have no plan for such face-to-face communications. Others should seek a discussion with some employees but do not because they are afraid they may get themselves out on a limb. They are not sure of their facts. Frequently superiors are fearful of questions the employee may ask during such a discussion. They don't know the answers. Some discussions with employees just naturally involve bad tidings. Many superiors are especially reluctant to undertake any discussion if unpleasant news or adverse comments are involved. They don't know how to approach the employees in such cases. For these and other reasons, superiors sometimes postpone discussions with employees until some action is absolutely necessary. They then undertake such an interview in an apologetic or brusque manner, with inner forebodings concerning the outcome. In these circumstances their fears are usually well grounded. The results of such discussions are disappointing to both parties, to say the least.

A part of the answer to this situation is understanding by the superior of certain fundamental principles involved in most of these discussion situations. Elton Mayo's Hawthorne study established that the intangible factor—employee attitude—the way employees feel about their work, their fellow employees, and the company—was the strongest influence toward increased productivity.[10] In order to discover more about this intangible which we call *attitude*, the researchers experimented with different interviewing methods.

At first, prepared questions were asked. Time and time again, the employees would mentally and verbally wander off. Clearly, they had something on their mind that while it might seem trivial to other people, was important to them. These questions, it appeared, tended to elicit opinions on topics which the interviewer rather than the employee, thought important. This so-called *direct* type of interview was therefore abandoned. Because of this wandering and in order to get at the fundamental troubles of the individual, a new technique was devised, one in which the employees were allowed to express themselves freely on any topic. It is known as the *indirect* or nondirective interview.

In the final two sections of this chapter we will discuss two of the most important purposes of indirect interviews used in organizational communication. The first involves an employee's problem. This problem may be brought to the superior by the employee or may be referred by some other superior. The *problem interview* is designed to help superiors help employees to help themselves. The second involves some aspect of the employee's work or attitude which can and should be improved. The *improvement interview* is designed to help superiors talk with an employee so that they can come up with a mutually acceptable plan to increase the employee's usefulness to the organization by building on strong points and correcting certain deficiencies.

THE PROBLEM INTERVIEW

Since the time of the Hawthorne study, several principles related to this indirect or nondirective interviewing method have become widely accepted. They have been established throughout twenty-odd years of experience and research. First, job dissatisfactions and personal problems cause employees to change jobs or remain away from work, or they affect efficiency so that productivity is lowered. For example, an employee who is having serious marital difficulties or who is harassed by a burden of excessive debts or who habitually drinks himself or herself into a stupor night after night will be unable to maintain the pace required by the job. While management cannot take responsibility for directing workers' lives, even if it knew how, it can accept the point of view that adjustment on the job involves a worker's total adjustment.

Second, a major purpose of many discussions with employees is to prevent problems rather than cure them. This means that the superior frequently needs to take the initiative. For example, an employee who has been prompt, alert, and enthusiastic becomes tardy, lackadaisical, and disinterested. The superior has every reason to believe that something is troubling the employee. One of two things can be done: wait for the employee to come in or to ask to go to the personnel office, or make an opportunity to talk things over with that employee in the hope of giving help. The wide-awake superior will try to prevent rather than cure problems.

Third, in general superiors will encounter two types of employee problems: those involving a solution which lies within their prerogatives and responsibilities, and those in which the solution lies outside their prerogatives and responsibilities. The former on-the-job problems involve such things as (1) Susan Pond is sore because she was passed over in regard to a promotion, (2) Jim Savage thinks his work load is too heavy, (3) Mary Hanson is worried about her ability to take hold of her job, and (4) George Parks wants his vacation to come in July. Those problems which are purely personal to the employee and which arise outside the work situation but which may affect their work are off-the-job problems. Typical examples of such problems are (1) Joe Baldwin has a housing problem, (2) Jane Brown is having money problems, (3) Carol Marks needs help with her income tax return, and (4) Henry Banks' wife is suing him for divorce, and he needs some legal advice.

Finally, the purpose of discussions with an individual employee is to help the employee help himself/herself. Interviewers do not ordinarily solve problems for

73

employees. They help. They give information, help clarify problems, and suggest an help develop solutions, after which they expect the employee to help himself or hersel Referral should be made elsewhere when necessary. It is important for interviewers t realize that they are not equipped to handle all employee problems which the encounter.

The problem-solving interview is a plan for holding a discussion with employee in an attempt to help them to adjust to a problem which interferes with efficient jo performance. In accomplishing this aim, the interviewer may perform any or all o three main functions.

Provide an opportunity for employees to "talk it over." Employees havin personal problems or grievances are emotionally disturbed and because of thi cannot give full attention to their work. By providing a "friendly ear" and by no directing action, the "friendly" listener gives employees a chance to get a grievanc or a personal problem off their chest. Other benefits forthcoming from the successfu discharge of this function are, first, that the interview has a tension-releasing effect o the employees which in turn tends to influence positively their attitude toward the jo and the company; second, the interview may act as a catalyst to the employees' ow thinking and may help them meet their own problems more effectively; and finally, th employees' desire for recognition may be satisfied by management's interest in ther as individuals.

Provide information for employees. The need for information of all sorts i pronounced, and discussions with employees provide one means of making badl needed information readily available. This need includes information on the inter pretation of company policies, programs, and regulations, as well as information o varied off-the-job matters, such as housing, transportation, hospitalization insurance community facilities, and sources of financial and legal help.

Provide information to top management. Superiors should serve as a channel o communication between top management and employees. They interpret policies an practices to individuals on the one hand and reflect back to management employe reactions to these policies and practices. The manager should also keep policy forming groups in touch with employee problems and attitudes in order tha preventive or remedial action may be taken by responsible officials.

Rules to Remember

In the problem interview, employees are not only allowed but encouraged to tal freely about those things which are worrying them. In order to enable the employee t do this, the superior must conduct the interview with care. The following rules hav been developed to make the interview effective. They point up the difference betwee ordinary social conversation and the interview as a tool for effective face-to-fac communications.

The interview needs information. If this information is to be useful, it must b valid. Observing the following guides will help the interviewer get valid information First, *the interviewer should remember that an obvious complaint may not be the rea trouble at all; it may simply be symptomatic of something deeper*. The interviewe should guard against accepting everything the employee says at face value. Rathe he/she should consider what caused that opinion, idea, or thought to be held. G below the surface complaint to get at the real problem.

The interviewer should listen not only to what the employee says, but for what i not said—for what the person does not want to say or cannot say without help. Durin the problem interview, the interviewer has many opportunities to note significant gaps and omissions in what a person is saying. The interviewer should note these omissions and mentally ask whether these areas have been omitted because the speaker does not care to talk about them or because he/she has never thought about them. Things about which a person does not care to talk are often likely to be connected with unpleasant or painful experiences. Such omissions are likely to indicate areas of emotional significance, which should be explored by the indirect approach.

The interviewer should not treat everything that is said as fact; one must remember that *he/she is dealing with feelings, sentiments, opinions, and attitudes which, while honestly expressing the employee's point of view, are not necessarily true or false.* The beginning interviewer tends to be concerned exclusively with truth or falsity. Everything is fact or error. Many statements are neither fact nor error; they are often subjective opinions, such as: "Working in this place is like being in jail!" or "This is the most wonderful outfit to work for!" Then, too, many statements, although believed to be the honest truth by the interviewee, may be based on false assumptions and considered false by other people. The converse is also true.

The interviewer should try to prevent the employee's feelings from affecting his/her own. The interviewer and interviewee are both the result of past and present experiences which may be distinctly different for the two. Because of the differences, the interviewer, unless he/she guards against it, may become annoyed or irritated at what the other person is saying. If one doesn't guard against exhibiting sentiments and feelings, they may destroy the very attitude on the part of the speaker that he/she is trying to express.

The interviewer should respect the dignity of the employee as an individual. One should remember that the relationship existing between interviewer and interviewee will help determine the outcome of the interview. This relationship may change, for better or worse, during the course of the interview. It is well to remember that this relationship between the interviewer and the interviewee is reciprocal. What the interviewer says and does affects the employee. A key point to remember here is that information given in confidence should always be held confidential. Many matters discussed are, of course, nonconfidential in nature. Occasionally, however, an employee needs an outlet for personal tensions or problems of a highly confidential nature. Unless the employee is sure that what is told the interviewer will not be divulged without permission, it is likely that the very information which might enable the superior to understand and help meet the problem will be withheld.

In addition to these guides for getting valid and useful information, there are certain rules to be employed during the conduct of the interview. *The interviewer should talk or ask questions only as needed to keep the discussion moving along a constructive course.* The superior is there to listen to the employee and not to express personal opinions or ideas. Everything said or done should be to the end of making it possible for the employee to talk freely. One may have to start the conversation with a little social conversation to put the employee at ease. The interviewer may want to ask a few questions about the employee's job, or family, or some other comfortable topic. It might be necessary to relieve the anxiety of the employee by reassurance that the interview is confidential. Questions might need to be asked to clarify some statement, to get all the information needed to summarize, or to help the employee reach a decision. In so doing, the interviewer makes questions work for him/her.

The interviewer should listen to the employee in a patient, friendly, and intelligent manner and avoid interrupting. This means that the interviewer is listening to what the employee has to say with complete interest and attention, trying to understand everything said or implied. We will discuss more about listening in the following chapter.

The interviewer should not display any kind of authority. The employee is likely to be resentful of any display of authority. The interviewer, therefore, should guard against displaying authority in any of its forms, i.e., contradiction, interruption, or subordination of the employee. Orders and threats are not techniques which basically alter human behavior anyhow.

The interviewer should never argue with the employee. It is wise never to argue with the employee about personal opinions, prejudices, or irrationalities. Any argument is in some way an attempt to direct employee actions or thinking and implies that he/she is wrong. Almost invariably it interferes with an effective interview. Furthermore, it often forces individuals to defend themselves rather than to examine their attitudes or behavior. If allowed to talk things out, they may often change, but argument seems only to reinforce emotions and attitudes and to prevent change.

The interviewer should not direct or make decisions or give moral admonition. One should not advise or direct employees or make decisions for them; neither should one pass judgment on them or point out what is right or wrong. The individual who has a good deal of independence rejects such suggestions in order to retain personal integrity. On the other hand, people who already have a tendency to be dependent and to allow others to make their decisions are driven deeper into dependency. Then, too, after listening to complex human problems, the interviewer is *not* equipped to come up with the answer in only a few minutes. This leads us to the conclusion that giving gratuitous and didactic advice will be vicious at the worst and useless at the best. If the worker says, "This is a heck of a place to work," or "Sam Davis is a gol-darn jackass," the attitude of the interviewer should *not* be: "Tut-tut, my good man, you're not displaying the proper spirit." Instead, the interviewer should prevail upon the worker to express attitudes more fully by asking such questions as "Why do you feel that way?"

Planning the Interview

When an employee comes to a superior and states that he/she wants to talk about something, or when a discerning superior has occasion to make an opportunity to talk to a troubled employee, the interviewer needs a plan for conducting the discussion. The use of this plan should assist in making the best use of time, in controlling the interview, and in guiding the employee's thinking toward a solution or at least a constructive course of action which the employee accepts. The phases of the plan may be varied from one situation to another. Sometimes all that is needed is to provide the opportunity for the employee to talk things out. In other cases, the employee is uninformed, or the facts as stated are in obvious conflict with conditions known to prevail. Sometimes a simple referral to a proper authority or agency will clear up the problem. Frequently, when the supervisor initiates a problem interview, he/she may not even begin to get the facts during the first contact with the employee. The very fact that the employer has proven interest, however, makes it easier for him to follow up with further contacts or for the employee to seek help later. The following stages should be included in almost any problem interview.

1. *Place the employee at ease*. The interviewer may start the discussion with a little social conversation designed to put the employee at ease. One might say: "Have a seat, Joe, and tell me how your family is getting along," or "How do you like your

76

new job?" The idea, of course, is to relieve any tension that may grip the employee. In addition, assurance may be needed by the employee that the immediate facts which are divulged will be maintained in confidence, and that discussion of the problem will have no bearing upon job status. This cannot, however, be carried to the point of indicating that *the problem* will be kept absolutely inviolate. In order to assure that the employee is at ease, the setting for the discussion should be one that is conducive to confidence and ease.

2. *Get the facts*. The interviewer encourages the employee to state personal problems—to get the facts on the table—to make clear references to the time, place, and circumstances surrounding any given situation or incident. To start the ball rolling, and to get as many facts as possible, one could say, "What's on your mind, Joe?" or "Now let's see if I understand this correctly," or "Do we have the whole story? Are these all the facts in the matter?" Especially at this point the interviewer needs to be a good listener. The superior will also want to be as objective and unemotional as possible.

3. *Weigh the facts*. With the facts about the problem at hand, the next move is to weigh the facts. This weighing of facts is not done with the idea that the interviewer is weighing the facts preparatory to giving a solution or answer to the problem. On the contrary, it is done with the idea of determining whether the employee is ready to undertake a decision or course of action. This may require additional questioning and should include an effort to recognize feelings and reactions and to distinguish them from the facts. The interviewer might ask here: "Have you anything else to tell me about this?" or "If this is taken care of, will that completely solve the problem?" Weighing the facts also includes an effort to get at causes which may go beyond the facts stated. Most people with a problem know that they are troubled, but the reasons they ascribe to the trouble may be more plausible than real. Sometimes one of the best methods of making an estimate of a personal problem is to trace back through the employee's past experience. What has happened in previous situations may provide a clue to the immediate problem.

4. *Consider appropriate action*. The interviewer and the employee then consider possible appropriate courses of action. This could be started with a question which will bring out what the employee thinks should be done. The superior might ask: "Well, Sally, what do you think ought to be done?" or "Do you think you might do this in view of the facts you've told me?" Such a question should be followed up with questions which prompt the employee to consider the proposed solution in relation to the facts which have been revealed. To accomplish this, the interviewer might ask: "Why do you think this idea will work?" or "Why do you suggest this course of action rather than any other?"

The superior may suggest consideration of given solutions through questions which begin with "Have you considered?" or "What do you think of going about it this way?" If this is done, care should be taken that the employee does not turn the question back to the interviewer and get the latter to support the implied suggestion with his/her own reasons. The interviewer may point up an idea, but the purpose of the interview is defeated unless the employee analyzes it and decides personally whether or not to use it. When the subordinate has reached a solution which appears to fit the facts, this phase in the interview is concluded.

Many times when the subordinate's problem is of a personal or off-the-job nature, the superior will have to refer the problem to the personnel office or elsewhere, where it can be handled most economically. For example, cases of ill health, emotional and mental unbalance beyond the variations of the normal range, and legal problems should be referred to physicians and lawyers for special aid. Some kinds of family and personal difficulties are best handled by referral to social agencies. The superior should never be afraid to refer problems which are beyond his/her capabilities.

5. *Check and review.* The final phase of the problem interview plan involves a summary—a check and review. This amounts to taking a running inventory with the employee of the facts as initially stated, related points which have been drawn out, solutions which have been considered, and the solution which the interviewee considers to be the best one. This review in effect puts the whole case together and makes certain that an understanding has been reached, as well as some agreement as to when the employee will take action. Here the interviewer undertakes to impress the employee with the fact that the solution represents what he/she wants to do and that the doing of it is up to him/her. This ordinarily terminates the interview, unless there is some point which the subordinate has agreed to examine further and discuss with the employer at a later date.

Conclusion

Emotional disturbances, feelings of anxiety or insecurity, and social maladjustments on the part of employees can affect their morale adversely and, as a natural corollary, their production rate and efficiency. An effective tool for dealing with such problems is the problem interview. This *listening* tool is an essential technique for every good superior. It allows the employee to unload problems through talking and then thinking through the problem to a personally satisfactory solution. It is also a communicative tool of management for discovering attitudes and feelings of employees toward company policies and practices so that adjustments of a preventive or remedial nature may take place. An effective problem interview can reflect organizational communication transmission at its best.

THE IMPROVEMENT INTERVIEW

Up to this point, we have spent considerable time in examining the problem interview, which is a useful communications tool for the superior when an employee comes forward with a problem. It is also useful to the discerning superior who detects a troubled employee and makes an occasion to discuss the problem. Communications with employees are frequently needed, however, in other situations. One of the most typical of these concerns the need to discuss with the employee his/her work performance. Let us examine an interviewing pattern which has been tried many times and which has proven to be an excellent communications tool. It has been used for building on or improving employees' strong points as well as for correcting weaknesses. We call this method the *improvement interview*. The improvement interview is used, then, to accomplish one or both of these objectives, first, in seeking to use to advantage an employee's capabilities and strong points, and second, in seeking to correct any phase of the employee's work performance or job behavior, such as his/her attitude or conduct.

There are four major stages in an effective improvement interview: (1) presenting the problem, (2) getting the employee's reaction, (3) considering appropriate action, and (4) stating the plan of action. On the following pages each of these major stages is
discussed, and at the end of the discussion the reader will find an improvement

interview chart depicting the interview's movement through each stage as well as presenting a coded indication of where the key phrases would most probably be used. The suggested key phrases are presented in the text with a number in brackets to correspond with the chart.

Stage I—Present the Problem

As a first major step, the superior will want to present the problem. The problem may involve capitalizing on an employee's strong points, correcting a weakness, or both. Of course, the superior must get the problem before the employee in such a way as to get a constructive reaction. Otherwise there is a failure of communications.

At the beginning of the improvement interview, the superior will try to put the employee at ease. One should recognize the employee's possible anxiety and quickly come to the point by telling the employee the reason for, or what the general purpose of, the interview is. Key phrases used to accomplish this purpose are: "Bill, I've called you in to talk *with* you about your job," or "Sharon, I thought we should take a little time to talk over your work."[1] It is important that the purpose as first stated be in general terms; otherwise one may get into specifics so quickly that it unnerves the employee and gets a negative rather than a constructive reaction.

If the objective is to build on the strong points and to improve particular talents of an employee, the superior presents these strong points, explaining to the employee that what will be discussed are some ways and means of further developing these talents for the betterment of the company and of the employee as well. An example of the way this might be approached is, "Bill, there are certain parts of your work which you're performing particularly well and which, with a little more emphasis, will make you a much more valuable employee. . . . Are you interested in developing more skill in your work? . . . Are you willing to assume more responsibility?"[2]

If, however, the specific objective of the interview is to correct certain job-related weaknesses, the supervisor will first want to show recognition and appreciation of the employee's value to the company. One does this by specifically mentioning the employee's good points. This may also help to get the employee to relax and will serve to "write off" the good points in the employee's mind, tending to keep him/her from resentfully thinking about all the good things while the superior concentrates on his/her weaknesses. The superior is then ready to present the specific problem—the employee's weak points. This is presented in terms of what the employee has done or failed to do, without indicating what might be proposed to be done about it. These weak points are stated as facts and are not referred to in terms of faults; the following is an example of this approach: "Barbara, there are certain places where you can do a better job, such as with respect to . . . ."[3]

Stage II—Get Employee's Reaction

After mentioning the employee's weak points, the superior will probably get the employee's reaction. Thus we move into the second major step of the interview. The interviewer should encourage the employee to give his/her side of the story, and this can be done by asking appropriate questions: "Do you think this states the case about as it really is?" or "Do you think these facts are correct?" or "Do I have the complete picture?"[4]

In general, the employee's reaction may indicate agreement or disagreement with the superior's conception of what the problem or situation is. Proper questioning should bring out that the employee's reaction of agreement or disagreement is not only with respect to the superior's statement of the subordinate's weak points, but also with respect to the superior's evaluation of the underlying reasons for these weaknesses. This means that in addition to getting the employee's agreement with the basic facts, the superior must encourage the employee to come out with the underlying reasons for the weaknesses. If the employee's reaction indicates agreement with the superior's statement of the problem and with the superior's opinion as to the underlying reasons thereof, then there is nothing to change the superior's original thinking, and they are ready to move on to the next step.

Stage III—Consider Appropriate Action

When the employee agrees with the basic facts, the superior then proceeds to consider the appropriate action to be taken. Actually, the superior will have some action in mind before beginning the interview, or it would have been most unwise to attempt it. Since what is wanted is to get the employee's cooperation in strengthening his/her good points and correcting the weak points, the interview is directed to that end. Thus, the next step is to get the employee's suggestion as to how the strong points may be developed and how the weaknesses may have developed or how the weaknesses may be improved. An example of this might be: "Do you have any suggestions as to what we can do?"[5] Any suggestion the employee makes here may be in line with the superior's plan, or it may be otherwise OK. In such an ideal case where the entire interview stays right on the main track, the superior will clinch the interview by indicating to the employee that the suggestion is OK and that everything will work out all right. In other words, one might say something like, "I'm sure we'll work this out," or "If you need any help, call on me."[6] The interviewer has thus moved into the fourth and final stage of the interview. One might want to restate the plan of action—to summarize and clarify it for all concerned. Some people also want to add that the employee can come to them for assistance at any time.

All improvement interviews are not that ideal, of course. Let's assume that the employee had no suggestions as to the appropriate action or that the suggestion was simply no good. If the suggestion is unsatisfactory, the superior might say: "I'm sorry, but I don't think that would work, because . . ."[7] and then add, "Suppose we try this . . . ."[8] In such case, the superior brings the subordinate back onto the main track by suggesting a new plan of action, which had been thought of prior to commencing the interview. In making a personal suggestion, the superior will indicate what assistance will be available from other sources. The employee may agree readily with the superior's suggestion, or there may be some discussion before agreement is obtained.

Another possibility is that the employee may come up with something that sounds pretty good and appears to have merit, but the superior is not prepared to commit himself/herself to putting the suggestion into effect. Some further checking may be needed—perhaps with a superior or the personnel office. Key phrases nine, ten, and eleven are reflected in the following possible comment: "Your suggestion has merit but it's going to require a little study and looking into. Suppose I check on it and discuss it with you later." [9, 10, 11]

Recognizing the value of getting the employee's cooperation, one should take the necessary time to check on the feasibility of the employee's suggestion. The interviewer will give the employee a *rain check* and come back later and tell the employee the results of the inquiry. For purposes of our analysis, we may then consider that the employee's suggestion *requires study*, and the superior then gives a rain check.

Stage IV—State the Plan of Action

Up to this point, the interview has proceeded along relatively straight and easy lines. But suppose the employee's reaction to the presentation of the problem is to disagree? The superior will then have to take into consideration the nature of the disagreement. If the employee disagrees with the idea of strengthening special talents or shows a negative attitude indicating indifference to developing particular strong points, the superior may deem it advisable to drop the matter for the present at this stage of the interview or to study it further and give the employee a rain check.

On the other hand, if the specific objective is to correct a weakness, the employee may disagree with the idea of needing certain improvements and, thus, may indicate that the superior was not correct in the statement of the basic facts or opinions as to the underlying reasons for those weaknesses. If any contrary information presented by the employee is sufficiently important to indicate a possible change in the superior's thinking, he/she may wish to reconsider the original plan for corrective action. This may require some time for proper investigation and study, and one may, therefore, wish to postpone the interview with the employee. Under such circumstances, we may consider that the employee has made a *point* which requires study, and that the superior has given a rain check. In such an instance the superior will advise the employee that in view of this new information, further consideration will be given the matter and they will continue the talk at some time later. To do this, the superior might say: "I'm glad you told me that. It may alter the picture somewhat. I'll check on it and discuss it with you further." [12]

The superior, however, may find that in disagreeing the employee may do quite a bit of talking but actually fail to come up with any information that seriously alters the original plan for corrective or improvement action. That is, while the employee may disagree, what is said may not change the superior's original thinking. The employee may make *no point*. The superior can then indicate that while recognizing the value of what the employee has said, there are still certain facts (mentioned under Stage I) which need attention. The superior may wish to reiterate these weaknesses in order to get the employee to recognize that all of the supervisor's points were not answered, and then proceed with the rest of the interview. One does this by simply saying, "Yes, but this . . . still needs attention." [13]

Before the interview is closed, both the superior and the employee should clearly understand any action that is planned. It may be a plan for corrective or improvement action suggested by the employee or by the superior, or it may merely be a rain check for another interview. Where some form of corrective action is planned, the superior should try to close the interview on a note of confidence and encouragement.

In order to obtain the best results from an improvement interview, the superior must continue to observe the subsequent performance of the subordinate. One must be quick to encourage the employee when improvement is seen. One must establish a day-to-day relationship on such a basis that comments on good work or suggestions for improvement of performance become a part of the ordinary give-and-take of superior-subordinate relationships.

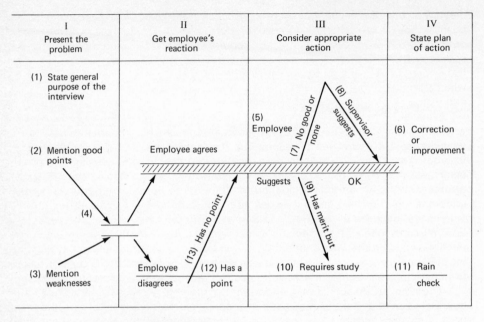

I Present the problem	II Get employee's reaction	III Consider appropriate action	IV State plan of action
(1) State general purpose of the interview			
(2) Mention good points	Employee agrees	(5) Employee	(6) Correction or improvement
(4)		Suggests OK	
(3) Mention weaknesses	Employee disagrees (12) Has a point	(10) Requires study	(11) Rain check

(8) Supervisor suggests · *(7) No good or none* · *(9) Has merit but* · *(13) Has no point*

Figure 3-5 **The Improvement Interview Chart with Suggested "Key Phrases" Coded by Numbers to Correspond to Point Where They Would Most Probably Be Used**

Conclusion

The supervisor must have a sound plan for communications with subordinates. Perhaps the most important communication one has with employees takes place during what is called the *improvement interview.* It is in this interview that the superior attempts to improve the employee by discussing strong points and weaknesses, work pattern, behavior, or attitudes, with the idea of securing from the employee cooperation in achieving improved work performance. The improvement interview should be the setting for improving and helping the employee, not for bawling him/her out.

The following chart, Figure 3-5, should be studied very carefully if one is to make the improvement interview effective. It has proven to be a highly workable indirect interview plan.

Summary

In this second section of Chapter 3 on communication transmission, we have tried to demonstrate some ways one might go about putting the basic principles of communication transmission into practice. The techniques we have presented here can, with slight modifications, be useful and important in all types of communication transmission situations, because the communication principles and the practices are more or less the same across all kinds of interaction situations.

In the first part of this section we pointed out how difficult it is to say what we mean. Voice tone, rate, force, quality, and pitch are all at least as important to us in the business world as our dress, neatness, physical appearance, manners, and other outward aspects of our personality because our personalities show through our speech. As Sara Teasdale once said, "All that I know, and all that I have not known, live in your voice." In that area we tried to suggest some rules for you to keep in mind when attempting to say what you mean, and some ways to begin improving your voice and expression.

We then attempted to suggest ways by which one can improve the meaning of what is said. We discussed the ways by which one transmits communication: words, gestures, sounds, ideas, and meanings. The fundamental ingredient for good face-to-face communication seems to be *humanity*. People do not communicate well because they have emotional blocks, have different frames of reference, are incapable of expressing themselves through the use of the spoken and written word, and are unable to use their personality effectively.

Finally, we turned our attention to the area of superior-subordinate communication. We examined when superior-subordinate communications take place, why they often don't take place when they should, and why they go astray. The principle of indirect interviewing was introduced and two major types of indirect interviews—the problem interview and the improvement interview—were examined very carefully.

The rules for obtaining valid information in the problem interview are (1) to go below the surface complaint, (2) to look for significant gaps and omissions, (3) don't treat everything said as true or false, (4) don't allow the employee's feelings to affect your own, and (5) respect the dignity of the individual. The rules for conducting the problem interview are (1) talk or ask questions only when necessary, (2) listen—don't interrupt, (3) don't display authority, (4) don't argue, and (5) never pass judgment or direct decisions. Finally, the plan for the problem interview is place the subordinate at ease, get the facts, weigh the facts, consider appropriate action, and check and review.

The stages of the improvement interview are (1) to present the problem, (2) to get the employee's reaction, (3) to consider appropriate action, and (4) to state the plan of action. Each of these stages was presented very carefully and a chart was provided at the end which noted the appropriate place for each of the key phrases suggested in the text.

REVIEW QUESTIONS

1. What are the key elements in the communication process?

2. Explain the three possible purposes one might try to accomplish with communication transmission.

3. What does the text mean when it says, "In most cases people will initiate communication only when they feel that their equilibrium state has been disturbed"?

4. What are some of the basic individual incentives and impediments to communication?

5. What are some of the basic differences between a defensive and a supportive organizational communication climate?

6. What are the basic differences in nature between the information which travels downward, the information which travels upward, and the information which moves horizontally in an organization?

7. What are some of the basic communication problems which can occur when information travels downward, upward, and horizontally in an organization?

8. What are the five important aspects of the voice by which people judge us, and what is the role of each?

9. List the ten basic rules of good vocal transmission.

10. How can people go about improving their vocal transmission ability?

11. What are the roles played by words, gestures, sounds, ideas, and meanings in communication transmission, and why are they so important?

12. Why is humanity toward a fellow human being such an important concept in communication transmission?

13. How do emotional blocks, frames of reference, vocabulary, and personality often lower the effectiveness of communication transmission?

14. Summarize the twenty do's and don'ts of face-to-face communication.

15. What are some of the problems which prevent better and more timely employer-employee communicative relations?

16. Why is the indirect or nondirective style more often preferred in interviews to the so-called direct style?

17. What are the main purposes and functions of the problem interview?

18. What are the main rules to remember during a problem interview?

19. How does one prepare for a problem interview, and what are the main stages of such an interview?

20. What are the main objectives of the improvement interview?

21. List the four major stages in an effective improvement interview and explain how one accomplishes the purpose of each.

EXERCISES

1. The following is a composite business speech, not a parody. It is based on a systematic count of the expressions and constructions most commonly used in current United States business speeches and includes the sixty principal clichés of reverse gobbledygook. The speech is reprinted from *Fortune* magazine.[11] You are to discuss 1) why a speech like this is often very effective, and (2) how one can prepare a speech which would improve on the one below.

It is a pleasure and a privilege to be here with you today. These great annual meetings are always an inspiration to me, and doubly so today. After that glowing introduction by our toastmaster I must confess, however, that I'd like to turn the tables and tell a little story on Chuck. When I say it's about the nineteenth hole and a certain gentleman whose baritone was cracked, those of you who were at the Atlanta conference last year will know what I mean. But I won't tell it. Chuck Forbes is too good a friend of mine, and seriously, I know full well we all realize what a tower of strength his yeoman service has been to the association in these trying years.

Yes, gentlemen, trying times. So you'll pardon me if I cast aside the glib reverberations of glittering generalities and the soothing syrup of sugar-coated platitudes and put it to you the only way I can, straight English.

We're losing the battle!!

From every corner the people are being weaned away from the doctrine of the Founding Fathers. They are being detoured from the high-speed highways of progress by the utopian highwaymen.

Now, the man on the street is a pretty savvy fellow. Don't sell him short. Joe Doakes may be fooled for a while, but in the end he wants no part of the mumbo jumbo the global saboteurs are trying to sell him. After all, he is an American.

But he has to be told.

And we're not telling him!!

Now let me say that I do not wish to turn the clock back. None of us do. All forward-looking businessmen see themselves as partners in a team in which the worker is a full-fledged member. I regard our employees as our greatest business asset, and I am sure, mindful as I am of the towering potentials of purposeful energy in this group of clear-sighted leaders, that, in the final analysis, it is the rock foundation of your policies, too.

But the team can't put the ball across for the first down just by pushing it. The guards and the tackles can't do their job if the quarterback doesn't let them in on the play. And we, the quarterbacks, are muffing the ball.

How are we to go over for a touchdown? My friends, this is the $64 question. I don't know the answers. I am just a plainspoken businessman. I am not a soothsayer. I have no secret crystal ball. But I do know one thing: before we round the curve into the home stretch we have a job to do. It will not be easy. I offer no panaceas or nostrums. Instead, I would like to suggest that the real key to our problem lies in the application of the three E's. What are the three E's? Enterprise. Endeavor. Effort.

Each and every one of us must appoint himself a salesman—yes, a missionary, if you will—and get out and do some real grass roots selling. And when we hit the dirt, let's not forget the customers—the greatest asset any business has.

Now, much has been done already. But let's not fool ourselves: the surface, as our chairman has so wisely said, has hardly been scratched. The program is still in its infancy. So let me give it to you straight from the shoulder. The full implication, gentlemen, depends on us.

So let's get on the beam! In the cracker barrel fashion, let's get down to earth. In good plain talk the man on the street can understand, let's remind Joe Doakes that the best helping hand he will ever find is the one at the end of his own shirt sleeve.

We have the know-how.

With sights set high, let's go over the top!

2. Your instructor will ask you to present one or more formal communications to your classmates. The following are some examples of the types of formal speaking assignments which would fit well with the material presented in this text. Be sure to also read Exercise 3 before making your presentation. It will provide some help in making the most of your vocal quality.

a. Find some situation which has disturbed your equilibrium lately, that is, something that has disturbed you or made you angry. Describe the situation briefly, including all of the problems involved and attempt to activate in your audience the same kinds of emotions that you experienced when the situation actually occurred. You will find it necessary to use gestures and your voice efficiently to accomplish your purpose.

b. Prepare an outline and present a speech on some aspect of your job (or one with which you are familiar) which is somewhat detailed and complex. The outline will be turned in to your instructor and compared with outlines the other members of the class will prepare from your talk as you present it. The object here will be to speak as clearly and accurately as possible so that all of the outlines will match. If you find that visual materials will help clarify your presentation, you are free to use them.

c. Visit a local organization in your community and collect whatever information you can about their safety regulations. Then you are to assume that the audience you are speaking to is a group of employees who have been disregarding the rules. Your job is to persuade them that all the rules are made for their own protection and that they should follow all of them to the letter. Remember, persuasive speaking is probably the most difficult of all formal presentations; so prepare this speech very carefully, logically, and emotionally.

3. While you are making one of the formal presentations listed above or one of your instructor's choosing, your speech will be recorded for later evaluation. When you do have a chance to listen to yourself, answer the following questions about your vocal quality. You should ask these same questions of yourself and others in every oral exercise done in this course (i.e., speeches, role playing, group meetings, etc.).

a. Was my vocal *tone* conducive to a productive communication? Was I calm and collected? Did I seem confident and sincere? Did I seem to respect the dignity of my listener(s)?

b. Was my vocal *quality* pleasing? How did I display the emotions I was feeling? Was I loud enough to be heard clearly? Did I use accurate diction and pronunciation? Did I express myself clearly? Did I use my personality effectively? Did I get too emotionally involved in the matter I was communicating?

c. Was my *pitch* monotonous? Did I accurately emphasize the important points? Did my pitch level tend to rise so high that I had nowhere to go for emphasis?

d. How was my speaking *rate?* Did I use pause effectively? Did I vary my rate to emphasize important points? (If it was an informal communication, did I leave enough room for others to express themselves and not interrupt too often?)

e. In what ways did I use vocal *force?* Should I have used it more often? Did I display authority by directing, making decisions, or giving moral advice?

4. You are to deliberately go out and find a communicative situation which is taking place. Do not enter into the situation, but stand or sit close enough to watch and listen to what is taking place. Try to determine if the words, gestures, sounds, ideas, and meanings being transmitted are being received accurately. When you listen and watch very carefully, you will be surprised to note how many gestures, meaningless sounds, omissions, and other mistakes go seemingly unnoticed in normal conversation. While you are examining this communication situation, review the do's and don'ts of face-to-face interaction discussed in this chapter and see how many of the rules one or more of the participants are breaking. After you have observed the situation for a while, remove yourself and write down the things you noticed. One or more of these reports will be shared with the whole class.

5. Select a recent informal communication transmission situation in which you were involved or know thoroughly. Describe the situation in some detail and then answer the following questions.

a. In what way had the equilibrium state of one or more of the participants been disturbed to warrant the communication in the first place?
b. What was the operational status of each participant with regard to his/her social needs; that is, did each feel accepted, recognized, and secure in his/her position with regard to both the organization as a whole and the other participants in the communication situation?
c. What were the reference groups of each of the participants, and did this have an effect on the communication?
d. What was the message, and how important was it to each of the participants?
e. Was the communication climate defensive or supportive in both the organization as a whole and the specific communication encounter described?
f. Would the basic nature of this communication be described as upward, downward, or horizontal, and did this have any effect on the nature of the communication?
g. Taking all of the preceding factors into account, as well as the end result of the communication, would you describe this communication incident as successful, semisuccessful, or unsuccessful, and why?

FOOTNOTES

1. Alan H. Monroe, *Principles and Types of Speech*, 4th ed. (Chicago: Scott, Foresman and Company, 1955), pp. 28–29.

2. This quotation and much of the discussion on group climate were paraphrased from "Defensive Communication," by Jack R. Gibb, in the *Journal of Communication*, vol. 11 (1961), pp. 141–148, and used by permission of the International Communication Association and Jack R. Gibb.

3. The organization chart is used by permission of the American National Bank and Trust Company of Michigan.

4. The West Coast Life performance evaluation guide is used by permission of the West Coast Life Insurance Company.

5. W. H. Read, "Upward Communication in Industrial Hierarchies," *Human Relations*, no. 15 (1962), pp. 3–15.

6. Harold H. Kelley, "Communication in Experimentally Created Hierarchies," *Human Relations*, no. 4 (1951).

7. W. C. Donaghy, "Status, Emotion and Small Group Interaction: A Field Experiment," *The Michigan Speech Association Journal*, vol. 8, no. 1 (1973), pp. 27–31.

8. Robert F. Bales, *Interaction Process Analysis: A Method for the Study of Small Groups* (Cambridge, Mass.: Addison-Wesley Publishing Company, 1950), p. 9.

9. The term "meaning of meaning" comes from an extremely interesting book on semantics: Charles K. Ogden and Ivor Armstrong Richards, *The Meaning of Meaning* (New York: Harcourt, Brace and Company, Inc., 1949).

10. Elton Mayo, *The Human Problems of an Industrial Civilization* (New York: The Macmillan Company, 1933).

11. "The Language of Business," *Fortune*, vol. 42, no. 5 (November 1950), p. 114, used by permission of the publisher.

RELATED TEXTS

Bormann, Ernest, G., William S. Howell, Ralph G. Nichols, and George L. Shapiro: *Interpersonal Communication in the Modern Organization*, Prentice-Hall, Inc., Englewood Cliffs, N.J., 1969.

Cronkite, Gary: *Persuasion: Speech and Behavioral Change*, The Bobbs-Merrill Company, Indianapolis, 1969.

Dance, Frank E. X., and Carl Larson: *Speech Communication: Concepts and Behavior*, Holt, Rinehart and Winston, Inc., New York, 1972.

Dooher, M. Joseph, and Vivienne Marquis (eds.): *Effective Communication on the Job*, American Management Association, New York, 1956.

Howell, William S., and Ernest G. Bormann: *Presentational Speaking for Business and the Professions*, Harper & Row, Publishers, Inc., New York, 1971.

Karlins, Marvin, and Herbert I. Abelson: *Persuasion: How Opinions and Attitudes Are Changed*, 2d ed., Springer Publishing Co., Inc., New York, 1970.

Knapp, Mark: *Nonverbal Communication in Human Interaction*, Holt, Rinehart and Winston, Inc., New York, 1972.

Mehrabian, A: *Silent Messages*, Wadsworth Publishing Company, Inc., Belmont, Calif., 1972.

Moncur, John P., and Harrison M. Karr: *Developing Your Speaking Voice*, 2d ed., Harper & Row, Publishers, Inc., New York, 1972.

Tracey, William S.: *Business and Professional Speaking*, Wm. C. Brown Company Publishers, Dubuque, Iowa, 1970.

Wilcox, Roger P.: *Oral Reporting in Business and Industry*, Prentice-Hall, Inc., Englewood Cliffs, N.J., 1967.

Wirkus, T., and H. Erickson: *Communication and the Technical Man*, Prentice-Hall, Inc., Englewood Cliffs, N.J., 1972.

COMMUNICATION RECEPTION

Did you look at your portrait in the mirror this morning? Probably you didn't see anything new or different. All you saw was that same old face. Well, take another look at that familiar face. What you will see is two eyes, a nose with twin breathing spaces, two ears, and only ONE mouth—twin receiving equipment and only one noise-making apparatus. Strange how we can talk more with one mouth than we can listen with two ears. Perhaps nature had a purpose in giving us two eyes and ears. In more primitive times those eyes and ears were highly important. People's very lives depended on what they were able to see and hear. The sounds early humans were able to hear were far more important to them than the noises their vocal cords could make.

True it is that our vocal instruments are of the highest order. True it is that song and speech are of the highest human achievements. We have been so busy developing these higher arts, we have forgotten the primary purposes of seeing and listening. Our ancestors survived in this world because they trained themselves to value the sounds their ears brought to them and the sights their eyes were able to perceive. Time and civilization have erased the need for keen hearing and accurate sight. It would be a mistake to think that these valuable aids to our enjoyment of life are to be used only for hearing music and viewing beautiful sights. It may well be that seeing and hearing are still of prime importance in our survival and work life. This is particularly true of hearing. We must learn to listen if we would hear.

Do you listen? Remember when you told Mr. X in your office that if anything went wrong with his work, just to come and tell you about it. And when he came to your desk, did you hear him out? Did you listen to him? Or did you say, "Oh yes, Jim, I'd sure like to talk with you, but excuse me, I'm busy now and I have an important date with Gatwhite Mufflesink." Maybe you did that. Maybe you did worse. Maybe you said, "Oh yes, Jim, sit down, I'll be with you in a minute." Then five minutes later while tapping on your teeth with a pencil, you heard him launch into his complaint. After one or two sentences, you cut in and said, "Well, now, I know all about that. I remember when I was with the Company in '69 or was it '59, an incident like that came up. I remember when the Old Man founded the company, you know. He called me in and said, 'Herman, I want you to handle this like that.' First time that policy was ever laid down. Oh yes, now what I would like you to do . . ." and so on ad infinitum.

Listening is not talking. Talking is not listening. Listening means *listening*. It means hearing. It means understanding. It means attempting to get at the basic elements of the other person's story. The old saying is that you cannot take any more water out of the well than the size of the pail you lower. How is your *listening ability*?

CHECK YOUR COMMUNICATION RECEPTION ABILITY

If you are interested in determining how well you listen as a matter of habit, answer the following questions. This "test" is easy to "beat," and if you like to cheat, go right ahead, but do not be fooled by your answers. However, if you are honest with yourself, you have a chance of estimating your listening ability. Just answer "yes" or "no."

1. Do you locate yourself in the room so that you are certain you can hear clearly?
2. Do you listen for underlying feelings as well as words?
3. Do you disregard a speaker's appearance and look only to the ideas he may have to present?
4. Do you "pay attention": do you look at a speaker as well as listen to what he has to say?
5. Do you allow for your own prejudices and feelings as you evaluate what a man has to say?
6. Do you keep your mind on the topic continuously and follow the train of thought being presented?
7. Do you try consciously to estimate the logic and the rationality of what is being said?
8. Do you restrain yourself (you do not interrupt or "stop listening") when you hear something you believe to be wrong?
9. In discussion, are you willing to let the other fellow have the last word?
10. Do you try to be sure that you are considering the other person's viewpoint before you reply, answer, or make a rebuttal?[1]

If you answered all of these questions with a positive "yes," then you are an excellent communication receiver. To the extent that you answered "no," you need work on listening. As you attempt to work on your listening performance, the preceding ten questions should be your guides. They include the most significant listening problems which occur in organizational communication.

BASIC FACTORS IN COMMUNICATION RECEPTION

Dr. Ralph Nichols of the University of Minnesota states that extensive research on his part into the listening capacities of individuals has led him to this general conclusion:

Immediately after the average person has listened to someone talk, he remembers only about half of what he has heard—no matter how carefully he thought he listened.[2]

• • •

Two months after listening to a person talk the average listener will remember only about 25% of what was said.[3]

In the same article, Dr. Nichols reported that an executive decided to determine how much of the day was spent in communicating with people, what percent of that time was devoted to talking to people, and how much time was devoted to listening. It was discovered, by having the secretary log the time used in communication contacts, that some 35 to 40 percent of total working time was given over to listening.

Interestingly enough, most people believe that as we move up the ladder of success, and as we find ourselves in positions of more and more responsibility, our activities shift from listening or receiving communications to more and more giving out or "telling" others what to do and even how to do it. This is exactly the opposite of the observable facts. The higher one moves in the managerial hierarchy, the more important listening and evaluating skills become. One must become an adept and experienced listener. One must evaluate literally hundreds of oral statements and written messages before taking one step or making one utterance. Permissiveness or willingness to listen carefully and thoroughly and the ability to abstract the key concepts and inferences are among the most valuable managerial attributes.

How does one, then, learn this ability to listen carefully and thoroughly and abstract key concepts? The authors believe that the first thing one must do is learn something about the basic factors involved in communication reception: attention, perception, comprehension, and acceptance.

Attention

Before we can ever hope to receive a message, we must somehow have our attention drawn to the message. People attend to messages either voluntarily or involuntarily. Involuntary attention is given to a message when the receiver feels it poses a threat to personal well-being. Attention given in this manner, however, lasts only to the point where the receiver no longer feels a threat. Such things as loud noises, bright lights, sudden movements, and other novel events fall into this category. Voluntary attention is normally given to those messages which are somehow seen as being interesting to the receiver. A listener will maintain this attentive state only as long as the message is of more interest than other activities one could be doing.

This fluctuating and selective nature of attention is one of the primary obstacles faced in establishing and maintaining good communication. The responsibility for establishing and maintaining attention falls on both the transmitter of the message and the receiver. If a salesman or saleswoman walks into your office, for example, he/she takes on the burden of attracting your attention and holding it until the message is completed. In this case, you as the listener have little reason to work at maintaining attention. On the other hand, when people you have invited come into your office, the burden of maintaining attention shifts to you as the receiver. Obviously, they have information you need, or they would not have been called to come in to begin with. They may be unwilling to give you the information or they may become involved in irrelevant facts while approaching the issue which interests you. In this circumstance a good listener will force himself/herself to maintain attention even though other things may be more interesting.

Perception

Perception is the process of recognizing the message in an unbiased manner. This naturally comes only after one has focused attention on the message. Accurate communication perception is determined not only by the degree of attention given the message, however, but also by a number of other personal factors.

Like attention, our perceptions are selective. We tend to accurately perceive only those things which we want to perceive or are prepared to perceive. Our personalities, past histories, and group identifications all play a role in the accuracy of our perception of any given message. When we perceive messages as potentially threatening, we tend to avoid them or distort them in the hopes of protecting ourselves. The manager who has an employee suggest that a procedure or policy is not working properly will tend to begin forming a rebuttal and to allow feelings and prejudices to interfere with perception.

As with the attention factor, the responsibility for achieving accurate perception can lie with either the speaker or the listener. The salesman or saleswoman, for example, mentioned previously, must attempt to guide the manager's perception by using the correct vocabulary, repeating when necessary, and using other aids where possible. The manager, however, who wants to accurately determine the effects of policies must take the responsibility for seeing to it that personal prejudices do not get in the way of perception.

Comprehension

Comprehension involves making sense out of the communication that is received. From our past experiences with the world and all of the people that inhabit our little portion of the world, we have developed mental categories into which we try to fit all new concepts and ideas that come our way through attention and perception. Very early in our childhood, we learned that these categories of similar things have names. Four-legged animals which bark and lick your face are called *dogs*, while four-legged animals which go "Moo" and give milk are called *cows*. The process by which we learn these categories and their names is called *concept formation*.

In order for us to comprehend new or unusual information, we must fit the new concept into our already learned categories. This process is called *concept attainment*. Different degrees of comprehension depend on the accuracy with which the new concept is placed in the existing categories, the quantity and quality of the original categories, and finally, the desire on the part of the receiver to accurately attain the concept. Many times good comprehension and, therefore, good listening are prevented by the fact that the listener is just not familiar enough with the subject area, does not question the speaker to make sure the concept is correctly placed in its proper context, or simply does not want to understand the message.

As with attention and perception, the speaker can aid comprehension by providing useful associations between new and familiar ideas, using understandable language, carefully structuring the message, and making all points explicit, but the receiver must also assume some responsibility for comprehending the message. This is done by asking questions, restating the message, and providing other forms of feedback to the speaker. Of all the basic factors in reception, the one that seems to be the most difficult is comprehension, because if the basic categories are not in the receiver's mind to begin with, all the talk in the world will not allow one to

comprehend the message as well as a listener who has the necessary background.

Acceptance

Acceptance is really not a determining factor in reception, but should be a product of successful speaking and listening. People accept messages, however, based upon a number of factors other than reception of the communication. Such things as the source of the communication, the nature of the message, and the message channel are all key determinants of both communication reception and acceptance. In the following section each of these factors will be discussed with regard to communication reception.

RECEPTION: THE KEY TO EFFECTIVE COMMUNICATION

As was mentioned in the preceding chapter on communication transmission, the four major elements of communication are the source or sender, the message itself, the channel through which the message travels, and the receiver. We have also previously discussed the fact that originally it was thought that in order to improve organizational communication all that was really needed was to improve the communication source and the message. Thus, there appeared a rash of books and articles dealing with ways business and industrial leaders could improve the quality of speaking and writing within their organizations. It is our purpose in this section to point out that improved writing and speaking will have little or no effect on the quality of organizational communication unless the relationships between the source and the receiver, the message and the receiver, and the channel and the receiver are fully understood. In other words, we intend to demonstrate why we believe *reception* is the key to effective communication and, ultimately, to sound morale within the organization.

Source of Communication

As listeners we tend to judge the creditability of sources by such things as their real or apparent social status, their appearance and dress, and qualities in their vocal and bodily actions that indicate sincerity. An employee, for example, when hearing identical communications, will tend to accept the one coming from a superior before believing the same message from a subordinate or a peer. Even the simple fact that one communicator is dressed differently affects the impact of the message for many receivers. The three factors that tend to determine which sources will be better received are: credibility, status, and opinion leadership.

CREDIBILITY

The Greeks referred to the credibility of the source of communication as *ethos*. The three main factors which determine a source's credibility or ethos are competence or expertness, trustworthiness, and dynamism. None of these three factors, however, are actually possessed by the source; they are instead ascribed to a source by the receivers of the communication. Thus the receiver, not the source, is playing the major role in determining source credibility.

93

Expertness

The qualification, competence, or expertness factor refers mainly to the source's perceived credibility with regard to the task. A person who rates high in this factor would be seen by listeners as trained, experienced, qualified, skilled, informed, authoritative, able, and intelligent. This type of credibility is normally situationally oriented, that is, a person is normally seen as being an expert in only one or two areas. One's influence over listeners is limited to those specific areas in which they see him/her as being competent. In other areas one is merely perceived as being a peer in the discussion.

Trustworthiness

The trustworthiness factor is much more wide-ranging than the expertness factor. A person perceived as possessing this attribute is not necessarily limited to a specific task or area for influence. A person who rates high in this factor is characterized by listeners as kind, congenial, friendly, agreeable, pleasant, gentle, unselfish, just, forgiving, fair, hospitable, warm, cheerful, sociable, ethical, calm, and patient. The trustworthiness factor really refers to personality characteristics of the source, and a source with this type of perceived credibility will have influence in most or all communication situations of which he/she is a part. These are the characteristics which receivers in our culture feel are important in a source regardless of the task.

Dynamism

The dynamism factor relates to a person's perceived motivation or enthusiasm with regard to communication. Another term for this factor is "charisma." A dynamic source is usually described by listeners as aggressive, emphatic, frank, forceful, bold, active, energetic, and fast. This attribute is especially effective when used infrequently. A person who is always dynamic will lose some credibility with listeners when opposed by a person who becomes enthusiastic only about certain matters of unusual importance.

Perhaps an example will make these three types of credibility clear. Suppose you, as a plant manager, have a problem which has reduced your unit's productivity. You decide to get two opinions on the matter: one from your most senior employee, Lou Longlife, and one from the company consultant on efficiency problems, Professor Productive. Before you even hear what they have to say, each of these people has a certain type of credibility in your mind. Lou's greatest source of credibility for you comes from his trustworthiness. He has been of help to you on other, though different, problems, and you and he get along quite well. The professor's credibility is primarily derived from her expertness. Although you do not know the professor very well, you do know that one of the other plant managers called her in once, and she provided some sound suggestions with regard to a similar productivity problem.

Once you get the two people together, after having first explained the problem to them and allowed them time to visit the plant and think about the problem, the dynamism factor comes into play. You might notice, for example, that one of them made what seems to be a more detailed analysis of the problem and presents the possible solutions in an energetic and frank way, while the other seems less concerned and, although a solution is presented, less confidence in it is shown.

When you get home that night you begin to think about what you will do to attempt solving the problem. You are inclined to go with Lou's suggestion because you trust him, and he is generally the type of person you believe, but the professor made some very good points and, from all you can tell, she knows her stuff. The aggressive presentation impressed you very much, but forcefulness certainly doesn't make one right. In the final analysis, the decision as to which suggestion to accept rests with you, the manager and the receiver of the communications. We each weigh these three credibility factors differently, based on our personalities and past experiences. If we have generally found expert opinion to be the most useful, we would go with the professor's suggestion. If we are the type of person who feels trustworthiness and friendship are more important than pure information, we would implement Lou's suggestion. If we feel that dynamism and motivation are more important than the other factors, then we would implement the energetically pre-sented message. We all weigh these things differently. What for you is the prime determiner of credibility? Think about it.

We have, of course, been talking about extremes of ascribed credibility. In actual communication situations, people are perceived (either consciously or unconscious-ly) as having some degree of all these credibility factors. The professor will have some degree of trustworthiness and dynamism as well as her expertness. Lou will have some degree of expertness and dynamism along with his trustworthiness.

Speakers can also manipulate their perceived credibility to some extent. They can mention the groups to which they belong and the things they have done, or they can cite certain authorities and examples which enhance their credibility. This is com-monly referred to as "name dropping." Lou could say, "You know, we had a similar problem in the previous company I worked for." In the same way, the professor might enhance her trustworthiness by accepting your invitation to lunch, mentioning that her son goes to the same high school as your boy, and generally being a warm and sociable individual. Of course, either the professor or Lou could have been the dynamic individual simply by getting motivated over the task assigned.

STATUS

A person's status depends in a large measure upon the role or position he/she is perceived as holding in the community, profession, or world in general. It does not matter what role one actually holds, but only whether that role is known and seen as important by the receiver of a message. Here again the listener is the key to understanding the effectiveness of the message. The manager of a company could walk through a plant and make suggestions, but his/her messages would probably not be accepted unless the receivers knew his/her status.

One's status is also relative to the position held by the receiver of the message. A plant supervisor holds a high-status or prestige position in relation to an assembly line worker but a low-status position in relation to the company president. Speakers can increase their status in the eyes of receivers in much the same way they increase their credibility, that is, by mentioning the authority and responsibility that go along with their various roles. Since we will be discussing the effects of status on reception of messages later in our chapter on groups, we have merely mentioned it here. In organizational communication, status is an extremely important factor that needs to be understood completely.

OPINION LEADERSHIP

One of the most interesting studies completed in the field of mass communication research was done by E. Katz and P. F. Lazarsfeld.[4] They examined the effects of radio, television, and newspapers on the attitudes and behavior of receivers. Upon immediate examination these media seemed to have little effect on message reception, but after several weeks with no new information, the messages had created a remarkable impact. At first Katz and Lazarsfeld were at a loss to explain the results, but after careful examination they found that the people who had received the message only allowed the communication to affect them once they had discussed its contents with others in whom they had a high degree of confidence. They dubbed the latter people *opinion leaders*. Later studies have found that these opinion leaders (1) were not of noticeably higher status, (2) differed with the topic at hand, like those with expertness credibility, and (3) tended to serve as models for the people they influenced.

The opinion leader concept is not limited to the mass communication setting. All of us have our own opinion leaders, be they our wives or husbands, our poker or golf buddies, our neighbors, our lunchroom comrades, or the person in the next office. They are people whom we have come to rely upon for advice and support and whom we check with before making important decisions. Very few of us are willing to commit ourselves to something until we know the reactions of those around us whom we consider important. Again, it is the receiver who is determining whether the communication accomplishes its purpose or not.

The source of a communication is one of the major factors which is affected by communication reception. There are, however, a number of other factors of importance in communication reception. They will be discussed in the following sections on the message itself and the channels employed to transmit the message.

Structure of the Message

The structure of one's message is also affected by the receivers. Many times there is a tendency on the part of people to confuse the style and structure of messages. The style of messages was discussed in Chapter 3 and includes such things as tone, quality, pitch, rate, force, word choice, gestures, and other sounds. Style is primarily a transmission phenomenon, while structure is more directly related to message impact and reception.

Every message has some kind of organization, even if the sender is unaware what it is. Some types of message organization or structure are more effective, however, in attracting the receiver's attention, focusing perception, increasing comprehension, and gaining acceptance than others. The question, then, is, What message structure is most effective for a given receiver, by a given source, in a given situation? Since people tend to like those message structures which are most familiar to them, the following traditional patterns will seem to be the most useful.

First is the *chronological structure*, where the main points merely follow one another in the order of their occurrence. In a discussion of some particular company, the first point might be the founding of the company, followed by the development of the product image, the problem of keeping the company going through changing times, and ending with some comments regarding the company's future. The beauty of this structure, as with most of the following structures, is that the listener is never in doubt where the discussion is going and, therefore, can sit back and listen easily to what is being said.

Second is the *spatial structure*, where the main points are arranged on some geographical basis. In a discussion of the company's current sales picture, the first point might be that sales in the West are up from last year, followed by the point that sales in the Midwest and South are down somewhat, and concluding with the fact that sales in the East are holding about the same as last year. The listener does not know exactly where the speaker is going next after each point but does have a general idea and, therefore, still feels comfortable.

Third are the *inductive* and *deductive structures*, where the main points go from the more specific to the more general (inductive) or from the more general to the more specific (deductive). Suppose that you want to tell your listeners that efficiency and productivity have increased in your plant since you took over. You could go about it either inductively, by first making your general point and then indicating how you did it through the use of computers, decreasing labor turnover and absenteeism, and maintaining manpower costs at a constant level, or deductively, by first demonstrating how you have been able to utilize the computer more, decrease labor turnover and absenteeism, and maintain manpower costs at the same level, with your conclusion being that efficiency and productivity have increased in your plant since you took over. In the following section on order effects we will talk more about listener preferences for inductive and deductive structures.

Fourth is the *problem-solution structure*, where the problem is first outlined and then one or more possible solutions are presented. If, for example, instead of wanting to comment on the increased efficiency and productivity in a plant, you wanted to suggest that there is an efficiency and productivity problem and solutions you are going to attempt to implement, you might well use the problem-solution structure. This communication structure is one of the most commonly used in our everyday conversation and is, thus, comfortable for listeners.

Finally, we have the *causal structure*, which is very similar to the problem-solution structure except that both the causes and the effects of a problem are presented. In the discussion of declining efficiency and productivity, for example, you would first present what you feel are the causes of the problem (labor costs, turnover, absenteeism, etc.), then the problem itself (decreasing efficiency and productivity), and end up suggesting the possible effects of the various policies and procedures you hope to implement (greater computer utilization will increase productivity and reduce cost, an improved working environment will lower turnover and absenteeism, and the reduction of overtime duty will reduce manpower costs). This is perhaps the most complete structure available for listeners. They get more information through this structure and are, therefore, happier as a result of attaining completeness.

Since we do not know very much about the comparative effects of each of these message structures, it seems safe to assume that they are all familiar enough not to disturb communication reception. Some of the effects of message structure on reception that we do know something about are those due to the order of presentation, those due to the presentation of one or both sides of the issue, and those due to the amount of logic contained in the message as opposed to emotional appeal.

ORDER EFFECTS

A communication message which gives the most important materials first is called *anticlimactic*, whereas a message with the most important information in the middle **97** is called *pyramidal*, and that with the most important information at the end is called *climactic*. For most receivers, placing the important arguments either at the beginning or near the end of a message has more effect than placing them in the middle, and the climactic order seems to have some slight advantage over the anticlimactic.

Some of the factors which confound the above generalization, however, are the level of receiver commitment, the amount of contradictory information the receiver has or is likely to receive, and the relevancy of the information to the receiver. When we have publicly committed ourselves to one side of the discussion, it is extremely hard to change our opinion. We do not like to get ourselves in a position of looking uncertain, indecisive, or inconsistent. Many closed-minded receivers will not even listen to comments made for the opposing point of view.

The amount of contradictory information which we as receivers possess or are likely to receive is also important. Regardless of the order in which one presents a message, if a previous message has been received, we are likely to believe the message we received first over any others. When you, as a source, are the first one to present listeners with a message, they will tend to believe yours over other opposing messages they might receive later. If receivers do not see the relevance of the message they are hearing to themselves, they may very well turn their hearing ear away and concentrate on something else. This is why sources normally introduce a communication by relating it directly to the listener. This is often done by saying, "Bill, you will be interested in this . . . ," or "We should all be aware of those new procedures for our unit." Not only is this useful for attracting the receiver's attention or focusing perception, but it increases the possibility of comprehension and acceptance regardless of the order in which the message itself is presented.

SIDEDNESS EFFECTS

When a communication message has two sides, an important determinant of the reception of that message is whether both sides are presented. When too much of the opposing side is presented, the listener may become more resistant to the original purpose of the message. When too little of the opposing side is presented, the receiver tends to feel that his or her intelligence has been insulted, and uses the opposing information to resist the main message. A supervisor would have the best effect on listeners if he/she could first determine what information they currently know, so that he/she will not give them any new information but attack that information which might endanger the effect of the message. He/she cannot, for example, convince them that a change in policy is necessary until they are convinced that the old policy is inadequate.

Other factors which enter into the sidedness decision are the educational level of the receiver, the receiver's current belief (which may be different from that of the source), and the likelihood of the receiver being exposed to contrary information. Receivers with a high educational level seem to prefer two-sided messages while those with low educational levels are more convinced by a one-sided message. Receivers who are initially in agreement with a message want no more material than is necessary, so the one-sided approach is best. When the listener initially disagrees with the message or is likely to hear opposing information, the two-sided approach seems to have the most lasting effect.

To sum up, it is a given fact of life that reception is best when the message presented is totally new, the listeners are not educationally or intellectually equipped to question the message, and there is little chance that opposing information will be heard. In these instances the receiver will most likely hear one-sided messages. Two-sided messages appear once receivers have formed their opinion, since that opinion must be defeated before a new one can be implanted. This again points to the importance of the receiver in the determination of the quality of communication.

EFFECTS OF LOGIC

All receivers would like to think that they are more susceptible to logical than to emotional appeals. In actual practice, however, this is not necessarily so. It is those messages which appear to be logical, even though they may not meet the tests of logical validity, that are better received than those that appear purely emotional.

Perhaps the main reason why logic is not very well attended to is that it is normally quite boring. Receivers would much rather listen to an interesting story or a hypothetical illustration than to a logical syllogism or statistics. This conclusion is more relevant perhaps to spoken communication than to written. Leaders seem to expect more logic in a written report or a formal memo than they expect from a telephone conversation or an informal discussion. In business and industry we tend to think that all or almost all of our messages are logical rather than illogical. If we carried a tape-recorder around with us for a day and actually listened to the communications that go on around us, we would find that nonlogical communications are at least as prevalent as the logical ones. This is not necessarily a bad thing; few of us have the training or the inclination to listen only to strictly logical messages. We should, however, be aware of the kinds of messages we receive and carefully examine those upon which we base our decisions.

A great deal more study needs to be given to the effect of message structure on communication reception. The evidence is clear, though, that the way a message is structured plays a significant role in determining how and even whether the message is received. Message patterns, such as the chronological, spatial, deductive, inductive, problem-solution, and causal, allow a receiver to follow a message more easily. The placing of important information at the beginning, middle, or end of a message in part determines its acceptance. Presenting one or two sides of an issue, as circumstances require, will make a message more believable, as will making it appear logical. In the final analysis, the receiver is the key to how one should structure a message for the most effect.

Communication Channels

The ways in which messages can be transmitted are many and varied. The most obvious froms of transmission are the spoken and written word, but we also communicate through our bodily movements, the pitch and tone of our voices, our facial expressions, our dress, our posture, our sense of touch, and many more ways. With the advent of books, magazines, newspapers, radio, telephone, television, and movies, we are able to transmit messages to large numbers of people quickly and relatively cheaply. Channel technology has become so sophisticated in the last fifty years that many communication experts claim we are undergoing an electronic revolution.

The foremost exponent of the importance of the message channel is Marshall McLuhan, Toronto director of the Center for Culture and Technology and author of such widely popular books as *The Medium Is the Message* and *Understanding Media* and articles in almost every major magazine in the country.[5] McLuhan's basic assumptions are the following.[6] First, ideas come from "information" received through all of our senses—seeing, hearing, feeling, smelling, and tasting. Second, the way that an idea takes shape in the receiver's mind is determined by the balance between various senses that provide the original information. Thus, before the alphabet and later print, humans took in information all at once with all of their senses. With the advent of writing and reading, they began to take in information one bit at a time and in sequence. But with the coming of the electronic age, we have returned to a state approaching primitive, all-at-once, simultaneous reception. Third, various modern communication channels "extend" our senses. The pen extends our sense of touch; the telephone extends our voice; film and television extend our sense of sight; and even clothing is an extension of our skin. From these three basic assumptions, Marshall McLuhan draws the conclusion that the channel of communication determines how much and what kind of information is received, because it determines the senses that will be useful and extends the senses we already have for receiving information.

An example of the implications of this conclusion might be in order here. Suppose we were interested in running an advertising campaign for our company's product. We might simply run a written advertisement in a newspaper or magazine; or we might decide to run the same ad on the radio, having someone read it; or we might decide to run it on television with a picture of someone using the product and an announcer reading the copy. Obviously, with the television advertisement more senses are brought into play (sight and sound), whereas with either the magazine or radio advertisement, only one of the receiver's senses is being used. The television would, then, provide the greater impact, according to McLuhan. For this reason, he says, the "medium *is* the message." This does not mean, in our opinion, however, that the medium determines reception. We believe that the amount of attention, perception, comprehension, and acceptance given to any specific message through any specific channel depends finally upon the receiver. We as receivers have tended to gravitate to the electronic, all-at-once channels because they are more useful and satisfying to use in the twentieth century; but we do have a choice, and for many purposes we do choose to take in information linearly.

McLuhan introduces the terms "hot" and "cool" to describe the channel and to explain the gratifications and effects of the various communication channels on the receiver. A "hot" medium is one in which receivers are not asked to take part in the communication process—as a matter of fact, they could not take part if they wanted to. Reading a memo or listening to a report, or looking at a diagram, for example, is using a "hot" communication channel. Participating in a discussion, watching television, talking on a telephone, and face-to-face interchanges are all considered "cool" channels, because the receivers are asked to respond or fill in visual or acoustical space; everything is not laid out for them, and they must provide some information themselves before they can fully understand the message. We receivers have chosen to move into an age dominated by "cool" channels because we have a desire to become an "involvement-participatory-oriented society." We are not satisfied with one-dimensional thinking. The complexity of our business and industrial society has made it impossible to deal with modern problems one bit at a time; we must know everything before we can do anything.

In the following paragraphs of this section we will be discussing the effect of some of the more important communication channels on message reception. We believe that again you will see that in the final analysis reception is the key to effective
organizational communication.

ORAL VERSUS WRITTEN CHANNELS

We have already used a great deal of space in this text talking about written and oral communication, but we have devoted relatively little space to discussing the differences between the two types of channels. A number of factors determine the effect of these two channels upon communication reception: (1) the difficulty of the material, (2) the number of receivers, (3) the desire for source-receiver interaction, (4) the personal preferences of the receiver, (5) the source of the message, and (6) the time and money available for the message.

Message Difficulty

Written communication is much more effective for transmitting difficult material than is the oral method. When business people receive a written communication, they have the ability to read and reread it until they have a complete understanding of the message. On the other hand, when they are called on the telephone, visited face to face, or have the material presented to them through an oral report, they must comprehend the message immediately or risk losing it. Often things like poor logic, weak facts, and incomplete research are masked by an oral presentation. Reception of difficult material presented orally can be improved through the use of repetition and summaries or by the addition of written or visual aids, but the written channel is still normally better for difficult or complicated messages.

Number of Receivers

For years the number of receivers reached was thought to be the only major difference between written and oral communication channels. Written communication was seen as reaching one person at a time, while a speaker could transmit to thousands of people at once. The fact of the matter is that as the number of receivers increases, spoken communication tends to lose some of its effect. People who listen in a large group tend to be more distracted than those listening in a smaller group or talking face to face. Television, of course, combines both of these advantages; it reaches large numbers of people but has the aura of a face-to-face discussion. There is, however, one other factor to consider with regard to this question of numbers, and that is "mob psychology." Receivers sitting or standing and listening to a truly effective speaker can, many times, get caught up in the atmosphere of the setting, and they will think and do many things which they would normally not consider or which they would consider wrong when reading the message or having it presented to them face to face.

Interaction Possibilities

For many types of messages, an immediate response is desired from receivers. This feedback is usually delayed when a written channel is being used. When it does arrive, it lacks the nonverbal cues which help one to interpret it. In the industrial world, for example, we receive thousands of memos a year, many of which make little or no sense, and we must ask the writers what they mean. The writers may very well repeat **101** the message in exactly the same words, but when they put the stress in the correct place and nonverbally amplify the message, we can understand it. Private face-to-face communication provides the greatest amount of interaction and feedback, but a source presenting material before a group also benefits by seeing the nonverbal (and sometimes verbal) reactions of the receivers. The feedback information a receiver provides for a speaker is helpful because it permits the speaker to determine the impact of his/her message and adjust or amplify it where necessary.

Receiver Characteristics

The personal characteristics of the listener or reader are also important. Many people in this country and around the world either cannot read or do not like to read because it is difficult for them. For these people oral communication is about the only communication channel to which they attend with any regularity. They watch television for their news. They go the movies to satisfy their esthetic interests. They listen to music on the radio for relaxation. They visit friends and coworkers to fulfill their normal social needs. For these people, the written channel is just not a part of their normal reception pattern. It has been demonstrated that people who get their information from written channels are usually highly educated, white-collar, and have a higher socioeconomic status (i.e., they have more money and prestige). Those who get their news and form their opinions from oral channels (radio, face-to-face discussions, telephones, television, etc.) are normally less educated and blue-collar, with a lower socioeconomic status. This is not to say that one form of reception is better or worse than the other; it's just that we should try to be open to all possible message channels.

Individuality

Many times a written communication channel does not seem to carry the warmth or individuality of a spoken message to the receiver. It takes an excellent writer to create a message such that it is immediately associated with him/her. Oral messages, on the other hand, bear the unmistakable stamp of the sender. A number of prominent people could read from the telephone book, and we, as receivers, would instantly identify them, just as you can your mother's or your boss's voice on the telephone. When we feel that our position or personality will aid in the acceptance of a message by the receiver, the oral channel is the most effective. Employers, for example, should theoretically communicate orally when they want to put their full authority behind their message; the impact is reduced when the message is written.

Time and Money

Finally, it takes a great deal of time and usually more money to utilize the written channel. Granted that a good oral presentation with high-quality visuals can also be costly in time and money, in general the oral channel is less costly. For many business people, it is well worthwhile to telephone a message rather than write it out and have a secretary type and mail it. The cost of a message may in many cases be the prime consideration, but one must realize there are costs involved in both communication channels.

MULTIPLE CHANNELS

As McLuhan argues, a communicator should try to involve as many of the senses in transmissions as possible. An oral presentation augmented with a written report, or slides, or a tape recording, or a short film, or charts, diagrams, and models may aid in gaining attention, improving perception, increasing comprehension, and perhaps creating acceptance. This is especially true where difficult and unfamiliar messages are involved.

There can, however, be a number of drawbacks to using multiple-channel presentations, especially when presentation time is a factor and when the various channels are used incorrectly. Receivers may tend to become distracted if there are too many things going on and may simply dismiss the message. People tend to distrust communicators or communications that look staged. A primary source of distraction for receivers is the communicator who stands with his/her back to them and speaks instead to the chart, projector, map, etc. Other sources of receiver distraction are failure to remove an aid once its purpose is served, not checking out equipment prior to the presentation and having it break down, letting the aid make the point rather than making it strongly in the presentation, fumbling around and playing with the "extra" materials, passing the aids around so that they further distract the receivers, and passing out written material at the time of the presentation rather than before or after it.

In the final analysis, then, the decision as to whether reception will be improved through the use of multiple channels is influenced by a number of factors: time available, message difficulty, message familiarity, source skill, and probably many more. Multiple-channel usage is definitely the trend of the future, and receivers tend to prefer it in many cases over single channels for those reasons mentioned earlier.

NONVERBAL CHANNELS

It is impossible not to communicate—that is, the absence of words does not mean that there is an absence of communication. The employee who sits in a crowded lunchroom looking straight ahead and the company president who is sitting and listening to a report with hands over eyes are both communicating that they do not want to speak to anyone or be spoken to, and the people around them usually "get the message" and leave them alone. Without saying a word they have communicated their wishes as clearly as if they had stood up and announced them over the loudspeaker.

Nonverbal channels are the ones of which we seem to be least aware in ourselves but are most aware of in others. We will listen to people, but believe them only if the nonverbal channels also tell us that we are not being deceived. In reading written communications, we receivers attempt to "read between the lines." Many words have so many meanings that they can be interpreted only in their nonverbal context: "How are ya?" does not demand an answer, but "How *are* you?" does. Understanding nonverbal communication is no simple task. It is complicated by a host of factors, some of them observable and others veritable booby traps. For example, Herman Barkobite, who is a supervisor in the Issuance Department, had a minor discussion with the little woman before he left for work this morning. When he got to work, his most valued and trusted employee, Enrika Gainaday, smiled and brightly said to him, "Good morning, Herman." Herman, who was still mulling over the events of the morning and who, on the drive over to the office, had figured out how to answer both his wife and his wife's mother in all domestic issues, did not notice Enrika's bright and cheery "Good morning." With complete lack of courtesy, he practically brushed her by with something resembling a growl emanating from the depths of his throat. Enrika was crushed . . . simply crushed . . . and began to think . . .

Nonverbal communication channels have been classified into three categories: sign language, action language, and object language.[7] *Sign language* refers to those nonverbal messages which have an almost universal meaning to receivers, for example, a hitchhiker's thumb, a rising inflection at the end of a sentence which indicates a question, a wave of the hand to indicate "goodbye," and the "come here" sign with one's finger. *Action language* refers to those actions which one carries on normally, like walking, sleeping, sitting, and others which can carry a great deal of meaning for those receivers who know an individual well and are sensitive to such messages. A husband, for example, is many times able to communicate something to his wife without even trying to do so or even being aware that he is communicating. Something about his walk, posture, or look gives her the needed information. *Object language* includes all the material things which we choose to use that also communicate something about the way we are or the way we would like to be seen. Dress, hair style, desk objects, wall decorations, and many other things tell receivers something about the man or woman who owns the objects.

Communication authorities are just now beginning to conduct serious investigations into the effect of nonverbal channels on message reception. We do know, for example, that people tend to develop a sense of personal space, that is, a distance at which they prefer to interact with others. This concept is fully discussed in the book *The Territorial Imperative*.[8] If one's receiver sits or stands too far away, one tends to move forward and reestablish the required space. A receiver can move senders clear across a room by merely backing up casually and having the sender attempt to reestablish the traditional space. Oral presentations seem to be more effective if the speaker walks forward and moves around while speaking. In writing letters, reports, and memos, there are certain degrees of formality or social distance which one can or cannot have in communication with a superior or subordinate. We also know that the seating pattern people establish with one another affects how they and their message will be received. Similar messages delivered by tall versus short, shaven versus unshaven, fat versus thin, neat versus tattered, and young versus old sources will have different degrees of attention, perception, comprehension, and acceptance. Speakers who gesture with their hands, face, and body generally are found to be better received than those who do not. People with pleasant, lively, enthusiastic voices and vocal patterns tend to get better reception.

For the most part, however, direct relationships between specific kinds of nonverbal communication and specific receiver effects have been only hunches. With the amount of study that is being given to this area, however, it should not be too long before we can draw some authoritative conclusions. Until then we must continue to agree with Sapir's description of nonverbal idiom as "an elaborate code that is written nowhere, known by none, and understood by all."[9]

MASS MEDIA CHANNELS

The evidence to date tends to show that all of the mass media channels are more effective as reinforcing agents for messages that are already accepted by receivers than as a means of changing opinions. The best means by which actual receiver opinion change is manifested through the mass media is in the operation of the two-step flow or opinion leader, as we mentioned earlier. Opinion leaders receive information from the mass channels and in turn change the attitudes of their receivers.

Although for many receivers the mass media channels have a great deal of credibility—that is, people tend to believe what they read in the paper or hear on the television more than what they get from other sources—the same matter of selective reception works here as it does in all other communication settings. Receivers allow themselves to hear and read only information which agrees with their preconceived opinions. In the case of the mass media it is very easy for receivers to skip over articles or switch channels when something threatens to run contrary to their previous beliefs.

What the mass media channels, especially television, tend to do is provide receivers with a dream world into which they can put themselves if they take certain steps, like buying mouth wash, wearing hair spray, or owning a certain type of car, furniture, or home. Listeners and readers of the mass media channels project themselves into the world created by television; they identify with television people, and these people then help them to make decisions they probably would have made by themselves if given enough time. Studies have failed to prove, for example, that watching a violent television program will cause even the youngest child to become violent. Violent tendencies, in the same way as a desire to buy a new car, come from within the receiver; television only serves to reinforce the attitude.

Summary

The basic premise of this section has been that reception is the key to promoting effective organizational communication. We have demonstrated how the receiver determines the way in which the source is perceived, the message is structured, and which communication channels are needed. We pointed out that the source of a message is dependent on the receivers to determine his/her perceived credibility (i.e., expertness, trustworthiness, and dynamism), status, and opinion leadership. The structure of the message must be familiar to receivers, and the arguments within that structure must appeal to the receivers' biases with regard to placement of the strongest arguments within the message, the number of sides of the issue presented, and the use of logical versus emotional appeals. Finally, the receiver is important in determining the type and number of communication channels that should be used. Written channels are well received when difficult material is involved, when large numbers of receivers are not involved, when there is little need for interaction and feedback, when receivers are visually oriented, when message individuality is not important, and when time and money are of little importance. Where one or more of these factors are not met, the oral communication channel may well elicit better reception. Even more important than the written and oral channels, however, in our modern industrial society are the nonverbal and mass media channels. Modern communication receivers are placing more and more emphasis on these media, and thus such media also should be taken into consideration when message reception and acceptance are being predicted. It is evident that reception plays a key role in the determination of communication effectiveness.

BARRIERS TO COMMUNICATION RECEPTION

A barrier to communication reception can have beneficial as well as detrimental results. People like Aldous Huxley in *Brave New World Revisited*,[10] George Orwell in *1984*,[11] and Vance Packard in *The Hidden Persuaders*[12] have told us that communication scientists will soon become so sophisticated that they will be able to control or "engineer" our lives. The fact of the matter is, however, that at the same time we are becoming very sophisticated receivers who have developed barriers which protect us from manipulation. The detrimental result of developing these barriers is that they can also impede our reception of relevant and important communication which needs to flow smoothly if the organization is to be productive. We will be discussing three of the major barriers to reception in the following sections: personal, semantic, and environmental barriers.

Personal Barriers

We have already discussed the fact that listeners and readers tend to expose themselves to those messages which agree with their previous attitudes. The simple process of selective exposure keeps us from receiving too much new information of either the productive or the unproductive variety. We turn off the television in a very conscious manner, but we can turn off the boss or the company newsletter or the union president in the same manner although we do it unconsciously.

Even when we do perceive communication messages, there is no guarantee that we will comprehend them. As someone once put it, "we often hear but do not listen." Inattention is especially prevalent with respect to highly repetitive material; we, as receivers, may pay attention to one "no smoking" sign, but when such signs are all over the shop we cease to comprehend them even if we do see them. Few of us can remember the color of our favorite restaurant even though we may go there once or twice a month. Even if we did receive the transmission at one time, we no longer comprehend it or "listen."

A further personal communication barrier is perceptual defense or perceptual sensitivity. Receivers tend to see only those things which they want to see even when the message is presented to them directly. People will either reject or misperceive messages that are against their values. Readers viewing the word "income" have reported seeing "learning," "tomorrow," "knowledge," and even "loving." The reverse is also true: receivers will tend to see messages quicker if the messages are important to them. An interesting study once compared the drawings of a dime made by children from wealthy families with those made by children from poor families. Invariably the size of the dime was drawn larger by the children from the poor families.[13]

Just as we receivers practice selective perception and selective exposure, we also practice selective forgetting. We cannot possibly remember everything we see and hear, so we remember those things which we want to remember. A receiver examined some weeks after hearing acceptable information presented by an unacceptable source tends to remember the message but not the communicator. If we do not totally forget information which does not please us, we also have the ability to distort what we remember to fit our needs. This is perhaps the reason why written contracts are required in business dealings. As much as we might like to make deals with a handshake, receivers of goodwill can distort things in the past as badly as men of ill will.

The preceding receiver defenses will come into play to a greater extent the more important the attitude involved. We have some beliefs which we hold tentatively and others that are central to our entire belief structure. If our egos are centrally involved with certain attitudes, we will fight with every means possible to prevent those attitudes from being questioned. A receiver with a lower degree of self-confidence will tend to hold most or all attitudes tentatively, while a very confident and dogmatic receiver will have very few inconsequential beliefs and, thus, will be more likely to receive communication messages selectively. In reception it pays to keep an open mind and to be willing to change one's beliefs and attitudes on the basis of new information provided.

Semantic Barriers

A number of semantic barriers to reception also exist. We have discussed some of these in earlier portions of the text but will go into a little more detail here. The most pervasive semantic barrier to efficient communication reception is the tendency that all of us have to classify and label things and people. Once we have labeled something, i.e., as *liberal, conservative, Negro, rate buster, management, worker,* etc., we tend to act as if we have captured the "essence" of the thing classified. Classification is not bad in and of itself; communication would be impossible if we had a separate word for every object in existence. Classifying does present a very real and detrimental barrier, however, when we receivers fail to realize that our classification is only one of many possibilities. A person, for example, may be tall or short, fat or thin, liberal or conservative, smart or dumb, black or white, redheaded or blond, and one of hundreds of other opposites, but none of these classifications captures their "essence" because each person is a unique individual, incapable of total classification.

The natural result of classification or stereotyping is to narrow our reception categories and to treat them as mutually exclusive. One cannot, we would say, be both smart and dumb, liberal and conservative, right and wrong, good and bad. The fact of the matter is, however, that people are both smart and dumb (smart about some things and dumb about others), liberal and conservative (liberal with regard to salary, but conservative with regard to promotion), right and wrong (right about what is needed, but wrong about how to get it), good and bad (good in the morning and bad in the afternoon). Semanticists call this tendency to believe that things are either one way or another *two-valued orientation,* as opposed to the better alternative of a *multivalued orientation.*

The other semantic barrier of major importance in determining reception is a receiver's tendency to confuse the symbols we use to classify the world with the actual, "real life" world. Franklin Roosevelt once told us that we have nothing to fear but fear itself; as Professor Condon points out, what Roosevelt meant was, "It is one thing to be afraid, it is something else to be afraid of being afraid."[14] We find the thing-symbol problem especially relevant in business organizations, where symbols become so very important. The symbol for a janitor, for example, has changed to *sanitary engineer,* but these people do the same work they always did. In the same way, many businessmen tend to value money, not for what it can buy, but merely for its symbolic value. Receivers who confuse words and things begin to live in a dream world and become incapable of translating ideas into actions.

107

Environmental Barriers

A major point that must be made with regard to acceptance of communication is that single messages will have little long-lasting effect on the receiver unless the source has some control over the receiver's environment. Very effective brainwashing centers, like mental hospitals, religious orders, and prisoner-of-war camps, maintain almost complete environmental control. Unwanted ideas are first suppressed by force, and later, when the propaganda has taken effect, receivers do not want to hear contrary messages (selective attention).

In this country the free and almost unrestricted flow of ideas prevents any one source from exercising too much control over the reception environment, although it may try. Advertisers try to saturate a market, politicians try to censure the news media, and management tries to isolate and eliminate any hostile rumors. Nevertheless, total suppression of contrary ideas is next to impossible. But to the extent that people are able to control the reception environment by eliminating unfavorable messages and promoting favorable communication, they will determine in large measure the amount of communication reception and acceptance.

The environment can be controlled by determining the size and nature of the receivers, the amount and kind of information they receive outside of the business setting, the intercommunication between receivers, the amount and kind of information they hear within the business setting, and so on. One problem with environmental control is that once the control is reduced, the receivers may very easily revert back to their old ways. Examinations of religious crusades, for example, tend to show that the environment created—singing, proclamations of faith, organ music, religious statues, etc.—has a tremendous effect in terms of raising money and getting people to repent; but once the crusade passes on and converts are sent to a more established church, they soon return to their former life style.

In this final section we have not exhausted the barriers to communication by any means. What we have tried to do is introduce some of the major personal, semantic, and environmental barriers to communication reception; others of lesser importance have been discussed earlier in the text and a few more will be discussed in the appropriate following sections. We must be constantly alert, not only to the ways we as receivers can be manipulated by communication transmission and reception, but also to the ways in which we can in turn distort and impede the smooth flow of messages. Personal, semantic, and environmental barriers to reception help us prevent the former but, at the same time, encourage the latter.

IMPROVING RECEPTION
ABILITY

Throughout the preceding sections of this chapter on the factors involved in communication reception, we have made a number of suggestions as to ways by which one can improve reception ability. By way of summarizing this chapter we will gather these suggestions together as well as other practical suggestions which if seriously practiced in organizations might double or triple communication effectiveness.

1. *Realize that listening is hard work.* Many receivers believe that listening is just a matter of sitting back and absorbing information like a sponge. We have pointed out that both the source and the receiver must share responsibility for communication effectiveness. McLuhan has pointed out that especially with a "cool" channel like face-to-face communication, television, and telephone conversation, the receiver must fill in visual and acoustical space, and this is not always easy. It has also been

pointed out in this regard that the higher we go in the administrative structure of an organization, the harder we must work at listening. As you continue to read through our suggestions for improving your reception ability, you should get the very definite impression just how hard it is to be a good communication receiver.

2. *Prepare to listen.* It has been pointed out a number of times in this and other chapters that people cannot communicate if they do not have some attitude, beliefs, or knowledge in common, that is, some common points of reference, and if they are not somewhat familiar with the subject under discussion. This means that listeners, if they do not already have the necessary background to understand the communication, must get it. It means being familiar enough with the subject of the message not to confuse the words being used with the things or objects they represent. Preparing to listen also includes getting into the correct mental attitude—one that is designed to maintain attention, increase perception, and elicit comprehension. Some of the following suggestions refer to just what the mental attitude of the receiver should be.

3. *Know your own biases.* All of us have certain biases with regard to the communications we receive. These biases are part of our mental classification scheme; but, as we pointed out earlier, we must recognize the value judgments we put on various things and prevent them from blinding us to new and different information or forcing us into two-valued, either-or thinking patterns. We must also recognize who those people are who provide us with opinion leadership and try to make sure that we take more into account when listening than just what we perceive their opinions to be. We also have biases with regard to the source of communication: some of us like experts, while others like people they can trust and still others tend to prefer listening to and believing persons who are dynamic. We must, however, try to break these prejudices and listen to all sources, because useful information may come from almost anyone. Some of us prefer certain kinds of message structures, organizations, appeals (logical or emotional), and sidedness in the messages we receive. We are in danger, though, in tuning out those messages that do not fit our bias if we are not constantly alert. Finally, we have channel biases which can also prevent us from attending carefully to those messages that do not come through what we believe to be the proper channel or channels. If we know our biases, we are much better able to control them and keep them from interfering with our reception ability.

4. *Choose your listening position carefully.* The key point to remember here is that you must sit or stand so that all the information presented is available to you. This can mean sitting up close when the audience is large or sitting away from distractions like street noise or projection equipment or even the television if you are reading. A second factor in choosing your listening position involves not limiting your reception environment or letting others do it to you. Actively seek the information you need, and don't expect it all to come to you. When you become aware that others are trying to keep you from the relevant information, do not be afraid to ask for it or to ask where you can find it. Even in this age of communication, many people do not even have the information they need to survive because they have not gotten themselves to a place where they can receive the messages they need.

5. *Take notes.* Many receivers have somehow gotten the impression that they look silly taking notes while listening. This is certainly not true; many of the most important management people active today take notes throughout all of their listening occasions. When you are reading, you should keep a pencil handy to mark important passages for future reference. Note taking is especially important where difficult or unfamiliar material is presented orally. When it is possible, a written copy of the presentation will take the place of notes. For many of us, note taking has become a lost art, but it should not be for the efficient receiver.

6. *Concentrate.* We have mentioned that attention is a fluctuating and selective

process. The natural attention curve for most people begins quite high, drops off as the message continues, and increases again at the end. As listeners and readers we must combat this tendency by increasing our concentration during the middle part of a message and trying to keep it constant. The runner, for example, who starts fast and ends fast will lose a long race to the runner who maintains a constant pace. We must also concentrate on not allowing our natural tendency for selective perception, exposure, and forgetting to make us miss useful information. We should also listen just as carefully to familiar as to unfamiliar messages and to the middle speakers as we do to those who speak first or last. Maintaining one's concentration takes a great deal of practice and must be done consciously first; in time it will occur unconsciously.

7. *Don't be distracted.* The ways in which we can become distracted are many; we can be distracted by the source's appearance, dress, vocabulary, style of presentation, use of visual, oral, or written aids, and many more factors. We can be distracted when listening with others in a group by letting our attention wander. We can also be distracted by something in the message or channel that keeps us from receiving the message clearly. We have discussed all of these earlier in this chapter, but you must remember that anything which distracts you from the main message is likely to lower your reception ability.

8. *Be open-minded.* Being open-minded means not feeling threatened, insulted, or resistant to messages that contradict your beliefs, attitudes, ideas, or values. It means not becoming ego-involved with the topic to such an extent that you are unwilling to listen to messages on the other side. It is difficult to listen to a one-sided message when you know the other side and want it dealt with. It is difficult to listen to an emotional appeal when you know that most of the logic points elsewhere. It is difficult to stay open-minded, but it is necessary, because at any time a point might be made or occur to you that would outweigh the information on which you base your current attitude. In many ways being a good receiver and being open-minded are one and the same thing.

9. *Be interested.* Efficient listeners are interested and attentive to everything around them; they look for ways in which each message might be relevant to them and their job. This means that you must be prepared to receive a message at any time, even when you are busy with other things. A vital message or valuable thought might need to be expressed immediately or it will be lost. When people are interested, they look at the communicator and let him/her know in many little ways that they care about what is being said. No one likes to talk to a "blank wall," and a couple of these experiences will hamper future communication.

10. *Be empathetic.* When we have empathy for the source of a message, we try to put ourself in the source's shoes and understand the problem from his/her point of view. This is different from "sympathy" in that the sympathetic listener feels sorry for the source and does not necessarily try to understand the problem completely. When listeners are empathetic, they create a climate that encourages others to communicate often and honestly with them. You as a receiver become a shoulder to cry on and an ear to bend. Empathetic listeners do not try to correct a problem right away, but they make sure they have all the pertinent information and see things from the sender's viewpoint. This is the kind of climate we have discussed in the previous chapter.

11. *Delay argument.* When you are efficient at delaying your arguments, you do so both mentally and physically. That is, you not only don't interrupt the speaker and argue with a point, but also don't prepare arguments in your own mind to be used later. Mentally arguing with a communicator is perhaps the chief reason why so little

listening takes place in discussions. Carl Rogers became so aware of this problem that he developed a game to delay argument.[15] He suggested that before persons can make a point in a discussion, they should first be able to repeat the last person's message to that person's satisfaction. Try playing this game sometime and see for yourself how difficult it is to keep from preparing mental arguments to the exclusion of messages that are coming to you.

12. *Delay judgment.* There is a very fine line that must be drawn between this suggestion and the following one—that people should listen critically. We are referring here to delaying judgments regarding the sender's personality, the sender's main message, and your own response. We many times allow the personalities of our sources to cause us to prejudge their messages. In the same way we many times prejudge whether the main point of the message is going to appeal to us, and thus we select that part to which we will listen and neglect the other. Finally, by judging too quickly we can easily get caught up in the "psychology of the mob" and do or say things we would not normally do under other circumstances or after some thought. It is always smart for the able receiver to delay judgments of this sort and attend to the message in an impartial way.

13. *Listen critically.* On the other hand, one should be critical and pass judgment on the assumptions, arguments, evidence, and logic behind the main communication message. One should not sit passively and accept uncritically the development of a point which has no foundation in fact or rationality. Some people seem to believe everything they read or hear without ever analyzing it. The good listener delays judgment on the personality of the source, the main points of the message, and a final response to the message, but he/she must listen critically enough so that when the time comes to pass judgment on these things he/she will do so in an enlightened fashion.

14. *Listen for more than words.* We have often mentioned throughout this text that communication involves more than words, but if receivers are not attuned to these other forms of communication, they will miss much of the message's meaning. The able listener looks for variations in vocal and bodily action and other nonverbal channels which give indications of the expertness, trustworthiness, and dynamism and the underlying feelings of the communicator. These channels can many times give us more of the information we need in order to respond than the words themselves.

15. *Look for main points.* If receivers can determine the main points of a message, they have a much better chance of comprehending and remembering the communication. In order to do this the listener must look for the structure of the message and mentally review the material that has gone before. Note taking is useful in this latter task. As we pointed out earlier, the main points can come at the beginning, middle, or end of a message, so the receiver must be always alert. If the message source gives a preview or summary of the communication, it is important to listen especially carefully to it. It is through the main points of a message that the receiver can determine its usefulness.

16. *Use listener responses.* We have not talked much about *listener responses*. These are very brief comments or actions that can be made to sources which convey the idea that you are interested and attentive and wish them to continue. They are made quietly and briefly so as not to interfere with the speaker's train of thought— usually when the speaker pauses. Five types of listener responses are nodding the head slightly and waiting; looking at the speaker expectantly without doing or saying anything; remarking, "I see," "Uh-huh," "Is that so," "That's interesting," etc.; repeating back the last few words the speaker said; and reflecting back to the speaker

your understanding of what has just been said ("You feel that . . ."). The value of listener responses is that they provide feedback for communicators and tell them that you are still with them and want them to continue speaking.

17. *Don't interrupt.* A pause, even a long pause, doesn't necessarily mean that the speaker has finished saying everything he/she wishes. Interrupting a message is the surest way there is of stopping further communication. It many times takes people a long time and some digression to make their point, but by interrupting, the receiver runs the risk of not ever having the point made. One of the most infuriating things some listeners do is to interrupt a communication when they think they have discovered what the main point is going to be, as if they were on a quiz program and must answer before their opponents. Even when you think the message has ended, it is best to wait a little while longer to be totally sure before you respond.

18. *Use reflecting phrases.* If you don't understand something that has been said or you want the sender to elaborate on a point, you may pursue the thought by beginning with a *reflecting phrase*, such as "you said," "you mentioned," "you cited before," or "you described." After repeating the idea, follow with a question beginning with "who," "what," "when," "where," "why," or "how." Reflecting phrases are designed to give you a second chance for receiving something you missed the first time around. One should not be used, however, until you are sure that it will not disrupt the source. Make a note of it and ask the speaker at the end of the presentation, if a better opportunity does not occur earlier.

19. *Ask for added information.* There are times when you as a listener are not satisfied that everything the speaker knows has been communicated. For example, the speaker may just present one side of an argument and you want to hear an assessment of the other point of view. This points up the fact not only that you are interested in what was said, but that you trust him/her enough to listen to more of his/her ideas. Asking for added information should definitely come at the end of the communication message, or it might very well give the source the impression that you are a hostile listener.

20. *Limit your own talking.* At the end of most communications there is time for discussion and for questions from the listeners. During these periods it is very easy for receivers to monopolize the conversation and not let the source have a chance to respond to the comments. An able listener always remembers that it is the speaker who is most important during this period. It is also important in this respect to allow the source of the main message to have the last word. This gives the sources a feeling that they are important and that the job was well done, and usually makes receivers feel they have played their role well. As a receiver, you should be proud when you have worked hard at your job and confident that you have enough information on which to base your acceptance or rejection of the message.

Throughout the preceding discussion of ways to improve your reception ability, as well as throughout the other sections of this chapter, there are a number of tips we believe are valuable for the transmission of communication. We will not list them here, since this chapter has mainly dealt with reception, but we hope they have not gone unheeded. It is only through both quality transmission *and* quality reception that organizational communication is improved.

REVIEW QUESTIONS

1. What are the most significant listening problems that occur in organizational communication?

2. Differentiate the four basic factors involved in communication reception.

3. What does the text mean when it says that attention and perception are selective?

4. How are our mental categories and comprehension related?

5. What are the responsibilities of a receiver as opposed to a transmitter in a communication interchange?

6. Discuss the three factors on which a communication receiver judges the source of the message.

7. What factors determine a source's credibility?

8. Why is status said to be a relative matter?

9. What is meant by *opinion leadership*?

10. Explain the five types of message structures.

11. Under what conditions are the anticlimactic, pyramidal, and climactic orders most effective?

12. Under what conditions should one present a two-sided as opposed to a one-sided message?

13. Why are Marshall McLuhan's concepts important in understanding communication channels?

14. What are the important factors involved in determining whether a message should be communicated orally or in written form, and why?

15. What are the advantages and drawbacks of using multiple channels of communication?

16. Explain the three types of nonverbal channels.

17. Why does the text say that the mass media are better opinion reinforcers than changers?

18. Why does the text say that reception is the key to effective communication rather than transmission, message, or channel?

19. Explain the personal, semantic, and environmental barriers to effective communication reception.

20. List and explain each of the twenty ways to improve your reception ability.

EXERCISES

1. Do a communication audit on yourself for an entire day, using a log similar to the one found below. In order to use the log, you must mark a check (✓) in the appropriate box for each of the divisions between the scored lines (i.e., ⁄⁄⁄⁄⁄⁄) and for the appropriate communication incident. The divisions represent, in consecutive order: (1) locus of the message, (2) media or channel, (3) direction of the message, (4) message content, and (5) message length. What does the information from this audit reveal about your communications during the day? How does your communication audit compare with those of other members of the class?   **113**

Communication incident number	1	2	3	4	5	6	7	8	9	etc.
Self-initiated										
Received										
Telephone										
Face to face										
Informal memo										
Formal report										
Dictation										
Superior										
Subordinate										
Equal										
Outside of organization										
Gave advice or opinion										
Gave information										
Gave decision or instructions										
Made correction										
Made request										
Sought advice or opinion										
Sought information										
Sought decision or instructions										
Persuaded or negotiated										
Praised or reprimanded										
Followed-up or checked										
Received advice or opinion										
Received corrections										
Received decision or instructions										
Received request										
Received information										
Small chitchat										
0-5 Minutes										
5-10 Minutes										
10-15 Minutes										
15-30 Minutes										
30-60 Minutes										
Over 60 minutes										

Figure 4-1 Communication Audit Log

2. This exercise is called the *rectangular demonstration*. Your instructor will give one person a copy of a picture made up of rectangles (such as the one pictured below), which he/she is to describe in such a way that the audience members can reproduce it, having never seen the picture themselves. For the first trial, the describer is to turn his or her back to the audience and no questions are allowed (one-way communication only). For the second trial, the describer will be allowed

114

to look at the faces and gestures of the audience (not the drawings themselves), but still there must be no verbal communication from the audience. Finally, on the third trial all types of communication are allowed (except showing the drawing). Which of the reception situations do you think will produce the best results? Why? Try it and see if you are correct. A different drawing will be necessary for each trial.

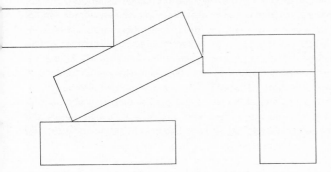

Figure 4-2

3. Examine the following three situations where faulty reception took place, and then write a paper on any one of them telling why the problems occurred, similar problems in reception with which you have come in contact, and how the problems could have been prevented had the transmitter and receiver been better informed regarding the communication process.

    a. Richard Kenney is a research engineer employed by the Oklian Oil Company. For the past two years he has been working on several projects related to waterflooding operations. He has conducted experiments to determine the causes of plugging when water is injected into sandstone reservoirs. Kenney's work, in cooperation with a production engineer, has saved his company many thousands of dollars.

    Other engineers in the company felt they could profit from Kenney's research. It was decided to call a meeting of the major members of the staff who were directly involved in waterflooding operations. At this meeting Kenney would present the results of his work and explain how such results could be applied to their operations.

    More than twenty-five company engineers from all parts of the United States arrived at the meeting place and assembled in an auditorium, notebooks in hand, prepared to listen to instructions about the new technique.

    Kenney began his discussion with a forty-five-minute outline of the nature of petroleum production, telling how oil was produced from an oil field by pressure decline until such methods became uneconomical. He then reviewed the entire history of watershedding as a means of recovering additional oil from such oil fields.

    This review was old stuff to the assembled engineers. By the end of this elaborate presentation, some of his audience were fast asleep; others were making elaborate doodles in their notebooks. In spite of the fact that Kenney's talk was illustrated by thirty beautiful slides showing apparatus, both pictorially and in scale drawing, the **115** audience failed to show interest in the material. He concluded by saying that he would be glad to answer any questions concerning applications to field problems. A few minutes passed with no questions. The chairman of the meeting suggested that perhaps people would prefer to think things over and write Mr. Kenney concerning their questions. Mr. Kenney is still wondering why he has not received any letters![16]

b. A group of technical men had just finished a long meeting in which air transportation was the main topic of discussion. The new jet age had made distances so much shorter in time that new travel schedules were essential. Greater areas for the various consultants to cover were being assigned. The group was deep in troubled thought about the ways in which faster planes had affected their jobs. Another of the executives had just arrived. He had not been present at the deliberations. After a few quick words of greeting, he looked at the clock behind him. Then he announced to the group, with upward inflection, "Jeet jet?" There was a puzzled silence. "What kind of a plane is that?" asked one of the participants. This completely confounded the executive. "Are you kidding me?" he asked. It took a little time before the astonished group realized that the original question had been: "Did you eat yet?" The general hilarity did not raise the prestige of the officer of the company.[17]

c. Before working hours, the men in the drafting room usually gather at the desk nearest the door. They talk about fishing, their children, the day's news, etc. Whenever Ron Norman approaches, the men look at each other meaningfully. They know in advance what his opening remark will be. It usually runs something like, "Boy, do I feel rotten today!" Without any encouragement, Ron will launch into a clinical description of his current medical symptoms. It is amazing how the group scatters when his lugubrious words depress the tone of the discussion. He wonders why he was passed over for promotion. He ought to be in a supervisory position by this time.[18]

4. Attend a speech or watch on television a formal presentation by some currently popular speaker. Then answer the following questions about the speaker's listener appeal. (These questions can also be used for guidelines in evaluating speeches in class.)

a. Did the speaker seem to get his/her purpose across to the listeners?
b. Did the speaker gain the listeners' attention?
c. Did the speaker structure the listeners' perception adequately?
d. Did the speaker accurately assess the categories in the listeners' minds and use them to increase comprehension?
e. Did the speaker seem to gain acceptance from the listeners?
f. Did the speaker manifest credibility (i.e., expertness, trustworthiness, and dynamism)?
g. Did the status of the speaker add to or detract from the presentation?
h. How do you think the presentation would have affected your opinion leaders?
i. What was the structure of the message, and how would this have affected the listeners?
j. Was the message of an anticlimactic, pyramidal, or climactic order, and how would this affect listeners?
k. Did the speaker present a one- or two-sided message, and how would this affect listeners?
l. Did the listeners perceive the speech as logical?

m. Did the speaker use the best channel for the greatest listener effect?

n. What nonverbal channels were used?

o. Do you believe the listeners had any personal, semantic, or environmental barriers to the communication?

5. The following is an example of a *reception-feedback card*. Your instructor will make up enough for four or five people to respond to each formal student presentation. Be sure you sign your name and circle one of the numbers for each category on the card. Added comments or explanations can be put on the back of the card. Starting with number 1, the numbers represent: excellent (1), good (2), average (3), below average (4), and poor (5).

Speaker: _____

Receiver: _____

Gained attention	1 2 3 4 5
Focused perception	1 2 3 4 5
Developed comprehension	1 2 3 4 5
Secured acceptance	1 2 3 4 5
Overall rating:	1 2 3 4 5

---

6. For your next face-to-face listening situation, write down all twenty (20) of this chapter's suggestions for improving your reception ability (i.e., realize that listening is hard work, prepare to listen, etc.) and intentionally practice each and every one. You will then be asked to report to the class which of the suggestions helped you the most and how you went about practicing each suggestion.

7. Your instructor will ask each of you to find a complex picture (i.e., with a lot of detail and many things going on at the same time) from a magazine, book, or newspaper. He/She will then choose the best one and send several people out of the room. He/She will then show the picture to all the remaining students and choose one student to describe the picture to the first of the excluded persons. That person will then be asked to relay what he/she has been told as accurately as possible to the next excluded person, and so on. Remember, only the first transmitter and the nonparticipating class members have actually seen the picture. This exercise demonstrates how a receiver's attention and perceptions are selective. That is, some of the details will be faithfully retained right down the line undistorted, other details will be added, some details will be dropped or lost somewhere along the line, and finally, many details will be distorted in one way or another.

8. With some of your classmates select and test one of the statements made in this chapter, such as:

a. "The higher one moves in the managerial hierarchy, the more important become listening and evaluating skills."

b. "Even the simple fact that one communicator is dressed differently affects the impact of the message for many receivers."

c. "Very few of us are willing to commit ourselves to something until we know the reactions of those around us whom we consider important."

FOOTNOTES

1. Lynde C. Steckle, *The Man in Management: A Manual for Managers* (New York: Harper & Brothers, 1958).

2. Ralph Nichols, "You Don't Know How to Listen," *Collier's* (July 1953), pp. 16–17.

3. Ibid.

4. E. Katz and P. F. Lazarsfeld, *Personal Influence* (Glencoe, Ill.: The Free Press, 1955).

5. Perhaps Professor McLuhan's most all-inclusive book is *Understanding Media: The Extensions of Man* (Boston: Beacon Press, 1960), which covers most of the things discussed in this section.

6. Some of the material and interpretation in this section were paraphrased from Bruce E. Gronbeck, "Beyond the Flannel Graph: Mass Media and the Christian Message," *Event*, vol. 9, no. 3 (March 1969), pp. 3–13.

7. For more on this subject, see J. Ruesch and W. Kees, *Nonverbal Communication* (Berkeley, Calif.: University of California Press, 1972), pp. 189–193.

8. R. Ardrey, *The Territorial Imperative* (New York: Atheneum Publishers, 1966).

9. E. Sapir, *Language* (New York: Harcourt, Brace and Company, Inc., 1921).

10. Aldous Huxley, *Brave New World Revisited* (New York: Harper Brothers, 1958).

11. George Orwell, *1984* (New York: New American Library, Inc., 1951).

12. Vance Packard, *The Hidden Persuaders*, Cardinal Edition (New York: Pocket Books, Inc., 1957).

13. J. S. Bruner and C. C. Goodman, "Value and Need as Organizing Factors in Perception," *Journal of Abnormal and Social Psychology*, vol. 42 (1947), pp. 33–44.

14. John C. Condon, Jr., *Semantics and Communication* (New York: The Macmillan Company, 1966), p. 62.

15. Carl R. Rogers and F. J. Roethlisberger, "Barriers and Gateways to Communication," *Harvard Business Review*, vol. 30 (1952).

16. Harold Weiss and James McGrath, *Technically Speaking* (New York: McGraw-Hill Book Company, 1963), pp. 13–14, used by permission of the publisher.

17. Ibid., pp. 52–53.

18. Ibid., pp. 127–128.

RELATED TEXTS

Barker, Larry L.: *Listening Behavior*, Prentice-Hall, Inc., Englewood Cliffs, N.J., 1971.

Bem, Daryl J.: *Beliefs, Attitudes and Human Affairs*, Brooks/Cole Publishing Co., Belmont, Calif., 1970.

Bois, J. Samuel: *The Art of Awareness*, 2d ed., Wm. C. Brown Company Publishers, Dubuque, Iowa, 1973.

Clevenger, Theodore, Jr.: *Audience Analysis*, The Bobbs-Merrill Company, Inc., Indianapolis, 1966.

—— and J. Matthews: *The Speech Communication Process*, Scott, Foresman and Company, Glenview, Ill., 1971.

Eisenson, Jon, J. Jeffery Auer, and John V. Irwin: *The Psychology of Communication*, Appleton-Century-Crofts, Inc., New York, 1963.

Johnson, Wendell: *Your Most Enchanted Listener*, Harper & Row, Publishers, Inc., New York, 1956.

Lee, Irving J.: *How to Talk with People: A Program for Preventing Troubles That Come When People Talk Together*, Harper & Row, Publishers, Inc., New York, 1953.

Nichols, Ralph G., and Leonard A. Stevens: *Are You Listening?* McGraw-Hill Book Company, New York, 1957.

Scheidel, T. M.: *Speech Communication and Human Interaction*, Scott, Foresman and Company, Glenview, Ill., 1972.

Stewart, John (ed.): *Bridges Not Walls: A Book about Interpersonal Communication*, Addison-Wesley Publishing Company, Reading, Mass., 1973.

Whyte, William H., Jr.: *Is Anybody Listening?* Simon & Schuster, Inc., New York, 1952.

CHAPTER 5

COMMUNICATION IN SMALL GROUPS

To this point we have treated communication primarily as an individual and/or interpersonal event. Individualized or personal communication is only one aspect of organizational communication on the oral level. The group meeting as an informational and decision-making methodology has become increasingly more prevalent in organizations. This growth is due primarily to the fact that all the information needed to make decisions in our increasingly complex business society can no longer be adequately assimilated, evaluated, and decided by one specialty without reference to other aspects of the organization. Modern organizations are truly dependent on group effort based on group interchange.

In this chapter the focus will be on small groups, that is, groups small enough to conduct their business without using parliamentary procedure or some other set of formal rules. In general, we are describing groups not exceeding ten to twelve people. The group this size, or smaller, is the most common in our business structure. It is generally referred to as *staff conference, task force meeting, luncheon meeting, policy meeting, briefing session,* and so on. Large-group meetings and the concomitant problems of leadership will be presented in the chapter that follows.

This chapter involves a discussion of the primary differences between individual and group communication, why people join groups in the first place, the factors relevant to an understanding of intra- or within-group behavior, and the factors relevant to understanding inter- or between-group behavior. In most cases the information presented is derived from currently available research and theory. Where research and theory are unavailable, the authors have made some educated guesses based upon their past experiences in the field of organizational communications.

INDIVIDUAL VERSUS GROUP COMMUNICATION

Three sources of information are available to every individual as it relates to any issue: (a) direct personal observation, (b) observation of other people's personal investigation, and (c) reports (oral, written, visual, etc.) from various sources. In our attempts to solve a problem by ourselves, we generally have direct observation and written reports available to us. In a group, however, all three forms of information are present and immediately available.

A highly skilled individual analyzing a problem alone may perform more effectively and efficiently than would a group. It is sometimes patently obvious, after a group discussion, that one or two of the participants might have reached the same conclusion without help. It is usually impossible, though, to determine beforehand which particular individual is truly skilled enough to solve the problem alone, or who will be the primary participants in any discussion. For these reasons, most organizations continue to rely on the group process for important decisions. The main differences between individual and group communication processes are found in the nature of the task, the presence of other people, and the increased information available.

Nature of the Task

Regardless of the task, groups in the proper communication climate produce more and better suggestions than do individuals working alone, but they take much more time to do it. There are, however, some tasks for which groups are uniquely qualified, and others for which the added benefits available through a group solution are not worth the time and effort it takes to accomplish the end result. The types of situations for which groups offer special advantages are those which call for some kind of division of labor, those for which creativity is desired, those where memory or recall of information is important, those where the object of judgment is ambiguous, and those where manual rather than intellectual skills are required. The reason for a group's superiority with tasks involving a division of labor or manual skills is obvious; ten hands are better than two and usually faster. Groups are better at judgmental, creative, and memory tasks because five heads can usually manage to make more accurate judgments, be more creative, and remember things longer than just one. It is important to remember in this regard that groups learn faster than individuals since there is less chance of a built-in bias disrupting learning.

Another interesting difference between group and individual thinking and communication is that persons are willing to accept a more risky decision in a group than they would alone. A number of theories have been proposed to explain this phenomenon. The two that seem to have the most popularity are (1) that people in groups can mentally spread the responsibility for their task decision over all group members rather than just bear it themselves, and (2) that groups may actually create a "value" for risk in that the participants prefer to conform rather than appear to be oddballs. Regardless of the reason, it is an interesting fact to remember that we can expect managerial decisions reached in conference to be generally more risky than the decisions of those same people if approached individually. For some organizational tasks a risky solution is desired, but for others we like to "play it safe."

In terms of man-hours, an individual working alone is far superior. This is because the individual does not have the problem of coordinating efforts with other individuals, does not have to listen to information already known, does not have to feel out the group climate before contributing, and runs no real risk of having his/her efforts duplicated by others. An individual decision maker has no one to communicate with. A small group can benefit from dividing the work, however, and can cut down the total elapsed time (not total man-hours) needed to complete the task. Thus, we should take the nature of the task and the available time into any consideration which would determine whether to use individual or group decision making for any particular situation. It also must be borne in mind that many situations require group decision making because of the nature of the organizational structure. For example, most governmental units, whether state, local, or national, necessarily use the group decision-making techniques in deference to the fact that each of the members may represent an electorate.

Presence of Others

Working together on the same task can act as a stimulant to greater productivity for the members of the group since group members often work to gain social approval. This can also lead to the problem of distraction through increased defensiveness. The presence of other people in a group may modify the means by which we seek our goal, the reasons why we seek it, and even the nature of the goal itself, since we must take our conferees' attitudes into account. This introduces the concept of *social motivation*, which affects group more than individual communication. That is, we must find out something about the frame or field of reference of five, six, or ten other persons—not of just one or two, as in the interview. Just as we must learn to understand and develop an empathetic climate with another person before we can effectively communicate interpersonally, we must learn to understand and relate to many others before we can work efficiently with them in a group. For this reason effective group participants tend to be less self-centered, more objective, more interested, and, under positive circumstances, more active.

The main disadvantage of the presence of others is the group pressure which may arise and influence people to agree with a mediocre decision. Group pressure need not necessarily lead to a mediocre decision, but groups value compromise, and compromise leads to mediocrity through the process of accommodation.

Increased Information

The added information which a group brings to a task can, like the presence of other people, have both positive and negative consequences. The added information makes it easier to find the correct solution and allows members to select from a number of alternatives, but it also increases the man-hours required to reach that solution, opens the possibility of duplication of information, and can, if not controlled, lead to conflict and a lower-quality solution.

Groups of people with widely varying experience regarding the task are often the most effective. The number of different ideas available tends to increase with group size and variety but levels off at five or six participants. It is not enough, however, for information merely to be present; it must be persuasively and legitimately presented for the group to accept it. The shy or reticent participant may not be able to get his or her point across even when the vital information is available. One must also remember that a decision which attempts to accommodate every individual contribution tends to become an unworkable conglomeration; therefore, selectivity is necessary.

The amount of information produced in a group, especially new, progressive, and creative information, can be artificially increased by suspending critical evaluation during the production period. One of the more interesting techniques devised to accomplish this was developed by Alex F. Osborn and is called *brainstorming*.[1] The rules for brainstorming are: (1) adverse criticism is taboo, (2) "freewheeling" is welcomed, (3) quantity of ideas is desired, and (4) combination and improvement of ideas are sought.[2] The first of these rules is the most crucial. Criticism or negativism inhibits thinking as well as communication. In a brainstorming group, evaluation of ideas is suspended until after the session is completed. A secretary or tape-recorder takes down the suggestions while the group members throw them out as rapidly as possible. One idea triggers another, and as a result much creativity emerges. The best thoughts usually come after participants have been working on the problem for a period of time and are removed from inhibitions and guarded poses. At this point all of the trite and simple thoughts have been mentioned. "Experts" are not allowed in brainstorming groups, since they tend to stifle ideas. They know too much about the task and cannot keep themselves from analyzing the suggestions.

The results of brainstorming groups in business indicate that through its employment, groups produce more ideas than they would otherwise and, for some problems, produce higher-quality suggestions. According to its promoters, brainstorming not only increases original thought on the part of participants but also teaches them to have greater empathy and tolerance for the ideas of others. It is certainly an organizational communication technique worth a try when the situation is appropriate.

INTRA- OR WITHIN-GROUP COMMUNICATION

Communication within small groups is determined by a very complex set of interconnected factors. In order to discuss intelligently any one factor in small-group communication, one must first know something about all of the factors, since they are interdependent and influence one another. The major factors in small-group communication are:

1. Cohesiveness
2. Roles
3. Status
4. Structure
5. Norms
6. Pressure
7. Influence
8. Size
9. Participation
10. Task
11. Performance

We will begin by discussing cohesiveness but immediately introduce information regarding most of the other relevant factors. It is very much like trying to decide where to cut into a freshly baked pie; it really doesn't matter too much where you begin, just get into it as soon as possible.

Cohesiveness in Groups

The term "cohesiveness" has generally been confused with the term "morale" in organizational literature. For our purposes, *cohesiveness* refers to one's desire to belong to a group while *morale* refers to one's desire to act toward a goal. By these definitions, cohesiveness represents an individual's attraction to the group and its members while morale represents one's satisfaction with these as well as other major aspects of the work situation. Morale is more closely related to satisfaction than to cohesiveness and will be discussed more fully in those sections on status, communication structure, and performance.

Cohesiveness is a circular phenomenon; that is, once established in a group, it leads to many desirable outcomes, which in turn lead to even stronger cohesion. We will discuss those factors which seem to promote cohesiveness and then its effects once established in an organizational group.

BUILDING COHESIVENESS

There seem to be as many causes of cohesiveness as there are people who belong to groups. Instances have even been found where people are attracted to groups with a history of failure. This occurs when an individual is more concerned with the group's membership than with its task. Some of the factors which promote cohesiveness in groups are size, status and mobility, and task.

Size of Group

A prime determinant of cohesiveness is the group's size. As the number of members is increased beyond approximately six, cohesiveness begins to decline. This effect is due primarily to the need for dividing tasks, the need for stronger leadership to keep order, and the number of cliques or factions which appear. A notable exception to this rule is the three-person group or *triad*. Triads are not very cohesive because they normally develop into a pair and a loner. The pair may be quite cohesive, but the loner normally experiences a very low degree of cohesion. Because of these unique characteristics, we will not be dealing too much with the triad in this chapter. The dynamics of a three-person group is more closely related to that of the interpersonal situation discussed in the previous two chapters than it is to that of the groups discussed here or in the following chapter.

Status and Mobility

People are most cohesive when there is some stability in the positions they hold with respect to other individuals in the group. Staff conferences, for example, where a different individual is the leader each meeting would not promote as much cohesion as one where the leader remained stable. Besides stability there is a natural tendency for people to be attracted to and have affection for others who have the same or higher status than themselves. We normally find in organizations that a supervisor will be happier and more comfortable with other supervisors or even managers than he/she will be with subordinates. When individuals perceive a group as containing persons of lower status than themselves, they will tend not to join that group. Many times
lower-status individuals choose higher-status persons as friends and believe that the

friendship is reciprocal when in fact it is not. Finally, one can see this equal- or higher-status attraction in group seating patterns; people of equal status tend to sit together in meetings of various kinds.

By the above reasoning, you might expect the leader or highest-status person to be the best liked; this is not always the case. The best-liked person is usually the second or third in status, since the leader or some high-status person must step on some toes and hurt some feelings to get the job done, while an associate or some other high-status member of the group can concentrate on soothing the ruffled feathers and being a friend to the group participants. These two group roles have been dubbed the *task* and *social-emotional* activities of group leadership.

Although the highest-status group members are not always the best liked, they are often the most satisfied and cohesive. Job cohesion across different levels of organizations shows an increase with each higher level. Those individuals who consider themselves in a mobile position with respect to status are generally less cohesive in their current group and with its members but highly attracted to members of the group to which they aspire. This mobility orientation is reflected in the communication that takes place. When people perceive a possible change in status either between groups or within a group, they will transmit briefer messages to current peers and longer ones to higher-status individuals. They will send fewer irrelevant communications and tend to criticize their current colleagues more and future colleagues less. People with upward aspirations also do a great deal of speculation about how things would be if they were promoted, and consequently they have lower expectations with regard to the productivity of their current group. In hierarchical organizations such as the military, this matter of status and mobility is especially important in determining cohesiveness.

Task and Competition

Two other sources of cohesiveness are the task or goal of the group and the degree of competition within and between groups. Normally cooperation, morale, and cohesiveness increase with task success and decrease with failure. Some studies have found little or no relationship, however, between performance and cohesiveness. The explanation for these results is that cohesiveness is not based solely on the task itself, but also on how explicitly it is formulated, its difficulty, the method by which it is to be attained, and its likelihood of success.

Competition can be either within a group or between two or more groups. Between-group competition generally leads to increased cohesiveness within each of the competing groups, but within-group competition generally lowers cohesiveness. Within-group competition lowers cohesiveness because it causes splinter groups to occur, and when splinter groups are prevalent, attraction to the group as a whole is lowered. Bickering, in-fighting, name calling, and group disintegration are the most extreme results of this situation. A mild degree of competition among group members taken in a kind of sporting manner can often produce increased motivation and production, but the problem is in knowing where to draw the line.

Other Factors

Another factor that tends to build cohesiveness between group members is the physical proximity they have to one another. Meeting chairmen should work toward a seating pattern which is comfortable but relatively small. The normal small-group pattern is a circle, since it allows everyone to see the person talking without difficulty. The style of group leadership is also a determinant of cohesion, as we will discuss in detail in the following chapter. Also, people tend to find groups attractive that provide them a full opportunity to participate and have a fair hearing.

To sum up the importance of building cohesiveness in organizations, it is necessary to paraphrase the findings of a number of studies that have been conducted in actual business organizations. Researchers have consistently found that those organizations where definite efforts were made to improve the bonds between new employees and the organization by showing them around the plant, introducing them to their fellow workers, having lunch with them for a week or so, and inviting them and others to take part in discussions of matters which concern them had less labor turnover, less absenteeism, and better all-around communication than organizations where everything else was approximately the same but no efforts were made to establish bonds between employees and established group members. Building cohesion in the organization and groups within the organization is not an easy task, but it is well worth the effort.

PRODUCTS OF COHESIVENESS

Cohesiveness is a key concept in group theory because it influences almost every other facet of group behavior: solidarity, conformity, social influence, interaction, motivation, performance, and satisfaction. In general, cohesive groups are more democratic, cooperative, friendly, better oriented, more coordinated, more orderly, more group-centered, more ready to accept the ideas of others, more attentive to one another, more insightful, and more productive than noncohesive groups.

Status and Responsibility

In highly cohesive groups, agreement has usually been reached on the duties and responsibilities of each member. When conflict does arise over what each participant is supposed to do, a cohesive group is more orderly, understanding, and willing to work together to solve the problem. In cohesive groups, people are normally opposed to highly differentiated jobs; they like to share responsibilities and not allow any one member to get too much status or power. It is difficult to have a cohesive group and still maintain a complex status system. An interesting study of carpenters and bricklayers who were accustomed to being assigned to work by their foreman but were suddenly allowed to choose their work partners showed that job satisfaction increased, labor and material costs dropped, and labor turnover decreased to practically zero.[3] This result occurred because the "buddies" did not have to spend as much time working out status problems.

Conformity and Social Influence

Perhaps the most important product of cohesiveness is conformity and the potential for social influence. This result is due to the fact that we are more susceptible to influence from friends or people with whom we are cohesive than from people we dislike. People who are attractive to us also have the potential to influence us more than unattractive people. Conformity and social influence occur where one is unable to obtain physical empirical information and must trust someone else's word. This situation provides us with a kind of "social reality" as opposed to the physical reality. To the extent that we trust a group and have found its past information to be acceptable, we will turn to them again. The group becomes a kind of "reference group" and its leaders become our opinion leaders. The effectiveness of reference groups is in large part determined by the cohesiveness we have for the group, and an effective reference group is one that can influence us socially, causing us to conform to its attitudes, beliefs, and values.

In groups where cohesiveness is high, deviation from the group will cause us to experience much pressure to conform. If conformity does not occur, expulsion from the group is a possible outcome. In attempting to bring a deviant member back into the fold, the other group members reinforce their own commitment to the group and, thus, promote even stronger cohesive bonds. People who do not feel totally accepted by a group will conform more than those who feel their position is secure. Any manager knows that the fastest way to get someone to listen to advice is to suggest that their job depends upon it. Such a suggestion has disadvantages as well, but it certainly works.

The fact that cohesiveness produces conformity does not necessarily mean that productivity will be increased. In fact, highly cohesive groups often tend to produce uniformly low-quality products. Anyone who deviates from the low norm will experience the kind of group pressure discussed above, and, because group members are cohesive, the pressure is more likely to work. Breaking up this kind of group is one way to increase production; the other way is to attempt to persuade the group to abandon their unacceptable philosophy.

Interaction

The rate and nature of group interaction are also influenced by the degree of cohesiveness. In groups with high cohesion, members tend to interact with one another to a greater degree, and the pattern and content of the interaction are usually more positive than in groups with low cohesion. The basis on which the cohesiveness is established determines the type of interaction that will occur. When people are cohesive mostly because they like one another as people, the interaction will tend to be one long, pleasant conversation with persuasion and task-related communication shunned. If the cohesiveness is based primarily on the performance of a task, group members limit their interaction to topic-related remarks and attempt to accomplish the task quickly and efficiently. They will participate in the discussion only so long as they feel it serves their purposes and make little effort to do anything but an adequate job. If cohesiveness is based on the prestige of the group, members tend to act very cautiously and not risk their status. Interaction will occur on irrelevant and, therefore, safe subjects with no definite stands being taken.[4]

There are, of course, other ways in which cohesiveness affects interaction. When we are a member of a cohesive group, we feel much more pressure to communicate and contribute to the group's product. One also finds much more communication designed to produce agreement in cohesive groups, as well as more open and honest communication. In general, interaction in a group where the degree of cohesiveness is high is rather smooth and relaxed, often to the point of wandering off the track. This, in turn, has an effect on the level of motivation, satisfaction, and performance.

Motivation, Satisfaction, and Performance

Perhaps the main procedural goal of every organizational group is to increase the participant's level of motivation and satisfaction, as well as produce a high-quality product. We have already pointed out how in some cases group cohesiveness can act to hold productivity down; but how can it work to increase productivity? All of us tend to work harder when we are happy with the job we are doing and the people we are doing it with. We are able to work harder because we are less anxious about how we will appear to the others. We trust them not to attack or belittle us, and therefore we can concentrate our efforts on the task at hand. We are more willing to suggest sound ideas which we might withhold in groups where we are not sure of our standing. In low-cohesive groups a leader is necessary to stimulate cooperation and purpose. Once the task is accomplished, members of cohesive groups tend to be more satisfied and confident that they will receive proper recognition for their contributions.

Cohesive groups also have less need for supervision. Workers are much less likely to "goof-off" if they know that their behavior will reflect upon their friends. For this reason there is less variation in the quality of performance by cohesive groups. There is a danger, of course, in letting groups get too cohesive and independent of leaders, resulting in their being more likely to question company policy and procedures which they do not understand or agree with. In short, such groups might refuse to be treated as robots and insist upon being recognized as hard-working and contributing men and women.

Roles, Status, and Communication Structure

In this section we deal with those factors that differentiate people in groups. Roles differentiate people on the basis of the nature of the function they perform in the group. Status differentiates people on the basis of specific attributes or characteristics which they possess and can transform itself into power over the other group members and the task. Communication structure differentiates people on the basis of their access to relevant information transmitted in the group. The three factors that operate to produce differentiation in organizational groups are the requirement for efficient group performance—which leads to specialization—the different motivations and abilities of the members, and the physical and social characteristics of the organization itself. Once differentiation of either roles, status, or communication structure occurs, a great deal of a group's energy goes into maintaining the differentiation.

Not only do roles, status, and communication structure reflect differentiation within a group, but they are all very closely related to one another. A person who performs an important role in the group's decision making also tends to have a relatively high-status position and a relatively central position in the communication structure of the group. Some writers even define *status* as the importance of a role in a group. For the sake of convenience, however, we have decided to discuss each of these factors separately in the following subsections.

GROUP ROLES

A *role* is defined as a set of expectations which group members share concerning the behavior of a person who occupies a given position in the group. The types of roles a

128

group has are determined in part by the physical environment of the group and in part by the nature of the group members themselves. Individuals vary in their ability to play certain roles, and the expectations of a group are more easily met if an individual's personality fits his/her role. Some people, for example, are not "cut out" to be managers and should not be promoted to such a position even though they qualify; otherwise one runs the risk of introducing the "Peter principle," i.e., people rising to the level of their incompetency.[5]

Groups form role structures because the members either feel a need for such structure or perceive that such a structure will facilitate goal achievement. If a group with roles is to be effective, however, the roles must be more or less interlocking. An interlocking role structure is most likely when the activities comprising the group's task can be assembled into some functional divisions, when the differences between the various roles can be made explicit, and when the group's path to its final goal is well planned.

Three basic problems can occur to disturb a group's role structure and, thus, reduce communication efficiency and overall group productivity: role collision, role incompatibility, and role confusion.[6] Role collision occurs when two different individuals in a group hold overlapping roles. Role incompatibility occurs when an individual must meet expectations for two different roles in different groups. A common example of this is the conflict between the somewhat powerful roles a manager has at work and the somewhat less powerful roles one plays at home or with neighbors after working hours. Some people are unable to make this adjustment. In most cases such role incompatibility will be resolved in favor of the group that is most important to the role occupant. Role confusion occurs when one finds that there are inconsistent expectations by other group members concerning the behavior appropriate to the role. This can occur if someone else had the role before and handled it differently from the way you and others perceive it, if there has been no formal agreement as to the definition of the role, or if other groups of which the individual is a member disagree regarding the nature of the role. Any one of the above problems will disrupt the individual holding the role and, thus, the total effectiveness of the group. If the individual happens to hold an important role, it could be disastrous.

STATUS AND POWER

Status is a person's relative position with respect to the degree which he/she possesses or embodies some socially approved or generally desired attribute or characteristic. High-status group members normally occupy some favored spatial position like the head of the table or being seated at the right hand of the president. Many times they are found to be physically and intellectually stronger than other participants. The three basic types of status—reflected, ascribed, and achieved—refer to the way in which it is obtained.[7] An employee, for example, who had high-status ranking in another part of the company and continues this status with a new group is said to have *reflected status. Ascribed status* is that which is assigned to individuals because of their role or position in the larger organization. An employee who was a member of the county board of education might have such status in company discussions of in-service training. Finally, status which is earned on the basis of outstanding performance in the group or organization is called *achieved.*

Power, on the other hand, is the influential force which high-status people use to maintain their positions. There are five basic types of power: *reward* power, whose basis is in the ability of one individual to supply rewards for another; *coercive* power, **129** which stems from the expectation on the part of one person of punishment by another; *legitimate* power, which is derived in some formal way such as appointment, election, or seniority; *expert* power, which is based on the perception by one person that another has certain desired knowledge; and *referent* power, which has its basis in one person wanting to be like another because of some quality admired in that person.[8]

Status Behavior

People with high status in a group behave differently from people with low status. They talk more often and are more often the target of communication in meetings. The nature of the received communication is often approval-seeking, and it is presented in a deferential manner. High-status individuals tend to express more criticism and threats than other participants. They often resist compromise longer and find it easier to neglect the demands of others. When a high-status person does communicate to subordinates, the message is usually less clear than those messages he/she receives. Powerful persons who perceive weaker group members' positions to be caused by "external" factors will be more willing to help than if they perceive the dependence to be caused by "internal" personal factors. The more power people have, the more likely they are to use it and the greater their influence upon the group.

Depending upon the security of their power position, high-status persons may be either more or less conforming to group norms than persons with low status. Relatively insecure high-status individuals will tend to conform as a way of maintaining their current status, even though, as more central members, they are less influenced by others. If they are relatively secure in their position and their nonconformity is not crucial to the task performance, they will be allowed more freedom than other group members. If their deviation does affect the performance of the task, they will receive proportionately more severe punishment and pressure than will their low-status comrades.

Productivity

The effect and importance of status and power on group productivity are somewhat more confusing. Well-organized groups with a strict division of labor, and high-status members controlling the group's output, will often be highly productive. On the other hand, for some tasks high-status group members may affect the free flow of information and restrict feedback, thus lowering productivity. This result occurs because group members are unwilling to commit themselves too early for fear of being on a side opposite the powerful member, and they will often go along, even when they feel he/she is wrong. Although none of us want to create "yes men" in our organizations, we do it all the time without even trying.

In predicting the effect of status on any particular group, one should certainly take the nature of the problem into consideration. A strong status structure is helpful where the task is more or less routine and mechanical, but less useful where the problem is complex and/or creative, requiring efficient communication. A high-status individual can often get around these effects on productivity by making it as clear as possible to the other group members that they are free to speak their mind without punishment or disfavor. This can be followed up by remaining as quiet as possible and not expressing an opinion until all others have spoken.

Cliques and Cabals

Two major status groups which tend to arise in all business organizations are called *cliques* and *cabals*.[9] *Cliques* are groups which serve to protect older employees whom the organization has bypassed. They have tended to withdraw from the situation as far as they can; their position in the age-grade hierarchy and their previous experience and qualifications have usually led them to positions whose functions are well defined but out of the mainstream. They maintain their self-respect and prestige in their own mind by being critical of new features and changes in the organization as well as of the people who have brought the changes about.

Cabals are made up of young people who have an intense desire to move up in the organization. Their membership in the group offers a possible way to improve their chances for success by either legitimate or illegitimate means, as well as a means of securing reassurance in case of failure. These groups are interesting because they can be found in most organizations, and they represent the results of the status and power systems in formal organizations.

COMMUNICATION STRUCTURE

A number of communication structures have been examined to determine the effect of such things as centrality, access to other members, open channels, communication linkages, and access to information on the group's participation, satisfaction, and performance. The most commonly studied structures are the circle, chain, wheel, and "Y" illustrated below. *Centrality* refers to the degree to which one person has easier access to others. The wheel is the most centralized communication structure, followed by the "Y", then the chain, and finally the circle, where no one has any greater access to the others. In the wheel, "Y", and chain structures, person *A* has the more centralized position.

Centralized and Decentralized Communication Structures

A number of things occur when a group is organized in a centralized manner. The person with the most centralized position tends to become the leader, regardless of whether he/she is the best qualified for the job. It normally takes a centralized group less time to get themselves organized and, therefore, they appear on the surface to be the most efficient. Studies have found, however, that once a decentralized group has

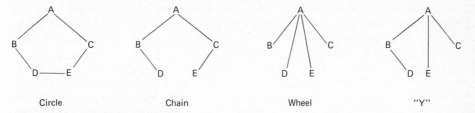

Circle   Chain   Wheel   "Y"

Figure 5-1 **Commonly Studied Communication Structures. Each letter represents a participant, and each line represents a communication linkage.**

established a stable work organization, they can operate as efficiently as a centralized group. It does take longer for the participants in a decentralized group to reach that stable work organization. Of course, other factors, such as the amount of noise in the system, the location of the relevant information, the kind of prior experience the members have had, and the nature of the task, also play a part in determining productivity.

With the characteristic of speedy decisions comes the problem of creativity and originality loss. It is a problem of bureaucracy versus innovation. Centralized groups tend to do better when the task is simple and the cooperative thought of all group members is not necessary. It is much easier to run out of suggestions and comments in a centralized communication structure since fewer people talk. Participants do not stimulate one another as easily as when the group is decentralized.

The final major area of concern is with the satisfaction of the group members. The only person really satisfied in a centralized structure is the leader or central person, whereas in a decentralized communication structure the peripheral members are satisfied as well. We are generally more satisfied with our group participation when we feel our contributions have some real importance, and this seems to occur more in a decentralized group.

Communication network studies have come under some criticism in recent years for not taking into account some of the factors which occur in real-life groups that do not occur in experimental studies.[10] It is claimed, for example, that actual group members do a lot of communicating to the group as a whole and not to any individual member. They suggest that we might learn more about a group's communication structure by examining how many communications a person receives from each other member, how many times a person sends a communication to each other member, and how many communications a person gives and receives from the group as a whole. Some of this research which is currently under way is designed to either confirm or reject the preceding ideas. We feel, however, that these two types of communication researchers are actually looking at somewhat different situations. The network researcher is looking at the type of situation that occurs in non-face-to-face groups (people, for example, communicating by memo from their offices), while the other type of research is dealing with the small, face-to-face group which one finds in staff meetings and other gatherings.

Other Factors in Communication Structure

Besides a group's centralization or decentralization, factors such as the openness of the channels, the group's size, and the types of communication allowed also affect interaction structure. For simple problems it appears that the more open the channels, the more likely it is that leadership will not occur, or, if it does, it will not be as strong as in groups where the channels of communication are restricted in some way. The kinds of restrictions we are talking about involve the length of the message, the speed with which it is delivered, the individual's accessibility to it, and so on. When a channel is restricted, the frequency of error increases. Group size affects communication structure just by increasing the number and types of channels that are available. This is a geometric, not arithmetic, progression of channel possibilities. The types of messages that can be communicated also affect the structure. Upward communication in an organization, for example, which is consistently screened so that unfavorable information will not reach the boss usually leads to a highly differentiated and well-planned structure. In business, especially, people at each level

132

of the organization are largely concerned with protecting their position and, thus, prefer the kind of structure in their groups where they have access to all important information.

In summary we can say that roles, status, and communication structure all operate to differentiate people into groups. The effects of these types of differentiation are both positive and negative, depending upon the importance of such things as participation, creativity, speed of decision, efficiency, honesty, power, satisfaction, motivation, and performance. How highly one wants to differentiate a group and the type of differentiation employed will dictate the nature of these three interrelated factors of role, status, and structure.

Group Norms, Pressure, and Social Influence

A *group norm* is an accepted way of thinking and behaving in that group. The group develops pressure and attempts are made to influence all participants to conform to the norms. For there to be conformity, there must be a conflict between one or more individuals' behaviors, beliefs, attitudes, or values and those of the other group members. We have already mentioned the fact that a group creates a kind of social reality for its individual members which accounts in part for the social influence it has over them. We are influenced socially in two different ways: first, we can be influenced merely because we like or admire the other people and desire to meet their positive expectations, and second, we can be influenced because we do not have access to the necessary information and we find the other person's information acceptable. The former is based solely on the personalities of the people involved; the latter is based solely on the information transmitted. The former tends to produce many cases of external conformity without internal change, that is, we do what we are told but don't like it. The latter usually accomplishes both internal and external conformity. In most social-influence situations, however, conformity is a matter not of one or the other, but of both types of social influence to some degree.

WHY PEOPLE CONFORM

People conform to a group's norms because of factors both within themselves and within the situation of which they are a part. These personal and situational factors will be discussed in the following two sections.

Personal Factors

There are four basic personal reasons why people yield to pressure in groups: (1) they see conformity as a way of gaining prestige and acceptance within the group, (2) they see conformity as a method of increasing their status within the group, (3) they feel that the other group members are correct and want to help them achieve their goals, and (4) anxiety remains very high and uncomfortable for those individuals who do not conform. In other words, conformity satisfies some kind of need within individuals which is more important to them than their need to be correct against all odds.

A great deal of our predisposition to conform or to resist conformity comes from our background. If we come from a home where our parents were extremely harsh and did not provide independence training for us until late in our life, we will most likely be easily influenced by pressure. There are also some personality characteristics which differentiate conformers and nonconformers. People who are rigid, conventional, self-depreciating, inconsistent, anxious, moralistic, constrictive, and "in the dominant life style" will conform more than those who are not. One's level of confidence is also important. If we perceive our own competence as less than that of the majority, then we will tend to conform.

Three other vitally important personal factors determining susceptibility to influence are intelligence, authoritarianism, and sex. Normally, intelligent people are less influenced by pressure than those who are less intelligent. If you are an authoritarian, that is, if you like to be the boss, you will tend to conform more in groups where you are not the leader and conform less in those groups where you are the leader. Finally, women seem to be more prone to conformity than men. Perhaps this is changing as women become more independent, but there is no current evidence to back up this hunch.

Situational Factors

Four basic situational factors affect the amount of conformity that will take place: the nature of the group itself, the influencing message, the size of the majority and discrepancy involved, and the type of task. Groups made up of individuals who are dynamic, competent, and trustworthy will be more powerful than groups of individuals perceived as not having those characteristics. When the group's leadership is participatory rather than supervisory, this also increases the possibility of conformity. This relates directly to the idea of centrality; groups with strong centralization, as opposed to a decentralized group, will have stronger influence over their members. Finally, mixed-sex groups, that is, ones with both men and women, tend to stimulate more conformity than all-male or all-female groups.

The nature of the influence message and the number of influence attempts made also have a great deal to do with the amount of conformity elicited. Punishing or critical remarks seem to increase conformity more than rewarding messages, but verbal reinforcement once conformity has occurred is an important method of cementing the change. Group members will conform more easily to vague messages than they will to explicit ones, because they have less information with which to argue. When group members perceive an influence attempt as being covert, they will tend to oppose it; but if they believe that everything is open and above board, they will be more likely to conform. It is usually the high-confidence individual who makes the most influence attempts in a group, and if these attempts fail, the individual usually becomes hostile. As the number of influence attempts increases, the amount of yielding that occurs also increases. We do not have to be physically present to be influenced by a message; it is sufficient for us merely to hear a group's or an individual's judgment or to see a visual display of the majority against us to make us conform.

The size of the majority against an individual and the degree of discrepancy between the individual's belief and that of the group are important situational determinants of conformity. Group size and conformity are proportionately related up to about four people, but then the effect seems to level off. For the maximum conformity to occur, a group should be unanimously against the deviant. If an individual has even so much as one ally, it will take much longer for conformity to occur. Like group size, the discrepancy between the individual and the group is proportionately related to the amount of conformity that will take place up to a certain point. When individuals perceive the discrepancy as being too great and out of their range of acceptability, a boomerang effect may take place, and they will resist that much harder.

With regard to the type and importance of the task involved, it has been found that obscure, difficult, and memory tasks yield much stronger group pressures and more conformity than attempts to influence attitudes on easily and immediately perceived tasks. As with vague and ambiguous messages, vague and ambiguous tasks force the individual to rely more on social than physical reality in order to make decisions. When the individual perceives the task as being important to the other group members, the more he/she will tend to go along with their decision.

WHY PEOPLE RESIST PRESSURE

We have already mentioned some of the reasons why people resist group pressure in the preceding section on why people conform. Some people resist group pressure because they are confident and have had a past history of success through deviation. Others resist for the obvious reason that they are convinced of their belief and more concerned about task success than about the social-emotional success of the group. Finally, some people deviate simply to draw attention to themselves. The situational factors determining conformity mentioned in the preceding section also apply here.

One of the most interesting aspects of resistance to group pressure is the process it evokes in the group itself. First, the other group members increase their communications toward the deviants, trying to persuade them to conform to their side. If they do conform, the level of communication drops off, and they are once again average members of the group. If they still reject the pleas and the group feels the effort is useless, the group will either cut them off from communication completely or totally reject them from the group in no uncertain terms. The reason groups want to exclude nonconformers is that the unconventional member usually inhibits group functioning and can spread his/her ideas to other group members. One of the positive effects of resistance to pressure is that it promotes cohesiveness among the other members by helping them establish their commitment to the group through negative communication to the deviating member. The more private the decision, of course, the easier it is to deviate. If you want to hear group members' honest opinion about some topic and not give conformity a chance to work, you will conduct the vote or ask for opinions privately.

PRODUCTS OF NORMS, PRESSURE, AND SOCIAL INFLUENCE

Norms, pressure, and social influence can be used by the group to produce either positive or negative results. Circumstances where social influence is likely to lower the quality of the group product are those where experts continue to receive respect as authorities even though the topic is outside their area of specialization, where the group members conform merely for social approval, where conformity sets in before all opinions have been aired, and where members become too dependent on others and do not make their own ideas known.

In business organizations we like to stress conformity because it introduces order into the group process and provides for the coordination of individual efforts. We must remember, however, that conformity and social influence tend to lower the quality of the group product because people do not feel free and unrestrained enough to suggest new and different ideas. One of the strengths of the American system of government has always been its tolerance of all ideas regardless of how ridiculous they might have seemed to some people. The question is: Can we carry this concept into our business organizations as well without reducing efficiency too much? It is only through an understanding of the processes that create norms, pressure, and social influence which we have discussed above that we can hope to create an open, honest, and accepting atmosphere for communication in organizations.

Size, Participation, and Group Interaction

One of the major questions managers must ask themselves regarding group or conference utilization is how large should they make the group. We have already mentioned how size affects the cohesiveness of the group, the status and communication structure, and social influence, and we will be discussing large groups in greater detail in the following chapter. There are, however, a number of other variables affected by group size. Individual participation and group interaction are closely related to the matter of group size. As we use the terms, *participation* relates to one individual's contribution to the discussion, while *interaction* refers to the relationship between various group members.

GROUP SIZE

As a group gets larger, the amount of information any single individual is able to contribute to the group decreases. There is also a greater chance that conflict will arise; people tend to give rather than ask for opinions, and agreement is harder to obtain in groups of around twenty as opposed to groups with around five people. With this decrease in the amount of information transmitted, in the number of people contributing, in the amount of opinion seeking, and in the degree of agreement come corresponding changes in the degree of satisfaction derived by the members of the group, the nature of the leadership that appears, and the group performance potential.

Participant satisfaction is obviously lessened when participation is limited. This dissatisfaction spreads from the operations of the group itself to the members of the group, the group product, and, finally, the organization as a whole. In large groups these dissatisfied people get together and form cliques, a development which further lowers the ability of the group to function effectively. The most satisfaction seems to occur in groups of around five people; as the group grows to over seven or eight, satisfaction begins to decline.

With regard to performance, the results are mixed. Large groups are usually better equipped to handle problems where remembering information is important, and they sometimes produce a somewhat higher-quality product if all of the various opinions are given a chance to be heard. On the other hand, they are much slower in solving a problem, have many more difficulties in reaching their decision, and have much more variable products. Group size does not seem to have a uniform effect on either individual performance or the proportion of correct solutions.

One of the basic problems facing a large group is its seating arrangement. Members usually sit in rows facing the chairman—an arrangement which cuts down on member interaction. A number of studies have shown that people more often interact with those sitting across from them than with people sitting adjacent to them. In large groups the most talkative and influential members usually sit near the front, and the rest of the group members are forced to become listeners.

As a general rule, more and stronger leadership is necessary when a group gets large. The leader must be a kind of mediator in the various disagreements that usually break out. This is one of the reasons why most large-group meetings are conducted according to parliamentary procedure. Except for these two or three exceptions, a leader's role is pretty much the same regardless of the size of a group, and leaders tend to speak about the same amount of time.

Although group size does play an important role in a group's behavior, it is one of the variables that is hardest to control. A group's size is very often determined by necessity or tradition and can be altered only under special conditions. A manager must, however, be aware of the fact that the size of a group may account for the quality and quantity of its product.

PARTICIPATION AND INTERACTION

The reasons why people either do or do not participate in a group's deliberations are many and varied. Perhaps the least understood group member is the quiet or silent participant. Professor Franklyn Haiman once asked his least talkative students in discussion classes why they did not actively participate and discovered the following eighteen motivations.

1. *A lack of confidence in one's own ideas:* "It doesn't make any difference whether I say anything or not, because I never have anything original to contribute."
2. *A lack of emotional involvement in the matters being discussed:* "I just didn't feel excited about the subject."
3. *A lack of skill in verbalizing ideas:* "The others can state their ideas so much more clearly than I can; so I'd rather just listen."
4. *An inability to think rapidly enough to keep up with the pace of the discussion:* "By the time I've mulled over a point long enough to have something to say on it, the rest of the group has moved on to something else."
5. *A deeper reflection of ideas:* "Some people just seem to think out loud; but I prefer to think to myself a while before speaking."
6. *An attitude of detached observation:* "I just like to hear what other people have to say about these things."
7. *Habitual shyness:* "I never talk very much."
8. *A lack of sleep or other physical disturbances:* "I could hardly keep my eyes open."
9. *Distraction of more pressing personal problems:* "The reason I didn't talk today was because I was worrying about a mid-term exam I have next period."
10. *Submissiveness to more aggressive members:* "A guy can never get a word in edgewise in this outfit, so I just keep quiet."
11. *An interpersonal conflict:* "I knew that if I ever got started I'd have told that —— off, so I decided not to say anything at all."
12. *A nonpermissive atmosphere:* "I don't feel free to speak when Miss —— is around."

13. *An overdominant leader:* "He doesn't care what I think. He just wants an audience to make big speeches."
14. *Fear of being rejected:* "I'm afraid everybody will think that what I have to say is silly."
15. *A solidified pattern of participation:* "Everybody in the group has gotten used to my not talking much, so I feel uncomfortable—as though everyone were surprised—when I do speak."
16. *A feeling of superiority:* "That was such a pointless discussion and nobody really knew what they were talking about. What a waste of time!"
17. *A disbelief in the value of discussion:* "Talk never changes anybody's mind, so why bother."
18. *Lack of knowledge or intelligence:* "The discussion was way over my head."[11]

Perhaps we can say, then, that people who do choose to participate are those who do not feel constrained or restricted by the preceding motivations, or if they do feel them, the motivation is not strong enough to stop them from actively communicating. For whatever reason group members either participate or choose not to participate, their behavior affects themselves, the other group members, and the group's performance.

Along with motivation, such personal factors as chronological age, sex, intelligence, and confidence in part determine participation. In most groups it is the older, more intelligent, and competent males who do most of the talking. With participation usually comes satisfaction, whether your ideas are accepted or not. The amount of communication you receive from the other members of the group is also dependent on the degree of your participation. This aspect is more important in determining quantity of communication received than other factors such as status and communication structure. Once you have begun speaking in a group, you will continue to participate as long as the rewards you are receiving for your contributions outweigh the difficulties you face in contributing. If you have participated in making the final decision, you are also more likely to accept and remember it and, thus, put it into effect more efficiently and quickly.

Actual task success is also enhanced when the total amount of participation is increased and when that participation comes from all or most of the potential communicators. More participation usually means more information from which to make a decision and increased feedback, which improves the quality of the product. It can be harmful, however, to force people to participate against their wishes. They become defensive and can lower the quality of and satisfaction with the product.

It might seem at this point that if we are able to increase participation, we will also improve group interaction. This is not necessarily the case. If just one or two members of the group are doing all the talking, total participation will be high but interaction (of all members) will be low. Barriers to interaction include such things as inequality of status, negative attitudes, a lack of cooperation, excessive formality, excessive control, poorly defined goals, excessive differentiation, and unfamiliarity with the other members. People feel free to interact openly and honestly when and only when they feel confortable. A sign of anxiety will be a sign to a sensitive group member or the leader that things should be changed in some way to maintain the maximum interaction level. If the cause of the anxiety is not readily evident, the group members should be consulted privately to determine what is causing the discomfort.

Group size, participation, and interaction are all very closely related. We will be discussing the problems facing large-group leaders more in the following chapter.

Participation and interaction levels of a group provide us with our earliest indication of the potential performance level of the group. If participation and interaction are high, we have every reason to expect that the group will be effective. Group members who are sensitive to the participation and interaction level of a group can make enormous contributions to the group because they will be the first to spot potential trouble spots.

Goal, Task, and Performance

Although performance is perhaps the most important variable in the study of group communication in organizations, we are left at this point with very little more to mention. We have, in effect, come almost full circle and have arrived back where we started. We have already discussed the effects of all the other major group variables on a group's goal, task, and performance. We will, however, discuss what little remaining information there is in the following paragraphs and then conclude by relating each of the factors back to productivity.

Every time people get together to communicate in groups, they have a task and a goal which determine their performance. Besides the task goal of the group, however, there are also personal goals which people create for themselves regardless of the group goal. For most people these goals involve things which enhance their acceptance, recognition, and security. A group may fail to meet its task goal, but if participants feel they have achieved one or more of their personal goals, the group has been successful for them. In some cases the success of a personal goal may depend on the failure of a task goal. The person who predicts a group's failure, for example, will gain recognition if the group does in fact fail. It is important in this respect to know the personal goals of group members and try to make sure they are in line with the goals of the group.

With respect to the task goal of a group, it is important that it be very clear and that the means by which the goal is to be reached are also clear. It is important in this respect that the first major project of the group be that it achieve fairly strong consensus on the goal of the group. Later group functioning and performance of the task depend to a great degree on whether the goals are heterogeneous or homogeneous. Goal and goal-path clarity have been found to be positively correlated with both the motivational characteristics of the group members and their efficiency. Motivation and efficiency are both, of course, prime determinants of task performance.

The nature of the task itself also determines, in part, the performance of a group. When a group is facing a difficult task, they should expect to spend more time at it and to make more errors. Difficult tasks also motivate more and stronger leadership attempts. Many people seem to feel that strong leadership is most important where the difficulty of a task is high. As a matter of fact, the evidence seems to point to just the reverse conclusion. When a task is difficult, group performance is facilitated when participants can freely communicate their feelings of satisfaction or dissatisfaction with the group's progress toward its goal. Strong leadership tends to inhibit such free communication and, thus, lowers the group's performance of difficult tasks. Democratic or procedural leadership, which we will discuss thoroughly in the following chapter, seems to be the most successful method of guiding a group with a difficult task.

Learning implies the acquisition of new information, while *performance* implies the use of already acquired information. One of the most important facts to remember about groups is that they facilitate efficiency when performance is required but

139

decrease efficiency when learning is required. The ways in which cohesiveness, roles, status, communication structure, norms, pressure, social influence, size, participation, interaction, goals, and task affect performance are not necessarily the same as the way they affect learning. Learning, for example, is facilitated by remaining silent in a group, but performance is decreased when members are silent.

We have been concerned in this section with improving not group learning, however, but group performance, so we will conclude this section by reviewing the most important ways we have mentioned in which group participants can improve their communication and ultimately their performance.

1. Keep the size of the group to around five members where possible.
2. Get the group members as close to one another as possible and comfortable physically, in a circle if possible.
3. Keep the task as simple as possible.
4. Formulate the task goal and the path to the goal clearly and carefully.
5. Encourage personal goals that complement the task goal and discourage those that do not.
6. Promote friendly conversations between group members before the meeting starts and during breaks, and be understanding if they also occur during the meeting.
7. Provide an informal and friendly atmosphere of acceptance and trust for every group member.
8. Encourage group cooperation and discourage intermember competition.
9. Discourage the formation of splinter groups, but allow members to choose their work partners when a division of labor is in order.
10. Keep the role structure as simple, explicit, and interlocking as possible.
11. Encourage members who are playing roles which facilitate group progress, and discourage those who are employing roles which impede the group.
12. Allow group members some latitude in the way they fill their role, but be on the lookout for role collision, incompatibility, and confusion.
13. Keep the status and power of all group members as close to equal as possible.
14. Be wary of those persons with upward aspirations and those with reflected or ascribed, rather than achieved, status.
15. Encourage a decentralized communication structure whenever possible.
16. Promote participatory rather than supervisory leadership whenever possible.
17. Keep the channels of communication as open and unrestricted as possible.
18. Make sure that every participant receives a full and fair hearing.
19. Encourage a physical rather than social testing of information whenever possible.
20. Allow group members some latitude for deviation from the norms of the group.
21. Keep influence attempts, threats, and coercive communication to a minimum; but when they must be made, make them overtly rather than covertly.
22. Try to understand the reason underlying a participant's deviation from the norms or decisions of the group.
23. Allow group members to relieve the tensions that build up in decision making through humor and other non-task-related conversation.
24. Provide for private vote by the group members whenever possible even when consensus seems to have been reached.

25. Remember that the preceding suggestions are most important where the task is difficult and intellectual; where routine and mechanical tasks are involved, they should probably not be handled by a face-to-face group in the first place.

INTER- OR BETWEEN-GROUP COMMUNICATION

Most of the research that has been devoted to group behavior has been devoted to studying communication within rather than between groups. Like individuals within a single group, separate groups can either cooperate or compete with one another. Obviously, the preferred relationship is one of cooperation, but how does one get groups to cooperate? That is like asking, "How can we bring peace to this old world of ours?" The only surefire answer to that question is to present the various nations on earth with a task which none can achieve alone and which they all feel they must achieve to survive. An invasion from outer space is the example provided us by the science-fiction writers. Perhaps someday when people become aware of the real destructive power of our current weapons, this will also force the various groups involved to cooperate.

This same principle of being faced with a task which is desirable but unattainable without cooperation is the most important one in understanding intergroup cooperation. Why, for example, do the various divisions of our organizations work together effectively? They do so only because they realize that none could accomplish the task alone. Matters of proximity, similarity, and respect are simply not enough to guarantee cooperation.

Let us backstep for a moment and discuss why between-group communication more naturally runs to competition than to cooperation. First of all, people are competitive in nature; when they are in groups, this competition naturally rubs off on the group as a whole. When group members, for example, are asked to rate their product in comparison with those developed by other groups, they will consistently rate their own better, even when it is obviously inferior. Another example involves people who come together to discuss a matter, each representing some particular group. They become very independent and resistant to pressure even when it means delaying a better solution.

In some meetings intergroup competition is promoted as a way of increasing within-group cohesiveness. Anticipation of intergroup competition creates anxiety in all of the group members, and this shared anxiety leads to shared determination and closer affiliative tendencies. Leaders of nations, athletic coaches, and military men are all very familiar with this process, and they use it to mobilize armies, inspire football teams, and win votes. That is why they paint a fearsome picture of their opponent; it provides motivation and solidifies the group. This is also the reason why people become cooperative during times of crises and the normal deliberative process is suspended.

In most other respects, as far as we know now, communication between groups proceeds in somewhat the same manner as communication between individuals in the same group, and the factors affecting intergroup performance are about the same as those affecting within-group performance. The number of groups involved should be kept as low as possible. The groups should be physically close to one another. Their task should be simple and the goals clear. Members of all groups should be   141 allowed to contact one another socially. Status and power differences between groups should be kept to a minimum. The channels of communication between the groups should be kept clear and unrestricted. This is especially difficult when one group does have a higher status than the other. Each group should have an equal hearing and share in determining the final product, if there is one. In other words, most of the comments we made in the preceding section also apply here.

In conclusion, then, to both this section and the chapter as a whole, perhaps the most significant point the reader should remember is that cooperation is the basis of effective small-group communication, and communication is the basis of productivity. We can improve organizational communication in groups through the same process we use to improve communication between individuals, by promoting cooperation.

REVIEW QUESTIONS

1. What are the major factors which underlie the differences between individual and group communication processes?

2. What are the basic rules of brainstorming?

3. In what ways are all the factors affecting intragroup communication interconnected?

4. How are *morale* and *cohesiveness* different?

5. How does group size affect cohesiveness?

6. How do one's status and mobility affect cohesiveness?

7. How do the task and the level of competition affect cohesiveness?

8. What other factors contribute to establishing a high level of cohesiveness and affection in small groups?

9. Why is it important to build cohesiveness within small groups in an organization?

10. How are status and responsibility, conformity and social influence, interaction, and motivation, satisfaction and performance all products of cohesiveness and affection?

11. How and why do roles, status, and communication structure differentiate people into groups?

12. What problems can occur to disturb a person's role structure?

13. Differentiate the three basic types of status.

14. Differentiate the five basic types of power.

15. How is a person's status reflected in his/her behavior?

16. What are some of the negative effects status can have on productivity (including cliques)?

17. How do the effects of centralized and decentralized communication structures differ?

18. What effects do channel openness, group size, and type of communication allowed have on group operations?

19. How are group norms, pressure, and social influence related?

20. What are some of the personal and situational factors that cause people to conform and to resist conformity?

21. What are some of the positive and negative results of conformity?

22. How does group size affect group participation, satisfaction, and performance?

23. What are some of the reasons why people fail to participate?

24. What can one do to increase participation and interaction in groups?

25. How does a group's goal and task affect its performance?

26. What are some of the important factors affecting intergroup communication and performance?

27. Attack or defend the statement that "cooperation is the basis of effective small-group communication."

EXERCISES

1. Your instructor will break the class up into groups of four to seven people. All groups will then discuss the same problem; it might be a problem of the instructor's choosing or one of the case studies found in the Appendix. Think your task through carefully before coming to class for the discussion, appoint a leader, and conduct the discussion. If possible, be sure that each group cannot overhear what is being discussed by members of the other groups. After each of the groups has come to some conclusions on their own, the leaders of each of the groups will get together in front of the whole class and try to come to some classwide conclusions. Prior to the discussions, you are to write down how well you think the first groups and the leader group will handle the discussion and what possible task and interpersonal problems might arise. When the discussions are finished, all of the class members will share these predictions and attempt to determine why they either did or did not occur.

2. For this exercise the same basic format will be used as in Exercise 1 except that instead of choosing one leader for the entire discussion, leadership will be changed every five to ten minutes. The group as a whole will vote at the end of the discussion on who should represent them before the entire class. You are to again write down ahead of time how well you think each of the groups will handle the situation. This time add where you think the differences between this group and the groups created in Exercise 1 will arise.

3. For this exercise the same basic format will be used again except that no leader will be chosen or designated. The group is to remain "leaderless," and again the representative to the final discussion will be chosen by the group members at the end of the discussion. You are to again write down ahead of time how well you think each of the groups will perform, as well as the differences that you believe will occur between these groups and the groups in Exercises 1 and 2.

4. An interesting variation on the format used in Exercise 3 is to give each group member a specific number of "communication tokens" (six to seven is about right for a five-person group in an hour discussion). Each time a person makes a substantial contribution to the discussion (more than just a "yeah" or short **143**

question), he or she must give up one of his/her tokens until none is left, at which time he/she may no longer speak. You can surely see the eventual possible results of this exercise. Once you know who the members of your group will be for this exercise, you are to attempt to predict what their behavior will be if and when they run out of tokens. You might also attempt to predict who will run out first, second, third, etc.

5. During any one of the preceding exercises your instructor might well ask someone secretly to deviate from the majority on some issue. In other words, that person and the instructor will intentionally attempt to introduce a disruption of this nature in the group. If this were to happen in each one of the groups of which you are a part, how do you think the group would handle such a situation? What do you think would happen if the deviate were to maintain his/her position, allowing no compromise until the very end of the discussion? What do you think would be your group's reaction if the deviate were to "slide" back to the majority opinion after a while? What do you think would be the group's reaction if another member of the group joined in the deviate opinion? After this exercise is completed, your instructor will inform you that a "confederate" was working in your group and ask all of you to discuss the effect of his or her behavior together.

6. As an experiment in sensitivity training, your instructor will ask each person in the class to attempt to accurately label each of the other members in the class, using no more than three roles for each person. Your instructor will provide you with a list containing everyone's name and indicate the people individually if you cannot yet remember everyone. Once all decisions have been made, your instructor will collect all the papers and total the number of votes each person received for each possible role. These results will then be announced, and each person should attempt to discover either in open discussion or by random dyadic conversation (instructor choice) why their behavior thus far in the course has merited the choices received. This exercise should be handled with some tact and care, since, like many sensitivity exercises, it can get out of hand and become threatening to some class members if not undertaken correctly.

7. Observe a group actually operating in some organization. While observing the group, or directly after it has disbanded, answer the following questions about the group. For some of the answers you may have to interview one or more of the group members. You can combine this exercise with the similar one in the following chapter if the group you are observing has a formal leader.

   a. What reasons do you feel motivated this meeting, instead of each person attempting to solve the problem individually?
   b. Were cohesiveness and affection evident in the group? If so, how did they develop, and what effects did they have? If not, why not?
   c. Was there much role, status, or communication structure differentiation in the group? If so, how did they develop and what were their effects? If not, why not?
   d. Were group norms, pressure, and social influence evident in the group? If so, how did they develop and what were their effects? If not, why not?
   e. Describe how size, participation, and interaction patterns within the group developed and their results.
   f. Discuss how the goal(s) and task(s) of the group affected its performance.
   g. If not discussed in one of the previous answers, describe which of the

twenty-five rules for improved communication and performance were not followed by the group.

8. Make a participation flow chart such as the one pictured below and record the direction and amount of communication which took place in the group. Once you have done that, you are to write a paper where you relate this record to the cohesiveness, roles, status, structure, norms, influence, size, and task of the group. A participation flow chart can be one of the most useful tools available for analyzing group behavior.

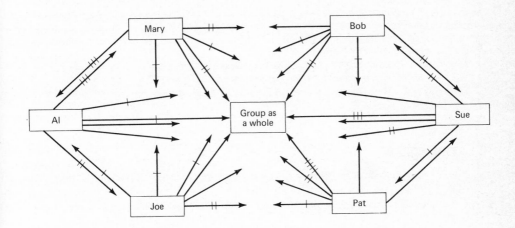

9. Attempt to use the brainstorming technique. In doing this exercise you must first choose a topic which lends itself well to brainstorming. You may use one of the several possible topics suggested below or you may choose one of your own. The topic must, however, be defined very clearly and be as specific as possible. Before starting the session, be sure everyone has reviewed very carefully the rules of brainstorming. Hold both an "ideation" session, where the ideas come fast and furious and are recorded by a secretary or tape-recorder, and a "judgmental" session, where each of the ideas presented in the "ideation" session is evaluated. Once this exercise is over, the class as a whole will discuss the differences between brainstorming and regular problem-solving discussion.

   a. How can we improve morale within our company?
   b. How can we use some of the waste products of our production process to make extra profit?
   c. How can we better prepare for the upcoming examination?
   d. How could the teaching of this course be improved?
   e. How could we make $20,000 in one year?
   f. How could we better publicize the achievements of our company?

FOOTNOTES

1. Alex F. Osborn, *Applied Imagination*, rev. ed. (New York: Charles Scribner's Sons, 1957).

2. Most of the information in this section on Alex F. Osborn's brainstorming technique was

paraphrased from Arthur M. Coon, "Brainstorming—A Creative Problem-Solving Technique," *Journal of Communication*, vol. 7 (1957), pp. 111–118.

3. R. H. VanZelst, "An Interpersonal Relations Technique for Industry," *Personnel*, vol. 29 (1952), pp. 68–76.

4. K. W. Back, "Influence through Social Communication," *Journal of Abnormal and Social Psychology*, vol. 46 (1951), pp. 9–23.

5. Laurence J. Peter and Raymond Hull, *The Peter Principle* (New York: Bantam Books, Inc., 1969).

6. Some of the information concerning role collision, incompatibility, and confusion is paraphrased from A. Paul Hare, *Handbook of Small Group Research* (New York: The Free Press, 1962), pp. 119–121.

7. K. Davis, "The Child and the Social Structure," *Journal of Educational Psychology*, vol. 14 (1940), pp. 217–229.

8. J. R. P. French, Jr., and B. Raven, "The Bases of Social Power," in D. Cartwright (ed.), *Studies in Social Power* (Ann Arbor, Mich.: Institute for Social Research, 1959), pp. 150–167.

9. T. Burns, "The Reference of Conduct in Small Groups: Cliques and Cabals in Occupational Milieux," *Human Relations*, vol. 8 (1955), pp. 467–486.

10. Robert N. Bostrom, "Interactive Patterns and Indicators of Group Structure," unpublished paper delivered at the Speech Communication Association Convention, December 1967.

11. Franklyn S. Haiman, *Group Leadership and Democratic Action* (Boston: Houghton Mifflin Company, 1951), pp. 145–146.

RELATED TEXTS

Auger, B. Y.: *How to Run More Effective Business Meetings*, Grosset & Dunlap, Inc., New York, 1964.

Bormann, Ernest G.: *Discussion and Group Methods*, Harper & Row, Publishers, Inc., New York, 1969.

Cartwright, Dorwin, and Alvin Zander: *Group Dynamics: Research and Theory*, Harper & Row, Publishers, Inc., New York, 1968.

Ewbank, Henry L., Jr.: *Meeting Management*, Wm. C. Brown Company Publishers, Dubuque, Iowa, 1968.

————and J. J. Auer: *Handbook for Discussion Leaders*, Appleton-Century-Crofts, Inc., New York, 1954.

Osborn, Alex: *Applied Imagination*, 3d ed., Charles Scribner's Sons, New York, 1963.

Phillips, Gerald M.: *Communication and the Small Group*, 2d ed., The Bobbs-Merrill Company, Inc., Indianapolis, 1972.

————and E. C. Erickson: *Interpersonal Dynamics in the Small Group*, Random House, Inc., New York, 1970.

Potter, David, and Martin P. Andersen: *Discussion: A Guide to Effective Practice*, 2d ed., Wadsworth Publishing Company, Inc., Belmont, Calif., 1970.

Rosenfeld, Lawrence B.: *Human Interaction in the Small Group Setting*, Charles E. Merrill Publishing Company, Columbus, Ohio, 1973.

Sattler, William, and N. Edd Miller: *Discussion and Conference*, 2d ed., Prentice-Hall, Inc., Englewood Cliffs, N.J., 1968.

Shaw, M. E.: *Group Dynamics: The Psychology of Small Group Behavior*, McGraw-Hill Book Company, New York, 1971.

CHAPTER
6

LEADERSHIP COMMUNICATION

Of all the areas of human behavior studied during the last several thousand years, leadership would rank near the top of a "most popular" list. The number of books, articles, pamphlets, and other printed documents on this subject would fill a library by themselves, without counting the number of speeches, conferences, workshops, and other nonprinted efforts that have been devoted to this subject. Yet, with all this attention directed toward it, leadership remains one of the least understood areas of human behavior. Four reasons have been suggested for this failure to develop a cohesive and unified theory of leadership: "(1) the failure of students of leadership to agree upon a working conceptualization of the leadership phenomena, (2) the pronounced tendency to view leadership as a subject matter unto itself, (3) the lack, until comparatively recently, of a significant volume of empirical work, and (4) the effect of the great bureaucracies which support and subtly channel much of the leadership literature."[1] We hope that you will find that the current chapter avoids the preceding failures and does indeed present a cohesive and unified theory of leadership as well as practical suggestions as to how that theory can be implemented to improve the practice of organizational communication.

In the first section of this chapter we will present a philosophy of leadership based upon the nature and types of contemporary leadership and the causes and effects of each type. In the second section we will present some practical suggestions regarding leadership communication in the staff meeting, conference situation, and organization as a whole. Finally, we will present a somewhat detailed discussion of parliamentary procedure and how its enlightened application can improve communication in large groups. If we do have a bias in this chapter, it would probably be in the direction of more democratic and less authoritarian leadership, but we tend to feel that this is also the bias of the current leadership literature. We believe that leadership should not be studied in isolation, but in light of the other forms of organizational communication. For that reason the material presented here should be placed in the context of the preceding chapters on oral communication transmission, communication reception, and communication in small groups.

WHAT IS LEADERSHIP?

The earliest approach to leadership definition has been called the *trait* approach; that is, certain physical, intellectual, and personality traits were felt to be possessed by leaders and not by followers. This notion persisted until the last decade and a half, but we can still see traces of it in some current writing. A sample of the traits which were believed to reflect leadership are: talkativeness, self-confidence, intelligence, dependability, moral straightness, fairness, firmness, initiative, sensitivity, extroversion, decisiveness, tact, enthusiasm, and good appearance. Although we would all probably agree that these things are important assets for a leader, the trait theory of leadership was abandoned when it was discovered that the minimal traits required of all leaders were also widely distributed among nonleaders as well, and that the traits of leadership necessary and effective in one group situation were often quite different from those requisite in another situation. In effect, it was discovered that leaders are "made, not born."

Dissatisfaction with the trait leadership approach led to what has variously been called the *functional* or *situational* approach to leadership communication. In this view the characteristics of the group and the situation in which it exists determine the nature and the amount of leadership communication necessary for effective performance. Leadership study within this orientation does not seek to discover certain invariant traits of leaders, but instead seeks to discover what actions are required by groups under various conditions if they are to achieve their goals, and how different group members take part and respond to these actions. This view also leads to the realization that any group member can exert leadership; one need not be the designated leader. This brings us finally to a definition of leadership.

The way in which people have studied leadership has directly affected how they define it. The military definition of *leadership* is an example of how leadership is often defined in strong hierarchical situations: "the art of imposing one's will upon others in such a manner as to command their obedience, their confidence, their respect, and their loyalty."[2] A current author's definition which harks back to the trait period defines the leader as "an individual who is endowed with dominant personality traits such as intelligence, knowledge, insight, responsibility, initiative behavior, and a 'sense of mission.'"[3] Other definitions stress the motivational aspects of leadership: "that process whereby an individual directs, guides, influences, or controls the thoughts, feelings, or behavior of other human beings."[4] Psychologists are fond of defining leadership by the functions performed rather than by influence: "The leader is an individual who is a planner, policy maker, group representative, arbitrator, and dispenser of rewards and punishments."[5] Finally, the pragmatists often define a leader in light of the group's goal, that is, as "an individual who, in interaction with others, performs actions that assist the group in achieving desired outcomes."[6]

All these definitions have one main drawback: they fail to separate leadership from leaders. A *leader*, for the purposes of this chapter, is defined as the individual *formally* given certain status through election, appointment, inheritance, revolution, or any number of other means. *Leadership*, on the other hand, refers to those behaviors performed by one or more individuals in the group which helps the group accomplish its goals. With these definitions, it is perfectly reasonable for a group to accomplish its goal without a "leader," a designated boss; but it is impossible for a group to function effectively without "leadership," i.e., persons performing functions to influence and move the group to its conclusion. This separation of leaders from leadership allows one to account for the very common situation where the person in charge is not the only person or even the most important person influencing the organization. The determination of whether a group needs a leader, the type of leader or leadership needed, and the amount of leadership required depend upon the nature of the task, the structure of the group, the personalities of the group members, and all the other factors discussed in the preceding chapter.

DETERMINANTS OF LEADERSHIP

Even though groups do not need leaders, they do need leadership—without it there is chaos. The reason why one person exercises that leadership at a particular time and in a particular situation and another does not is related to a number of very subtle factors. The factors on which a group's leadership is based, in turn, determine in many respects the performance of the group.

One of the main factors determining leadership is the nature of the other group members. Leadership is an interaction between the influencer and the influenced, between the leader and the follower. It is not, as many people seem to believe, a one-way street. In most cases people expect leadership in group situations, and groups seem to be most effective when the participants' leadership expectations are met. Some people prefer strong leadership in organizational and group situations; they like to be told what to do and panic when given responsibility of their own. Other people like responsibility and, thus, prefer more democratic leadership communica-tion. The preferences of the followers, then, are one of the primary determinants of both the amount and the type of leadership necessary.

Different kinds of leadership are required at different stages of a group's progress. An individual who is able to provide leadership at the problem-orientation phase of a staff meeting may not be capable of providing effective leadership during the decision-making phase. This is one of the major reasons why having a single designated leader can often impede progress. That leader is simply not flexible enough to relinquish his/her leadership when it does not fit the group's needs. The most extreme example of this is the group in an emergency or stress situation. In these situations even the most powerful and dogmatic leaders will be disposed of if they are incapable of handling the situation. It is up to leaders to be sensitive to the group's leadership needs at a particular time and to try to meet them; but when they are unable to fill these needs, they should be willing to admit it to themselves and the other group members. Most designated leaders, however, feel threatened when they perceive that they are doing a poor job or merely an adequate job, and they make overt attempts to maintain their leadership role.

Perhaps the most consistent determinant of leadership is the power to reward and punish. The more coercive power people have at their disposal, the more likely they are to exercise leadership. If the power is very great, they will tend to become dictatorial or strong leaders. When they perceive their followers as having almost as much power and prestige as themselves, they tend to become more democratic. The converse of this is also true: group members who perceive themselves as having a high degree of independence, interdependence, and interaction tend to prefer more democratic leadership. A meeting of foremen, for example, would usually be more democratically led than a meeting of one foreman or forelady and his/her subordinates because of the differentiation of power in the latter group. Some of the most interesting and effective groups are those where one of the participants does have more power to reward or punish but does not exercise that power unless things really get out of hand.

As we mentioned in the previous chapter, a person's position in the communication structure also determines his/her leadership potential. If one has a central position or has control of certain vital information, he/she will be more likely to exercise leadership than the other individuals with less central positions and information. Access to information and communication gives people another kind of power; they can withhold the information or block the communication as a form of punishment. It is for this reason that ambitious people try to move into central positions and monopolize information in an organization.

In the preceding chapter we also mentioned how the difficulty of the task also affects leadership; it is especially important in determining the type of leadership desired and the type of leadership needed. It usually works out that these clash. When the task is routine and mechanical, people tend to prefer less leadership, but this is the type of task where strong leadership works best. It is with difficult tasks where both creativity and satisfaction are desired that followers usually want strong leadership and little responsibility but where more democratic leadership communication usually yields the best product. About the only role a designated leader can play in a group with a difficult task without impeding the group's progress is a procedural one, that is, calling on people to talk, summarizing, and so on.

Leadership is also determined in part by the talkativeness of the participants. The quality of what is said does not have as much importance as the quantity of participation. The people who do the most talking are not only perceived by the other participants as being the leaders, but they do in fact seem to have the most influence on the group. Perhaps this is so because many people in our organizations are unable to separate the quantity from the quality of communication. The amount of talk only seems to determine the highest leadership rank; however, those who are most frequently second and third in speaking are not necessarily perceived as providing the second or third degree of leadership, nor do they exercise that amount of influence.

Other less important determinants of leadership are the group's size, the intelligence level of the group, the friendship that exists among participants, the external rewards for solution, the group's atmosphere, the seating positions, and even the amount of wit. Larger groups tend to need more leadership than small groups, and such things as parliamentary procedure become important in large groups. Groups made up of highly intelligent members tend to need and desire less leadership. When group members are quite friendly, they also resent too much leadership. If the participants perceive some kind of reward for their solution, they tend to want less leadership and more personal responsibility. The atmosphere of the group or organization is, of course, important in determining all types of communication. If the organization and/or group climate is open and honest, democratic leadership practices seem to follow, but in a cold and secretive climate more autocratic leadership styles appear. Leadership is also determined in part by where one sits; people sitting at the head of a table are normally more prone to exercise leadership than those sitting elsewhere. Finally, people with sarcastic wit tend to be influential in groups but unpopular, while people with a comical wit are often popular but without influence.

150

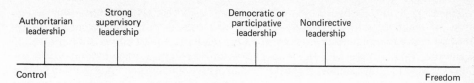

Figure 6-1 **Placement of Various Types of**
Leadership on a Continuum
Ranging from Complete Control
to Complete Freedom

These, then, seem to be the most important determinants of leadership in organizations and groups within the organization. None of the preceding factors normally determine leadership by themselves, but a combination of various factors determines the amount and type of leadership exercised. In addition to those factors we have just mentioned, for people to attempt to influence a group two conditions must be present: (1) they must be aware that the function is needed, and (2) they must feel they are able to perform it, have the skill to perform it, and are safe in performing it. We have discussed to some extent in this section the type of leadership one can exercise if one chooses to do so and if the conditions are right. We have mentioned terms like "strong leadership," "democratic leadership," and "autocratic leadership"; in the following section we will discuss these types of leadership in more detail.

TYPES OF LEADERSHIP

Perhaps the best way to visualize the types of leaders and leadership communication is to place them on a continuum ranging from complete *control* over the situation to complete participant *freedom*. The above Figure 6-1 approximates the place of each of the leadership types we will discuss on such a continuum. Since no leadership would exist in situations of complete freedom, that end of the continuum is blank. You will notice that authoritarian leadership and strong supervisory leadership are fairly close to one another on the control end of the continuum while democratic or participative and nondirective leadership are close together on the opposite end. This is generally how one should think of them: authoritarian and nondirective leadership are the extremes, while supervisory and participative leadership are modified versions of the two extremes.

Authoritarian Leadership

When one person determines all policy, dictates task steps one at a time, decides tasks and assigns work partners, and does not reveal any standards of praise and criticism, he/she is exercising authoritarian leadership. There are a number of ways one can spot a group with authoritarian leadership. First, the group members will be highly dependent on the leader for guidance; they will be afraid to make any move, even the simplest, without approval. Second, the participants will tend to have a low motivation level and, thus, will appear to be robot-like people doing the task because they have been told to. Third, the group members will always agree with the leader when asked their opinion, but they will have little agreement when talking among

151

themselves. Fourth, when they are talking to one another or listening to the leader, they will seem to be forcing attentiveness to the message. Fifth, such groups will have a great many complaints expressed when the leader is not around and a high rate of turnover. Sixth, there will be little expression of satisfaction either verbally or nonverbally, i.e., few smiles, laughter, and expressions of pride. Finally, there will be little total interaction either between the leader and the participants or between the participants themselves. With regard to the group's productivity and effectiveness, the quantity of output may be very high but the quality will usually be quite low.

Strong Supervisory Leadership

It is difficult to differentiate people exercising strong supervisory leadership from those using authoritarian leadership. It is simply a matter of degree. The participants look pretty much the same as those just described, and if the leaders were asked, they would probably state that they believe full responsibility for what happens in a group should reside with the leader, that group members need the services of a strong leader, that task attainment requires an efficient and orderly procedure, and that productivity is more important than the social-emotional state of the group members. A supervisory leader is not quite so dogmatic as the authoritarian leader and is usually more willing to listen to and be persuaded by subordinates or other group members.

For many people, working under a supervisory leader is very appealing. They do not have the responsibility for making very many decisions, and they are less likely to get themselves into trouble when something goes wrong. Working under an authoritarian leader, they would not be able to maintain any real level of recognition and self-respect, but under a supervisory leader they can be quite happy with the little responsibility they are given, and they know that at least the leader will listen to them. Supervisory leaders are really like an extension of one's father: they are kind and usually very gentle; but they maintain the last word on any subject.

Democratic or Participative Leadership

People exercising democratic or participative leadership would normally respond, when asked, that they believe all individuals have a personal worth and dignity that should be respected, that all members of a group should have the opportunity to excel and show initiative, that a free exchange of ideas must be encouraged, that individuals should be able to satisfy personal needs in the group as well as the group's task needs, and that substantial consensus is usually attainable through discussion. One can usually spot participants working under democratic leadership for a number of reasons. First, the people are usually much more satisfied. They smile and will tell you they like what they are doing and the way in which they're guided. Second, they are usually more cooperative with one another and with the leader, offering to share work and information. Third, they will refer to themselves as *we* or *us*, not so much *I* or *me*. Fourth, they will not be afraid to say when they are not convinced of the leader's ideas or directions. When they do say they agree, they usually mean they are both externally and internally convinced. Fifth, they will tend to have a higher level of morale and cohesiveness. They will go to lunch with one another, get together after work, and be more willing to defend their group and organization if attacked. Finally, they will usually talk much more to one another and

152

to their leader. They will go to the leader with information and suggestions rather than make the leader come to them and ask.

Nondirective Leadership

Because even the most democratic of leaders often leaves something to be desired in certain situations, a new leadership pattern has been more or less perfected within the last ten years. This type of leadership has been called *nondirective, client-centered, group-centered, leaderless, sensitivity group, T-group,* etc. In each case the primary purpose of this type of leadership is to get every member to "find" himself or herself and discover excellence and satisfaction purely through personal efforts. Nondirective leaders, often called *trainers,* perform very few of the functions usually associated with a democratic, supervisory, or authoritarian leadership. Those directive functions which they do perform, they usually try to carry out below the level of awareness of the other group members (i.e., by asking questions, responding nonverbally, or making very subtle suggestions). They would never, for example, try to structure the group procedurally or give solutions, or even attempt to define the group's goal. Everything must grow out of the group members themselves; the group members must feel almost all of the responsibility for the product themselves.

We would not suggest that this is the type of leadership that should be encouraged within a business, educational, or political organization. We tend to favor the less extreme democratic leadership style, but there are a great many people in business and education who have been attracted by groups offering training in nondirective leadership and paying a great deal of money for the experience. For certain kinds of problems, perhaps the nondirective approach, if handled correctly, could be a useful method of improving organizational communication, but we believe it would certainly be ineffective as a general leadership policy.

Emergent and Designated Leaders

We have already talked about formal leaders versus informal leadership. What we are talking about in this section is whether the formal leader emerges from the group and is then given leadership through election or some other means, or whether the leader receives status by appointment or some other method outside of the group itself. It is important that we know something about the means by which one receives leadership if we are to fully understand the types of leadership. The type of leader one eventually becomes is in part determined by whether authority comes from outside or from within the group.

Contrary to what one might expect, emergent leaders are more likely to become authoritarian than appointed leaders are. They usually emerged in the first place because they were aggressive, forceful, and dominating. They also usually attained their role through a strong concern over substantive rather than procedural or social-emotional matters. One sees many leaders who have emerged when divergent interests have occurred in the group and they have been strong enough to bring the group back together. In other words, emergent leaders have had to fight for their role, and they intend to use any means to keep it.

Designated leaders, on the other hand, usually feel more secure in their position. Thus, they are able to spend more of their time asking questions, initiating action, and **153** responding to the group members. Designated leaders can afford to be democratic because they do not have to worry about someone taking their place. A designated leader is not afraid of a shared leadership situation. In summary, then, appointed or designated leaders have the ability to choose the type of leadership they want to exercise, whereas emergent leaders have much less freedom of choice if they are to remain on top.

LEADERSHIP EFFECTS
AND EFFECTIVENESS

Good leadership does not necessarily lead to a high level of group effectiveness. The leadership communication phenomenon is much more complex than any such simple analysis would indicate. We know, for example, that groups behave differently because of the nature of their leadership, and that leaders exert more influence on a group than other members do; but we are not certain exactly what kinds of leadership communication produce what kinds of behaviors or even what kinds of influence are uniquely those of leadership. What we will try to do in the next several paragraphs is summarize some of the most important effects of leadership that we do know with some degree of certainty and then attempt to sketch the outlines of an effective leader as best we can from the current literature. An in-depth discussion of specific ways in which people can improve their leadership behavior follows this section.

Leadership Effects

Because leaders tend to influence the group's attitude and opinion more than any other member, they are normally better able to assess the group climate at any particular time. This sensitivity allows them to act more in conformity with the group's norms and desires. This conforming behavior builds up a kind of credit for the leaders and allows them to deviate from the group's norms at some future date. In other words, they are said to have "paid their dues" and, thus, are allowed more freedom without the normal types of pressure that come with deviation.

Once a leadership hierarchy has been established in a group or organization, there is a tendency for that hierarchy to remain constant. As was mentioned earlier, high-status individuals will fight to maintain their status. No matter whether they are good or poor, leaders will attempt to take a larger share of the initiative in the discussion than the other participants. This increased participation does not make them better leaders, but instead may stifle more capable people in the group who should be exercising the leadership. It is enough for the high-status individual simply to be present to create this dampening effect.

The way in which powerful people are approached also reflects this differential attitude. Those in power are approached nondirectly and very carefully. In some cases they are even emulated by others regardless of how poor or mean they may be. In an organization this means that management may be creating "yes men" without even trying. Any communication which leaders make either verbally or nonverbally regarding their attitude about a particular issue is unconsciously picked up by subordinates and adopted as their own. This obviously causes a great many problems, especially when originality and creativity of thought are desired.

Finally, the person who normally enjoys a group experience the most is the one in charge. People, regardless of their culture and social class, want to discuss and have some control over the matters that affect them directly. In a group, the leader has the most control over decisions and is, thus, the most satisfied with the discussion. If the decision does not work out the way it should, most leaders will look for a scapegoat. It takes a very self-confident person to accept the responsibility for the group's decisions if they prove to be incorrect. In some cases, leaders attempt to delegate responsibility for leadership but retain control of the rewards and punishments which normally go along with leadership power. When this happens, ambiguity and apathy descend upon the participants and the quality of performance declines.

What Constitutes Effective Leadership?

Perhaps more has been written about this question than any other in the leadership area. The most reasonable answers, however, seem to come from observing and interviewing both effective and ineffective leaders and their subordinates. No better objective test has yet been found to evaluate leadership effectiveness than interview and/or observation.

In general, research of this nature has indicated that an effective leader is one who builds a working team with a friendly and cooperative atmosphere and high group loyalty through the encouragement of full and honest participation and other recognized techniques which we will discuss more fully later in this chapter. Effective supervisors, for example, are normally found to spend most of their time in planning what is to be done, providing the necesary materials, and initiating future action. They have also been found to delegate much of their authority to other capable individuals. They do not check up as often on their subordinates and are generally more supportive than their ineffective counterparts. Finally, they usually work quite hard at promoting cohesiveness and affection among the participants. The sex of the leader does not seem to have any effect on the leader's performance, but the degree to which the leader derives satisfaction from status and subordinate performance is extremely important.

In summary, then, leadership affects a member's deviation ability, his or her participation, the communication directed to him or her, and his or her satisfaction with the job. Effective leadership involves building a friendly, cooperative, dedicated working team. In the following sections we will provide some suggestions as to how, specifically, one can improve overall, staff, and conference leadership.

IMPROVING OVERALL LEADERSHIP ABILITY

Supervisors or leaders who are bossy or who issue commands on the dead run are firing from the hip. Those who boom out orders like a drill sergeant, who attack first and ask questions later, who give orders that can mean six different things, or who let their temper show through their voice are riding for a fall and don't know it. *The ability to give orders is an art*, and in all probability, no other single factor will make your success or failure in management so much as your ability to give orders.

There is a reason why this is true. This reason is based on the "psychological makeup" of average employees. They are by their inherited nature difficult people to order around. They resent it. The pioneers who settled this country were people who resented dictatorial authority. This is why they left their native land to make their homes in a free country where people are equal by accomplishment, not by inherited power or birth. Research studies have shown that it is not the lack of intelligence, ability, know-how, reliability, or even cooperativeness that accounts for the failure of the executive, line supervisor, or foreman or forelady. Their success or failure as reported by top management depends on how well they can get people to cooperate and work with them.

Giving orders properly is a cornerstone of leadership communication. The executives who bark out orders with a "Yours is not to reason why, yours is but to do or die" attitude may get people to work (grudgingly), but they will not be developing the kind of working atmosphere that builds themselves, their employees, and their firm in the long run. Their departmental output will drop the minute their backs are turned. These supervisors could not get people to *want* to work at the job. And why can't the "bosses" get people to do things willingly, obligingly, and interestedly? A large share of the blame must be laid on this inability to give orders properly. Every supervisor or foreman or forelady can learn how to give orders.

The first ingredient in this learning recipe is the supervisor's own attitude. The leader must learn to think *objectively* about what he or she is going to say and to whom he or she is going to say it. It was once said, and very appropriately too, that the greatest occupational hazard of management is the "open mouth." Here are some rules to follow. Put them into practice, and your rating as a competent boss will soon climb. These are rules not to memorize, but to read and digest and then to apply every chance you get until they become a part of your working technique.

WHAT TO DO

1. *Remember that you are a leader*. People look to you for direction. Give your orders in a firm, confident tone.
2. *Whenever possible, explain the "why" of the order with some comment*. People are reasoning creatures. They will cooperate more readily if they can see the reason for so doing. You might point out the advantages or disadvantages of doing something a certain way.
3. *Give your orders clearly, carefully, and fully*. Remember that you may have been thinking about the problem for some time. The person whom you are requesting to do something may not have been thinking about the problem at all or may be entirely unfamiliar with it.
4. *Be sure that you get the entire attention of the person to whom you are speaking*. All of us are engrossed in many different thoughts during the working day. Be sure you have undivided attention before proceeding.
5. *Never leave a worker to whom you have given unusual orders until you are certain he/she understands the orders*. It is very easy to misperceive an unusual order for a routine one.
6. *Know the person whom you are directing*. This may sound like a large order in some cases; nevertheless, understanding the person you are directing will help you in getting orders across.
7. *Talk to people in the language they understand*. Don't use big or technical terms to beginners or people who may not understand what you mean. Don't use abbreviations or other terminology that is not perfectly clear.

WHAT NOT TO DO

1. *Don't give orders in an irritated manner*. Your irritation is contagious and creates an antagonism before the task gets under way.
2. *Don't raise your voice*. Loud noises are disquieting to people. Psychologists have reported that the voice is one of the most dramatic instruments for portraying emotions. When you use your voice in anger, disgust, or recrim-

ination, you disturb people and cause emotional reactions of hate, fear, and anger.

3. *Don't start your orders with an accusation.* An example would be: "Didn't I tell you to do this in such-and-such a manner once before?"

4. *Don't give orders while you are in a "sweat" or are emotionalized about something that went wrong.* Wait until the air has cleared somewhat and you are in possession of yourself.

5. *Don't give orders in a bossy tone.* Refrain from the attitude that everyone has to jump when you say something. Remember that all people resent domination.

6. *Don't take it for granted that your order is understood.* Take the time to ask the people you are directing how they intend to tackle the job. Have them explain to you their understanding of your order. This is particularly important if the task is new or different or if the person you are directing is unfamiliar with the work.

7. *Don't give orders that are open to several interpretations or choices.* The determination of what is to be done is the function of the order-giver. Make sure that you know what it is that you want done—then give the order. Make it clear, definite, and to the point.

Our schools, our society, and our home life have all fostered democratic concepts. We are not a nation accustomed to master/servant relationships. We all feel our personal value and worth keenly. If you would win respect as a real leader, learn to give your orders in a cooperative, understanding, true leadership manner! It is in the manner of giving orders that we find skillful leadership exercised. Leaders who would get people to do things willingly must *think* before they talk. They must give their orders in reference to the conditions that surround the situation. Here are some of the things they must think of:

1. Timing: Is this the right time to tell them? Can this wait? Need I tell them?
2. Place: Should I tell them at their desk or call them into my office?
3. Method: Should I attack or explain?

As we mentioned earlier, leaders are made, not born, and one of the better ways to make leaders is to expose them to a leadership training course.

Leadership Communication Training

The two main questions with regard to leadership training are how to identify the persons with the greatest leadership potential and how best to develop that potential. Perhaps the best way to determine leadership potential is to observe how various candidates operate in groups of their peers; if they tend to emerge as leaders in those situations, it is likely that they could profit from having their skills perfected through a leadership training course.

The kinds of results one can expect from an enlightened leadership training program are improved attraction, enthusiasm, holding power, efficiency, self-discipline, and both quality and quantity of work. The Society for the Advancement of Management proposes the following four essentials for any leadership training program.[7] First, the program must impart information concerning leadership theories and practices. Second, it should aid the potential leader in developing leadership skills through actual practice. Third, a program should attempt to modify a trainee's attitudes that might be detrimental to leadership by giving him/her direct, personal insight and experience. And finally, it is essential that the program create an environment conducive to trying new methods and testing new ideas and skills. A good, well-prepared leadership training program affects not only new leaders, but all of those people who follow their leadership and, indirectly, the entire organization.

HOW TO IMPROVE YOUR LEADERSHIP IN MEETINGS

Have you ever come out of a meeting with the thought in mind, "Well, just what did we accomplish?" It may be that the meetings you yourself have called have left people thinking those very thoughts. Meetings can be of great value to your group—or they can be just time wasters that merely add to the general confusion. Do you want to guard against having your meetings fall into the "wasted time" category? Do you want your meetings to accomplish what you were driving at? You can help ensure the success of your meetings if you follow some of the suggestions listed below:

ACTION STEPS TO TAKE BEFORE CALLING THE MEETING

1. *Make sure the physical setup is adequate.* The physical situation should allow people to see one another and be acoustically capable of permitting interaction. Everyone should be comfortable during the meeting.
2. *Decide the purpose of the meeting.* State this purpose in a single sentence. Write this sentence down and circulate it to people who will be attending, if possible.
3. *Check with your associates to determine the "climate" of the problem.* This means that you should find out how and why people are thinking about the problem as they do. This will prevent you from becoming surprised by an unusual turn of events in the meeting.
4. *Plan your meeting and work your plan.* How do you propose to accomplish the purpose of your meeting? Are you going to call on various members? Are you going to advance only your own ideas? Are you going to use someone in a higher authority level as your agent? How are you going to get done what you hope to accomplish?
5. *Write down two or three possible solutions that might be advanced.* What do you think would be the best solution? Write this down so that you will be aware of your own prejudices on the subject.
6. *As chairman of the meeting, be sure that you yourself are thoroughly conversant with the topics you are going to have under discussion.* You should know as much or more about the subject than do the members of the group.
7. *Put on your "proper frame of mind."* You must be ready to invite criticism. You must be agreeable to suggestions from all members of your committee or group. You must take the time to listen to each and every member present. If someone doesn't readily speak up, try to find out why and don't overlook him/her when he/she wants to speak.
8. *Give everyone proper notification.* Do not wait until the last minute. Give people time to plan their day.
9. *Set a definite starting time and a definite stopping time.* The members of your committee can then make the necessary arrangements.

10. *Have all the material you are going to use ready for distribution*. Be sure you have enough copies of the materials. If you are going to use a blackboard or other devices, have them ready.

ACTION STEPS TO TAKE AT THE MEETING

1. *Start the meeting on time*. If certain participants do not show up, start without them. By waiting you only encourage late attendance.
2. *Be sure that all participants are thoroughly informed as to the purpose of the meeting*. Be sure that all participants have copies of the material, if you were distributing prepared material, or have read it beforehand.
3. *Hold the meeting on course*. Do not permit extraneous matters to enter unless they are designed to relieve tension that has built up. Do not let someone sidetrack your meeting. Permit few side discussions. Channel the meeting toward its goals.
4. *Encourage "sounding off."* The expression of hostile feelings has a release value. Unless the participants are allowed to "get it off their chest," they may be detrimental or at least apathetic to the discussion.
5. *Promote discussion and active cooperation*. People learn better if they are allowed to participate actively in the decision. Use open-ended questions and frequent summaries to promote this purpose.
6. *Inflate egos*. This is particularly important for reticent members. Although other group members may do this, it is up to the leader to be on the lookout for good contributions and to praise them.
7. *Reflect*. This involves rewording what a person says and clarifying or drawing out the feeling tone behind a statement. This encourages participants to continue with what they are saying and does not reflect either agreement or disagreement. This comes directly from the nondirective type of leadership mentioned earlier.
8. *If at all possible, do not take phone calls at your meeting*. It has a tendency to throw you off course, and it may occur at a crucial place in your meeting.
9. *List the points that have been settled or agreed upon*. Make a statement to the effect, "On this point, we have agreed to do . . . ."
10. *Adjourn the meeting on time*. Make this a rule.

ACTION STEPS TO TAKE AFTER THE MEETING

1. If the meeting has been a formal or semiformal meeting at which a definite decision has been reached, each participant at the meeting should get a *written résumé* of what was decided.
2. A *follow-up* should be made to see to it that the action decided upon at the meeting has been incorporated into the operating procedures or into the method of handling a particular item. You may think you got your point across at the meeting, but you may find that some did not understand.
3. *The door to further action should be left open*. Check to see how the decisions of the meeting have been accepted. No decision is so final that it cannot admit of improvement at a later date. Action determined should be thought of as the best possible means that could be devised for the present.

Handling Large Meetings

For our purposes in this section a *large*-group meeting will be defined as one where full audience participation cannot be secured through ordinary discussion methods. **159**

This usually means around twenty people or more. A large-group meeting usually has one of two possible purposes, either to promote *individual* learning and problem solving or *group* learning and problem solving. In the first case there is no need for a group decision, and the action resulting from the meeting will be performed by individuals acting alone. The second type of large-group meeting does require a group decision, and the action which follows usually involves interaction and cooperation among the participants. The effectiveness of a large meeting should be evaluated according to one of these two purposes. Unfortunately, other criteria are normally used to evaluate a large group's success: the skill in diction and presentation of the leadership, the emotional uplift that comes from the meeting, or even the reputation or charm possessed by the speaker, panel, symposium, or forum. As a result, little effort has been made to improve the conduct of large-group meetings.

THE TYPICAL LARGE MEETING

A number of phenomena usually occur during the typical large-group meeting. First, the people normally sit in rows facing the leadership. They become a kind of "audience," which denotes that they sit and listen rather than participate. With pure listening come apathy and passivity and a readiness to be told. If the purpose of the meeting is to bring about a change in the participants or action on their part, this passivity creates a barrier to the accomplishment of the meeting's goal. All of our research indicates that people learn better and have more carry-over if they are involved in the problem and participate in solving it. The second result of most typical large-group meetings is the feeling of anonymity on the part of the participants. They are not really a group because little or no interaction takes place among them. By being anonymous, individuals are able to shirk the responsibility for the group's decision; as a matter of fact, they are not even allowed to take on responsibility. With no responsibility, as with no involvement, the participant learns less and has practically no change of mind or resultant action.

Two other contradictory phenomena that occur in typical large groups are identification with the leadership and rejection of the leadership. For some participants the leadership will be so attractive that they will accept whatever is proposed without ever learning it and, thus, not really changing their mind. On the other hand, some participants will reject the leadership outright, saying, "They don't know anything about our problems," or "Maybe they can do it, but that doesn't prove that we can." Because there is no interaction between the leadership and the participants, these reactions never surface.

Finally, communication in large-group meetings is normally of the one-way variety, from the leadership to the participants. Little or no opportunity for an interchange of points of view is allowed, or if it is, it is usually at the end of the meeting just to fill in time until the meeting adjourns. Efforts to improve communication in large-group meetings normally comprise efforts to improve speaking ability, choice of vocabulary, and ways in which the material is presented.

IMPROVING THE LARGE MEETING

A number of techniques have been developed to improve the large-group meeting. Five of the most successful are audience listening teams, buzz sessions, audience

representation panels, role playing, and post-meeting reaction sheets. Audience listening teams are audience members selected to give critical evaluation of material presented by the leadership or others. They usually meet for a short time after the presentation and select one of their members to present a summary of their responses. This is especially useful when information is being given, problem diagnosis is in progress, or problem definition is taking place.

The buzz session is designed to elicit information from the participants by getting them together to talk in small groups and again having one of the group members present their material to the large group. This is an especially effective technique during phases such as planning strategy, gathering information, and solution testing. Audience representation panels involve selecting various members of the audience to take part in a discussion of the problem. This is valuable because the representatives are perceived as peers rather than leadership, and the members of the larger group usually find expression through them. They do not, however, represent some specfic group, as do the listening or buzz group representatives.

Role playing is a way of illustrating various kinds of human relations problems and analyzing them. Usually various members of the audience are asked to play the various roles. This allows the audience to identify with the situation more easily. Finally, post-meeting reaction questionnaires allow members of the audience to express their views anonymously. This is the most effective way of determining just how effective the meeting was for the majority of participants. It is normally found that those meetings are most successful where full participation is at least encouraged even though it is almost impossible to accomplish.

Several of the preceding suggestions can be used in combination with one another to get the participants involved. Even if these procedures are not applicable for your particular group, at least allow enough time at the end or periodically ask during a large-group meeting if anyone has anything to contribute. If the group's agenda is too crowded to allow room for such interaction, you should question whether any of the items could be delayed to allow interaction time. Along with the promotion of interaction in large groups, the leadership should have a working and democratic means of arriving at a decision. The most successful process yet devised is parliamentary procedure. When used correctly, it is most satisfying for both the leadership and the participants. When misused, however, it can become a powerful weapon by which democracy and full participation are subverted. In the following section we will discuss in some detail this very commonly misunderstood process. We hope that, with it, some of the methods we have suggested briefly above, and your own creative imagination, your large-group meetings will be enhanced and more beneficial than the typical large-group meeting.

USING PARLIAMENTARY PROCEDURE

Early rules to protect the rights of all group members first found expression among the ancient tribes of Germany. The first orderly system is credited to King Edgar of England, and thus we get the name "parliamentary procedure" from its use in the English Parliament. One of the earliest American contributions to parliamentary law was Thomas Jefferson's *A Manual of Parliamentary Procedure*, which he wrote for conducting the First Continental Congress. In 1874 General Henry Robert, an army engineer, finished his first edition of what he called *Rules of Order*, which has since become the classic publication in this area. Since that time there have been a number of other publications on parliamentary procedures, the best of which seems to be Alice Fleenor Sturgis' book called the *Sturgis Standard Code of Parliamentary*

Procedure (first edition in 1951 and second edition in 1966) and her accompanying volume called *Learning Parliamentary Procedure* (1953). The following comments are based on the Sturgis publications.[8]

When used correctly, parliamentary procedure is a perfectly acceptable means of providing large-group meetings with structure. The system is simple and easily understandable; it need not take long to master the basic rules of parliamentary procedure. In this section we will discuss those basic rules, and with a little practice you should find the system quite usable.

In all business meetings using parliamentary procedure, a core system is provided; that is, certain steps are necessary for the orderly presentation and disposition of a piece of business. The core procedure usually consists of six steps:

1. A member rises and is "recognized" by the chairman, and he/she then has the floor; only he or she may speak.
2. The member proposes a motion which provides a precise statement of the proposition before the group.
3. The motion is "seconded" so that one knows that at least one other member believes the motion deserves consideration.
4. The motion is restated by the chairman to indicate that it is in order, fully understood and recorded, and open for discussion.
5. After discussion (if any), the motion is put to a vote to learn the will of the assembly.
6. The vote is then announced to indicate the decision and that the matter is settled.

These basic steps are designed to accomplish the four basic principles of democratic decision making: equal rights for all, free and open debate, protection of the rights of the minority, and rule by majority. The six steps mentioned above should account for the vast majority of communications within a meeting. There are, however, a number of situations in which a group or individual desires to depart from the usual routine, and certain processes are provided for those situations. In the following pages we will discuss the major issues involved in using each parliamentary procedure, and a summary and order-of-precedence chart will be provided at the end of this section.

The Main Motion

In parliamentary procedure the first three words of a motion are fixed: "I move that . . . ." The essential qualities for the statement of any main motion are clarity, brevity, precision, simplicity, and completeness. One of the most common mistakes in framing motions is trying to deal with more than one thing at a time. For example, someone might move that the organization sell some parcel of land at $1,000 per acre during the next year. This is too much for one motion to handle; the question of whether to sell the land, the price for which it should be sold, and the date when it should be sold each requires an individual main motion.

Three other types of motions fall under the category of a main motion: the petition, the recommendation, and the resolution. A *petition* is used when the group does not itself have the power to do something, but wants instead to ask the appropriate administrative or governing body to take the action they deem necessary. The wording of such a motion should begin, "I move that we petition . . . ." A *recommendation* is used in approximately the same situation as a petition, but it is not as strong. It merely puts the group on record as favoring a certain action or position. A recommendation is usually worded, "I move that we recommend . . . ." A *resolution* normally carries several arguments prefixed by "whereas," along with an additional paragraph or two stating the motion or action to be taken.

Once one has introduced a main motion and it has been recorded and restated by the chairman, the proposer of the motion is given the first chance to speak for the motion. Once that person has spoken, the chairman should ask if there is anyone who would like to speak against the motion, and the discussion should continue in this fashion with alternate speakers for and opposed to the motion. There are, however, several things that can happen to that motion *before* it is voted upon, and these are the subject of the following eight items.

DIVISION OF THE QUESTION

If some members of the group feel that a proposed main motion, like the selling of land cited above, which really demands two or more separate considerations (i.e., several main motions), then they are entitled to call for a division of the question. Such a motion cannot interrupt a speaker, requires no second, is not debatable, cannot be amended, and requires no vote. In such a situation, the chairman merely rules on whether the question is dividable. If some members wish to question the decision on this matter or any other decision of the chair, they may appeal the decision of the chair, which will be discussed later. Normally, however, a simple ruling from the chairman allows the proceedings to continue.

WITHDRAWING A MOTION

If, in the course of discussing a main motion, the proposer of that motion wishes to withdraw it (for any reason), he/she may be recognized and do so. The withdrawing of a motion requires no second, cannot interrupt a speaker, is not debatable, is not amendable, and requires no vote. If someone else in the group feels that the motion should be discussed, it must be restated as a new motion. Any motion withdrawn by its proposer need not appear in the minutes of the meeting.

THE AMENDMENT

Perhaps the most often misused and misunderstood motion of all is the motion to amend. When used effectively, the amendment process makes democracy work in large groups. Through the amendment process it is possible to seek a better solution, one that is tailored, if not to the unanimous taste of the group, at least to the point of substantial majority support. When used improperly, it causes a group to get bogged down in parliamentary detail and increases frustration to the point of breaking the group apart. Nothing is more disconcerting than to listen to a group haggle over who has the floor and which amendment or amendment-to-an-amendment is being discussed or voted upon. Handling amendments is really where chairmen earn their stripes or fall in the eyes of their assembly.

Let us begin this discussion by stating flatly that all amendments which are hostile to or reverse the intent of the original motion are out of order. A chairman must constantly watch for this kind of amendment. It is possible to have any number of **163**

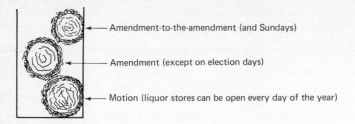

Amendment-to-the-amendment (and Sundays)

Amendment (except on election days)

Motion (liquor stores can be open every day of the year)

If the amendment-to-the-amendment is defeated (or accepted) then another amendment-to-the-amendment can be added. For example, if "and Sundays" is defeated, the words "and holidays" might become another amendment-to-the-amendment, or if "and Sundays" is passed, the words "before 1 P.M." might be proposed as another amendment-to-the-amendment. Once all the amendments-to-the-amendment have been proposed and voted upon, the log pile looks like the one below.

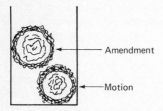

Amendment

Motion

Now the group would vote on the amendment and any other amendments proposed before voting on the main motion itself.

Figure 6-2   **Example of How Handling Amendments and Amendments-to-the-Amendment Is Like Stacking Logs**

amendments and amendments-to-an-amendment for a motion, but it is possible procedurally to handle them only one at a time. That is, once a main motion has been presented, another group member may rise and move to amend that motion, at which time the amendment will either be debated and voted upon or further amended (by an amendment-to-an-amendment). If it is further amended, then the stack is voted upon in reverse order; the amendment-to-the-amendment first, then the amendment itself, and finally the main motion. This sounds confusing, but if you think about it as a stack of wood piling up and then being removed, the process is easier to understand. The woodpile can hold only three logs at a time (a main motion, an amendment, and an amendment-to-an-amendment) before some action must be taken. Only when the amendment-to-the-amendment has been voted upon can a new one take its place, and only when the original amendment has been removed can a new amendment be proposed. The main problem a chairman must watch for is allowing too many amendments and amendments-to-the-amendment to pile up before any action is taken. It is easy for this to happen when all the participants are on their feet and shouting out amendments, but the wise chairman calls for quiet, sits everyone down, and takes things one at a time.

If an amendment is proposed which seems to the proposer of the main motion to be a good addition to the motion, the proposer may bypass the whole debating and voting process by simply standing and stating, "I accept the amendment." In certain situations this saves time and simplifies the amendment process. Many good chairmen make it a first order of business when an amendment is proposed to ask the originator of the main motion if the amendment is acceptable. This is not always possible, of course.

Another process which is often used to overcome amendment problems is called *amendment by creating and filling blanks*. This involves amending a motion to create a blank where some controversial matter is involved (like a date or a sum of money) and voting on the main idea of the motion first. If the motion with a blank is approved, the chairman can then list possible alternatives to fill the blank and through a process of elimination find the one with majority support. This technique averts arguing over trivial matters before the group has determined if the proposal is worthwhile.

Normally, however, there are only three ways in which a motion can be amended: by adding something to the motion, by deleting something from the motion, and by substituting one thing for another in the motion. Every amendment, then, should begin with one of the following: "I move to amend the motion by adding . . . ," "I move to amend the motion by deleting . . . ," or "I move to amend the motion by substituting . . . for . . . ." All amendments, be they of first or second order, require a second, are debatable, and take precedence over a main motion but cannot interrupt a speaker. All amendments require a simply majority vote even when they apply to motions which themselves require a two-thirds majority or more.

OBJECTING TO CONSIDERATION

The purpose of the motion objecting to consideration is to prevent discussion of a proposal which may be harmful, objectionable, embarrassing, contentious, or merely useless. This motion, however, is often misused for cutting off a proposal which is none of the above before its proponents have even had a chance to defend it. To prevent this misuse most parliamentary procedure texts require that it be proposed immediately after the question has been proposed and that two-thirds of the group concur. Unlike other methods of killing a motion, this one, when passed, is sudden death, with interruption of a speaker allowed, no second required, no debate allowed, and no amendments.

POSTPONE TEMPORARILY (LAY ON THE TABLE)

There are times in meetings when a motion is under consideration but another issue is deemed more urgent. It is at these times when the motion to postpone temporarily is in order. A motion tabled is considered on the table until the end of the following meeting. If it has not been taken up before that time, it is dropped. It can, however, be brought up again, but only as a matter of new business and as a new main motion.

Because of the requirement that a motion not acted upon be dropped after a certain period of time, this motion is often misused to kill a main motion. By using the motion to postpone temporarily in this way, we lose the ability to use it in the manner in which it was intended. When this motion is used to kill a main motion, the democratic process is thwarted and a majority prevents a minority from being heard. The proper motion to use in this case would be the motion to postpone indefinitely. The only real difference is that postponing indefinitely allows for debate while the motion to postpone temporarily does not. When one's motion is being killed, he or she should be allowed to debate the matter.

POSTPONE DEFINITELY

Because a group does not always have the information on which to base a legitimate vote readily available, the motion to postpone definitely becomes very important. This motion allows a chairman to appoint a committee to study the problem and report to the group, or to ask that the proper materials be made available to the group.

When a piece of business is postponed to a certain time, it becomes a *general order* or *order of the day* for that time. This means that it will be considered after the business of the house is completed. When the group desires a more exact time for discussion of the issue, it is made a "special order" and this is noted in the postponement motion, which means that it can interrupt whatever is on the floor at the time it is to be considered. It is not normally in order to postpone a matter beyond the next regular meeting unless there is a clear and logical relationship between the time suggested and the motion itself.

It has become an accepted practice in many groups to create orders of the day as main motions; for example, one might move that "the question of . . . be made a special order of business for tomorrow morning at ten o'clock." This is especially useful when issues have to be discussed and some members are interested in discussing some more than others. It prevents members from wasting their time listening to matters with which they are not concerned and makes it certain that urgent business will be taken up during the meeting or conference. Such a motion cannot interrupt, requires a second, is open to restricted debate (as to time only), can be amended (with regard to time only), and requires a majority vote.

POSTPONE INDEFINITELY

We have discussed this motion earlier; when it is passed, the matter is dropped. Many people refer to this motion as a *straw vote*, as it is often used by opponents of an issue to get a "test" vote without risking its passage. This motion also allows a group to do away with an issue which they do not want to be on record as either favoring or disapproving. Semantically, it sounds better to outsiders to say, "*We* postponed the matter indefinitely" rather than "*We* passed (or defeated) it." This motion cannot interrupt a speaker, needs to be seconded, must allow debate, must have no amendments, and must be passed by a majority vote.

REFER TO COMMITTEE

A motion is *referred to committee* when it is felt by the assembly that further research, consultation, or other measures may prove helpful. The proposer of such a motion may also suggest that certain instructions be given to the committee (and is usually made the committee's chairman). There are normally two types of committee in any group: *standing committees*, which are a permanent part of the group, like finance, membership, rules, etc.; and *special committees*, which are appointed to deal with only one matter. In some groups, like the United States Congress, the *reference committee procedure* is used, which means that all proposals coming to the group are submitted in advance for consideration by a reference committee.

A third type of committee used by some groups is called a *committee of the whole*. When this is used, the whole group has decided that they want to discuss a matter without the necessity of parliamentary procedure, motions, amendments, etc. It is accomplished by first moving to suspend the rules and then going into a "committee of the whole." Minutes are not kept in such a session, and the group can discuss a matter "off the record," so to speak.

Structuring Discussion and Voting

All the eight motions discussed above are ways in which a group can dispose of business without actually voting on it. The following five motions refer to ways in which the group can organize the structure of the discussion, question the vote, and change the decision once it has been made. They are limit debate, close debate, division of the assembly, reconsider, and repeal.

LIMIT DEBATE

In the beginning, most codes of parliamentary procedure allowed all motions to be debated fully, as was done in the United States Senate, but it was soon realized that a point can be reached where little more remains to be said and there is little chance that the minority will swing more votes. At this point a motion is in order to limit debate. One can also extend debate with this same motion. It cannot interrupt a speaker, requires a second, is not debatable, and can be amended only as to the time allowed for debate, the length of speeches, the number of speakers, or other similar proposals. In order to protect the minority rights, a two-thirds vote is required to pass a motion to limit debate.

CLOSE DEBATE (MOVE THE PREVIOUS QUESTION)

When people move to close debate (or move the previous question), they are, in effect, doing more than simply stopping debate; they are stopping all consideration of the motion, including amendments, postponing, referring, and any other possible action short of a vote on the motion. It is a way of killing several procedures with one motion. If this motion is passed, a vote on the main motion must follow immediately. The motion to close debate cannot interrupt a speaker, requires a second, is not debatable or amendable, and requires a two-thirds vote for passage.

DIVISION OF THE ASSEMBLY

One asks for a division of the assembly in order to substantiate a vote which is in doubt or to secure a more accurate vote count. If a voice vote has been taken and the result is close, someone may ask for a show of hands or a roll call vote. The decision as to the advisability of a revote is left to the chairman; of course, the chairman's decision can be appealed. A division of the assembly can interrupt a speaker and requires no second.

RECONSIDER AND REPEAL
(OR RESCIND)

These two motions are discussed together because they are often confused. One can move to reconsider a motion only at the same meeting during which the motion was decided, and it must be made by someone who voted on the prevailing side. The latter rule prevents someone on the losing side from using this motion to rehash a lost cause.

The motion to repeal or rescind is a much stronger action, which can be proposed at any time after a decision has been made. In effect, it asks the secretary to *expunge* the motion from the record, and if passed, the secretary actually writes "expunged by order of the assembly" across the original action in the minutes. This not only repeals the action but also shows a strong disapproval of the action. This is the closest thing available in parliamentary procedure to blotting out the record. Both the motion to repeal and the motion to reconsider require a second, are debatable, cannot be amended, require a majority vote, and cannot be renewed at the same meeting, but the repeal cannot interrupt a speaker while the motion to reconsider can, because in the latter case there is a one-meeting time limit.

Other Motions

We now come to that vast array of motions designed to allow a large-group meeting to run more smoothly. They include the point (or question) of privilege, appeal from the decision of the chair, point of order, parliamentary inquiry, request for information, suspension of the rules, recess, and adjournment. Aside from main motions and amendments, these are often the most-used parliamentary actions. For the members' own personal comfort and peace of mind, they must be willing and able to use each and every one of these motions.

POINT (QUESTION) OF
PRIVILEGE

Every member of a large group is entitled to satisfactory conditions (within reason). When one or more members of the group feel that this right or privilege is not being met, they may call for a question of privilege. This may amount to nothing more than opening a window or leaving to obtain a drink of water, or it may refer to more important matters such as speaking louder or holding down distracting noise. Such a motion can interrupt, requires no second, is not debatable or amendable, and requires no vote.

APPEAL THE DECISION OF
THE CHAIR

When, in the course of a meeting, the assembly wishes to correct its leader, the proper method is to appeal the decision of the chair. This appeal must be made immediately after the decision has been made and prior to the introduction of new business. Once an appeal has been made, the only comments accepted are those of the chairman in explanation of the decision and those of the appealer as to why he or she disagrees.

This happens most often when a point of order has been raised and denied by the chairman, although it may occur anytime, as was mentioned previously.

The danger of this procedure is that an obstinate majority could sustain an appeal which is contrary to a good and proper ruling by the chairman and in effect nullify the constitutional rules which guide them. One could also use this technique to discredit the chairman. Parliamentary procedure accepts this potential danger, however, as a better alternative to leaving a group without legal recourse against an improper ruling by a dictatorial and dishonorable chairman.

POINT OF ORDER

Whenever members feel that a rule is not being enforced, a member is acting improperly, or the assembly is moving incorrectly, they may raise a point of order. This motion can and often is misused by those members of groups who want to be the center of attention. A point of order should be used only when the problem is of some consequence and not for minor irregularities or technicalities. When the problem involves a speaker who is using abusive language, showing disrespect for the group or other members, a member may, instead of rising to a point of order, simply say, "I call the gentleman to order."

When a point of order has been called, it must occur immediately after the error, except when the problem involves a violation of the law, constitution, or bylaws of the group. These can be corrected anytime. The chairman rules on all points of order as either *well taken* or *not well taken.* No action can be taken on any pending motion until the point of order has been cleared up. A good chairman will refer a point of order to the group as a whole when in doubt, but unless he/she asks for discussion, none is possible.

PARLIAMENTARY INQUIRY

A point of parliamentary inquiry is used either to get *parliamentary* information or as a polite way of calling the chairman on a point of order without embarrassment. When information other than procedural is needed, the "request for information" is the proper motion. Some modern parliamentary texts list "request for information" or "request to ask a question" under parliamentary inquiry (Sturgis, for example). A parliamentary inquiry is always addressed to the chairman and is answered by him/her. When chairmen perceive such a request as purely designed to annoy, they should call it out of order.

REQUEST FOR INFORMATION AND REQUEST TO ASK A QUESTION

Both a request for information and a request to ask a question are to be directed to the chairman; but when such a request is to be answered by some other member of the group, the chairman will first ask if the questioned will yield to a question. The questioned may respond either "yes" or "no." If the answer is "yes," then the chairman is no longer involved, but if the answer is "no," the request goes unfulfilled. **169**

MOTION TO SUSPEND THE RULES

There come times in the life of a large group when they feel that it is necessary to take emergency action or to do something which is forbidden by the rules or program adopted. When this circumstance arises, a motion to suspend the rules is in order. Such a motion is allowed only for a specific purpose and for a limited time. When the problem involves the group's constitution or bylaws, their suspension must be allowed for by specific provision. No rules which are designed to protect absentees, such as rules requiring notice of meetings or fixing a quorum, can be suspended at any time. A motion to suspend the rules must be made when no other questions are pending or while some question is pending only if it refers to that question.

RECESS

The motion to recess is a *privileged motion,* which means it can be made even when the assembly is engaged in other business; the proposer must be recognized by the chair, however, and cannot interrupt another speaker. When the specified time for a recess is completed, the chairman calls the meeting to order, and it proceeds as if there had been no interruption. A recess cannot be extended beyond the time set for the next meeting.

ADJOURNMENT

This motion is a quick, direct way to end a meeting. It can be proposed at any time, even though other business is pending. The motion to "fix the time at which to adjourn" is necessary only for groups that do not meet regularly.

Precedence and the Nature of Motions

In the preceding discussion of parliamentary procedure, we did not refer to motions according to the way they are listed in the following table; that is, we discussed them according to jobs they perform rather than according to their order of precedence or whether they are main, subsidiary, privileged, or incidental motions. For a text of this nature we felt that the latter arrangement would be less useful. In order to read the following table, however, some discussion of precedence and the nature of motions is necessary.

Order of precedence allows motions to be taken up according to their importance and urgency. If such an order were not built into parliamentary procedure, it would be nearly impossible to organize the many possible motions that come before most large organizations. The following chart gives each possible privileged, subsidiary, and main motion a number—beginning with adjournment as number 1 through general and specific main motions as number 11. This means that once a motion has been made to limit debate (number 6), motions to postpone definitely (number 7), refer to committee (number 8), and so on, are out of order and only motions such as vote immediately (number 5) through adjourn (number 1) are allowable. For meetings to

Order of precedence*	Can interrupt speaker?	Requires a second?	Debatable?	Amendable?	Vote required?	Applies to what motions?	Motion can have what applied to it (in addition to withdraw)?	Can be renewed?
I. Privileged motions								
1. Adjourn	No	Yes	No	No	Majority	No other motion	No other motion	Yes[2]
2. Recess	No	Yes	No	Yes[1]	Majority	No other motion	Amend[1]	Yes[2]
3. Point of privilege (question of privilege)	Yes	No	No	No	No Vote	No other motion	No other motion	No
II. Subsidiary motions								
4. Postpone temporarily (lay on the table)	No	Yes	No	No	Majority	Main, amend, appeal	No other motion	Yes[2]
5. Close debate (previous question)	No	Yes	No	No	2/3 Vote	Debatable motions	No other motion	Yes[2]
6. Limit debate	No	Yes	No	Yes[1]	2/3 Vote	Debatable motions	Amend[1]	Yes[2]
7. Postpone definitely	No	Yes	Yes[1]	Yes[1]	Majority	Main motion	Numbers 9[1], 5, and 6	Yes[2]
8. Refer to committee	No	Yes	Yes[1]	Yes[1]	Majority	Main, amend	Numbers 5 and 6	Yes[2]
9. Amend	No	Yes	Yes	Yes	Majority	Variable in form	Subsidiary motions and reconsider	No
10. Postpone indefinitely	No	Yes	Yes	No	Majority	Main motion	Numbers 5 and 6	No
III. Main motions								
11. (a) General main motion	No	Yes	Yes	Yes	Majority	No motion	Specific, subsidiary, and object	No
(b) Specific main motion								
Reconsider	Yes	Yes	Yes	No	Majority	Main, amend, appeal	Numbers 5, 6, and 7	No
Repeal (rescind)	No	Yes	Yes	No	Majority	Main motion	All subsidiary motions	No
Resume consideration	No	Yes	No	No	Majority	Main, amend, appeal	No other motion	Yes[2]
IV. Incidental motions								
Appeal	Yes	Yes	Yes	No	Majority	Decisions of chair	Numbers 4, 5, 6 and 7	No
Point of order	Yes	No	No	No	No Vote	Any error	No other motion	No
Parliamentary inquiry	Yes	No	No	No	No Vote	No motion	No other motion	No
Request for information	No	No	No	No	No Vote	No motion	No other motion	No
Withdraw a motion	No	Yes	No	No	No Vote	All motions	None	Yes[2]
Suspend rules	Yes	No	No	No	2/3 Vote	No motion	No other motion	Yes[2]
Object to consideration	Yes	No	No	No	2/3 Vote	Main motion	No other motion	No
Division of a question	No	No	No	No	No Vote	Main, amend	No other motion	No
Division of assembly	Yes	No	No	No	No Vote	Voice votes	No other motion	No

*Numbers refer to order of precedence.   [1] Restricted.   [2] After change in parliamentary situation.

Figure 6-3 **Principal Rules Governing Motions**[9]

proceed smoothly, precedence must be strictly followed. A good chairman should have precedence memorized and be willing to call motions out of order when necessary. Incidental motions are not included in the order of precedence because they may be proposed at any time and must be decided when they arise.

Although we have discussed the nature of motions briefly in the discussion of individual motions as well as in the preceding discussion of precedence, it might be well to review the types here, since they neatly summarize the purposes of all the motions to which they refer. A *main motion* refers to the ways in which questions are brought before large groups for consideration. Main motions have the lowest precedence and are of two types: *general main motions,* which refer to possible issues other than reconsideration, repeal, and resuming consideration, which are *specific main motions. Subsidiary motions* include all of the possible ways of dispensing with a main motion under consideration. They include the three types of postponement (temporarily, definitely, and indefinitely), amendment, reference to committee, limitation of debate, and the call for immediate voting. *Privileged motions* have nothing to do with main motions, but are considered of such importance as to demand immediate action. They include adjournment, recess, and question of privilege. *Incidental motions* are all of those miscellaneous motions which cannot be placed in any of the above categories. Appeal, point of order, parliamentary inquiry, withdraw a motion, suspension of the rules, object to consideration, division of the assembly, and division of the question are all incidental motions.

Summary

In this chapter we have tried to deal with all types of leadership communication. It was pointed out that the old "trait" theory of leadership has given way to contemporary "situational" leadership theory. We tried to draw and maintain a definitional distinction between a *leader* and *leadership.* A number of factors that determine the nature of leadership communication, such as the personalities of the other group members, the nature and stage of the problem or task, the power and status of the leader, the structure of the group, and the talkativeness of the other members, were discussed in some detail. We reviewed briefly the four most common leadership types—authoritarian, supervisory, democratic, and nondirective—and the effects of each type. A number of differences were found between emergent and designated leaders. We described the factors which we believe constitute effective leadership and detailed a number of ways in which overall leadership ability can be improved. And finally, we pointed out how leadership communication in small and large formal group meetings could be improved through taking action steps before, during, and after the meeting, through the use of creative techniques to elicit full and open participation, and through an enlightened use of parliamentary procedure.

This ends our unit on oral communication, but it must be remembered, as you go on to read about written organizational communication, that many of the comments we made in this unit apply equally well to the next. The reverse is also true; you will learn a great deal in the next several chapters that will be important to improving your oral communication skills. As you continue reading, we think you will find it worthwhile to stop and consider from time to time how the material in these various chapters interrelates.

REVIEW QUESTIONS

1. Why is leadership still a greatly misunderstood concept?

2. Why has the trait approach to leadership been abandoned for the situational approach?

3. How would you define *leadership* and why?

4. How do the natures of the other group members, the stage of group process, the power to reward and punish, the position in the communication structure, the nature of the task, and the talkativeness of the participants each determine in some degree the type of leadership needed?

5. Discuss how all the four types of leadership mentioned (authoritarian, strong supervisory, participative, and nondirective) differ from one another in both participant and task effects produced.

6. How do the attitudes and behaviors of each of the above types of leaders differ?

7. How do emergent and designated leaders differ?

8. What are some conditions when good leadership would not necessarily lead to a high level of group effectiveness?

9. What are some of the effects of leadership?

10. What does one have to do and not do in order to be an effective leader?

11. How does the nature of the situation affect leader behavior?

12. What things should be part of a leader-training program?

13. What should one do to improve his/her leadership in meetings?

14. What are the possible purposes of a large-group meeting?

15. What are some of the problems in a typical large-group meeting?

16. What are listening teams, buzz sessions, audience representation panels, role playing, and post-meeting reaction sheets, and how can they improve large meetings?

17. What is the parliamentary core procedure and what does it accomplish?

18. Discuss the purposes and issues involved in using each parliamentary procedure.

19. What is meant by "order of precedence"?

20. Differentiate between main, subsidiary, privileged, and incidental motions.

EXERCISES

1. The following are three examples of leadership rating forms. (A fourth very excellent leadership rating form can be found in *The Dynamics of Discussion,* by Dean C. Barnlund and Franklyn S. Haiman,[10] but it is too long to reprint here.) You are to evaluate each of these forms (including the "Barnlund-Haiman Leadership Rating Scale" if you can get to it) as to their usability, reliability, and validity. Also note anything you think they have left out. Then you are to design your own leader

rating form, which will be compared with those developed by other members of the class. Finally, the class as a whole will develop an "ideal" leader rating form.

a. (From *Discussion and Conference*, 2d ed., by William M. Sattler and N. Edd Miller[11])

Discussion subject: _____
Group: _____ Date: _____
Leader: _____ Rater: _____

Check (✓) the number which represents your judgment and add comments which explain your rating.

1. When it was necessary for the leader to carry out procedural leadership functions, how effectively did he perform these functions??

1	2	3	4	5	6	7	8	9	10	11

Highly   Moderately   Moderately   Highly
Ineffective   Ineffective   Effective   Effective

Comments:
  a.
  b.

2. When it was necessary for the leader to ask problem-solving questions, how effectively did he perform this task?

1	2	3	4	5	6	7	8	9	10	11

Highly   Moderately   Moderately   Highly
Ineffective   Ineffective   Effective   Effective

Comments:
  a.
  b.

3. When (or if) it was necessary for the leader to give problem-solving answers, how effectively did he perform this task?

1	2	3	4	5	6	7	8	9	10	11

Highly   Moderately   Moderately   Highly
Ineffective   Ineffective   Effective   Effective

Comments:
  a.
  b.

4. When (or if) it was necessary for the leader to carry out social-emotional functions, how effectively did he perform these functions?

1	2	3	4	5	6	7	8	9	10	11

Highly   Moderately   Moderately   Highly
Ineffective   Ineffective   Effective   Effective

Comments:
  a.
  b.

b. (From *Discussion, Conference, and Group Process*, by Halbert E. Gulley[12])
Does the designated leader, or do those carrying the leadership responsibility:
  I. Have an adequate knowledge of group process?
     A. Understand interaction?
     B. Understand the influence of power relationships?
     C. Understand the influence of interpersonal relations?
     D. Understand the influence of group size?
     E. Understand the nature and types of leadership?
     F. Have ability to be impartial?
  II. Have an adequate knowledge of the problem?
     A. Have sufficient information?
     B. Recognize when a topic has been adequately discussed?
  III. Have adequate reasoning abilities?
     A. Have the ability to think quickly?
     B. Check for fallacies?
  IV. Have respect for others?
     A. Have social sensitivity?
     B. Display tact?

c. (From *Effective Group Discussion*, by John K. Brilhart[13])

Date _____ Leader_____
Time _____ Observer _____
Instructions: Rate the leader on all items which are applicable; draw a line through all items which do not apply. Use the following scale to indicate how you evaluate his performance:

5 – superior
4 – above average
3 – average
2 – below average
1 – poor

Leadership Style and Personal Characteristics
_____ Was the leader poised, calm, and self-controlled?
_____ Could he be heard and understood easily?
_____ Did he show enthusiasm and interest in the group and in the problem?
_____ Did he listen well to other participants?
_____ Did he show personal warmth and a sense of humor?
_____ Was he objective and open-minded to all ideas?
_____ Was he resourceful and flexible in handling suggestions from members?
_____ Did he create a permissive atmosphere?
_____ Did he make it easy for all members to share in functional leadership?
_____ To what degree was he democratic and group-oriented?
Preparation
_____ Were all physical arrangements cared for?
_____ Were his preparation and grasp of the problem thorough?
_____ Did he have questions prepared to guide the discussion?
_____ Were members notified and given adequate guidance for preparing?
Procedural and Interpersonal Leadership Techniques

_____ Were members introduced and put at ease?

_____ How well did he introduce the problem and supply necessary background?

_____ Did he guide the group to a thorough investigation and understanding of the problem?

_____ Did he suggest a suitable organization or pattern for group thinking?

_____ Were members encouraged to modify his plan or agenda?

_____ Did he state questions clearly?

_____ Did he rebound questions to the group (especially requests for his opinion)?

_____ Did he make appropriate attempts to clarify communication?

_____ Did he keep the discussion on one point at a time, encouraging the group to complete an issue before going to another?

_____ Did he provide summaries needed to remind, clarify, and move the group forward?

_____ Were reticent members encouraged to speak without being coerced to do so?

_____ Did he stimulate imagination and creative thinking?

_____ Were aggressive members controlled with skill and tact?

_____ Were misunderstandings, conflicts, and arguments handled promptly and effectively?

_____ Did he determine group consensus before moving to each new phase of discussion?

_____ Were important information, ideas, and agreements recorded accurately?

_____ Were plans made for follow-up and future meetings?

2. You are to make a list of all the groups to which you belong and the philosophy of leadership which you feel is evident in each most often. Then you are to evaluate the results of that philosophy on member satisfaction, communication, and performance. If possible, check the accuracy of your evaluation by interviewing or polling the membership.

3. Your instructor will divide the class into a series of small groups discussing problems similar to those suggested for the first exercises in the preceding chapter. Each group will have a leader appointed, and that leader will be asked to be one of the following: (1) authoritarian, (2) a strong supervisor, (3) participatory, or (4) nondirective. If you are chosen to be one of the leaders, you are to first prepare a brief description of the mental attitudes and behaviors which you will try to manifest while serving as the leader and keep it in front of you while playing your role. At the end of the discussion the group members will try to determine what things you had written down from the way you behaved.

4. A leaderless discussion will be planned by your instructor. Following the discussion, your group is to determine which two people best fit the role of task leaders, which two people best fit the role of social-emotional leaders, and which two people displayed the least leadership. If your instructor decides to get individual rather than group choices from all of the participants, a *sociogram* similar to the one presented below can be developed which could provide some very interesting information about the group. Each arrow represents a choice. What is the reason for many of the differences in leadership choices?

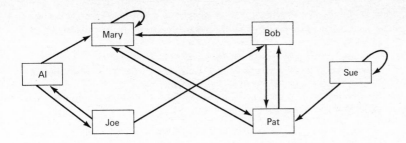

5. You are to intentionally find a group which is having difficulties of either an interpersonal or a task nature. Describe the problems and their causes in some detail and then suggest how a well-prepared and informed leader might attempt to get the group back on the right track.

6. Choose a group within your community or organization which uses parliamentary procedure at its meetings. Take your text along and note how the procedure operates in actual practice. Also note where differences occur between what is described in your text and what actually happens. Often different procedures are developed by organizations to meet their own particular needs. How would you assess the group's efficiency?

7. Your instructor will organize the class into one large-group meeting and set up a schedule for each class member to be chairman, secretary, and parliamentarian. Small committees will also be established and given a project and title (i.e., finance, membership, new projects, program, etc.). Each committee will prepare one or more resolutions and introduce them to the whole group. You are to attempt to use each and every motion at least once and try, on occasion, to trap the chairman. Before you try to trap him, however, be sure you are familiar enough with parliamentary procedure to know if he acted correctly. This exercise will be conducted as much like a real-life business meeting as possible.

FOOTNOTES

1. Robert T. Golembiewski, *The Small Group: An Analysis of Research Concepts and Operations* (Chicago: The University of Chicago Press, 1962), pp. 128–129.

2. L. A. Pennington, *The Psychology of Military Leadership* (New York: Prentice-Hall, Inc., 1943), p. 102.

3. William M. Sattler and N. Edd Miller, *Discussion and Conference*, 2d ed. (Englewood Cliffs, N.J.: Prentice-Hall, Inc., 1968), p. 194.

4.Franklyn S. Haiman, *Group Leadership and Democratic Action* (Boston: Houghton Mifflin Company, 1951), p. 4.

5. Sattler and Miller, p. 194.

6. Ibid.

7. Society for the Advancement of Management, *Planning and Training for Effective Leadership* (Ann Arbor, Mich.: the Society, 1956).

8. Alice Fleenor Sturgis, *Sturgis Standard Code of Parliamentary Procedure* (New York: McGraw-Hill Book Company, 1951); most of the material in this section on parliamentary procedure was paraphrased from Alice Fleenor Sturgis' second book entitled *Learning Parliamentary Procedure* (New York: McGraw-Hill Book Company, 1953) and used with the permission of the publisher.

9. Sturgis, *Learning Parliamentary Procedure*, cover pages, and used by permission of the publisher.

10. Dean C. Barnlund and Franklyn S. Haiman, *The Dynamics of Discussion* (Boston: Houghton Mifflin Company, 1960).

11. Sattler and Miller, pp. 476–477, and used by permission of the publisher.

12. Halbert E. Gulley, *Discussion, Conference, and Group Process* (New York: Henry Holt and Company, Inc., 1960), p. 358, and used by permission of the publisher.

13. John K. Brilhart, *Effective Group Discussion* (Dubuque, Iowa: Wm. C. Brown Company Publishers, 1967), pp. 107–108, and used by permission of the publisher.

RELATED TEXTS

Bass, Bernard: *Leadership, Psychology, and Organizational Behavior*, Harper & Row, Publishers, Inc., New York, 1960.

Drucker, Peter: *The Effective Executive*, Harper & Row, Publishers, Inc., New York, 1967.

Fiedler, F. E.: *A Theory of Leadership Effectiveness*, McGraw-Hill Book Company, New York, 1967.

Gordon, Thomas: *Group-Centered Leadership*, Houghton Mifflin Company, Boston, 1955.

Kepner, C. H., and B. B. Tregoe: *The Rational Manager*, McGraw-Hill Book Company, New York, 1965.

Likert, Rensis: *The Human Organization: Its Management and Value*, McGraw-Hill Book Company, New York, 1967.

———: *New Patterns of Management*, McGraw-Hill Book Company, New York, 1961.

Maier, Norman: *Problem-Solving Discussions: Leadership Methods and Skills*, McGraw-Hill Book Company, New York, 1963.

McGregor, Douglas: *The Professional Manager*, McGraw-Hill Book Company, New York, 1967.

Merrilue, Willard V.: *Managing by Communication*, McGraw-Hill Book Company, New York, 1960.

Stevenson, Fred G.: *Pocket Primer of Parliamentary Procedure*, 5th ed., Houghton Mifflin Company, Boston, 1972.

Sturgis, A. F.: *Learning Parliamentary Procedure*, McGraw-Hill Book Company, New York, 1953.

PART 3

WRITTEN
COMMUNICATION

CHAPTER 7

WRITING AS A MANAGEMENT FUNCTION

A generation ago old-style business entrepreneurs managed a relatively simple organization. If they were successful, in all probability they had the capacity to be all things to all people. They had the opportunity to converse with the relatively few employees almost daily. They probably knew all of their customers and were not particularly concerned with labor relations, income taxes, quality control, engineering, and a whole list of other technical aspects of modern business operations. They were in a position to note all of the activities of their business. They could walk through the enterprise with little effort. They could inspect, judge, correct, direct, order, or change policy on the spot. In fact, they were a whole team rolled into one, and they represented all phases of the modern business organization chart.

Today, business and industrial firms are teams—requiring teamwork. The modern team is composed of specialists. Each specialist is by training and experience the most qualified to carry out his/her specific duties. They are in most instances staff workers. A *staff worker* is one who is not directly working with production. Staff workers may be personnel people, purchasing agents, sales executives, accountants, research people, traffic experts, or any of the other manifold specialists that are commonly found in a business enterprise of any size. These specialists must communicate their ideas to one another as well as to the production department. The specialist must also communicate ideas to management, as well as to those who are under his/her direction. Production or *line management* personnel submit reports governing their problems, their ideas, and their results to their superiors as well as to the staff people who are charged with the responsibility of seeing to it that the operations in production are proceeding according to overall planning.

Accurate information from well-trained specialists who present their findings in readily understood terms will materially assist management in its decision-making activities and is vital to business success. If it is true that an army "marches on its stomach," then it is equally true that a business operates on flow of information.

THE IMPORTANCE OF WRITING

Writing is necessary because business is complex. A complex business can be likened to a human being, who must have eyes to see with, ears to hear with, and a memory which receives information, assimilates it, analyzes it, and records it for future use and decision making. Written communications, or, as we will call them, *reports*, serve as the eyes, ears, and memory of the business. In the final analysis, management determines how the information is to be employed. Some of the information management receives is acted upon immediately, some of it is stored, and some of it is relayed back to the other members of the organization just as your mind sends signals to the various parts of your body.

The successful manager must study and interpret the information that comes into his/her hands. On the basis of the information received, he/she formulates sound plans and policies and passes these along to superior officers in a clear and convincing form ready for action. Subordinate management must also analyze, study, and interpret the message it receives from superior management in order to transmit it effectively to those individuals for whom subordinate management is responsible. The end product of effective writing is *action*, either by superiors or by subordinates.

Summarizing, it may be stated that the reasons why writing has assumed increasing importance and significance in our business, professional, and economic lives are:

1. The increasing specialization of fields of knowledge.
2. The increase in research in every phase of activity.
3. The development of large organizational business structures.
4. The creation of staff and line organizations in modern business structures.
5. The decentralization of business activities conducted by large national firms.
6. The development of the staff specialist and research specialist whose work must be coordinated at various managerial levels.
7. The development of management as a professional occupation.
8. The need for accurate information in a very competitive economic system.
9. The development of research in marketing, design, system, methods, purchasing, and personnel, along with well-known research in the basic sciences as well as agricultural pursuits.
10. Information must be coordinated prior to the time that action is taken in complex business organizations.

Reports as Related to the Functions of Management

Most writers on executive duties and administrative action are in agreement that the following five basic steps must be performed in any organization:

1. *Planning*: This means developing policy on what shall be done, how it should be done, on what level it should be done, and what you are actually driving at. For example, if we were going to build automobiles, should we compete in the low-cost field or the high-cost field?

2. *Activating*: This means getting together all the personnel, materials, money, machinery, and other things which are necessary to get the project under way.

3. *Organizing*: This means setting up the machinery of a system so that each department or area knows what its objectives are and is in a position to go ahead with its duties.

4. *Directing*: This area covers the actual "running" of the operation. It embraces all phases of top-management and middle-management functions that are commonly associated with the word "managing." It means solving the various problems that arise from day to day.

5. *Controlling*: This includes those activities which are evaluative. They imply the type of control that sees to it that the overall operation of the business is in conformity with the original plans.

In order to fulfill the various functions of management that were sketched above, management of necessity must receive many reports as well as issue reports of its own. It may be accurately stated that business today is done on a "remote control" basis, and that in a certain sense we are in the era of "pushbutton" management insofar as most medium-size and large corporations are concerned. Control, direction, and other activities must be exercised through the medium of the written word.

Reports and the Organizational Flow

The organization chart is the nerve system for an organization. Through this nerve system must flow all of the information vital to its continued operation and existence. Most organizations have operating or executive committees that make overall or policy determinations. At the committee meetings it is necessary for the people in charge of the various activities to make presentations, either orally or in the form of a report. In passing, it should be carefully noted by the neophyte management man or woman or the management aspirant that the oral presentation and the written report at this point become very significant tools in the hands of the specialist.

In general, there are two types of reports presented at these meetings, routine and deliberative. As we shall see as we progress in the study of reports (i.e., writing), *routine reports* tell what has happened and the relationships that exist in such activities as production, sales, purchasing, budgeting, accounting, and other measures of performance. The term *deliberative reports* refers to all of those activities which have been undertaken to find and prepare information for management consideration in those areas in which management must make decisions based upon the information it has at its disposal. Deliberative reports may emanate from research activities, investigative reports, sales planning, production planning, and new techniques and devices, as well as from new products and new markets.

Management Viewpoints on Reports

Long-range planning, market and other research programs, and new technological products all must run the gamut of the managerial decision-making process. This creates an ever-increasing volume of reports which executives must digest in order to   **183** keep in touch with problems in the organization and contribute toward sound decision making. In an informal survey conducted among presidents and vice-presidents of various-sized organizations an attempt was made to determine what they and their companies thought ought to be fundamental in the reports submitted to them. General agreement seemed to be apparent on the following factors:

1. Reports are necessary in order to control the business.
2. Reports should be written, although a strong vocal minority favored oral presentations.
3. There are too many reports.
4. There is poor quality in the reports they receive. There was general agreement that the quality of presentation, especially in technical reports, is below the standard the presidents want. One executive stated: "Our reports were pretty deadly, reading like college treatises."
5. Reports submitted by one man or woman tend to be a standard for judging the competency of the man or woman. One statement was, "The quality of a report becomes almost subconsciously a measure of its author's ability."
6. Although no arbitrary rule should be placed on the size of reports, they should be as short and direct as possible.
7. The meat of a report should be summarized in a page or two so that the reader can decide how deeply he/she needs to delve into the supporting details that follow.
8. The language employed should be simple and nontechnical insofar as the recommendations or results are concerned. Technical language should be used only to back up the results obtained in a supplementary section.
9. Conciseness and objectivity in the recommendations should be achieved.
10. The concept of *completed staff work* should be employed so that the reader will know exactly what course of action the writer advocates and the reasoning based on the facts presented.

Reports Are a Two-Way Street

Reports provide the opportunity for two-way communication. It is by means of reports that management is able to build a channel through which ideas may be brought upward in the same manner as orders and information are funneled downward from top-echelon management. It is obvious that high-level management and middle management must get much of their information from basic sources if they are to be soundly and accurately informed. Every phase of organizational activity creates information. The aspects of business that concern management are created in manufacturing operations, in shipping departments, in packaging rooms, in power plants, in maintenance, in sales, and in engineering, to mention but a few phases. An organization which hopes to function effectively must make it possible for information to flow upward as well as downward. Accurately informed management is in a position to make sound decisions and to communicate with line and staff in keeping with the action steps it has taken.

Report Writing and Management Capacity

The writer of a report is in a unique position in relation to his/her superiors. He/She has the opportunity of entering their office via the written word, and it is obvious that the writer of a sound report is judged as being a sound person. Although executives would rarely promote a person solely on one's ability to write effectively, nevertheless, it is one of the tools which an astute, competent person can wield intelligently to one's own advantage while at the same time serving the organization to his/her best ability.

Writing a coherent, sensible, interesting, and informative report entitles one to respect among one's associates and superiors. Writing forces a person to use the knowledge gained through experience and observation. It places upon him/her the burden of thinking like management in that he/she must remain objective, carefully weigh the results of one's thinking, and demonstrate that he/she has the capacity to analyze lucidly a problem and reach a sound decision.

Reports as a Tool of Management

Reports permit management, regardless of its distance from direct operations, to obtain a first-hand account of what is going on. Reports enable management to review all of the operations of the business in a condensed form. Reports furnish information that serves as the basis for top-level thinking and action. Reports are also the means by which management itself is measured. Whenever concrete evidence is needed to show the extent to which management has measured up to its responsibilities, reports furnish the evidence for the final decision by the owners or their legal representatives.

As we are discovering, written reports may serve management in one or more of the following ways:

1. Serve as a permanent record.
2. Give management time to analyze and study a proposal.
3. Make information available to management in keeping with management's convenience and needs.
4. Serve as a basic device for internal communication. This means as a medium of two-way communication—from top management downward and from basic sources upward.
5. Be the basis for planning and policy formation.
6. Serve as a control device.
7. Serve as an evaluation device.
8. Be used to make the stockholder aware of the progress of the firm.
9. Serve as a device for receiving and disseminating information.
10. Be a basic pattern for research and study for any specific area or problem.

Management Must Have Information

The information needed by any particular management man or woman depends on his/her level of working authority and scope of supervision, the type of operation which he or she directs, and the degree of responsibility that has been assigned to him or her. Certain levels of top management, for example, must have information which will show the overall condition of the business at any one time. Specifically, the sales manager may want to know how certain salespeople are performing and whether or not quotas are being met in various territories.

Back in the production departments, the factory manager and superintendent of a particular department are forced to keep a sharp watch on their operations. They must know their reject rate. They must know their production rate. They must know where they stand on their production schedule. They must know what maintenance work must be done on the equipment and machines under their jurisdiction.

It is obvious that management must rely upon reports to help get the job done. There is a mistaken notion prevalent that management's chief function is to "boss" people around. This is a far cry from the truth. It is true that middle management and supervisors in business and industry actually do direct people, but they direct them in accordance with the information that has been handed them by their management.

WHAT IS A REPORT?

Simply stated, a *report* is information that has been carefully gathered and logically presented. Generally speaking, the information covers a specific item or event. Later in this text a sample letter is presented. Although this written message could logically be classified under the heading of "letter," nevertheless, it is in every essence a report. This message tells the story of an event in writing. It can serve as a record, and it may be sent through the "chain of command" so that everyone who needs to have this information can be given a copy. Since it is in writing, it may serve as a permanent record for as long a period of time as is deemed necessary to the solution of the problem.

Since the information this message contains is submitted in the written form, it gives all who have to work with it an opportunity to weigh, judge, analyze, and deliberate upon the problems it presents. In addition, it provides the writer with the opportunity to review his or her thinking after he or she has set down thoughts logically and in order. The readers are given the opportunity to study or reread the message at leisure or after they have obtained additional information or other viewpoints.

The report is a device of internal communication. It is the method and means which most business organizations must of necessity adopt in order to "talk" or communicate within the framework of the many activities that encompass the operation of the company. Although the written report may have many various purposes in the technical, professional, and business world, its most common use is to transfer information within an organization.

Reports are a means to an end—not an end in and of themselves. The function of the report is to help someone reach a decision or to motivate someone to a course of action which it is hoped will be effective. A report presents to management or the intended audience the story about a particular incident or problem in a terse, direct, objective, and lucid manner. When informal reports are used, they may be as varied as the nature and diversity of the problem may call for. It can be safely stated that there are as many report types as there are informational situations. It is in the area of formal reports that we find a more or less standard type of presentation.

There Are Reports and Reports

A partial list of the various types of reports that may be found in an ordinary type of business or industry is given later in this text. This listing is only a sampling of the many varying types of reports that might flow across an executive's desk during the course of his or her work. In addition to those on this list, literally hundreds of reports, some of them formal and some of them informal, would come to his or her attention. These reports would cover diversified areas ranging from community relations to a stockroom inventory analysis.

Informal Reports

The large bulk of everyday occurrences are covered by informal reports. These informal reports may range from accounting information listed on prepared forms to brief memos in response to definite questions. Most of the informal reports in business are of the performance variety. This type of report tells management how much was produced or what the dollar volume of sales was. They are essentially informative. They may cover periods varying from hourly, daily, weekly, monthly, quarterly, to annually. Very little writing enters into this type of informal report. For this reason, we are not too concerned with this type of reporting in this text.

The phases of informal report writing which we are concerned with are those types of reports which require one to find information, to report upon an event, to investigate a given condition, to suggest a method, to comment upon a process, and to submit this information to management. This type of reporting is done with little or no reference to commonly accepted research methods and techniques. There may be as many types of internal reports as there are situations and people.

Formal Reports

Writing formal reports has been in the past usually associated with the special fields of chemistry, engineering, psychology, education, and other scientific and pseudo-scientific fields. This is no longer the case. The province of business has taken over formal research as a tool. When research is carried on, its results must be reported. Report writing is an important aspect of research since it makes known to management the results of the research.

Formal research comes into being, generally, through two channels. One channel is the regularly constituted research department maintained by the firm. Such large corporations as General Motors, General Electric, Sylvania Electric Products, Dow Chemical Company, Bell Telephone Company, etc., have regularly constituted research departments. These departments are separate from the other staff functions. Their prime purpose is pure research. Reports of their work reach management through normal channels set up to evaluate, analyze, and interpret the research results. In addition, various staff departments are constantly undertaking research problems.

Another channel from which research finds its way into the organization is the analysis of the reports from such nonprofit research activities as those conducted by university and government staffs. From time to time certain research studies are presented in scientific journals or in texts such as this one which have an impact upon the research and development activities of the corporation. The elements of formal research and research reporting will be fully dealt with in later chapters. For the present, we can say that formal research is carried on under definite rules for its proper conduct which are designed to safeguard the findings.

Management Initiates an Informal Report

Let's take a specific example to see how management uses informal reports to help make countless decisions, answers, and adjustments. Mr. Adams, general manager of the Empire Pharmaceutical Manufacturing Company, receives a telephone call from Western Drugs in Chicago. The upshot of the call is that Mr. Biddle, the buyer for Western Drugs, a chain store organization, has lodged a complaint to the effect that **187** the last shipment of drugs arrived in damaged condition. He wants to know what Empire is going to do about it. He wants an adjustment. He wants to be sure that from now on it doesn't happen again. He is "mad." He lets his hair down and tells our Mr. Adams a thing or two.

Mr. Adams, as general manager, of course knows nothing about this specific incident. He assures Mr. Biddle of Western Drugs that he will personally take care of the matter and that all will be well in the future. Of course, Mr. Adams cannot take care of this matter personally. He is too busy. If all he did was handle complaints, he would soon be so bogged down in this detail that he would be unable to see the larger aspects of his job. Mr. Adams does what every good executive does. He calls in his secretary and dictates a memo.

```
From:  Mr. A. Adams, General Manager

To:    Mr. Homer Arnett, Traffic Manager


     Biddle of Western Drugs complained about last

shipment.  States that drugs arrived in damaged

condition.  Says this has happened too often.  Assured

him that this would not happen in the future.  See to

it that it does not.  He wants adjustment.  Whose

fault -- ours or shipping agency's?  Will you please

check on this and give me report on matter soon as

possible.


                    S/ Adams
```

A Report in the Making

Our traffic manager, Mr. Arnett, is faced with the need for information on the following four aspects of his problem concerning the midwest drug company shipment.

1. What went wrong with this shipment?
2. Why did it go wrong?
3. Whose, if anyone's, fault was it?
4. How are we going to correct it?
5. Should he recommend making an adjustment?

The first step, then, is to get the information. Mr. Arnett could proceed to do this in a number of ways.

1. He could telephone the chief clerk in the shipping department and have him give his version of the matter.
2. He could call the transportation company and have them give their version of how they handled the shipment.

3. He could walk down to the shipping department and personally interview a number of the shipping department employees while at the same time inspecting the various packing activities to check to see that everything was being done according to standards.
4. He could have his assistant run down all the information.
5. He could ask his secretary to make the phone calls and get the information.

What our man Arnett decides to do will hinge on a number of things. It will hinge on how he has learned to work with his superior. It will hinge on his interpretation of the importance of this specific event. It will hinge on the degree to which he trusts his assistant. It will hinge on the degree to which he can rely on the ability and integrity of his secretary. If he feels that it warrants careful attention, he may decide to tackle the problem personally.

After Arnett has gathered all of the information, he still has a lot of work to do.

1. He must decide on what is pertinent to this problem and what is irrelevant.
2. He must decide on just how he is going to make good on the promise that "it won't happen again."
3. He must decide on just how, where, and for what reasons he accepts the blame or rejects the blame.
4. He must now write the report and make it sound as factual, logical, thorough, and definite as possible.

The problem of Mr. Arnett, our traffic manager, was embraced in what is commonly called an *informal report*. By far and away the majority of reports that are used in business are *informal*. It is through the medium of the informal report that you will have the opportunity of gaining attention from your immediate superior or the next level of management.

THE ART OF WRITING REPORTS

There is a notion prevalent that those who can do act, and that those who cannot act can only write about action. In other words, the persons who have ability to get things done are not literary-minded. These action-oriented people presumably find it difficult to put down their thoughts in writing. This is a highly unwarranted assumption. The person who can act must of necessity have the ability to think logically and to express that thinking both orally and in writing. Writing down thoughts is one of the most potent devices for learning to organize, analyze, and evaluate one's ideas.

Writing is one of the highest arts to which mankind has attained. It is an art which must be learned through work, practice, and effort. There is a natural tendency on the part of men and women to shy away from activities that require them to write. This is understandable, since only those minds that are eager and able and coupled with a will to work are able to master effective writing expression. The ultimate rewards are, however, worth the painstaking effort involved in the learning process.

The Tools of the Report Writer

The tools of the report writer are equally available to all. Just as the difference between a good artisan and a poor artisan may often lie more in the manner in which the tools at hand are used than in the quality of the tools, so it is with the neophyte report writer. He/She must learn to make effective use of the tools he/she already possesses.

All individuals, whether they are in the industrial, business, or scientific world, or whether they are as yet students, have been employing the tools of the report writer all of their lives. They may not be conscious of the possession of skill with these tools, but possess them they do. These tools can be enumerated as follows:

1. Observational powers
2. Memory
3. Imagination
4. Vocabulary control
5. Ability to think through a problem
6. Ability to find information
7. Ability to read and assimilate information
8. Ability to analyze written information
9. Ability to write and organize one's presentation
10. Ability to discriminate (judgment)

It is obvious that no one particular course in school can endow you with all of the above knowledge and skills. They have been acquired by you over a period of years. You have gained strength in many of these areas from the many subjects you have studied. The good report writer knows how to weave in all of his or her varied background in building a specific report.

Report writers are constantly faced with the problem of keeping their report-writing tools in good working order. This they can do by constantly keeping alert to all the sources of information that affect their profession directly or indirectly. One of the greatest assets report writers can possess is a wide store of information. This is, in fact, their stock in trade. It gives them depth upon which they draw for any specific report. It gives them balance, perspective, and an insight into the problems with which they are presently working. Information is obtained daily. The man or woman who is to be an executive must learn to use easily all his or her powers of observation, questioning, retention, analysis, and synthesis of every sight, idea, thought, and problem that crosses his or her path. There are several methods by which an individual learns and learns to learn.

Development of Good Reading Habits

The management man or woman or the student who would aspire to mastery of report-writing techniques must learn to keep his or her report tools in good working order. This they can do by keeping alert to all the sources of information which affect their profession and company directly or indirectly. As we pointed out above, one of the greatest assets report writers can possess is a wide store of background information. This is what gives them depth, balance, perspective, and an insight into the problems with which they are working.

A management man or woman must read widely, and not in literature of his or her specialized field alone. It is true that management people must continue to read widely in their own field, but, what is even more pertinent, they must also learn to read intelligently and effectively in related fields. Management people must be aware of broad social trends, the ever-changing economic scene, the problems inherent in labor relations, and a host of other major and minor categories. Good reading habits and effective reading skill are thus an indirect aid to report writing, and they subtly turn into a direct aid when the time for writing is at hand. It is vitally important that one learn to read efficiently and effectively.

In fact, one of the fundamental requirements of report writers is that they learn to judge and evaluate written material. It is frequently necessary to question written material. The alert reader learns to ask:

1. Who wrote this?
2. What were his/her qualifications?
3. What was he/she trying to do?
4. How valid were his/her assumptions or statements?
5. Who agrees with him/her?
6. Who disagrees with him/her?
7. What line of reasoning did he/she follow?

In addition to evaluating written material, it is very helpful to assume a critical attitude when reading. This does not necessarily imply a negative attitude. It means making the material you are reading square with your own experience and judgments.

The aspiring report writer must, then, learn to read, and then read some more. He or she must learn to read widely, quickly, and retentively. Reading is one of the best entrees into all of the world about us. One can learn everything from the principles of electrical wiring to how to build a good lawn through proper reading. Reading for the purpose of assimilating a wide store of information is not quite like reading to meet the test requirements of a college course. To read for information assimilation, one must ignore the trivial and read for the broad background and the general information which the material presents. Textbook reading in the collegiate environment stresses diligent reading for exact detail and mastery of principles. Post-college reading and "experienced-businessman" reading imply addition to a basic store of knowledge, along with comparisons, analysis, and increasing one's range of interests and ideas.

Ten Basic Rules for Continued Learning

Reading is only one way of broadening background. There are other avenues by which an individual learns and learns to learn. For our purposes, we can say that the management man or woman who would master writing as a function of management should learn to:

1. *Observe.* The Chinese proverb that "one picture is worth a thousand words" is true insofar as learning experience is concerned. Learn early in life to see every process that you possibly can. Never visit a strange city without determining what business or industrial firm is the key enterprise. Then make it a point to visit that firm. In New York visit the stock exchanges. In Battle Creek visit the food manufacturing firms. In Detroit visit the many automotive firms. In Toledo visit the glass firms. In Kalamazoo visit the paper mills. Dr. Ray Palmer Baker made the following keen analysis of the use of the powers of observation to gather facts for writing:[1]

> What in particular do you wish to see? What kinds of facts is your subject concerned with? Walter Reed went to Cuba and observed all the conditions surrounding yellow fever. The man who studies glaciers goes, if he can, to look at mountains where glaciers exist or have existed, but he also watches snow, how it thaws and freezes, and perhaps, he contrives some special way to observe the viscosity or thick-syrup consistency of ice. The man who is interested in farm management looks at farms. The man who is interested in the drama goes

to the theatre and sees plays. The man who is interested in bookbinding examines the bindings of books, takes a book to pieces, and hunts up a bookbinder's shop.

With a discerning eye and inquiring mind, you can often find a world of information of which you had never even dreamed. A city street may be a veritable museum of architecture where you can see almost anything from Greek temples and Gothic churches to skyscrapers. A country roadside on a wet day will show you as much about rainfall, erosion, flood prevention, and the effect of deforestation as you will learn from many treatises.

The corner grocery can teach you something about the laws of supply and demand, the cost of living, and the economic condition of the country. In Molière's play, you may recall, there was a man who was astounded to discover that he had been talking prose all his life. You may be surprised to discover that you have been living among the facts of your subject all the time.

The truth is that we are generally so close to facts—they happen so constantly in such numbers all about us—that we have to get away from them occasionally in order to be able to think about them at all. But in thinking and reading about them, we must guard against forgetting that the very facts with which our minds are busy are perhaps sticking up before our eyes or roaring in our ears.

2. *Ask the man or woman who knows how.* When you see a workman performing an operation, whether it be painting, carpentering, or cement laying, ask him about his job. You will be amazed to discover that most artisans are more than willing to talk about their chosen fields of work. You can learn a great deal from these men. Develop the attribute of curiosity. When you are in a store, ask the proprietor about any specific item or sales effort and you will be rewarded with a practical lecture on the problem. Ask, listen intently and courteously, and assimilate.

3. *Learn by doing.* Try to do things for yourself. Build something, paint something, make something, work with your hands, and you will learn some of the basic problems that confront business and industry in this nation. The man who has not worked with his hands, even if it is only as a hobby, has a blind spot in his education and his ability to understand.

4. *Build your own library in the field in which you work.* The reporter writer should regularly read many of the current business magazines. In addition, he/she should be familiar with the many trade journals published for specific fields. Building a library does not mean that you stack up magazine after magazine, or book after book. What it does mean is that you learn to cut out items that interest you. Place these in a binder, folder, or ring notebook. Soon you will have an accumulation of good material in your field.

5. *Study the men and women with whom you are working.* The chief purpose of a report is to move the minds of men and women. The more you learn concerning the people with whom you are working, the more able you will be to direct your reports at their thinking, their interests, and their motivations. This does not mean that you should sacrifice the accuracy or structure of your report. It does mean that you should possess enough common sense to recognize that, in order to get action, you must work with and through people.

6. *Study the organization structure of the firm with which you are associated.* It is important that you know the company's history and policies. Familiarize yourself with all of the written policies and regulations. In this way, your report will be tied in with known facts. You will also have a good grasp of the channels through which your report will have to flow before any action can be taken.

7. *Learn all the possible sources for information for various types of reports.* In

a later chapter in this text, considerable time will be spent discussing the various sources through which the report writer may have access to information. These sources may provide first-hand information or they may guide one to secondary references such as government manuals, periodicals, magazines, and books. One of the tools that the report writer should be very familiar with in this whole area is his or her sources of information.

8. *Know your library.* This is another area which will be fully explored in a later chapter. It is sufficient to state at this point that report writers should be familiar with the resources of libraries which are available to them. More and more industrial and business firms are developing their own libraries. Every good-sized community has excellent library facilities. In addition, those communities in which institutions of higher learning are located often make available their library resources to researchers and established business firms.

9. *Welcome the opportunity to work at many different types of jobs.* The more jobs you have had, the more you should have learned. Use your work experience to learn. Don't worry about the pay. Get the job where you can learn the most. Work at it. Learn your job. Now learn the job of the person working next to you. And if you can't learn about all the jobs around you, you can do the next best thing: ask the person how he or she does the job. This know-how is your stock in trade if you are going to be the person who can write the report. It is the kind of knowledge that the person who makes the decisions on reports needs to have in hand.

10. *Study examples of good report writing.* Good report writing may be more or less easily observed. Most of the well-known business magazines feature good examples of report writing. Such well-known periodicals as the *United States News and World Report, Business Week, Dun's Review*, and *Modern Industry* have excellently presented reports. Some of their reporting, it is true, is flashily designed and eye-catching, but the majority of the work is well thought through and professionally presented. Other good examples of report writing may be found in such financial newspapers as *Barron's* and the *Wall Street Journal.* Additional examples of report writing may be found in many companies' annual reports. Many trade associations and quasi-public organizations also publish excellent examples of report writing.

THE POWER OF CLEAR THINKING

The ten rules which have just been presented are basic foundation stones of the report writer's ultimate competence. However, without one additional competency, that of the *power of clear thought*, the report writer will never achieve success. The arts of clear thinking have often been associated with the sciences, but they are equally applicable to all fields. The most useful rules for the report writer directed toward mastering the art of objective and clear thinking are well stated in a small booklet by Dr. Roy C. Bryan.[2]

Dr. Bryan stated that what is needed is straight thinking on our problem-solving activities. He stated that the difference between clear thinking and unclear thinking is that clear thinking results in correct solutions to problems based upon adequate information or evidence which is pertinent to the problem. He stated that the clear thinker generally uses procedures which produce good results while the poor thinker uses procedures which produce poor results. Dr. Bryan also noted that individuals whom we respect as having good judgment are those people who, when not fairly sure of themselves, withhold judgment. Those individuals who have good abilities in   **193** reaching decisions are respected by their fellow men and women as possessing good reasoning powers. It is suggested that those individuals who possess the characteristics of correct thinking do so because they either unconsciously and unknowingly use sound rules of clear thinking or else consciously use sound rules of clear thinking which they have acquired through experience or education, or both.

The Rules Governing Clear Thinking

Dr. Bryan presents the following seven guide rules to clear thinking, which are applicable to all report writers.

1. Prevent your feelings from dictating your thinking.
2. Suspend judgment until you are justified in reaching a conclusion.
3. Strive to identify assumptions.
4. Insist on adequate cross-section samples.
5. Beware of analogies.
6. Call for evidence of cause-effect relationships.
7. Organize your thoughts.

In the following paragraphs we will attempt to give full understanding and explanation of Dr. Bryan's seven rules as they apply to report writers.

Rule 1 concerns itself with the emotional quality of man's basic nature. One great philosopher has stated that "our thought is but a speck floating upon a sea of emotion." Feelings create the climate of our thoughts. Our feelings tend to master our thinking and color the manner in which we analyze and view everyday occurrences. This is true of objective, concrete problems in the fields of purchasing, sales, and all management effort. We *think* we are buying the best product, but may it not be because our thoughts are colored by a certain presentation by a salesman or saleswoman whom we like or innately trust? By *feelings* we generally mean such emotions as love, prejudice, jealousy, religion, class loyalty, provincialism, geographic differences, language variations, home concepts, race, name-calling, and personal interests. The greatest single obstacle to clear thinking is the tendency of people to believe only those things they want to believe. It is a hurdle to clear thinking in every working group of individuals.

Rule 2, although applicable to all phases of report writing, is even more applicable to management per se in all its manifold efforts. If out of your report-writing efforts this one aspect remains with you, it will serve you well throughout your career as a management man or woman. On this one facet of management ability and competence hinge many a promotion and many a failure. Heed well rule 2: *Suspend judgment until you are justified in reaching a conclusion.*

Suspending judgment is, or should be, a simple matter. When solving problems, the following steps will lead to a reliable conclusion:

1. Define the problem.
2. Plan a solution.
3. Gather the evidence.
4. Draw conclusions.

One should never take step 4, that of drawing conclusions, until he/she has first taken the three previous steps. The poor or illogical thinker makes a regular practice of jumping at conclusions.

Rule 3, that of identifying assumptions, warns us of the dangers to which those who deal with humans are always prone. We make a judgment based upon only the slimmest of evidence. We press forward because we are fearful that our jet-guessed opinion won't hold up under the light of careful scrutiny. We therefore fall under the delusion that skating on thin ice is sound philosophy as long as the ice doesn't give way. Therein lie the beginnings of many a management man or woman's downfall. Assumptions that endanger profits or cause the production of wrong items are serious errors in our economic life stream.

Assumptions are often slippery customers. An assumption is simply an opinion, guess, or theory, the truth of which remains to be determined. Whether an assumption is true or false can be determined only after sufficient evidence has been brought to bear upon it. When sufficient evidence has been assembled to prove that an assumption is true, it ceases to be an assumption. It can then be regarded as truth or fact. The first step which needs to be taken by one who desires to eliminate false assumptions from his/her thinking is to identify them. Once an assumption is identified, one can avoid acting on it until its truth has been tested.

Dr. George Gallup uses the principles enunciated under rule 4, that of obtaining an adequate cross-section sample, in his American Institute of Public Opinion. Dr. Gallup defines his use of the cross-section sampling technique in the following words:

> As the new surveys of public opinion venture into another Presidential year, their distinguishing mark is the use of the cross-section principle. Briefly it means that interviews must be obtained from each of the important and heterogeneous opinion groups in the United States in *exact proportion to the size of that group in American life or in proportion to its numbers on election day.*
>
> Essentially there is nothing new in the principle of cross-section sampling. The country bacteriologist who takes specimens of water in a neighborhood stream at different points to determine its purity, is making use of the principle. So is the ore-tester who calculates the richness of a lode iron ore by thrusting a scoop into the ore at different points.[3]

Our next rule, rule 5, warns us against analogies. Most of you are familiar with an analogy. When someone starts a line of reasoning with, "I remember a case," or "For example," or "An incident just like that occurred during the last conversion from war to peace." Analogies are generally fallacious in the basic comparative valuations they imply. No two specific events are exactly alike, and one cannot compare one set of events with another set unless they are strictly controlled under scientific laboratory conditions. Generally those who employ analogies are proving their point from a concrete example and wish to make a sweeping generalization from the one specific incident.

In all analogies, a comparison of two or more things is either obvious or implied. Most speeches you hear over the radio or at church on Sunday are usually well sprinkled with analogies or comparisons. However, analogies are best when used to clarify points or ideas or to suggest new ideas or solutions to problems. When they are used as proof, they are wrongly used. Remember this rule: Beware of analogies; even though they help to make thoughts clear and suggest solutions to problems, they never prove anything.

Pronouncements of cause-effect relationships, which is enunciated under rule 6, if quickly or loosely arrived at, may cause considerable trouble. All causes produce effects, and all effects have causes. Because of this fact, we are constantly called upon to learn the causes of observed effects and to predict the effects that will result from given causes. The clear thinker will not *assume* that one event is the cause of another event. He will insist on evidence that a true cause-effect relationship exists. **195**

For example, an investigator wanted to learn what effect education has on financial success in life. He studied the life history of 500 men and found a marked superiority in earning power of college graduates over that of high school graduates. He said, "By all means, go to college."

This conclusion needs to be examined critically. Even though the investigator has established the relationship between earning power and a college education, it does not follow that education is the cause of the greater earning power. It is one of the possible causes. Other possible causes are the intelligence of the group and their ability to carry out plans, apart from the length or intensity of their education. This is not to say that education does not increase earning power. Probably it does. But when seeking causes, we should not confuse a cause with factors tied to the cause, nor should we rule out the possibility of other causes after we have found one.

The final rule, organization of one's own thoughts, is the most difficult of all the rules. When one writes or speaks to another, his/her main objective is to be understood. Organized thought contributes to this understanding. The three steps which are frequently used in organizing thoughts are:

1. Identifying the points that one wishes to emphasize
2. Determining their relative importance for presentation
3. Placing the results in writing

For all practical purposes, organizing and outlining are one and the same thing. When we outline, if we have the knack of it, we simply arrange the major and minor points in proper relationship. If we organize our thoughts and place that organization of ideas in writing, we have an outline. It might be pointed out here that the ability to organize one's thoughts is not an inherited or natural ability. It is necessary to learn how to develop orderly processes of thought which enable us to attain a level of clear and straight thinking.

Summary

Today's management man or woman, as a participant in policy formation and direction of economic effort, must learn to speak with clarity, with forthrightness, and in the language that all will understand, appreciate, and trust. This is so whether the report is, as in the great majority of cases, addressed to other individuals in the management group or among the line supervision of his/her own company, or whether it is addressed to stockholders, labor, or the public. The management person must grasp the significance of the particular material, must understand the appropriate degree of detail to use, and must master expression. As we have stated, much depends upon his or her assiduous search for adequate background and determination to follow the rules of clear thinking.

FOOTNOTES

1. Ray Palmer Baker and William Haller, *Writing* (New York: The Ronald Press Company, 1929), pp. 94–95.

2. Roy C. Bryan, *Seven Rules of Clear Thinking* (Ann Arbor, Mich.: Edwards Brothers, Inc., 1947).

3. George H. Gallup, "Polling Public Opinion," *Current History* (February 1959).

CHAPTER 8

GETTING INFORMATION

The purpose of your report is *to tell* someone about something. It is obvious that you are going to tell about some specific item, thing, event, or idea. You therefore have to obtain information in order to write. The information you are presenting is the foundation upon which your report rests. It is axiomatic that your report can be no better than the information it contains and transmits.

Knowledge covering the "how of information gathering" is an important phase of an individual's management potential. Information gathering may run the gamut from face-to-face interviews, printed questionnaires, and actual observations through scholarly library research to scientific laboratory methods. Certain aspects of information gathering are technical in their very nature, springing from the laboratory research, while other reporting efforts may be based on daily industrial or business occurrences. The various aspects of information gathering for report writing will be examined in this chapter.

GUIDEPOSTS
IN INFORMATION
GATHERING

The first step in getting information is to decide what it is that you are attempting to do. It would probably be wise for the report writer, even before he/she starts out on the quest for information, to list a number of questions with which to structure the information needed for the report. These questions are:

1. Is this to be a formal (research) report or an informal report?
2. How accurate must it be?
3. How thorough and demanding are the requirements of this particular report?
4. What action might be taken on the basis of my report, and what might be the consequences of that action should the report be inaccurate or misleading?
5. How many checks will be made on this report?
6. What limiting factors exist as to: (a) time? (b) money? (c) special conditions?
7. Does the information sought lend itself to objective analysis and interpretation?
8. To whom is the report to be directed?
9. How much time do I have to complete the report?
10. Will it be necessary to run a follow-up report to check on the original report?

The scope and intent of the report you are preparing will, in the main, as outlined in the preceding ten points, dictate the amount and kind of information needed. After the report writer has decided on ''how far he/she is going to go,'' the task of gathering the information for the report begins. A ten-point *information checklist* presented below was developed by the writer as a guide to the *what, who, where, when,* and *why* of information gathering for report writers.

INFORMATION CHECKLIST

1. What specific information do I need?
2. What are the best possible sources for obtaining this information?
3. What is the best-known method for obtaining this information?
4. What possible objections to this method or source of information can I think of?
5. What steps am I going to take in getting this information?
6. What checks, if any, can I establish in order to protect myself in my information-gathering activity and to ensure accuracy?
7. Is there anyone who has already done work in this field? What has his or her company done about it? Is this information available to me?
8. Would it be practical to work out a trial study to see if the way I propose to do this is plausible?
9. Have I checked all information sources?
10. Have I listed in outline form the proposed steps I have decided to follow in order to obtain the necessary information?

Below is a checklist devised by a college senior to determine the method he was going to use to gather information on a report on opportunities in junior administration positions.

REPORT ON JUNIOR ADMINISTRATIVE POSITION

1. Check the newspapers to see what types of jobs are being advertised and predict how much of a demand exists for this type of job.

   a. Local papers
   b. Nearest large-city paper
   c. New York papers
   d. Wall Street Journal

2. Check with the State Employment Service.
3. Check with private employment agencies.
4. Check federal civil service literature for this type of job.

5. Check state civil service literature for this type of job.
6. Go directly to a selected list of corporations or companies and talk directly to the personnel manager about this type of job.
7. Read reports in business magazines as to this type of job.
8. Talk over the possibilities with the college placement officer.

SOURCES OF INFORMATION

The basic sources of information available to the report writer can be broken down into two main classifications:

1. Original sources
2. Secondary sources

Both of these sources will be discussed at length in this chapter. It must be pointed out that the use of secondary sources is often a prelude to the undertaking of original research and, thus, one would necessarily include in a report material from both the secondary sources and the original sources. Either source may be found in the formal or informal type of report writing. It should be borne in mind by the report writer that the use of either of these sources requires the exercise of initiative, persistence, judgment, and other well-known attributes of management-level thinking and decision making.

It should also be noted that the method employed for collecting, analyzing, and controlling factual information would of necessity vary as between formal and informal reports. Although the sources might well be the same for both a formal and an informal report, the exercise of objective control over all the information-gathering activities must be greater for formal reports.

Original Sources

A partial list of the methods and techniques for obtaining information from original sources would include the following:

1. *Observation.* The observation can be objectively planned, as in the case of the person who is making a real estate appraisal on the basis of a standardized form, or it can be subjective, as through the use of the trained eye, and can include experience, as in the case of a person who is sent out to estimate a roof or painting job or some such other task.

2. *Interview Method.* This method consists of asking competent people or so-called experts. The interview may be *patterned,* that is, it may follow a very definite form, or it may be unrehearsed. This phase of information gathering is used frequently in both informal and formal report writing. On the informal level it means just asking the person "how it happened." One of the biggest problems in interviewing people is how to focus the conversation. One of the best methods you as the interviewer may use to converse at the interview is to take along a card on which have been typed in brief form the most important questions which you want answered. In this way you can direct the line of conversation to the specific objectives which you are seeking. Under certain circumstances it may be unwise to attempt to take notes. Note taking may cause suspicion on the part of the person being interviewed and limit him or her

in the amount of information he or she will readily disclose. If this condition exists, you should write up your notes as soon after the end of the interview as is practicable.

3. *Questionnaire.* This is the more formal method of obtaining first-hand information. It is a device that is commonly used in formal research. Its strengths and weaknesses will be discussed when we review this aspect of information gathering in the chapter "Formal and Informal Writing."

For our purposes here we can say that the questionnaire is being looked upon with some disfavor by many research workers as well as by the recipients of the questionnaire. The reason for this is that the questionnaire barges in on one's busy time and asks many difficult questions that may or may not be readily answerable. The questions may often be vague or may require people to commit themselves on issues where they would rather not take a stand in black and white. There is much to commend the questionnaire as a technique for obtaining information. On the other hand, the indiscriminate use of this device by amateur research workers has brought a great deal of discredit to the method and to the validity of the results under certain conditions.

If the questionnaire is to be used, it should be constructed with exceptional care. A number of good suggestions to help you make your questionnaire an efficient information-gathering device are:

1. Write short questions. Avoid long or involved statements.
2. Be sure your questions are direct. Avoid ambiguity.
3. Be specific in the information you are seeking. How do you propose to collect, analyze, and present the information gathered?
4. Develop your questions, insofar as possible, so that simple checking of yes-or-no answers will elicit the information. Make the answers you receive easy to work with.
5. Be sure that the questionnaire is the proper device for getting the information you are seeking.
6. State your questions in a neutral fashion so that you will not influence the answers.
7. Arrange your questions on the sheet in some kind of logical manner.
8. Select your *sample*—those to whom you are going to mail the questionnaire—with forethought.
9. Test your questions on a sampling (a small group) before you make up the final list. You may discover that what seems simple to you is confusing to someone else.
10. Use a good format or layout in your questions so that they will be easily read, answered, and returned.

4. *Expert Opinion.* The use of "expert opinion" is a phase of the interview technique for obtaining information. This method may be used where one can find someone who is sufficiently recognized as an authority in the field so that one's written opinion or report is based upon his/her broad experience and background.

5. *The Letter Technique.* This is still another phase of the interview or opinion method. In this method you simply write someone who may have been in similar situations to inquire what their experience has been.

When you write letters requesting information, you should remember that you are asking busy people to work for you free of charge. You should, therefore, think through the matter with great care and determine exactly what it is that you are attempting to find out. Your letter should be the absolute top in judgment, tone, and selection of terminology. Your letter must of necessity create a favorable impression.

It should be so couched that the recipient will willingly provide the information you want. You should make it easy for the person being questioned to answer. Your letter should arouse interest in the problem and should motivate the reader to a positive action on your behalf. A few don'ts governing the writing of the request-for-information letter are listed below:

1. Don't ask for information that might be confidential.
2. Don't make your letter hard to understand.
3. Don't send your letter to the wrong person.
4. Don't ask too many questions.
5. Don't make your question too involved.
6. Don't ask the person to do "research" work for you.
7. Don't expect that the person will lay aside all of his or her work just to answer your questionnaire.
8. Don't expect anything. Be grateful for what you do receive.
9. Don't make a pest of yourself by writing again seeking enlightenment on the answers you have received. Work it out to the best of your ability.
10. Don't scatter your effort. Narrow down your range of questions.

6. *Telephone Interview.* In this method, you call the "expert" or the one who you believe would have the answer and ask your questions over the phone. This method is widely used by business and industrial firms who may have need for certain information very quickly. The telephone technique is very effective if it is used correctly. Here are eight rules which the author developed to guide office people in their use of the telephone request-for-information procedure.

RULES GOVERNING TELEPHONE REQUESTS FOR INFORMATION
1. Determine specifically the information which you are seeking. Make sure that you know definitely what it is that you want to know.
2. Put the question in the form of a definite, understandable statement so that the answer will fit specifically the question you are asking. You want the answer to fit your question. For example, "Do you have a completed survey on wages in this area?"
3. Decide what firm, individual, office, governmental agency, organization, or business might possibly have at hand the information you are seeking.
4. When you call the place you have decided upon, be specific. Don't say, "I wonder if there is someone around there who could tell me if this is O.K., etc." Put your proposal in this form: "I have a question which I believe your office could answer. It is: _____. If you cannot help me, could you please give me the name of the person who can?"
5. Do not become discouraged if the first place you try is not able to give you the information you want. Try another place. Keep trying. You will find what you want if you keep trying.
6. Be sure that you are talking with the proper person. Ask to talk to the "sales manager" if you are seeking information regarding that phase.
7. Write down the information immediately. Do not trust to your memory. Write it down while you are receiving it over the phone. Read it back to the person interviewed if necessary.

SOURCES AVAILABLE FOR TELEPHONE OR DIRECT INFORMATION REQUESTS
1. The public library
2. Business and related offices: (*a*) travel bureaus; (*b*) railroad offices; (*c*)   **201**

banks; (*d*) real estate firms; (*e*) insurance offices; (*f*) public utility offices; (*g*) trade association offices; (*h*) schools and colleges

3. Chamber of commerce
4. Newspaper offices
5. Municipal and county offices
6. State offices
7. Stock brokerage offices
8. Government agencies such as: (*a*) census bureau; (*b*) labor bureau; (*c*) commerce department; (*d*) agriculture department; (*e*) employment offices
9. Technical and trade associations
10. Professional societies
11. Research organizations

Use of Sources Available for Telephone or Direct Information Requests

1. *The public library.* Most public libraries, especially in the larger metropolitan areas, have departments devoted entirely to business subjects. These reference departments are staffed by expert workers who are able to find information on almost any question pertaining to the business world. Libraries exist, in their very nature, because of public demand. It is the wise report writer who makes the fullest use of these facilities.

2. *Business and related offices.* Almost all business offices have a desk labeled "Information." This pertains directly to information concerning that particular business or office. The office is inviting questions. A glance through the many pages of the classified section of the telephone directory will reveal that there are literally thousands of firms which in their very nature are specialists in their fields. Make use of them. It is readily apparent that they can give one more information of an up-to-date and dynamic nature than can many condensed reference books. The important thing to remember in this connection is to be sure that you are talking to the right person. Among the wide range of possibilities in this category can be listed: travel bureaus, railroad offices, banks, real estate firms, insurance offices, public utility offices, trade association offices, schools and colleges.

3. *Chamber of commerce.* The chamber of commerce office in practically every city gathers valuable information about the business life of the particular community. If the chamber of commerce office cannot answer your question, it can, more often than not, tell you where you can find an answer. How effective the chamber of commerce office can be is best illustrated through the following true incident:

> A young man was contemplating investing several hundred dollars in a newly organized business venture. He did not know the man with whom he was going to associate and, naturally, was dubious of the advisability of investing his funds. He decided to ask the Chamber of Commerce if it had any information concerning the merits of the venture. Imagine his pleasant surprise when the official at the Chamber of Commerce office pulled out a file and told him what their estimate was of the probable future success of the business and the past experience and position of the man with whom he was going to associate.

4. *Newspaper offices.* Newspaper offices, of necessity, are required to keep many and varied source books containing an infinite variety of information. In addition, their files contain valuable information that is local in nature. Newspapers pride themselves on being able to furnish the latest information. Certain departments of the newspaper always hold themselves in readiness to serve the public.

5. *Municipal and county offices.* Certain offices of the municipal and county government are available as sources of information to the public. The officials in these offices will courteously answer any questions on which they are free to give information. Among the offices in this group are: clerk of the courts, treasurer's office, department of vital statistics, county recorder's office, and fire department office.

6. *State offices.* State employment offices, state bureaus, state departments for economic development, etc.

7. *Stock brokerage offices.* These offices, as a rule, have employees whose duty it is to make investigations as to the financial standing of firms listed on the New York Stock Exchange. Since the brokerage company makes its livelihood by dealing in securities for its customers, it is at all times willing to give whatever information it possesses to those interested in certain securities.

8. *Technical and trade associations.* The U.S. Department of Commerce issues a book called *National Associations of the United States.* Listed in this book are 16,000 organizations of businessmen on local, state, and national levels. These associations, commonly referred to as *trade associations,* are a veritable gold mine of information ranging all the way from turnover figures for retailers to public relations programs for manufacturers.

Many of these trade and professional associations have been leaders in industrial research and trade promotion. For example, according to the National Research Council, the American Gas Association now has 125 research workers engaged in testing the various types of domestic and commercial gas-burning equipment and accessories. The industry-sponsored Institute of Gas Technology in Chicago carries on research in the production, purification, and utilization of oil- and coal-manufactured gas and natural gas; it also does research in gas appliances and heater development. The Anthracite Institute has approximately fifty research workers in its laboratories near Philadelphia.

In the February 15, 1952, issue of the magazine *Modern Industry* the following appeared:

> One group, the Portland Cement Assn., did the following last year: it received 300,000 requests for information from the various publics it served. Each request received prompt attention, whether it was from an engineer working on a skyscraper or a farmer who wanted to build a concrete barn floor. To service these requests, and promote the use of Portland Cement, the Association has more than 400 publications, ranging from technical design booklets to simple folders on small improvements in homes.
>
> This association channels its efforts towards promotion, research, technical service and educational work.[1]

Information Services Available from Trade Associations

The following is a list of services and information one can obtain from a trade association:[2]

1. *Government relations* (Information on legislative or administrative action; representation of industry before legislative or administrative bodies)
2. *Advertising* (Seeking to create goodwill for the industry and a better understanding of its products or services; promoting increased sales through advertising or other publicity)
3. *Statistics* (Compiling and distributing statistics on production, inventories, sales, costs, accounting, etc.)

4. *Employer-employee relations* (Information, advice, special services on wages, terms of employment, etc.)
5. *Standardization* (Voluntary or recommended standards defining a product, process, or procedure)
6. *Cooperation with other organizations* (With other associations, chambers of commerce, schools, government agencies, etc.)
7. *Education and training* (Development and promotion of training for persons in the industry or prospective employees)
8. *Business practices* (Developing codes of ethics, standard business forms and contracts, and trade practices)
9. *Field service* (Providing for contract and service in the field)
10. *Library service* (Maintaining a library and/or making available abstracts, lists, or reviews of books and articles)
11. *Legal service* (Retaining counsel to prepare bulletins, special reports, etc.)
12. *Product research* (Searching for new products, new uses for standard products, or improvements)
13. *Traffic and transportation* (Studying the problems of, or furnishing services for, improved transportation of products)
14. *Taxation* (Research and information)
15. *Accounting* (Developing and furnishing information on accounting methods, principles, and procedures)
16. *Insurance* (Assisting in problems)
17. *Marketing research* (Facts and methods that influence buying and selling, or how best to reach the market)
18. *Exchanges* (Arranging for exchange or resale of excess items or equipment)
19. *Market research* (Making studies of location, volume, or other trends)
20. *Elimination of trade barriers* (To remove obstacles to the free flow of commerce)
21. *Commercial arbitration* (Specifying rules and procedures governing disputes rising out of commercial transactions; providing service in arbitrating them)
22. *Credit and collection services*
23. *Awards and contests* (Designed to bring out ideas, methods, designs, etc.)
24. *World trade* (Information or services in connection with imports and exports)
25. *Merchandising* (Conducting studies and providing data on improved methods)
26. *Public health and safety* (Educational programs directed toward the public or to users of the industry's products)
27. *Conservation* (Promoting measures to conserve raw materials and natural resources)
28. *Copyrights, trademarks, designs, patents, and trade names* (Maintaining a registration bureau or providing information)

Secondary Sources

Secondary sources of information are an important and fertile field for those seeking information for reports. One of the noticeable trends during the past few years has been the increased reliance upon published information for the solution of current business problems. In fact, a number of business firms maintain their own libraries. It is also of interest to note that a number of major cities, such as Newark, New Jersey, Chicago, Illinois, and Boston, Massachusetts, maintain business libraries.

The increase in published information for the field of business has grown out of the increased research that is currently being carried on not only in educational institutions but also in research institutes and industrial organizations. In keeping with the increase in trained people in the business field, there has been a wholesome increase in the number of persons who are willing to write, to speak, and to discuss their common problems. Through these processes there has grown up a new area of specialized writing which is invaluable as background to the report writer. Almost all known fields in industry and business have a sizable amount of literature available to the student.

The novice seeking published reference material should guide his/her efforts in terms of the following questions:

1. What digest, guides, or reference works will enable me to determine if information exists in the areas in which I am working?
2. Is help available to me from libraries or other public or quasi-public organizations to assist me in my information search?
3. How should I go about finding the information I need?
4. Am I using the best method for locating the information?
5. How can I make sure I am not overlooking good sources?

The library system in the United States has provided most researchers with the foundation materials covering practically all of the areas which fall under the heading "business activities." A number of libraries over the past few years have added specialists to their staffs who are trained in the field of business information. This is particularly true in the larger cities. College and university libraries, where available to the researcher, have specialized libraries in the field of business subjects. Libraries not only have large collections of books, pamphlets, and magazines, but they have this material systematically arranged with proper guidebooks and reference cards for quick survey and ready determination as to content and availability.

Every report writer should have access to two well-known business texts that deal exclusively with business information source materials: Coman's *Sources of Business Information*[3] and Johnson and McFarland's *How to Use a Business Library*.[4] Both of these books should be an integral part of the library of anyone who undertakes to write anything more than a very limited report. Larger companies that maintain a library for their employees and staff workers certainly should have these available to their users. In order to give the reader a good résumé of the scope offered in both of these excellent works, the table of contents of each of these books will be presented. The report writer should become familiar with both of these volumes, as they fully catalog, analyze, and refer to the known sources of published business information.

In particular, the first two chapters in Coman's *Sources of Business Information* are a must for the report writer. It would be well for the reader of this book to acquaint himself or herself thoroughly with the listings and information given in these two chapters. This will give a basic foundation for finding information for report-writing activities that will prove invaluable in later life.

CONTENTS OF THE BOOK
"SOURCES OF BUSINESS INFORMATION"
Chapter
    1. Methods of Locating Facts
    2. Basic Time-Saving Sources

3. Locating Information on Firms and Individuals
4. The Business Scene
5. Statistical Sources
6. Financial Information
7. Real Estate and Insurance
8. The Literature of Accounting
9. Automation
10. Management
11. Personnel and Industrial Relations
12. Marketing, Sales Management, and Advertising
13. Public Relations
14. Basic Industries
15. Foreign Trade
16. A Basic Bookshelf

CONTENTS OF THE BOOK
"HOW TO USE A BUSINESS LIBRARY"
Section
1. How to Use a Library
2. Handbooks and Yearbooks
3. Periodicals, Reports, and Pamphlets
4. Directories
5. Business, Economic, and Financial Services
6. Business Directories
7. Government Publications
8. Publications of Regulatory and Quasi-Governmental Bodies
9. Research Foundations
10. Trade, Industrial, Commercial, and Technical Organizations
11. Encyclopedias, Dictionaries, and Almanacs
12. Preparation and Presentation of the Research Report

USING LIBRARY RESOURCES EFFECTIVELY

Both of these books also have excellent material on the effective use of the library. Since the use of the library is a must for the report writer, he/she should familiarize himself/herself with the fundamentals of effective library usage. In addition to the two books mentioned in this chapter, there are a number of pamphlets and booklets on *how to use the library.* Your librarian will willingly steer you to these sources and help make you proficient in the use of library facilities. Anyone contemplating extended research or report-writing activities would, of necessity, need to become expert in finding and using sources of business information.

Levels of Information

There are three concepts which the report writer must understand as a basic condition to working with library sources of information; they are:

1. A general knowledge of what the library contains
2. A general understanding of the plan on which the library is organized

3. A recognition that knowledge about a particular subject exists on many different levels

The third point affects the report writer searching for facts to a considerable degree. First of all, it must be recognized that different subjects often have different difficulty levels and that books and collections of books about these subjects are to be found on these various levels. We all accept the fact that there are history books written for high school pupils, history books written for college students, history books written for graduate students, and, last of all, history books which are purely in the realm of narrow research and investigation. The same might hold for economics, psychology, or philosophy of marriage.

The report writer who begins to work on his or her research has to determine what level of information he or she wants for this report. How deep do you want to go? We have already discussed this in the preceding chapter, but it is still one of the controlling factors in your attack on finding information. If you have a working background in the area covered by your report, you can skip elemental sources. If, on the other hand, you know nothing about the subject, you will have to be on the lowest rung of the information ladder.

After you have specifically determined what information you want, you must determine how deep you are going to go. Is this to be a long or a short report? At first glance it might seem that a short report would call for less information than a long report, but this is not necessarily so. The short report may represent the distillation of many months, weeks, and days of research, while the long report may just run on.

Reference books such as encyclopedias, which contain information about the whole range of human knowledge, can provide the report writer with summary or overall types of information. They may serve as a review and a check. They are also important because they are an authoritative source. A newspaper article, for example, may say a good deal on a subject, but it may not say it authoritatively.

A list of the major areas of sources of secondary information is presented here for reference. Full information as to the exact type and scope of information that they present can be determined by referring to your library or through reference to the two volumes referred to in the preceding pages as basic sources of business information.

A PARTIAL LIST OF BASIC AREAS OF
PUBLISHED BUSINESS INFORMATION

1. Encyclopedias
2. Handbooks
3. Directories
   a. City
   b. Telephone
   c. Manufacturers
   d. Trade and professional groups
4. Yearbooks
5. Almanacs
6. Dictionaries
7. Bibliographies
8. Catalogs
9. U.S. Superintendent of Documents (governmental publications)
10. Indexes to periodicals
    a. *Readers' Guide to Periodical Literature*
    b. *The Engineering Index*
    c. *The Education Index*

    d. *Chemical Abstracts*
    e. *Public Affairs Information Service*
    f. *The Industrial Arts Index*
    g. *New York Times Index*

11. Loose-leaf services
12. Biographies
13. Economic news services
14. Magazines
15. Textbooks
16. Association bulletins
17. Research association publications
18. University research bureau publications
19. Foundation research findings
20. Newspapers
21. Pamphlets

Each of the areas listed under the preceding twenty-one basic areas has many volumes and types of information under each heading. In order for the user of this book to get an idea of how diversified the information can be under any one of the major headings listed, the author has selected one phase of governmental publications for further treatment. It must be borne in mind that this is not a full appraisal and evaluation of the material to be found under this particular heading, but it is sufficient to show the wide range to be found under any particular area.

GOVERNMENT PUBLICATIONS

The governmental agencies have, during the last several decades, played an increasingly important role in the affairs of the business world. There is every reason to believe that this trend will continue. The government has created bureaus and spent large sums of money in the interest of obtaining information that will assist the businessperson and give understanding of the direction of the producing and consuming life of our nation.

The numbers and scope of these publications are so vast that it is fairly safe to say that they cover all fields of economic activity in the United States.

The Bureau of the Census takes the national census of population, occupations, mines and quarries, etc., every ten years; of agriculture, horticulture, and irrigation, every five years; and of manufacturers, every two years.

It has conducted a census of construction and of distribution of sales of manufacturing plants; of national employment; of retailing, wholesaling, and hotels covering the various years; and of business services and amusement enterprises. Censuses have been made covering advertising agencies, broadcasting companies, financial institutions, insurance companies, real estate agencies, and transportation (automotive) companies.

The Bureau also collects monthly or quarterly data regarding the production or supply of many commodities, including cotton, wool, hosiery, shoes, men's and boys' clothing, fabricated steel plate, air-conditioning equipment, clay products, fats and oils, paints, varnish, and lacquer products. Information gathered by the Bureau of the Census may be obtained by writing to the Department of Commerce, Bureau of the Census, Washington, D.C.

Department of Commerce Publications for Business People

The Department of Commerce, through its various bureaus and departments, is constantly turning out a vast volume of studies, statistics, research reports, and other material which can be of vast importance and interest to the researcher, report writer, and business people. It has been said that so many different divisions of the department are grinding out surveys, studies, interpretations, guidebooks, directories, and other business studies that it is hardly possible to maintain up-to-date cumulative bibliographies of this material.

METHOD TO EMPLOY IN OBTAINING INFORMATION FROM DEPARTMENT OF COMMERCE

1. If you would like to determine whether or not the Department of Commerce has ever published any material on a specific area, write or visit the field office nearest you. If you do not know their nearest field office, you may find out from your post office.

2. If you cannot locate any information in this manner, write to the Office of the Department of Commerce, Washington, D.C., or to the division in which you think the study would have been undertaken. *Make sure that you state specifically what you want, why you want it, and how you are going to use it.* It is this full disclosure of what you are driving at that will permit them to determine if they have what you want.

3. You can obtain original material or original studies if your request is based on data which the Census Bureau or the Department of Commerce has in its possession. This material is punched on IBM cards. If you wish to determine special information which logically may be in the Census Bureau data, you can have this done for you if you are willing to pay for the clerical costs involved. These costs are, for the most part, very nominal.

A PARTIAL LIST OF REPORTS, STUDIES, AND PAMPHLETS PUBLISHED BY THE DEPARTMENT OF COMMERCE AND OTHER GOVERNMENTAL AGENCIES WHICH ARE BASIC SOURCES FOR BUSINESS INFORMATION

1. Census reports
2. Labor force reports
3. Income statistics
4. Housing
5. General business and marketing

Summary

One of the best summaries governing the information-finding activities of the report writer is to be found in Coman's *Sources of Business Information.*[5] This summary of general techniques for locating business information is presented below.

COMPLETE TECHNIQUE FOR LOCATING INFORMATION FROM SECONDARY SOURCES

1. The problem must be defined accurately. Be sure that the type of information required is clearly understood, and use the dictionary to clarify the meanings of unfamiliar words.

2. The next step is to go to the library where the greatest accumulation of pertinent material is available. If the public library has a business branch and the topic being researched is a business one, the search is made that much easier. However, if the business firm conducting the research has its own library, the latter is the first place to start.

3. The general background of the subject is acquired by consulting the Encyclopedia Americana, the Encyclopedia Britannica, and the Encyclopedia of the Social Sciences. The annual yearbook volumes should be examined, too, and references at the end of each article should be noted.

4. Examine the almanacs and yearbooks, such as the *World Almanac,* the *Statesman's Yearbook,* the *American Yearbook,* and the various regional yearbooks if the topic is within the limits of their subjects.

5. The next step is to consult the subject index of the card catalog to locate books containing the needed information. Various selective reading lists, such as *A Reading List on Business Administration,* by Dartmouth College, Amos Tuck School of Administration and Finance, and the previously mentioned publications of the Business Branch of the Newark, N.J., Public Library, Special Libraries Association, and Alpha Kappa Psi Fraternity, all emphasize the better books.

6. Locate the pertinent government publications by consulting the *United States Public Documents Monthly Catalog* and the semi-monthly *List of Selected United States Government Publications.* If the subject is included in one of the U.S. Superintendent of Documents price lists, this source can be a real timesaver.

7. An even more direct method for locating exact information on laws and regulations is to utilize the appropriate loose-leaf service which presents the desired information directly to the reader without further research on his part.

8. The most recent data on the topic should then be secured from magazines, pamphlets, and newspapers, especially the *New York Times.* Consult the *Industrial Arts Index*, the *Readers' Guide to Periodical Literature, Public Affairs Information Service,* and the *New York Times Index.*

9. If the preceding steps do not unearth the information desired, visit or write trade associations, technical societies, and chambers of commerce for help. It is quite possible that they may have unpublished information which will solve your problem.

SHORT METHOD FOR LOCATING INFORMATION
FROM SECONDARY SOURCES

1. Consult the library card catalog.
2. Examine the various almanacs and yearbooks.
3. Review briefly the various government document catalogs.
4. Complete the job by checking the various periodical indexes.

HOW TO TAKE NOTES

In using either primary or secondary sources of information, it is necessary for the report writer to maintain a record of the information gathered as he/she goes along. It is obvious that if one were to write a rather short informal report covering a single incident, it would be possible for the writer to carry the facts in his or her head. However, even the interruption of several hours or the need for a trip back to the main office before undertaking the writing of the report will often result in the report writer's forgetting important aspects of the problem.

Taking notes is an art in and of itself. If you take too copious notes, you will become bogged down in a morass of detail. If you take too sketchy notes, you will not have anything when you come to work with your materials. There is no one best way of note taking. Various people work in various ways. You must learn a system that will fit your temperament and style of work. Different people adopt different methods. You probably have a method of your own at the present time.

Two methods that are in common use are described below:

Use of 3- by 5-in cards. In this method one places the topic heading on each card. The source is noted on the card. The excerpt is then written on the card. This method permits shuffling, filing, and easy reference when working. It is limited to the size of the reference and the fact that in any extended work the amount of cards one comes to possess is too great for easy handling.

Use of loose-leaf notebook. Many researchers like this method of note taking. A notebook is easy to carry around. Since the sheets are fastened, they will not easily become lost. Indexes of separate sheets make it easy to keep various phases of the study intact. The 8$\frac{1}{2}$- by 11-in. size paper gives much more room to work with. When or if one notebook is filled, another may be started.

Using either method, the best advice that can be given is encompassed in the following points:

1. Be sure that you have the complete reference of the material on which you are taking notes. This includes author, name of book or magazine, date, page, volume number, and any other pertinent data.

2. Learn to scan the entire article before beginning your note taking.

3. Learn to take notes over only the most pertinent points. Do not fall into the error of writing down too much. Make certain that your notes are clear enough so that if a period of time elapses between the time they originated and the time they are put into use, they will still be effective for you.

4. If you find that you will need to use an entire page, find out if the library can make a photostatic copy for you. This will cost only a few cents and save you valuable time.

5. If at all possible during extensive research work, find out if you can bring a portable typewriter into the library.

6. Check out, even if it is only for overnight, as much material as possible from the library. This will give you time to copy on the typewriter or have it copied under better circumstances.

7. Check to make sure that you are not taking notes over the material you have already covered. You will find that an "original statement" will be quoted over and over again by those who "chew on a bone."

8. Do not make your notes too full. They will only cause you ultimately to have too loaded an inventory of notes to work from.

9. Write plainly, simply, and accurately to ensure that you can translate that which you are going to use.

10. If you want such a concept without resorting to any direct quotes, then write the idea in your own words, which will ensure that you know exactly what it was that you wanted to work with.

Recently, a successful management consultant was asked how he maintained notes for the reports he wrote both for his home office and for the management for whom he was conducting his surveys. This particular management man stated that he did the following:

> Generally when I am out on the job, I carry a pad of $\frac{1}{4}$-size plain paper in my pocket. This is particularly true if I have to go out in the shop or on the production line. If I am going to attend a meeting or conference in an office, I generally bring along a pad of lined paper. If

I am in a situation where it would not be proper to take notes because of the surroundings or because I wished to allay the fears of the individual whom I am talking with or interviewing, I immediately record the notes as I recall them on the paper I have with me. I do this by going to an unused office, or even writing them in the hallway. I do not go to another duty or interview without recording the one which I have just finished. In most cases, however, I deliberately begin taking notes as soon as I begin working with the people or the job.

In the conference type of meeting I take notes almost constantly as through habit I find I can do this even though I keep up with the conversation and with the progress of what we are working on. I even take notes on my own remarks, sketchy as they may be, in order that I might later follow the trend of thoughts.

As soon as the day ends and I go to my hotel room, I sort out my notes and put them in order. If I have a portable at hand, I prepare a rough draft of the day's proceedings from my notes. *I do not let my notes get cold because when they do, I find that I have omitted much relevant material that makes the report more accurate and more to the point.* If I do not have a portable, I sometimes dictate the report into a Dictaphone at the end of the day. I frequently ask the management of the firm to loan me a Dictaphone for that purpose. If I use a Dictaphone, I mail the records into the home office and have a rough draft ready for me to work on when I return to headquarters.

In the event I have neither typewriter nor Dictaphone at hand, I sit down and write as best as possible in long hand a summary outline of my tentative report and try to put down all the key ideas so that they will be suggested to my mind quickly and accurately a few days or weeks later when I get back to the home office. *I never permit my notes to get cold, nor do I like to leave one day's notes get piled up and overlaid by subsequent days' notes.* When this happens I find that I have to interpolate, and I lose the sense of accurate touch and realism that are vital to my report writing.

EXERCISES

1. Using staff directories and university annual reports, develop the current organization chart for your university or college.
2. Arrange for an interview with an individual who holds the type of position in an organization that you aspire to hold. Make sure you have prepared your questions much in advance of the appointed interview time. Write a report describing what the interviewee said.
3. Develop a questionnaire to distribute to business school students about what courses students think are lacking in the current curriculum. Write a summary report from the data collected.
4. Ask your librarian at your college business library to point out to you where major business indexes are located. Develop a floor map showing this information.
5. Try a different note-taking system for one week in each of your classes. At the end of the week try a completely different method. Try taking outlines, using 3- by 5-in. cards, a loose-leaf notebook, or a tape recorder as various alternatives. After experimenting with several methods, decide which is most suitable for you.

FOOTNOTES

1. List is adapted from February 15, 1952, issues of *Modern Industry,* article entitled "The Trade Association: What It Can Do for You," pp. 66–77.

2. Ibid.

3. E. T. Coman, Jr., *Sources of Business Information,* rev. ed. (Berkeley, Calif.: University of California Press, 1964).

4. Webster H. Johnson and Stuart W. McFarland, *How to Use a Business Library* (Cincinnati, Ohio: Southwestern Publishing Co., 1951).

5. E. T. Coman, Jr., *Sources of Business Information,* rev. ed. (Berkeley, Calif.: University of California Press, 1964).

CHAPTER 9

WRITING
THE REPORT

WRITING THE ROUGH DRAFT

It is readily recognized that the design of a product is one of the basic elements in relation to its use and purpose. An automatic washing machine must be *designed* to perform a specific task. It must wash a given amount of clothes in a given time using a given amount of water and producing a measurable result. Without design, we would be running the risk of getting a product that does not meet a specific need.

Design is of equal importance in building a report. Design gives specific direction to what the report writer is attempting to accomplish. The experienced report writer aims his or her work at a well-defined target. He or she knows and understands the objectives. The report writer has already sketched the design when he or she begins the search for information. In the preceding chapter, it was pointed out that "the first step in getting information is to decide what it is that you are attempting to do." The report writer should have *defined the objective* before beginning.

PUTTING THE REPORT TOGETHER

We are now concerned with the "how" of putting the report together so that it will deliver the message with force, clarity, and sureness. We hope that the report will compel the action which it concludes is the wise course. We hope it will convey the ideas, our thinking, our structuring of the situation, to those who are depending upon information so that they might act correctly and wisely. Remember, you are writing because you have a specific thing to say about a particular matter to a certain person.

You are hoping that he or she will understand the problem as you understand it and that he/she will, therefore, respond in the way in which you want. It may be that you hope to impress him/her with the grasp of knowledge you possess and the keenness of your analysis. It may be that you want him/her to move in a way that would enhance the earning power of the organization. You hope that the person to whom you have directed the report will read it with interest and appreciate it; that is why you must structure the report so that it is not only logical and convincing but also appetizing.

How do we go about this business of planning the writing of the report? How do we get ready to write our report so that it will flow naturally from a basic premise through logical steps to a sound conclusion? This job of planning is based on several easy-to-master routines. Presented below are five fundamental steps to report-writing mastery:

Step 1: Boil down your objective into one sentence. This sentence is referred to by some writers as the *topic sentence.* Some writers say, "Put the gist of it into a single sentence." Some writers refer to this one sentence as a *limiting sentence.* This they hope to attain through the use of the report. This purpose permits you to bend your energies to the development of a report that will fit a specific need. Among the different purposes which your report may serve are:

1. To provide information
2. To make a recommendation or move someone to action
3. To give an account of stewardship
4. To keep someone informed as to progress
5. To analyze a specific event, situation, or problem
6. To establish a program of action
7. To report on the results of a survey
8. To report on scientific research or the comparison of methods of performance
9. To report on the result of a test or experiment of a specific or general nature
10. To report the results of action taken to correct a problem or solve a situation

Step 2: Design the manner in which you are going to unfold your story; i.e., what is the best method for telling what you have to say? What is the most natural method? What method will have the greatest impact? What method will hold the reader's interest the best? What method will lead him/her to a proper conclusion in the most direct manner? See the earlier section in the chapter "Communication Reception" on message structure for methods you might employ.

Step 3: Analyze the material you have collected and have ready for use. This is a difficult step. It should not be, but it very frequently is. The trouble with this step starts with the fact that people are not prone to throw anything away. We find it difficult to say, "This just doesn't fit in here, and I might as well not use it." This culling job gives the novice report writer the greatest amount of trouble, for he/she frequently fails to determine what is relevant and what is irrelevant. Several tests can be put to your information, such as:

1. Does it hit the mark?
2. Does it help clarify the main point?
3. Does it help explain?
4. Does it do its work simply?
5. Is it economical information? Does it save time and help streamline what it is you are trying to do?
6. Is it important?
7. Does it duplicate other information that you are going to use?

8. Will the report be better for the inclusion of this material?
9. Does it make for easier reading and quicker understanding?
10. Is the information valuable and authoritative?

There are many methods of analyzing material. No one method will be the exact one for your use. Remember, all of your material is not of equal importance. Arrange your facts in some logical sequence so that your report will flow naturally from one premise to another until it falls logically together in your conclusion. Your own work habits and background dictate what you should do. Here is a summary of some recommendations that various report writers have made for the best means of handling information for analysis and synthesis in the report-writing process.

Dummy out your outline in terms of what steps you believe you will take in order to tell your story. This outline need not be the outline you will finally wind up with. This is merely a "working" outline. Don't let the details of this outline floor you. Write it down. When you have made out this outline, let it be your first guide. Don't worry about whether it embraces all your final concepts. It is just a basic road map. It tells you whether you are heading north or south, east or west. It doesn't need to have detail at this point. Here are two outlines. Study the form which they take:

THE DEVELOPMENT OF A RAW MATERIALS CONTROL PROGRAM AT BREAKNECK MANUFACTURING COMPANY

1. The setting of the problem
   a. Products and production at Breakneck Manufacturing Co.
   b. Special raw materials control problems arising out of the type of production efforts in use at Breakneck
   c. Control program. Objectives of effective raw materials
2. Present methods of material procurement and control
   a. Types of items purchased
   b. Methods employed in purchasing
   c. Purchasing control
   d. Storage controls
   e. Problems arising out of present methods
3. Suggested system for improved material and inventory controls
   a. Production and inventory control
   b. Stockroom control
   c. New alignment of management control over inventory
4. Advantages to accrue from installation of new system
   a. Improved inventory control
   b. Reduction in costs
   c. Reduction in waste materials and items
   d. Improved production scheduling

THE TRAFFIC DEPARTMENT'S ROLE IN INCREASING SALES

1. The setting of the problem
   Defining the problems which make it imperative to consider the traffic department as an important element in the sales effort
2. The traffic department as an aspect of the sales-service problem
   a. The service aspects of delivery dates
   b. The price aspects in relation to traffic
   c. Traffic in relation to quality standards
3. Pool car sailing—the basic problem of the traffic department
4. Conclusions and recommendations

Step 4: Fit your information to the outline. After the outline is tentatively completed, many report writers sort their material and notes in accordance with their outline needs. One can arrange the materials in any one of many ways in order to have them available to fit into the outline. Your facts should be arranged so that they present themselves logically and in orderly procession. If, for example, you use cards, you could arrange all your cards in accordance with your outline needs. You could do this by writing the outline number, such as IV. A., etc., on the card and filing the card in your card box under the proper heading. If you had your notes on larger sheets of paper, you might employ file folders with the topic heading written on each folder, and then arrange your material by sorting it into the proper file folder. You could arrange your notes in outline order in your notebook, if you find it easy to maintain your findings in this manner. Other methods may suggest themselves to you as you work with your materials.

Step 5: Start to write the report. State your governing sentence. This is your aim. This is your objective. This governs everything you are going to say. Write this down. This sentence should be both inclusive and exclusive—inclusive of all you intend to report on, exclusive of areas you are not going to write on. Your second step will be telling your audience—the one who is to read your report—just why you are doing this. Say it simply, say it concisely. The third step is where you begin to work with your outline. Just follow the outline. Fit your materials to the outline, and let it run along.

ALTERNATIVE METHOD OF REPORT WRITING

Some people find it difficult to work from an outline. They are the kind of people who see things in their entirety. The psychologists call this the principle of *gestalt* learning. This means seeing the entire situation through a process known as "insight." For those individuals, the outline method seems slow and cumbersome. They would prefer to tackle the problem by starting right in. It is recommended that these individuals use the intuitive or "whole method" of report writing. Read over all of your material carefully. After you have absorbed it thoroughly and have made your material become a part of you and you feel that you are steeped with the concepts of your problem, put the notes aside and begin to write your first draft. Make as few references to the notes as possible. When you start to write the draft, let the material just flow out. Don't stop at the details—keep going. Write with sincerity. Try to tell the other person what it is that you know about this problem. Tell it to him or her just as you see it. Tell it to them in the same language as you comprehend it. Don't worry about whether it seems elementary to you. Remember that you now know more about this area of information than do many other people in the organization. You have become sufficiently acquainted with the problem with which you have been working so that in a certain sense you are an expert. When you start to write, write through the *whole* report. Do not pay any attention to form, grammar, design, or mechanics. Just get the facts.

INTEGRITY IN REPORT WRITING

One important aspect of the information you are about to present must be singled out. It is the quality of honesty which you bring to the report. *Your intent must be honest.*   **217**

You must adhere to the *spirit* of honesty as well as the letter of honesty. You can, by taking out of context or so arranging the material you have on hand, contrive to give an altogether different concept than one that intrinsic honesty would demand. It is in your hands either to show facts in their correct light or to distort them. It may be that certain aspects of the facts you have do not please you. It is a simple matter to distort the whole subject by suppressing the unwanted or undesired facts.

It is also easy to slant information toward certain goals. This can be done by omitting facts that question the materials that are supporting your evidence. Since these other facts may point to conclusions other than what you desire, it is tempting to suppress them. You may, unconsciously or consciously, exaggerate or minimize still other aspects of the information you have gathered. In the effort to design the ends of the report, the writer may be committing one of the cardinal sins of the neophyte report writer—dishonesty—to himself or herself and to those who will rely upon his or her presentation.

CHECK SHEET FOR PLANNING THE REPORT

1. Have I determined exactly what it is that I am attempting to do?
   a. Have I asked sufficient questions of management or myself so that I am sure of the task to which I am assigned or the project on which I am working?
   b. Have I a fair idea of what it is I am driving at?
2. Have I evaluated all the various methods of obtaining information?
   a. Have I searched all known sources?
   b. Have I selected the method which will give me the material and correct background on which to base my report?
3. Did I make the best use of the material and facts on hand?
   a. Did I use the proper sources?
   b. Did I use too much or too little information?
   c. Does the information fit my objectives?
4. Have I outlined my report so that I know that the information I have collected fits my objective?
   a. Have I determined how I am going to present this information?
   b. Have I selected an outline form that will keep the interest of the reader and lead from the introduction through to the summary in a logical and compelling fashion?
5. Have I determined my audience level, and have I kept my writing level to the audience I am addressing?
6. Have I made up my mind just exactly what it is I am trying to convey in the report? What specific thing am I doing in this report?
7. Have I used the best possible presentation in terms of:
   a. Language selection?
   b. Writing crispness?
   c. Illustrations?
   d. Other devices?
8. Is my report tastefully presented in terms of typewriting and printing?
9. Is the report bound correctly, and does the cover sheet or folder do it justice? Does it look representative of me or my department?
10. Have I provided for sufficient copies so that all interested management men and women might have a copy for reference?

WRITING INFORMAL REPORTS

Most of the reports which flow through the organizational bloodstream of a company can be logically and readily classified as *informal* reports. When viewed in this manner, one can immediately see that "informal" reports in fact cover the whole category of the transmission of written materials. The only exceptions are those types of reports which may be classified as *formal* or *research* reports.

Based on this type of approach, it is obvious that informal reports may cover a whole host of written types of information, such as:

1. Letters
2. Memos
3. Forms
4. Daily reports
5. Weekly reports
6. Monthly reports
7. Quarterly reports
8. Bulletins
9. Special reports
10. Staff reports

In general, one can say that informal reports are internal in character and for the most part used to transmit information up or down the organizational ladder or between units and departments. It may also be said that they tend to deal with the working problems of the business.

One does not need a great deal of formal training in order to prepare and transmit the ordinary informal report. The key to this type of reporting is simplicity, accuracy, timeliness, and pertinence. There should be sufficient information to make the communication complete insofar as the needs of the reader are concerned. The following are several examples of ordinary reporting as it occurs in the business world.

Multiplicity of Reports

There are literally thousands of reports in daily use in the business world. In fact, there has been a concerted effort on the part of some management consultants and systems and procedures people to question the widespread and indiscriminate multiplication of reports channeled to management.

The following list is only suggestive and partial. There may be as many reports as there are activities and variations in business, professional, or governmental undertakings.

A SAMPLE LIST OF VARIOUS TYPES OF REPORTS

Usually Informal	*Informal or Formal*
Production	Wage and salary survey
Inventory	Personnel hiring methods
Accident	Methods survey
Complaints	Time and motion study
Sales	New machine techniques

. . . .

INTERCOMPANY CORRESPONDENCE

From: M. J. Goloff September 28, 1971

TO: Bob Bristol   cc: Jack Hartung

     Accounting Dept.   F. C. Goodwill

SUBJECT: SURVEY OF COAL PILES, P. P. "G" and P. P. "H",

            AS OF SEPTEMBER 1971

    The Engineering Department has made a survey of the coal
storage yard of Power Plants "G" and "H", with the following results:

    Based on a weight of coal of 50 lbs. per cu. ft., there
was in storage at 8:a.m., September 28, 1971:

P. P. "G"	6,865 tons
P. P. "H"	300 tons
Total	7,165 tons

/s/ MJG

MJG/hw

. . . .

. . . .

H. E. Sweetland   June 20, 1971

F. C. Goodwill

Mel Killian

Ed Wilde

On the Production Schedule for the week of June 20 - 25, using average production figures for the items involved, the estimated production is as follows:

	Mon.	Tues.	Wed.	Thur.	Fri.
Estimated Paper Production Tons	105	143	138	102	79

Allowing the filler in the furnish in proportion to the standard ash test in the finished paper and using the percentage of converted paper stock called for by our standard furnishes, our consumption of paper stock should be approximately as follows:

	Mon.	Tues.	Wed.	Thurs.	Fri.
Converted Paper Tons	65	86	80	61	48

The conversion plant is to check the consumption of finished stock very closely and be sure to notify Mel Killian if mills are not pulling to capacity.

The above breakdown includes only tonnage shown on the Production Schedule for the week of June 20 - 25.

Production-Scheduling Dept.

HES/sk

. . . .   **221**

....

January 29, 1971

Mr. John Botts

Brush-Beryllium Co.

Elmore, Ohio

Dear John:

Would you kindly advise us as to the type of chain now installed in
the tubular conveyor handling the Dross at the Elmore plant, in
Elmore, Ohio. Also, could you advise us as to whether or not these
chains have any seal on the chain pin which would prevent the Dross
from coming in contact with the conveyor chain pin. We understand
that this chain has been changed from the one originally proposed.

Your immediate attention to this request will be greatly appreciated.

With best personal regards,

                                        Very truly yours,

                                        HAPMAN CONVEYORS, INC.

                                        Division Hapman-Dutton Co.

                                        C. Sigardson

                                        Chief Engineer

CS:dr

cc: N. W. Hapman

....

• •

INTER-DEPARTMENT MEMO

TO: J. Dietz   DATE: January 26, 1971

FROM: C. Sigardson

COPIES TO: W. H. Phillips, V. Downs

SUBJECT: Our Proposal #265

—————————————

Please request best price and delivery on ten (10) transfer cans, as per attached Specification #466 R2. Construction and fabrication are to conform to Specification #466 R2, dated 1/7/71.

Attached find one (1) print of sketch #122153-1, one (1) copy of form #RWB-2, one (1) copy Conditions and Instructions; one (1) copy Specification #466 R2, sheet 1 of 2, and sheet 2 of 2. All these items are to be returned with our quotation. Therefore, it will be necessary that your vendor furnishing quotation return all the attached material with his proposal.

Should you require further information, please contact the Conveyor Engineering Department.

—————————————————

C. Sigardson

CS:dr

• •

Quality control	New plant requirements
Absenteeism	New processes
Overtime	Company relations
Purchasing	Opinion survey
Traffic	Sources of raw materials
Shipments	Sources of suppliers
Storage	Substitutes
Accounting	Design changes
Retirements	Material handling
Advertising plans	Market survey
Training program	Educational needs for execu-
Union-management meetings	tive training program
Disciplinary action	Property appraisal
Grievances	Underwriting appraisals
Special area costs	Sales reports
Breakdown	Customer analysis
Car appraisal	Product analysis
Credit reports	Purchasing research
	Compensation

Controlling Informal and Repetitive Reports

Because report writing and report preparation have assumed such important proportions in the modern business world, there has been a strong reaction to their
indiscriminate preparation. This is particularly true of the repetitive type of informal
report. Office executives and management consultants frequently suggest a careful
scrutiny of all the reports that are prepared for management consumption. A check
sheet used for the purpose of determining whether a management man or woman
uses many of the reports that he/she receives is shown below. This check sheet was
devised by the authors for a specific situation to determine if the many reports
reaching the management's desk were actually necessary.

Report Analysis Blank

Name of report you receive. Is it on time?	Important		Can do without	Remarks
	Must have	Informational but not necessary		

Management Usages of Reports

Executives at various levels and in various categories need the information which
reports supply in order to fulfill their directing, controlling, and evaluating functions.

In order for management to keep its hand on the pulse of the business, a constant flow of various reports is almost a must.

With the increase of automation for recording purposes it is possible to have more information in various forms covering more areas than ever before. This creates its own problems, since this information permits the management man or woman to keep in touch with the organization's health but at the same time develops a flood of reports which someone must wade through in order to execute the evaluating process.

Management persons differ as to what they want to report. There are some who feel that any report should be condensed into a one-page presentation. Others believe that although a report should be summarized for rapid digestion, there should be enough substantiating materials to permit the senior management person to delve deeper into the problem if he/she feels the report warrants it.

Most management people agree that one cannot divorce the report from the writer of the report. In the main those people who have the capacity to present their ideas in logical, clear, concise, and nontechnical language, along with the ability to see the nub of the problem and to make good recommendations, are those whom the management man or woman tends to depend upon. It is axiomatic that an individual ought to be something more than just a good report writer, but this skill and ability is one of those attributes that give added strength to the selection process.

Mr. Arjay Miller, former president of the Ford Motor Company, made the following pertinent observations on the usages of reports in the organization with which he was associated.[1]

> The principal objective of top management reporting is to provide the facts so that management is in a position to evaluate: decide and act. To meet this objective, the Ford Motor Company's reporting system includes both regularly scheduled formal reports, which supply background information on recurring management matters, and special informal reports, scheduled as necessary for management discussion of particular issues.

> . . . This does not mean that all our reports are read and given consideration at top levels. Many reports deserve only occasional attention. At the risk of being heretical, we often find such "dead end" reports useful; in many instances, the fact of their preparation forces subordinates to review periodically elements of the business that might otherwise be neglected.

> . . . Probably we make use of special reports outside the formal reporting system more than most companies. One danger in such informal reporting is that only problems of immediate urgency will be considered, while other problems will be forgotten until they become urgent.

> *Reporting to Committees:* In Ford Motor Company, central committees establish policies and review the day-to-day problems of the Company. Responsibilities of particular committees cover, for example, product planning, styling, scheduling, engineering research programs, merchandising, and appropriations. The Committees consist of top management personnel, both staff and operating.

> A large part of our special, informal reporting is made directly to these committees. Meetings are scheduled regularly; committees have permanent secretaries; agenda are distributed in advance; and reports to be presented are based on well-defined ground rules and coordinated before the meetings.

The role of staff work for any of our committees is to obtain agreement on general assumptions and to give direction, through the reports presented, to the discussion of necessary action, including the determination that action *is* required. Through the establishment of ground rules and prior coordination, the committee is less likely to be plagued by what have been aptly termed "unfacts." Reports to the committees usually include recommendations, and often a discussion of possible alternative solutions to the problems raised. Every effort is made to supply all the data necessary for a decision, but not to usurp management's prerogative to make the decision.

In addition to the committee work, our informal reports include analyses made directly for top management. In these reports, there is a wide variation in the form of reporting, depending upon the preferences of the recipient. Some of our officials prefer to work directly with tabulations of data and to develop their own conclusions; others prefer an analysis of the data, with possible conclusions.

Executive Development through Reporting:

One aspect of business reporting often overlooked is its relationship to executive development. In most businesses, particularly those expanding rapidly, the shortage of potential executives is acute. This is especially true where demand for managers is large, as in a decentralized business. Although a great many executive development programs have been established in recent years, business may be overlooking an effective device for such development—its reporting system.

At Ford, both the committee work and the Financial Reviews are designed to serve this function. The special committee reports, usually presented by the person who prepared the analysis, allow the individual to demonstrate his ability to present the report and to answer questions about it. Knowing that he will have an opportunity to present his conclusions develops in the young analyst initiative and creative intuition, and affords him personal satisfaction. It introduces him to top management, and provides an opportunity to observe management in action. Further, the coordination entailed in most of our reports gives him the chance to discuss a problem in many of its facets with a wide variety of technicians and analysts, as well as with top staff and operating personnel.

Criteria of Effective Reporting:

The description of how Ford's management operates in making its decisions and the relationship of our reporting system to these methods probably illustrate our criteria of an effective reporting system to top management. Although we have not formulated a set of such criteria, we do have certain ones in mind:

Data should be designed to improve the quality of business decisions. This implies, wherever possible, showing advantages and disadvantages of alternative courses of action, all profit-oriented.

Data should be limited to subjects properly the responsibility of top management. The important should be differentiated from the unimportant.

Reports should emphasize "reasons why," not just "how much." They should evaluate rather than describe; objective yardsticks should be used wherever applicable.

226

Approximations, even guesses, if clearly labeled, may be useful. Assumptions of the estimates should be included. Management need not accept the estimates, but it is entitled to an informed opinion by a presumed expert. Analysis of errors in projections may be useful in improving techniques.

Information should be presented objectively, with interpretation as free as possible from bias. It is difficult to overemphasize the importance of integrity throughout the reporting system.

Reports, recurring and special, should be simple and easily understood. They should be prepared in accordance with precise terminology and accepted ground rules. It is important that there be prior clearance of data so that those affected have an opportunity to offer suggestions.

Characteristics of Sound Informal Reports

Authorities in the field of informal report writing generally suggest that regardless of the informality of the report, it should adhere to certain standards of presentation in order to be effective for management's use. The following list may serve as basic criteria for effective informal presentation.

1. Is the report clear as to what is being reported? Know your objective and stick to it.
2. "Better late than never" is not apropos to informal reports. Perhaps it may be wiser to state, "Better never than too late for proper action." The report should be presented in consideration of the nature of action in terms of the time span which it controls.
3. Is the period of time which the report covers accurately stated?
4. Does the report clearly and specifically state what happened? Are the comparisons made in the report based on the measurements used by management as standards?
5. What does the report reveal? Does it clearly state the differences or the areas showing good results or poor performance? Make sure you have all the facts and have checked the reliability of these facts and their sources.
6. What's to be done about it, if anything? Does the writer of the report have any comments to make, and are they in keeping with the information revealed in the report?
7. Is the report practical? The report writer must be a realist and present his or her findings in the proper order and in logical sequence.
8. Is the report complete? We must provide adequate proof for either favorable or unfavorable conclusions.
9. Is the report concise? Here length is not the criterion. The subject must be covered, telling in as few words as possible what the report writer wishes to express. The reader must be kept in mind in that he or she must be informed as clearly, simply, and briefly as possible.
10. Is the report readable? Clarity of presentation is a must on the part of the report writer. You should use simple words and simple sentences—correct word usage is important. Clear presentation is important. Make it easy for the reader to grasp your ideas.

WRITING FORMAL
REPORTS

What is *formal* research? The difference between the everyday, garden-variety types of reports and formal research reports lies in the nature of the research and the methodology employed. *Research* is the systematic search for the truth. The main conditions surrounding formal research reporting are:

1. Insofar as it is possible, the facts presented are measured and validated with scientifically calibrated instruments.
2. Controls over the various aspects of the study are maintained.
3. Every facet of the study is so detailed and so recorded that it can be repeated by any research worker in the field.
4. There is no attempt at the outset to prove any preconceived concept or conclusions.
5. To the greatest extent possible, judgment factors are reduced to the lowest possible element.
6. All previous activities in the particular area of study are researched for the light which they may shed on this particular problem.

In general, formal research covers two fields: applied and basic. *Basic research* embraces those activities which push forward the horizons of man's knowledge. It is the quest for the new—for ideas, discoveries, and concepts which will add to man's store of total knowledge. The ends of basic research need not be immediately applicable to any specific purpose. On the other hand, *applied research* bends its efforts toward finding, analyzing, developing, or synthesizing a new product, method, machine, or drug. It is the application of existing knowledge in new relationships.

In the early phases of our cultural and educational growth, the university was one of the few institutions that had as one of its objectives the continuation of basic research. Business and industry, for the most part, stayed in the fields of applied research. Today this distinction has more or less broken down as many types of business and industrial organizations carry on manifold activities which can be described as basic research. However, business and industry still expect to make those applications as readily as possible from any basic research which they may have been able to perform.

Today business and industry have been paying increasing attention to research and development work. Further, there is a continually broadening base to what legitimately constitutes the activities of management as it relates to research. The "experiment" has been moved from the clinical laboratory and moved over to cover the many activities which the corporation must undertake. There is pure research not only in the research and development departments, but also in the departments of personnel, purchasing, marketing, traffic, industrial management, and product adaptability, to name but a few areas. It is well recognized by alert management that profitable research can be undertaken in almost every activity of the corporation.

During the past decade there has come an acceptance of the concept of *operations research* in the business world. In general, it refers to the process of analyzing and probing into business and its environment, using the recognized scientific methods employed in formal research.

Of necessity, this text does not concern itself with the methodology of formal research. Each discipline tends to develop certain methods which are peculiar to its particular field. It may be stated that the safeguards which are established, the controls which are instituted, and the preciseness and the ability to repeat the work are the keystones of what is commonly called *scientific research.*

One writer has developed an eleven-step classification of the procedures involved in the use of the scientific method as it relates to business research.[2] For purposes of review, we are listing them below:

1. Becoming aware that a problem exists.
2. Defining problem and purpose(s) of the research.
3. Set forth hypotheses as to cause(s) and/or solutions of the problem.
4. Determine what information will be required.
5. Decide which methods to use in collecting information.
6. Collect information or evidence.
7. Compile findings in systematic form.
8. Analyze findings to determine whether they substantiate or eliminate hypotheses set up in Step 3.
9. Write final research report to bring out full significance of findings and any indicated conclusions.
10. Make specific recommendations as to feasible actions. The usual procedure is to include this step in the final report mentioned in Step 9. (Sometimes, however, the researcher is not supposed to go through this tenth step. It may be considered the job of the management.)
11. Follow up (*a*) to aid in application of recommendations, and/or (*b*) to determine results of application of recommendations.

Organization of the Research Report

The accepted academic way of organizing formal research papers is not necessarily the most appropriate one for writing a report for a busy management man or woman. The accepted organizational structure for academic papers, such as theses and dissertations, is roughly of this order:

1. Acknowledgment
2. History and background (or review of research)
3. Statement of the specific problem
4. Procedure followed
5. Results
6. Conclusions
7. Summary of conclusions
8. Bibliography
9. Appendices

A research report is generally submitted to management in order to communicate a set of facts which will assist in a management decision. The busy management decision maker, however, unfortunately is frequently too busy to wade through all the background material to find out exactly what happened in the research being reported on. The findings of the research project must be so presented that it can be readily read and assimilated. Managers, of necessity, must weigh information in terms of the decision-making process.

Basically, one can see, then, that an academician or theoretician may be reading the report from the standpoint of understanding the entire process being reported on. **229**

Only with the complete set of facts which went into the research can the trained researcher tell whether the study was adequately done, is consistent with other studies in the field, and fits the knowledge pattern of the subject under scrutiny. The management person relies upon his or her research staff to accomplish these things before presenting the findings.

The organization of a formal research report should, therefore, follow these lines:

1. A brief statement of the problem which is under consideration and the major purpose or purposes
2. The background to this problem and the need for research in this particular area
3. What questions it is hoped that the investigation may answer
4. The research method employed
5. The principal sources of the information or data
6. Significant findings and their interpretation
7. Recommendations (if applicable to study)

Although there are times when the background of a research report must of necessity be more detailed, the report writer should bear in mind that the statement of the problem under consideration presents an adequate background to the research being reported.

Physical Makeup of the Report

With regard to the physical makeup of the report, it is usually best to present each of the sections mentioned on a fresh page. Even though the introduction may be only one sentence, it would still occupy one page of the report. This serves several purposes. First, it points out that although the author did not have much to say, he or she felt that it was so important that it should be on a page by itself. Secondly, if there is a lot of white space on a page, it is much more likely that the page will attract attention and be read. Third, this paucity of material on each page early in the report tends to make the reader think that the job of reading it is less formidable than might be surmised by looking at the total size. It tends, therefore, to lead the reader on to at least the next page.

There are numerous studies in which it may be wise to present only the statement of the problem and the findings to management. In this situation the second section of the formal research report would be either a summary of results or summary conclusions, depending upon the nature of the research. Generally speaking, if there are any conclusions which are derived from the research effort, a summary of the important ones should be stated here. If no legitimate conclusions can be drawn from the study, then a summary of results would come second. For purposes of illustration, the summary conclusion section from the report mentioned earlier is presented here. Notice that these are *conclusions*, because they are not a specific reporting of results. They are, rather, inferences drawn from those results and can be supported by them. But they are, nevertheless, not results directly reported.

SUMMARY OF RESULTS

The third section of the formal report may be a summary of results. Here the report writer will want to choose those results which would have most bearing upon the particular problem to which the reader is addressing himself. If the report only reports facts and is not directed toward a particular problem or set of hypotheses, then the most important results in terms of magnitude would be reported. This section should also be brief and concise. If it is found after reviewing the research that there are a large number of summary results to the report, the writer should give serious consideration to developing several reports, one on each facet of the problem, and publishing them separately rather than presenting too many different sets of facts in one spot.

After the summary of results are presented comes the usual statement of the problem. This states specifically what was done, how it was gone about, and what specific questions the report was attempting to answer and in what specific way. In another research report by the junior author, the initial problem to a particular study was stated in a single paragraph in the following way: "The extreme speed with which State Farm has expanded in urban-metropolitan areas in recent years has raised the question of whether or not we have obtained this expansion at the expense of the development of our rural territory. This study is an attempt to arrive at the answer to this question." This is a general statement of the problem; the specific statement of the problem which was listed in the report was as follows:

THE PROBLEM
This market study was designed primarily to answer the following ten questions:

1. a. Is our representation in terms of number of agents decreasing or increasing in the rural as compared with the urban areas?
   b. What is the relative level of our representation in terms of number of agents in the rural and urban areas?
2. a. Is our representation in terms of performance decreasing or increasing in the rural as compared with the urban areas?
   b. What is the relative degree of our representation in terms of performance in the rural and urban areas?
3. a. Is our representation in terms of market potential decreasing or increasing in the rural as compared to the urban areas?
   b. What is the relative degree of our market saturation in the rural and urban areas?
4. a. Is our representation in terms of business-in-force as a measure of market saturation increasing or decreasing in each area?
   b. How do the rural and urban areas compare in terms of degree of market saturation as a function of business-in-force?
5. a. Is our market saturation in terms of total production increasing or decreasing in the rural as compared with the urban areas?
   b. What is the relative standing of the rural and urban areas on the basis of market saturation as a function of total production?

METHODS EMPLOYED

The section which usually follows the statement of the problem in an academic thesis is the one titled "Procedure or Methodology." This usually incorporates the specific data which were obtained and the manner in which they were obtained. Sometimes it is advisable in a management research report to have a specific section titled "The Data" and describe what the data were without going into great detail concerning the way in which they were treated or the procedural methodologies involved. The type of information which is presented in this particular section should be extremely detailed

231

and very specific. There should be no doubt on the part of the interested management person who is reading the report about where the data came from. For instance, if the term "Monthly Sales from the Eastern Region" is listed as one of the data, the numbers used should be described in full as, "This is the monthly sales of widgets for the period of January 1, 1968, through January 31, 1968, for the Eastern District as recorded in the Home Office records. This is the figure which is shown on the report titled 'Regional Results of Monthly Sales in Relation to Quotas' (published by the General Accounting Department). The figures in this study are those shown on this report for February, 1968." If this extreme care is taken when defining the data, the management person will know exactly where they came from and what possible pitfalls there are in these particular data.

PROCEDURE

The next section of the report would be titled "Procedure." In this part of the report the writer tells exactly what he or she did with the data which were had and what methods were used to arrive at the results shown. If, however, the report is about an extremely technical subject with which the management reader is not expected to be thoroughly familiar, the section in the body of the report should tell only in general terms what was done and describe only procedures which the management person can be expected to understand. If a technical procedure has been used and it is known that the reader would not understand a description of it, then reference can be made to it and it should be placed in a technical appendix. Technically trained people can then determine the adequacy of the procedure for the problem, but the nontrained management person will not be confused (or intimidated) by technical jargon.

DETAILED RESULTS

Immediately after the procedure section, the detailed results may be presented. In this section, charts, graphs, and tables are presented showing exactly what happened to the data under study in a very detailed fashion. In some instances it might be desirable to place the detailed results section before the data section, going from the broad, general conclusions to summary results. The nature of the problem and the reader of the report will determine this order in some measure.

The next section in the report would be an appendix which gives specific instruments used in conducting the research and/or other material which substantiates the report but which is not basic to the body of it. We mentioned above the problem of presenting a research procedure which is of such a technical nature that the management person will not understand it. Frequently, one use of an appendix might be to give a layman's explanation of a technical procedure used, so that if the management person is interested in the procedure, he or she can then look in the appendix and get a simple explanation of what took place.

Needless to say, these kinds of things are very difficult to write and require a highly developed knowledge of the subject. Another section of the appendix might contain the technical presentation of the subject specifically prepared for technical people without any apologies for use of technical language and visual devices. The problem of the use of technical language when communicating results which are in a field foreign to the training of the management reader is a very difficult one. The technically trained researcher is always faced with the dilemma of being precise and technically accurate but attaining no communication of the findings or of failing to present the results so that they can be understood by the untrained person and perhaps in the process taking some liberties with the facts as they actually are. How this problem is solved in any one individual situation will depend upon many things—the degree of communication desired, the degree of possibility of distortion, and so on.

The only purpose of writing a report at all is communication. Certainly if after the report is written it does not communicate, then it is of no value whatsoever. It is also true that the burden of accomplishing this communication lies with the communicator, not with the communicatee. If the management person reading your report can't understand it, it is your fault, not his or hers. Because of this, it is extremely important that technical people as well as nontechnically trained people who use technical language and technical research tools devote much time to the question, "How can I say this in nontechnical language?" or "How can I tell the manager (a layman) what I am doing, what I have done, and what it means for him or her and for the corporation?"

General Suggestions

Even though we have been talking about formal research reports in this chapter, remember that, in order to communicate well, one should avoid officialism. An informal style of writing and short sentences should be employed in writing the formal research report. It is formal only in that it has a relatively stable structure and that the activity which it represents is characterized by careful, thoroughgoing, methodical research work.

You will notice there was no suggestion for a section in the research report labeled "recommendations." This was deliberate, as the research report is designed to give management a portion of the facts necessary for the making of a management decision. Management decisions, by their very nature, are such that they require something more than what research can give. This is the reason why research efforts in most corporations are located in a staff as opposed to personnel in a line relationship to top management. Within this frame of reference, then, it is usually not the case that a research report would contain recommendations for management action. To the extent that the researcher acts as a part of management and makes inferences from the research report he or she can, of course, suggest recommended courses of action. In this regard, however, he/she is serving as a line management person rather than a research person. Therefore, it seems appropriate that recommendations for action should be included (if at all) in the letter of transmittal which accompanies most research reports. In this fashion, the writer can give top management recommendations apart from the objective results reported. It is also true that recommendations presented within the body of a research report tend to give the report an appearance of being somewhat less than completely objective. Recommendations by their very nature contain some suggestion of bias, since they represent, even at best, only an informed opinion.

The following is an example of what a well-written formal report should look like: **233**

FRANK BLOCK ASSOCIATES

Dr. Alfred H. Nadleman
Head of Department of Paper Technology
Western Michigan University
Kalamazoo, Michigan 49001

Dear Dr. Nadleman:

Dean Schneider of the College of Business referred me to you regarding
a contemplated survey of the waste paper industry. Because of your
close relationship with the paper industry I am sure you will be interested in such a study.

I am enclosing a brief outline covering the five phases of this industry
that I feel will be important in any study undertaken. I am sure that
additional phases will be uncovered during the actual study. These, of
course, will be either included or discarded at the time of the uncover-
ing. I wish to reiterate my objective in undertaking this study--the
facts and figures uncovered during this study will be compiled in a book
or series of books that will serve as a guide for the waste paper industry
for the next decade.

This type of survey, of course, must be pursued in some depth in order
that sound conclusions may be drawn. These conclusions then would be
projected to show trends and changes in the industry in the future.

I realize that this outline will undoubtedly raise a number of questions
and I will be glad to clear up any questions that I can, either by phone
or by letter. If the project is undertaken with your school, a great deal
of planning, of course, will become necessary before actual work is
begun.

I would be most interested in your comments and suggestions as to the
best possible way of undertaking this survey.

Sincerely,

FRANK BLOCK ASSOCIATES

Harold C. Harvey

HCH:nt
Enc.
cc: Dean Arnold E. Schneider

1.   A STUDY ON THE SOURCES OF WASTE PAPER

1. A fact-finding study to determine where waste paper originates today
   and to determine any changes in the origin of waste paper that might
   be forthcoming in the next decade
   Suggested sources of information:
   a. Waste paper dealers
   b. Waste paper-consuming mills
   c. Industrial plants
   d. Retail Stores
   e. Commercial buildings
   f. Urban and rural households

2. A study to determine the tonnage of waste paper automatically flowing
   to consuming mills regardless of market conditions
   Suggested sources of information:
   a. Waste paper dealers
   b. Waste paper-consuming mills
   c. Industrial plants
   d. Commercial buildings
   e. Retail stores
   f. Urban and rural households

3. A study to determine the present and future trends in architectural
   planning of new buildings in regard to the disposal of waste paper
   Suggested sources of information:
   a. Architects
   b. Architectural associations
   c. Architectural schools
   d. Building superintendents and managers

4. A study to complement the architectural study to determine if industrial decentralization will affect the sources of waste paper
   Suggested sources of information:
   a. Large industries
   b. Waste paper dealers

II.   A STUDY ON THE PROCESSING OF WASTE PAPER

This study will cover the progress of waste paper through a dealer
plant from the time it is received until it is loaded for consumer shipment. It will also project present trends in processing of waste paper
and will draw conclusions as to future changes in the processing of waste
paper.

1. A study of the receiving methods within the dealer's plant
   Suggested sources of information:
   a. Dealer-broker plant operations

2. A study of the grading and cleaning of waste paper in a dealer's
   plant
   Suggested sources of information:
   a. Dealer-broker operations

3. A study of bales and balers within a dealer's plant. (This study
   should cover technological developments in balers that would increase
   the per-cubic-foot density in waste paper bales.)
   Suggested sources of information:
   a. Dealer-broker operations
   b. Baler manufacturers

4. A study of storage methods and facilities in a dealer's operation
   Suggested sources of information:
   a. Dealer-broker operations

5. A study of the shipping practices in dealers' operations and possible future changes
   Suggested sources of information:
   a. Dealer-broker operations

III. A STUDY ON THE TRANSPORTATION OF WASTE PAPER

This study will cover the transportation of waste paper from the dealer-broker plant to the ultimate consumer. It would dwell on present transportation practices and would take in technological developments in the trucking and rail industries which might be projectable into future trends.

1. A study of loading practices in the waste paper industry
   Suggested sources of information:
   a. Dealer-broker operations
   b. Midwest Consumers of Waste Paper files
   c. Consuming mills

2. A study of the importance of bale size and density requirements in loading waste paper
   Suggested sources of information:
   a. Dealer-broker operations
   b. Midwest Consumers of Waste Paper files
   c. Consuming mills

3. A study of the present types of loading equipment and use and projected trends taking into consideration technological developments
   Suggested sources of information:
   a. Waste paper dealer-broker operations
   b. Loading-equipment manufacturers
   c. Consuming mills

4. A study of costs and incentives that affect loading practices prevalent in the waste paper industry and suggested changes
   Suggested sources of information:
   a. Waste paper dealer-broker operations
   b. Truck and rail freight rate committees
   c. Midwest Consumers of Waste Paper files

IV. A STUDY OF STORAGE METHODS OF WASTE PAPER

This would be a study of the storage methods used by consuming mills for waste paper. This study would determine the best present method of storage of waste paper and would project trends as to future methods.

1. A study of waste paper handling and storage equipment
   Suggested sources of information:
   a. Consuming mills
   b. Handling equipment manufacturers

2. A study of the best types of protective structures to be used in the storage of waste paper
   Suggested sources of information:
   a. Consuming mills
   b. Building manufacturers, i.e., Butler buildings
   c. Midwest Consumers of Waste Paper files

3. A study of the mill inventory policy
   Suggested sources of information:
   a. Consuming mills
   b. Mill associations
   c. Midwest Consumers of Waste Paper files

4. A study of the cost of the inventory of waste paper
   Suggested sources of information:
   a. Consuming mills
   b. Midwest Consumers of Waste Paper files

V. A STUDY OF <u>PRESENT AND FUTURE USES</u> OF WASTE PAPER

This study would determine the present usage of waste paper and would project usage trends into the future.

1. A study of the changing requirements of the consuming mills in waste paper furnish
    Suggested sources of information:
    a. Consuming mills
    b. Mill associations
    c. Midwest Consumers of Waste Paper files
    d. Waste Paper Utilization Council

2. A study to determine the flexibility of substituting one grade of waste paper for another in mill furnish
    Suggested sources of information
    a. Consuming mills
    b. Midwest Consumers of Waste Paper files
    c. Mill associations

3. A study of possible new uses of waste paper by the consuming mills or related industries, present and future
    Suggested sources of information:
    a. Consuming mills
    b. Fibre Box Association
    c. Packaging associations
    d. Midwest Consumers of Waste Paper files

EXERCISES

1. You are Joe Billige, manager of systems. You have been asked to recommend an individual from your staff who will be allowed to attend a seminar on new technological developments in your field. It is your opinion that the best person to attend this seminar is yourself. Write a memorandum to Dick Jones, director of systems, whereby you attempt to convince him that you should be the person to attend this seminar.

2. Write a memorandum to your business communication professor comparing and contrasting your best and worse academic experiences.

3. Obtain a corporation's annual report from your library. Write a report about the strengths and weaknesses of that annual report.

4. As the public relations officer in your corporation, you want to inform all the workers in your plants of the importance of safety practices on the job. Design and develop material that could be placed on the various factory bulletin boards to demonstrate this point.

5. Your boss, Clayton Rugglehouse, is most disturbed by the number of personal long-distance phone calls charged on company phone accounts. He has asked you to send a directive, indicating that this practice must cease, to every employee in the company. This directive will be included in their next paycheck envelope. Write the directive.

6. Attend a meeting on campus. Write a set of minutes describing that meeting.

FOOTNOTES

1. Arjay Miller, "Reporting to Top Management at Ford," *California Management Review*, vol. 1 (Fall, 1958, Berkeley, Calif.: The University of California Press).

2. Vernon T. Clover, *Business Research: Basic Principles and Techniques* (Lubbock, Tex.: Rodger Litho, Inc., 1958), pp. 15–16.

USING THE COMMUNICATIVE ARTS IN REPORT PRESENTATION

LANGUAGE USAGE FOR EFFECTIVE PRESENTATION

The purpose of your report, as has been said in a previous chapter, is to tell someone about something. As the writer you are faced with the problem of determining not only *what* you are going to tell, but also *whom* you are telling it to. The writer has to think of two things:

1. What do I want to say?
2. To whom am I saying it?

Up to this point in this text we have dealt largely with the problem of determining *what* is to be said. In this chapter we will begin to concentrate on the person to whom we are addressing our message.

One of the basic principles which the effective writer of business reports must observe is that *people are different*. Various members of a management team possess personal characteristics and personal capacities in the same degree that report writers, for example, possess different abilities. If one has expectations of delivering a message or moving someone to action, one must fully understand the language symbols which the recipient of that message will readily understand.

Specialized Vocabularies

One of the elements that tend to differentiate people is the use of specialized language. The various professional, technical, and scientific fields, as well as the major fields of business and industry, such as oil, railroading, insurance, banking, and electronics, have developed over the years a communication network of meanings that are very clear to the initiated and generally meaningless to the uninitiated. This communication network is composed of a vocabulary of words, abbreviations, and signs. Any specialized jargon was dubbed "gobbledygook" by Maury Maverick, who as a congressional representative from Texas became irate at the involved writing of the bureaucrats.

As we have learned from earlier sections of this text, each human being is an individual receptive organism different from every other receptive organism that walks on the face of the earth. Even if you were to use exact picture and exact sound recordings, you still would not have the same reception and the same interpretation among different viewers and listeners. Now, let us magnify the problem. Written reports are one-dimensional, whereas sound and visual presentation are two-dimensional or three-dimensional. When we add to the preceding facts that the science of semantics teaches us that even ordinary words have different meanings to different people and even different meanings at different times, depending upon the situation in which the word is used, we begin to realize the difficulty of communicating to someone with simplicity, clarity, and directness. It is no small matter to make oneself readily understood through the use of the printed word.

The Science of Semantics and Report Writing

The need for knowledge about semantics as it concerns the report writer will become evident from the following simplified explanations of a very minute proportion of the work of the semanticist as reviewed earlier.

1. *The word is not the thing.* Semanticists correctly point out that we human beings generally use words to describe things, but that the word and the thing are not identical. If we say "apple," what kind of apple do we mean—apple with a worm in it, Delicious apple, Winesap, Roman? Is the apple large or small, green or red, tart or sweet? "Apple" is a word that may have many shades of meaning, and all words have shades of meaning depending on the experience of the reader versus the intent and experience of the writer. Be sure that what you are describing is described fully and accurately so that there can be no misconception between your understanding and the readers' interpretation of what they think you mean.

In order to test this theory the writer asked the members of a report-writing class if they had ever visited an ore dock. Four members of the class raised their hands. "Describe what you saw," asked the writer. The writer was amazed to hear the students describe "unloading ore docks" of the type found in Cleveland and Detroit. The writer had worked as a youth on the "loading" ore docks of Northern Wisconsin and Minnesota and had expected the students to describe this type of dock.

It is evident, therefore, that the meaning of one word or group of words that the report writer may use is not necessarily identical with the meaning which will be given to the same word or group of words by the reader. Stating this another way, each of us carries mental pictures of the meaning of words as they relate to us, and these mental pictures rarely have a common-denominator meaning for all people.

2. *Find the referent.* When one is speaking of Communists, juvenile delin- **239**

quents, methods of improvements, or job evaluation, one must of necessity be specific so that the reader and the writer converge on the same concept. If one is discussing a type of methods improvement, and the reader is conditioned to and understands another phase of methods improvement, then a true meeting of the minds will not occur. It might be that "the parking situation at colleges" is under discussion. One of the discussants may be talking about the paved lot with an attendant, and the other may be thinking about the unpaved mud hole without an attendant. Our minds cannot meet because the words that are used are not referring to the same object.

3. *A fact is not an inference; an inference is not a value judgment.* This at first blush appears to be a somewhat involved statement, but it has value to report writers because an awareness of this general rule will protect them from making errors of judgment under false language colors. Stuart Chase analyzes this statement of Korzybski's with the following illustration:

(1) This train is going at 20 miles an hour. *A fact*
(2) At this rate we'll be an hour late. *An inference*
(3) This lousy railroad is never on time! *A value judgment*
(4) Passengers should avoid the unreliable railroad. *A purposeful communiqué*[1]

The majority of us cannot examine each and every sentence we speak or write in terms of the vast conditions set forth by the semanticist, but we can be made aware of the pitfalls of language usage and can write with our audience in mind. We are not then so prone to become involved in our own thinking and our own language usage to the detriment of those with whom we are trying to communicate. An understanding of semantics will make us aware that our problem of communicating rests just as much with the receiving mechanism of those with whom we are communicating as it does with our sending capacities.

Writing as an Art

So much for a slight brush with some of the scientific aspects of communication. The realities of communication lie in the manner in which we put together words to make sentences, sentences to make paragraphs, and paragraphs to be welded into a whole report. Writing is an art and not a science. It is the art of building, with the bricks of words and the mortar of thought, a lasting yet appealing edifice. One can read volumes on the subject of how to write a report, but only writing reports will teach you the art of report writing. In this area, as in many other phases of life, one must learn by doing.

We start our writing with words, those simple little building bricks with which we have been working all our lives. These are the same words with which we have made our daily adjustments to parents, friends, school, and society. We know more about words than almost any other aspect of our environment, and at the same time we know least about them because we have not given conscious attention to their effect on our own lives and the lives of those around us. The unique power of words lies in their inherent ability to make people move or stand still, to accede or refuse, to be happy or to be sad. Words give meaning to action, explanation to intentions, and color to events. Words are the tools of thought, and with words we are able to transmit our thinking, our observations, our ideas, and our motivations to those whom we wish to persuade, condition, or change. It is also true that words, like the notes on a musical score, can carry the melody of life.

Words make sentences, sentences make paragraphs, and paragraphs make up your report, yet in each paragraph, in each page, it is the words that basically create the meaning. Visualize, if you will, the moving electric news flashers. Only two or three words are spelled out at a time. Your eye reads them, your mind retains the words, and after enough words have flashed across your mind, you have the entire meaning. This is the way your words make sentences and your sentences create the total thought picture.

When you use words, try to use them as a rifle bullet. A rifle is a high explosive aimed to carry a great distance. The shotgun technique employs many little pellets and hopes to hit through scattering. In writing, the rifle technique is preferred because your objective is to get through to the minds of readers. Examine your report word by word. Make sure that each word means what you intended it to mean. If necessary, have someone else read the report to get the intent of the words and the feeling that the words convey in context.

Meaning in Context

In order to illustrate the effect of meaning in context the following example is cited:

> A consultant to an executive of a large manufacturing firm was asked by the executive to review a very important report which the executive was preparing to send to the top management of the corporation located in New York City. After reading the report the consultant asked the executive, "Mr. Hunter, are you asking them or are you telling them?" Mr. Hunter, after several minutes of deep silence, said, "I'm asking them." The consultant then said, "Mr. Hunter, you may think you are asking them, and you may intend to ask them, but the words and tone of your report are those of someone who is 'telling them.'"

Subsequently, the report was rewritten and the word usage and tone of the language employed were that of a report which conveys a proper feeling of asking for assistance.

Increasing Your Word Power

There are a number of books written on this subject of increasing your word power. There is no magic formula or series of exercises that will, per se, develop your word power. The common methods are known to all who are reading this page. One grows by continually making an effort to grow. One gains word power through working in those fields in which words are the basic tools. One must read to gain word power. One must read widely, thoroughly, interestingly, and willingly. The pervasive reader is the one who ultimately achieves a large vocabulary. If you have limited equipment as a report writer, your first task is to begin to read with enthusiasm, relish, and understanding.

Novels written by experts may be as educational to the engineer as a scientific treatise. The novel may not be educational from the viewpoint of scientific knowledge, but it is educative in the sense of increased word power. Some writers have said that to be a great writer, you must be a great reader. Reading is the process whereby we unlock the minds and thoughts of great people who have preceded us and with whom we can now converse through the medium of the written page—through the word images and word pictures that previous writers have used, we gain insight into the mastery of their craft. We share with them how they constructed thoughts which endured and which have the power to convey meaning even though the writer has long since faded from the scene and civilization has marched on.

But reading is not enough; the great reader will never become the great writer until he or she sets aside the reading and begins to restate in the light of his or her own understanding that which he or she saw, felt, read, and understood. It is at this point that the reader and the writer merge to form new thought processes and new expressions. Report writers who would write exceedingly well must first of all have read widely. They then must learn the art of personally interpreting what they have read and observed. Lastly, through practice and effort, they must learn how to express thoughts accurately in their own language and in their own style.

Making Words Work for You

Words tend to have value in and of themselves. The inherent meaning of words gives the reader, under normal circumstances, the kind of reaction which the writer wishes to achieve in the mind of the reader. Writers in advertising firms may spend literally hours dreaming up an exact word to fit into advertising copy. This phenomenon is particularly true in selecting a brand name for a new product.

For our usage, we can divide commonly used words into several categories, such as:

1. Concrete words:

    house
    brick
    glass

2. Emotional words:

mother	hate
son	love
father	desire
wife	traitor
baby	deserter

3. Abstract words:
    loyalty
    democracy
    honor
    faith
    trust

4. Negative words
5. Positive words
6. Nonacceptable words

The report writer has the opportunity to use the exact word that gets the job done. His or her words will in and of themselves frequently have the capacity to move their readers. Knowing good words is important, but knowing when to use them is even more important. A word which in ordinary usage may be classified as good may be the wrong word if used at the wrong time or in the wrong place.

The writer can only bring to the reader what the reader is able to abstract from the written message of the writer. Therefore, the language or word level of the reader is the paramount controlling factor in the choice which the writer makes of words to use in the report. This is not an easy task and it highlights the obvious, yet little realized, fact that writing that is easy to read is often hard to write, and that not infrequently writing that is hard to read has been easy to write in the jargon and style of the writer.

Word and Sentence Simplicity for Easy Reading

Prudential Insurance Company of America wanted to make sure that the written material going out from its offices could be thoroughly understood. So it recently distributed to its people a folder containing a "yardstick" for gauging the effectiveness of their writing. The yardstick was developed by Dr. Rudolf Flesch, author of *The Art of Plain Talk*[2] (Harper & Brothers, 1946). Contained in the folder are these three rules for effective writing:

1. Shorten your sentences to an average of 17 words.
2. Shorten your words to 150 syllables per 100 words.
3. Use about six personal references (boss, clerk, children) per 100 words.

These criteria, referred to on the yardstick, are considered "standard writing." Prudential considers standard writing as being easy to read for most of its policyholders. A quick glance at the material that goes out from an executive's office and that which comes in will reveal that far too much business writing is difficult to read. It is not unusual to find some reports, for example, with sentences averaging from 50 to 75 words. And using those big, impressive words is like making your reader travel a bumpy road in a jeep. Shakespeare identified the inconsiderate business writer when he said, "He draweth out the thread of his verbosity finer than the staple of his argument" *(Love's Labour Lost)*.

Whether you are writing to a Ph.D. or a sixth-grade student, you will be doing him/her a favor by keeping your sentences straightforward, simple, uninvolved. And you will be doing yourself a favor, too; for simple writing is more likely to get across your exact meaning.

It Takes Courage to Write

In our particular culture we are prone to look upon courage as something that can best be exhibited on the football field or on the ice sheet of a hockey arena. There are various shades and types of courage with which some of us are familiar. For example, there is the quiet courage that most people exhibit in mastering their daily problems of life, or the quiet courage of the young man or woman who must serve in the interests of their dependent families. This type of courage is frequently called *moral courage*.

Writing takes courage. It may not be the courage of the warrior, the mountain climber, the ski jumper, or the deep-sea diver, but writing does take a courage that the most zestful performers may not possess. The kind of courage that report writers must have is of the moral variety. They must sit at their desk and work in a severely self-disciplined manner at grinding out words that express their meaning. They must write and rewrite. They must grope for a word that brings the exact shade of meaning to their presentation. They must overcome the temptation to put down just anything, to quit, to perform a mediocre task, to circumvent rough drafting, or to leave well enough alone by not rewriting the original draft. All these temptations they must fight, while constantly evincing the necessary self-discipline to move forward, to continue to work on through the morass of undefined thinking to the ultimate higher level of articulate exposition.

Writing for Reader Audienceship

The editors of *Adult Leadership* summed up what they expected in the well-written article with these statements which are particularly apropos to the effective report writer:

> The best advice we can give to our prospective writers is simply this: Write neither up nor down, but tell your story straightforwardly, with economy of words, and with one eye on your subject and the other on your audience.

> Our experience is that many people write honestly and with competence about things in their field, but give little attention to "selling" the article to prospective readers.

> The article for us if we could get it would be precise and mature enough to interest the scholar, and down-to-earth enough to contain useful ideas for the busy practitioner in any of the many fields of adult education.

> Now how does an article come by these qualities? Each writer works his own magic, of course. It's technique and personality and maybe some other things. On the technical side, it might be worth while to list a few of the things that cause trouble.

> 1. *Overwriting:* Many articles as they come into our office are overwritten for our readership. Introductions are repetitious, and endings linger. The middle wanders. We've often wanted to suggest to a contributor that after he's written his article, he take another look at the beginning and ending. Is there too much wind-up? Too much hemming and hawing before he gets going?

> Often we find the article starts with paragraph four, or at the top of the second page or the third. The importance of an opening that grabs a magazine reader's attention cannot be overemphasized.

> Endings are another special problem. Some endings fail to wrap the subject up in a neat package. They just dribble out. Or they chop off and leave the reader hanging. More often than not, the perfect ending comes half a page or so before the actual one. A fillip saved for the end will sometimes throw a light over the whole article, and maybe help it to stick in the reader's memory.

> 2. *Too much straight exposition:* We prefer articles lightened up, illuminated with a few case histories and concrete examples. Contributors, even when dealing with factual happenings, are prone to keep piling up the expository sentences and generalizations. It sparks a piece immeasurably to say once in a while, "Here's what I mean. It happened to Joe." Whether it really did happen to Joe or not is beside the point. It only has to be something that could have happened to Joe . . . something the writer dreams up, if necessary, to illustrate his point.

3. *Cumbersome phrasing:* All sentences don't have to be short, but it helps if some of them are. A change in pace keeps the reader awake and breathes life into an article. Sometimes when a reader finds an article heavy going, it's because too many sentences deal with more than one idea. The reader then has to concentrate so hard on the individual sentences that he loses sight of the overall meaning.

4. *Gobbledygook:* Every specialty develops its own jargon, and adult education is no exception. A certain amount of this jargon is healthy. It's efficient. It adds vitality. Some of it gets into everyday talk; more of it probably ought to, and sooner or later will. But take it easy; use moderation in this. Some readers are scared off by "professor's talk."

5. *Just plain dullness:* Sometimes it's desirable to emphasize something by saying it several times, sneaking up on it from different directions. But too much repetition is a sure way to lose a reader.

A little attention to putting in a colorful word or phrase now and then helps banish dullness. Even punctuation and paragraphing help. Sometimes things can be effectively pointed up by listing: one . . . two . . . three. . . .

6. *Organization:* Occasionally, a piece comes in that hasn't been very well thought out. The scurrying practitioner—the action man—is the one most likely to trip up here. Some sober thought about effective presentation often saves considerable time in rewriting.

Please keep our readers in mind while you're writing, and stop writing when you're through, and don't wind up before you start. That's all.[3]

FIFTEEN RULES FOR REPORT WRITING

1. Write like you talk and keep in mind the image of the person to whom you are talking. Use commonly understood words or those words which the person you are directing the report to will readily grasp.
2. Keep your sentences short. Research shows that reading becomes more difficult when sentences exceed twenty words. Sentences in *Time* and *Reader's Digest* average only 16 to 17 words. This length sentence needs little or no punctuation except the ending period. If necessary, "break up" long sentences.
3. Simplicity is the keynote to clearness. Simplicity and clearness are the outcomes of clear thinking. Think through what you have to say, then write it, then correct your writing to add to its simplicity and clearness.
4. If your writing or explanations become involved, stop. Start again with a new approach using new ideas.
5. After you have completed your writing, read what you have written carefully. Now start crossing out all extraneous words. Do not "fall in love" with some of the pet sentences and phrases which you have used. Every word that is not necessary should be crossed out. Extra words make sentences involved. The simplest sentence carries the fewest words, but they are the words that do their job effectively.
6. When you are writing your original draft, don't worry about grammar, punctuation, or the mechanics. Keep going so that you will get the feel of what you are doing and the action of your thoughts as you project them on paper.

7. Keep the paragraphs short and uninvolved. Keep each paragraph on a central idea.
8. Do not "shadow box" in your writing. Step right in and start talking about what it is that you are presenting. Long, involved introductions risk losing the reader before he/she gets around to learning what you are writing about. Stick to the main concept about which you are writing.
9. Use an introduction that will attract attention. Readers are generally busy people and their curiosity must be aroused sufficiently so that they will want to read your entire presentation.
10. List or summarize main points throughout your presentation so that the reader will be able to quickly grasp the major concepts.
11. Whenever possible, employ visual devices such as charts, graphs, tables, and other summarizing devices.
12. Give your writing style sufficient variety to keep reader interest alive. Avoid monotony of effect or anything which dulls the interest of the reader.
13. Give your writing "action" by using active verbs.
14. Use words that move people to action and which are acceptable to them insofar as you can judge.
15. Never become satisfied with what you have done. Read, criticize, write, and rewrite, and then meet your deadline.

STATISTICS AS A MEANS OF PRESENTATION

Numbers are everywhere within an organization, for numbers are the chief means of recording and determining facts about the organization. The growth of sales, the cost of manufacturing an item, the time involved in delivering a shipment—all these and more are recorded in numerical form. In addition, numbers may serve as names for classification codes, as, for instance, an employee's time-card number or the number of a payment voucher or the numbers in an intricate number system governing inventory control.

As you can readily see, numbers may serve as the measuring stick or even as the language of a segment of a business enterprise. It is obvious that the accounting function of an organization relies almost exclusively on the function of numbers to achieve its end purpose. From the recorded activities of business, whether they spring from finance, sales, purchasing, or other endeavors, come the statistical data which serve as the fundamental measuring and relationship tools which management must use to determine not only where it has been but where it is going.

Ordinal Numbers and Cardinal Numbers

It can be said for our purposes here that statistics are those numbers which designate facts about an organization or activity. Since numbers are in the province of mathematicians, mathematicians have, for their purposes, divided these numbers into two basic groups: ordinal and cardinal numbers.

Ordinal numbers give only the order or the ranking of the facts which they represent. For example, a group of salespeople may be ranked from best to worst, with the best one given the rank of first, the next best given the rank of second, and so on. All that ordinal numbers tell us is the "order" of the things they represent.

Statistical work, for the most part, is related to cardinal numbers. A *cardinal number* can not only tell us the order of things, but it can be added, subtracted, multiplied, and divided. Since ordinal numbers cannot be treated and worked with as can cardinal numbers, it can be readily seen that it is with cardinal numbers that statisticians and mathematicians carry out their investigations and inquiries. For example, we know that the production of 12,000 tons is two times as great as that of 6,000 tons. We do not know, however, that the salesperson who is ranked twelfth is twice as bad as the one ranked sixth. He may be ranked twelfth on the basis of only a few less sales than the person ranked sixth.

Index Numbers

Another classification of numbers found in business organizations is included under the general class known as *index numbers.* These might be percentages, ratios, densities, rates, and so on. These will be discussed in more detail later on. Meaningful numbers which may form the basis for management decisions may be found in practically all areas of business activity. It is up to responsible management people to make use of these numerical facts in the decision-making processes.

It is for this reason that many corporations maintain large statistics-gathering and statistics-processing departments within their organizations. The recognition of the need for accurate up-to-the-minute numerical information about the various aspects of the business activity as a sound basis for management thinking is commonplace today.

It will be noted that we have talked about numbers rather than statistics up to this point. In common usage, "statistics" is employed synonymously with the word "data" or "numbers," as "statistics of highway accidents." It is really more precise not to use "statistics" in this sense, but to say "data or figures of highway accidents." *Statistics* really refers to the collection, presentation, analysis, and interpretation of numerical data. It is not a science in itself, but rather a method of science and is an indispensable tool for the report writer and the research worker, as well as for the management person.

Statistics May Be Inferential or Descriptive

The science of statistics can be divided into two general categories: descriptive and inferential. The area of descriptive statistics is concerned with the use of numbers—cardinal, index, etc.—for describing facts, conditions, or situations. One instance of the employment of the methodology of descriptive statistics would be the annual report of a corporation. Here we would in all probability find various relationships expressed governing such basic facts as the corporation's share of the market, the production per employee, rates of investment, ratio of capital to total assets, sales, gross payroll expenditures, and average hourly rates. Sometimes the annual report gives index numbers.

There are groups of statistical information which are presented in annual reports which fall under the general terminology of *accounting reports.* Accounting information is in reality statistical information as it relates to the dollar value of the corporate activities. One may know how many hours of direct labor it takes to produce product A, but in accounting terminology the hours are expressed in "cost" which is the price paid for the hours of labor. In general, accounting information deals with profit and loss concepts and balance sheet concepts as measures of the effectiveness of the organization.

Statistics is the numerical reporting system of the organization. In this sense, statistics presents historical data to be reviewed, analyzed, and evaluated by management. This may be done in a comparative fashion or through charts and graphs depicting in visual form the statistical relations which have occurred.

There is, however, an even greater usage that can be made of statistical information—from a managerial viewpoint. This is in the area of planning based on the predictive value of information as it is translated into trends. This body of statistical manipulation is commonly referred to as *inferential statistics.*

Inferential statistics, however, rather than describing what the state of things now is, makes predictions (through the use of probability language) about the state of things to come. In general, this is done by using the technique of sampling and requires a much greater technical background on the part of the user. In this book we will be concerned primarily with the utilization of statistical methodology in its descriptive rather than its inferential sense. However, the report writer should be as familiar as possible with the area of inferential statistics. The more he or she knows of this area, the more valuable the writer will be as a member of the management team.

Statistical Safeguards

It is presumed that report writers have a working acquaintanceship with normal statistical methodology. The possession of the tools of statistics does not automatically guarantee that report writers will observe the underlying soundness of the information they are transmitting to their management and upon which their management may act. For this reason, it is well to review a number of benchmarks which the researcher or report writer should constantly keep in mind in the form of check points or questions when he or she presents statistical data:

1. To what extent do the numbers which I am going to use accurately represent the underlying facts about my subject? An illustration of what we mean is cited by Sir Josiah Stamp in his book *Some Economic Factors of Modern Life.*

> Harold Cox, when a young man in India, quoted some Indian statistics to a judge. The judge replied, "Cox, if you were a bit older, you would not quote Indian statistics with that assurance. The government is very keen on amassing statistics—they collect them, add them, raise them to the nth degree, take the cube root, and prepare wonderful diagrams. But what you must never forget is that every one of those figures comes in the first instance from the village watchman, who just puts down what he damn pleases."[4]

2. Have I accurately and properly applied the technology of statistics to my data? The report writer, in working on a problem, can either develop new statistics or analyze those which already exist within the organization. As we mentioned before, a broad, theoretical knowledge in statistics is an important management tool. The individual trained in statistics has a much wider range of possibility in the presentation and development of quantitative data.

Statistical concepts with which the researcher should have at least a working knowledge are as follows: average, arithmetic mean, mode, median, central tendency, weighting, range, index numbers, time series, frequency distributions, arithmetic progression, geometric progression, percentages, ratios, and normal curves.

The statistical subjects with which a researcher should have at least a nodding acquaintance and a general idea of how they are employed are: geometric means, harmonic means, dispersion, skewness, kurtosis, standard deviation, coefficient of correlation, nonlinear correlation, multiple correlation, partial correlation, regression equations, curve fitting, standard error of mean, T tests, critical ratio, chi square, factorial design, analysis of variance, factor analysis, nonparametric statistics, operations research, queuing theory, and statistical quality control. It should be made clear that one's level of statistical knowledge is not necessarily limiting as long as the report writer knows what he or she is doing and recognizes limitations in the data at hand. In the following paragraphs are listed a few improper uses of data which under certain circumstances could destroy the value of a study which otherwise might be technically acceptable.

First is sheer carelessness. Obviously, all of the numbers recorded in a statistical analysis should be accurately computed. The arithmetic should be correct. Although this seems obvious, one should not underestimate the degree of negative impression created in the reader by mistakes of this kind.

Second, the presence of bias is to be avoided. If a report contains bias, it will be easily identified by a nonbiased reader. Although biases and preconceptions may be expressed by the report writer to management, when this is done it should clearly be labeled as such.

Statistical information should always be presented in as objective a fashion as possible. One of the frequent misusages of statistical information is to present noncomparable data in comparison tables in statistical reports. One frequent example of this is the comparison of two percentages which are based upon entirely different magnitudes of numbers. The percentages may or may not be statistically comparable—although usually they aren't. Another error committed by the novice in the use of statistical information is the confusion of association and causation. For instance, it has been demonstrated that there is a relationship between the consumption of alcoholic beverages and the average wages paid to ministers. To draw a logical conclusion from this type of statistical relationship is obviously erroneous.

Other instances of the possibility of error in statistical reports are insufficient data, unrepresentative data, concealed classifications, failure to adequately design the units measured, misleading totals, and poorly designed experiments. Some of the ways in which error can creep into statistical reports will be pointed out in the following sections on presentation of statistical data. A book by Darrell Huff, entitled *How to Lie with Statistics,* is a well-written and cleverly illustrated compendium of most of these sources of error.

The Transfer of Data into Meaningful Concepts

Our last concept in this chapter deals with the manner in which the researcher and report writer can transfer statistical concepts into meaningful managerial concepts. Generally speaking, the research writer should remember that management decisions are *by definition* always based upon something other than a complete set of facts. Therefore, it is highly unlikely that statistical information (which should be nothing other than an accurate representation of facts) will give an unequivocal answer to a management question. Hardly ever will the results of statistical inquiry result in the statement to management, "This is what you must do and the only thing you can do under the circumstances."

The final area of concern to the report writer is so pervading and to such a great extent one of the prime requisites of sound reporting that we find it necessary to devote a full section to its presentation. This area can be stated from the report writer's viewpoint in the following words: "How can I best present the statistical information which I have worked with in such a way that it will be readily meaningful to and usable by management?"

PRESENTING STATISTICAL INFORMATION

As we have learned from the preceding section, the function of our statistical information insofar as management is concerned may be historical, comparative, or predictive. It is the function of the researcher or report writer to so present the statistical information that the management person may abstract from it the most pertinent concepts. It is obvious that the meaning of the report must be understood by those whom it is meant to assist in decision making. In order for the statistical report to fulfill its mission, it must give the reader its information rapidly, lucidly, and fully.

John McElroy of Readability Associates[5] once determined that:

1. Of each $10 spent for voluntary reading for employees, $3 is wasted.
2. Of each $10 spent on copy for customers and the public, $4 is wasted.
3. Of each $10 spent on writing to stockholders, $9 is wasted.
4. Of each $10 spent on required reading for managerial employees, $8 is wasted.

Although we would not go along with Mr. McElroy in his guess estimate of the amount of waste involved in materials presented for reading, nevertheless, a great danger does exist in relation to the cost of preparing statistical data and their end usage. This is particularly true of those organizations that employ data-processing machinery. The possible flow of information is so great and the relationships can become so involved that mere mass in and of itself may bar one from objective and interpretive employment of what is at hand. For this reason, a still greater burden is placed upon the researcher and report writer to use those relationships which are meaningful and to select to present to management from a number of possibilities those statistical findings which are critical.

For the purposes of this section, the authors have designated eight separate modes of presentation of statistical information with which the management report writer should be familiar. Although these divisions are more or less arbitrary and other writers in the field might come up with a different classificatory system, it is believed that these are sufficiently broad in scope to give the report writer a wide latitude in selecting the best vehicle for the presentation of the data contained in his or her report. The eight methods selected are:

1. Textual presentation
2. Tables
3. Graphs
4. Charts
5. Pictograph
6. Component part
7. Charts and graphs
8. Statistical maps and overlays

Textual Presentation

Textual presentation is not a particularly effective way of presenting statistical information because there is no visual organization of the data presented. Most people cannot easily understand data when they are set forth this way, and it is particularly difficult to find a particular figure which has more or less meaning than any other figure. The report writer can, however, direct attention to or emphasize certain figures even in this type of presentation, and can call attention to comparisons deemed important. An example of a textual presentation follows:

> An automobile manufacturers association gives the total of 5,982,342 new motor vehicle registrations in 1967 in the United States as opposed to 5,955,248 in 1966. The State of California had the most new registrations with 571,185 in 1967 against 556,164. New York was second with 544,567 in 1967 against 511,096 in 1966.

Tabular Presentations

Tables are the simplest form of visual aid and consist of the orderly arrangement of figures in columns and horizontal lines, enabling the reader to grasp the significance of the figures presented and at the same time to discard from consideration those figures which are irrelevant. Anyone who has ever had to read extensive figures in texts will immediately recognize the help which tabular presentation can provide.

By arranging the figures that were presented in the textual statement above in tabular form, one can see how much more readily comparisons can be made.

NEW MOTOR VEHICLE REGISTRATIONS BY STATES
Five Leading States and U.S.

	1966	1967
California	556,164	571,185
Illinois	398,174	398,523
New York	511,096	544,567
Ohio	387,257	380,900
Pennsylvania	386,977	374,465
Total U.S.	5,955,248	5,982,342

It is obvious from a comparison of the table with the textual statement that the tabular presentation of this data is briefer and more concise. Also, the logical arrangement of the rows of the table makes it clearer and easier to read. Using columns and rows for the figures also facilitates comparisons.

A semitabular presentation can also be used. For instance, the discussion in the text might be broken down and the data listed as follows:

The three largest states with respect to new automobile registrations in 1967 were:

California	571,185
New York	544,567
Illinois	398,523

In tabular presentations, every table will have at least four essential parts. They are the title, stub, boxhead, and body. There may also be a prefatory note and one or   **251** more footnotes. If the figures in the table are not original, a source note is also included. The following gives an example of a table with all of these parts delineated.

GENERAL CONSIDERATIONS
FOR CONSTRUCTING TABLES

There are two general types of tables. One kind is the reference table, which is primarily used to store information. One example is the official airline guide published by American Aviation Publications, Inc., which in its quick-reference edition is one single table 1,104 pages long. The U.S. Department of Census publishes many tables which are of this nature.

The second type of table is the summary or text table, which is smaller and designed to demonstrate one finding or a few closely related findings in as effective a manner as possible. Generally speaking, the summary table should be simpler in construction than the reference table. Any statistical presentation in a management report should be simple and easy to understand. Particularly is this true with respect to tables, as the tendency of most readers is to skip the tables in any report.

A summary table can be designed and arranged so that emphasis can be placed where it is needed and the rows and columns can be so designated as to demonstrate important comparisons. One of the big uses for tabular presentations is the making of comparisons between two sets of data. Simply setting the data in tabular form does not guarantee that the most important comparison will be emphasized, however. Different juxtaposition of the boxed heads can make a difference in what is most easily compared. For instance, look at the parts of the two tables shown for car and truck registrations by state for 1967.

Comparisons are also aided (and sometimes only possible) if averages, ratios, or percentages are given so that the true similarity can be seen. Frequently, this is the only way "apples can be compared with apples" rather than "apples compared with oranges."

There are many ways of giving emphasis to a particular item in a table. Certainly, the arrangement of the items in the table makes some difference. For instance, if the total figures are to be emphasized, they should be at the top where they are most likely to be seen. If they are to be given less emphasis, they will appear at the bottom of the table. Usually, the extreme right-hand and extreme left-hand columns are also most noticeable to the average reader. Other ways of emphasizing entries are to underline them, to make them in boldface, and to give them italics.

Arrangements of items in the stub and caption of the table are also important in the design of the table, since the basic statistical data may refer to many different kinds of classifications. These different classifications will more often than not appear in some fashion in the stub of the table. If the classification is in either chronological or geographical order, the stub items could be placed in some sort of orderly fashion. That is, if the classification is in terms of years, then the years can be put in ascending or descending order. If the classification is quantitative, then again increasing or decreasing order might be appropriate ways of arranging the stub of the table. Again, for emphasis, it would be possible to rank the items by their magnitude in the most important column of figures or to place the stub classifications in an order of magnitude of that particular column. Obviously, there are no hard-and-fast rules in this respect. The primary concern of the report writer should be to obtain maximum communication of his/her subject matter. Here are some hints for assisting in the detailed construction of a table:

1. *Title and identification:* Obviously, every table should have a title. The title

should be clear, concise, and brief. If possible, within the framework of being brief, it should be so worded as to tell what data are shown in the table. In general, table titles state in order what, where, how, and when. When a title uses several lines, the longest line is first, the second longest second, the third longest third—the lines are arranged in descending order of length. Remember that a title should not be a complete explanation of every figure in the table. If the title is long, perhaps a summary title or identification title can be given, with the lengthy title shown as a footnote or a subtitle. In addition to having a title, every table in a presentation should be numbered so that the table can be referred to by number rather than by title.

2. *Footnotes:* Footnotes should be keyed to entries in the table in some uniform fashion. Frequently, the footnotes dropped from column headings and row headings are referred to by means of numbers, but footnotes to specific entries in the table are identified by some symbol such as an asterisk.

3. *Sources:* The data shown in a table when they are not representative of the material which the investigators collected should be identified with respect to their source. This is true not only because it is courteous to mention the source of data, but because this information gives the reader an idea of its reliability.

4. *Index numbers:* When any index number is used in a table, the caption entry of the row of columns should clearly indicate to what figures these indexes relate. Therefore, the term *percent* or *percentage* alone should be avoided. *Percentage of total* and *percent of increase* or *decrease* are preferable.

5. *Ruling:* Generally speaking, text tables are open at both sides. Certainly, they should never appear with one side closed and one side open. Frequently, also, double-line ruling is used, but this tends to make the table appear more complicated than it really is. All vertical rules in a table separating columns of figures also appear between the box heads which they separate but do not extend above these box heads. There seems to be an increasing tendency to use text tables without ruling of any sort. Below is an example of a table with no ruling involved.

AVERAGE SIZE POLICY IN FORCE
In the United States

Year	Ordinary	Group	Industrial	Credit
1920	$1,990	$ 960	$150	$200
1925	2,270	1,330	170	220
1930	2,460	1,700	210	200
1935	2,160	1,590	220	180
1940	2,130	1,700	240	150
1945	2,100	1,930	270	170
1950	2,320	2,480	310	360
1955	2,720	3,200	350	530
1956	2,850	3,360	360	530
1957	3,040	3,580	370	580
1958	3,220	3,740	380	610

LIMITATIONS OF TABULAR PRESENTATION

Regardless how superior tables are in comparison to textual presentation, they may be limited in their usefulness under certain conditions. If complete tables are employed covering a mass of statistics, they may become too bulky or overwhelming.

TABLE A

Title:

DISTRIBUTION OF GAINFULLY EMPLOYED PERSONS CLASSIFIED BY METHOD OF HOME-TO-WORK TRANSPORTATION WITHIN EACH OCCUPATION GROUP

By Occupation Group	Method of Home-to-Work Transportation					
	Passenger Car (percent)	Passenger Car and Public Transportation (percent)	Public Transportation (percent)	Walk (percent)	All Other Means and Not Reported (percent)	Total (percent)
Professional and semiprofessional	72.3	1.4	12.0	10.0	3.4	100
Proprietors, managers, and officials*	77.9	0.8	5.1	12.6	3.6	100
Store and office clerks, salesmen (excluding traveling), etc.	58.2	1.8	24.5	13.6	1.9	100
Traveling salesmen, agents, etc.*	87.1	0.6	6.0	3.7	2.6	100
Craftsmen, foremen, skilled laborers, etc.	78.1	1.1	10.3	8.0	2.5	100
Operatives, semiskilled workers, unskilled workers, and laborers	67.3	1.0	13.8	14.9	3.0	100
Protective services	72.6	1.7	10.2	7.4	8.1	100
Personal service workers	39.3	1.4	29.5	25.8	4.0	100

Stub:

Footnotes:

NOTE: Excludes persons for whom no travel was required, such as self-employed farmers, proprietors of small stores living at the place of business, etc.

Includes farmers and farm managers who were required to travel to work.

Source Note:

SOURCE: Compiled by U.S. Bureau of Public Roads from motor-vehicle-use studies conducted in 16 states (Ark., Calif., Del., Ky., La., Miss., Mo., Mont., N. Mex., Okla., Ore., Penn., S.D., Wash., Wis., and Wyo.).

TABLE B

1967 CAR, TRUCK, AND BUS REGISTRATIONS BY STATES

| | Privately Owned | | | | Privately and Publicly Owned[1] | | | |
	Passenger Cars	Buses[2]	Motor Trucks[3]	Total	Passenger Cars	Buses[2]	Motor Trucks[3]	Total
Ala.	905,680	2,126	199,276	1,107,082	908,629	6,291	208,101	1,123,021
Ariz.	380,030	950	99,037	480,017	383,017	1,711	104,700	489,428
Ark.	435,546	1,174	181,852	618,571	436,453	4,052	186,498	627,003
Cal.	5,783,057	11,220	951,470	6,745,747	5,808,837	17,066	1,006,047	6,831,950
Colo.	627,927	1,893	173,021	802,841	631,571	2,460	181,519	815,550
Conn.	879,632	3,147	121,330	1,004,109	882,839	3,375	126,943	1,013,157
Del.	129,885	630	38,013	168,528	131,085	665	39,090	170,840

The mass of data presents obstacles to the reader who is looking for simplicity and not involvement. In order to overcome this fault it is sometimes best for the report writer to use only those parts of a table which present meaningful data and which are indicative of the total situation.

When only a part of a table is used, good report-writing practice, particularly in formal presentations, dictates that the writer include the complete table with the report, in the form of an appendix. If this is not advisable or practicable, it may be well to indicate by footnote or other means where the reader or researcher may find the complete published table. It should be pointed out that the latter method is not suggested where the publication is an obscure one not conveniently available to most readers of the report.

For example, census figures in their entirety are readily available in a number of sources. On the other hand, a reference to a table in a specialized trade magazine of some five or six years in the past might not be too easily found by most of your readers. In order to assist them, it would be wise to include this table in the appendix of your report. It would save a lot of trouble for the reader who might find it necessary to verify certain of the data presented.

Visual Presentation

The purpose of illustrations in a report is threefold:

1. To relieve monotony
2. To show a trend or relationship
3. To give the reader the maximum amount of information as quickly as possible

The next six methods of presenting statistical information are all related in that they are all visual representations of the data. That is to say that the data are presented so that the magnitude of the figures is delineated by the visual agreement representation. For instance, in a bar graph the distance on the paper from the bottom of the bar to the top of the bar is in some fashion proportional to the magnitude of the number represented. This is not true in tabular presentation, where the number 2,000 is no different in visual size from the number 1,000. This visual way of presenting statistical data is extremely effective. In many instances, it is possible to comprehend a trend or larger amount of data by one glance. Also, readers are not as likely to skip a chart as they are to skip a table. Since most charts have the symbolic presentation of data also, more information is available. A simple, well-constructed chart or graph is also easier to understand than a table.

There are certain limitations, however. First, charts cannot show as many facts as a table. Second, although exact values can be given in a table, actually only approximate values are shown in a chart or graph. Charts, therefore, are generally useful for giving a quick picture or summary of a situation but not to show the details. The third disadvantage is the fact that charts are more difficult to construct, require more time, and frequently present a problem of reproduction.

GRAPHS OR LINE
DIAGRAMS

In representing statistical data with graphs, curves, or line diagrams, the points are plotted in reference to a pair of intercepting lines called *axes*. The horizontal line is known as the *X* axis or *ordinate*, and the vertical line is known as the *Y* axis or *abscissa.* Positive values are shown to the right of zero on the *X* axis and above zero on the *Y* axis. The point at which the two axes intersect is zero for both *X* and *Y* and is called the *point of origin.* Both axes increase as you move away from the zero point, or the point of origin.

Line diagrams and curves may use any or all of the four quadrants formed by the intersecting axes. Generally speaking, when we are dealing with statistical data, both *X* and *Y* variables are positive, and so we, therefore, use only the upper right-hand quadrant. Frequently, however, one statistical measure may be positive and the other both positive and negative, in which case we would use two quadrants, either the left and right or the upper and lower on the right-hand side. Since both *X* and *Y* values are negative in the lower left-hand quadrant, this quadrant is very rarely used in presenting statistical data. One point should be made. In all instances, at least one axis should have a zero point shown on it. Later in the text we will demonstrate why this is so.

Curves and line drawings are used most often for picturing time series and for showing frequency distributions. Qualitative data are rarely depicted by curves because a line drawn between one measurement and the next generally indicates a continuous (as opposed to a noncontinuous) variable, and qualitative classifications of data rarely lend themselves to this assumption. When plotting data in a time-series curve, the method used depends upon the type of data to be plotted. There are period data and point data. *Period data*, such as total sales per month or per year, refer to a description of the data for the entire period of time. *Point data*, on the other hand, such as price quotations and temperature readings, refer to a particular point in time. When chronological data are shown on a curve, the chronological classification—for instance, years, months, or days—is placed on the horizontal or *X* axis. The primary difference between the use of point data and that of period data is in labeling the intervals on the *X* axis. When presenting point data, label the vertical lines in the graph as if they extended. The curve is then plotted from one line to the next. When period data are being represented, spaces rather than lines should be labeled, and each observation is plotted within the space at the point in time to which the data refer. An example of a curve showing period data plotted is shown in Figure 10-1.

Line charts are also used to depict frequency distributions. Figure 10-2 gives an example of a frequency distribution plotted as a line chart. Obviously, these data could also be shown in a bar chart with each point in the chart representing the height of a bar. Ordinarily, the decision between making a line chart and using a bar chart depends upon the nature of the data. Again, if the data with which the frequency distribution deals are discrete or noncontinuous, the data are represented by bars; if, however, the underlying variable is continuous, such as the one shown, it is represented by a curve.

Here are some rules for representing statistical data in line-graph fashion: The most important rule is the inclusion of a zero point on the vertical scale. Although you will see this rule violated in many places, omitting a zero point almost invariably results in giving misleading information because the visual impression is erroneous. The reason for this is that the height of the points on the curve are not in direct proportion to the magnitude of the numbers which they represent. In some instances, it is difficult to show the zero point and still show the fluctuation in the line graph adequately. When this happens, it is possible to show the zero point and then a definite break all the way across the chart before beginning the additional numbers. Sometimes the bottom of the chart is serrated; other times a jagged edge is placed on the bottom of the chart.

The research writer should emphasize the zero line by making it heavier than the other marginal lines. In similar fashion, a 100 percent line or other base might be

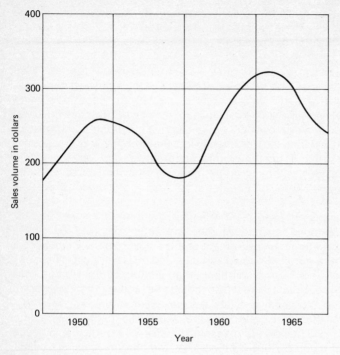

Figure 10-1

stressed. Coordinate lines should be drawn very lightly; no more coordinate lines than necessary should appear. Frequently, all coordinates are omitted. So that the reader of the report may understand completely what is in the chart, each scale should be clearly labeled. Not only should the nature of the data be given, but the specific units

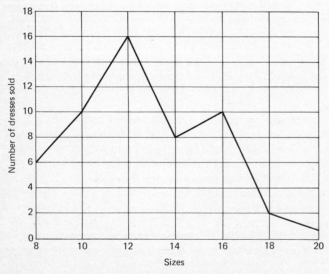

Figure 10-2 **Sales Volume by Sizes for**
Month of October, 197-

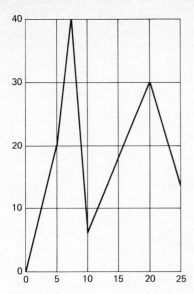

Figure 10-3

used should also be stated. The rules with respect to giving sources, designing titles, and so on, which were given for constructing tables, would apply.

In addition to the rule concerning always using a zero point, the choice of the size of the scale, both vertically and horizontally, has a marked effect upon the final appearance of the line chart. Notice Figures 10-3 and 10-4. Both of these line charts present the same statistical information. Condensing the values on the *X* axis on one and elongating the *Y* axis gives an impression of much greater fluctuation in the data presented than when presented as in Figure 10-4 where the *Y* axis is compressed and the *X* axis is extended.

All lettering on any type of visual presentation, including the scale labels, the values, the legend, the curve labels, and any other words or figures, should be placed horizontally if at all possible. Occasionally, space limitations may make it imperative

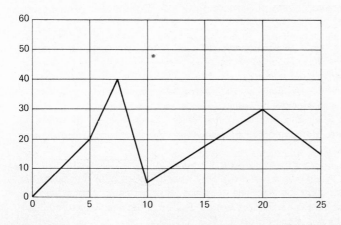

Figure 10-4

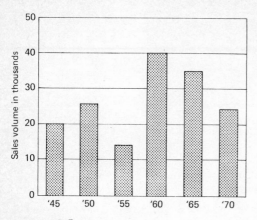

Figure 10-5

that a vertical scale label be used, but this should be avoided. The report writer can obtain a number of lettering devices which may help him in making charts and graphs. Any store which handles engineering drawing equipment can supply these devices.

BAR CHARTS

The simplest form of bar chart, of course, merely shows the relative degree of magnitude of the data being presented from one classification to the next by the height of the bar. The simplest form of this is shown in Figure 10-5. All bar charts should have a scale which is constructed in the same manner as one axis of a line chart. The same caution about the use of a zero point applies to a bar chart. Bar charts may be presented either vertically, as is the customary procedure and as is shown in Figure 10-5, or they may be shown horizontally, as in Figure 10-6. Vertical charts are used when chronological data or other quantitative data are presented. When making comparisons of data classified qualitatively or geographically, most often horizontal bars are used. For example, this is usually done by showing two separate sets of bars of different coloring or different types of cross-hatching. Here are some rules given by Croxton and Cowden in *Applied General Statistics,* Second Edition, for drawing bar charts.[6]

1. Individual bars should be neither exceedingly short and wide nor very long and narrow.
2. Bars should be separated by spaces which are not less than about one-half the width of the bar or greater than the width of a bar.
3. A scale is generally useful. It should be about one-quarter the width of a bar from the top bar or from the left bar if the bars are vertical.
4. Guide lines are an aid in reading the chart. Sometimes a chart is enclosed and the guide lines are extended through the entire chart. Sometimes the chart is not enclosed, and the guide lines are cut off.
5. When showing a time series graphically, a bar chart or a curve may be used. The curve permits the reader to obtain a notion of the general change which is taking place in the series, while the bar chart permits him to make specific comparisons between designated years. Sometimes a bar chart can be used to show positive and negative values by changing the direction of the bar.

PICTOGRAPHS

The *pictograph* is a pictorial unit bar chart in which each symbol is given a numerical value. Although the pictograph has been used quite a bit in the past, if the report writer is not careful, use of it can lead to distortion of the facts. Each unit should be given a specific value, and differences in magnitude should be shown by greater or fewer units rather than by increasing the size of any unit. An example quoted from a previously mentioned book, *How to Lie with Statistics*, indicates what is meant.[7]

> First is shown the dollars per week earned in the U.S.A. Shown in a bar chart, they look like the chart below. However, in translating this into a pictograph, a money bag could be drawn to represent the foreign country's $30, and then a second money bag which is twice as tall to represent the United States' $60. That's in proportion, of course. The catch is that because the second bag is twice as high as the first, it is also twice as wide. Therefore, it occupies not twice but four times the area on the page. The numbers still say "two to one," but the visual impression, which is the dominating one most of the time, says the ratio is four to one. (Actually, since these are pictures of objects having three dimensions rather than two, the second money bag also looks twice as thick as the first. So the volume of the $60 bag is eight times the volume of the $30 bag, or, in proportion, $240.)

Although pictographs have been in wide use in recent years, the trend seems to be to use bar charts on a background of appropriate art work rather than to incorporate the pictorial representation into the specific statistical representations. An example of this is shown in Figure 10-7.

Here are some rules for drawing pictographs as suggested by Rudolph Modley and Dino Lowenstein in *Pictographs and Graphs,*[8]

1. Symbols should be self-explanatory.
2. Changes in numbers are shown by more or fewer symbols, not by larger or smaller ones.

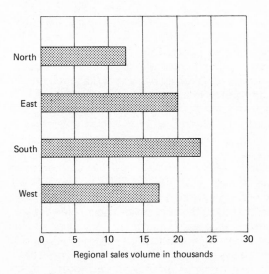

Regional sales volume in thousands

Figure 10-6

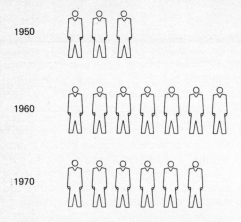

1950

1960

1970

Figure 10-7 **Sales Department Employees**

3. Pictograph charts should give an overall picture, not minute details.
4. Pictographs make comparisons between things; they do not make flat statements about one particular thing.

COMPONENT-PART CHARTS

Because almost all management utilizes percentages and proportions, a useful tool of the report writer is the *component-part chart*, which gives the percentage proportion represented in terms of representative proportions of a particular area on a chart. Figure 10-8 gives an example of a component-part chart. Frequently, this kind of information is demonstrated in the traditional pie diagram, as shown in Figure 10-9. Actually, accuracy of judgments made from studying the chart is about the same whether it is a bar chart or a pie diagram. Naturally, pictorial representation of data can be accomplished this way, too, and a bar may be used to represent a dollar bill or a pie can be used to indicate a coin. Figure 10-10 indicates how a bar chart can be combined with a proportional component-part chart. The charts could show the increase of magnitude from one year to the next of taxes, and the subdivisions could show pictorially the proportion of the total taxes taken up by each of the four different types of levies. Although a bar chart can be used in this fashion very well, curves and line charts can also be used in this way.

STATISTICAL MAPS

Statistical maps are a particular type of graphic device for showing quantitative information geographically. Statistical maps consist of representations of geographic areas shown either hatched, shaded, or colored. Statistical maps also include dot and pin maps. Figure 10-11 shows a shaded map which gives an indication of the penetration of various sales throughout the United States. Dot maps are also used, the frequency of dots indicating the relative density of the statistic being shown. Sometimes in some instances the size of the dots is varied as the magnitude of the data being presented varies.

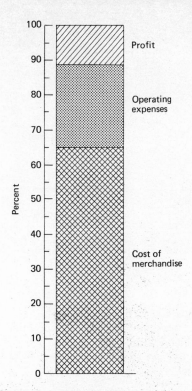

Figure 10-8 Distribution of Sales

Figure 10-9 Distribution of Sales

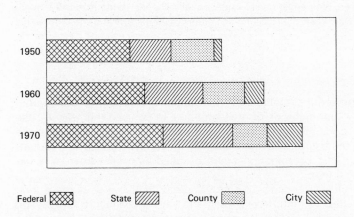

Figure 10-10 Taxes Paid

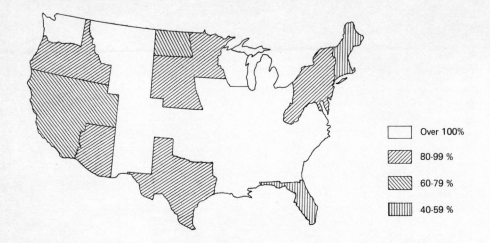

☐	Over 100%
▨	80-99 %
▧	60-79 %
⊞	40-59 %

Figure 10-11 **Sales Increase, 10-Year Period**

It is also possible to combine bar charts and statistical maps. Colors can be used also and geographical areas separated so that the reader may visualize exactly what territory is referred to. One caution should be given about the correct use of geographical maps. These maps also can be distorted. An example is quoted from *How to Lie with Statistics.*[9]

> A map was shown which gave the proportion of our national income which was now being taken by the federal government. He did this by shading the areas of states west of the Mississippi, except Louisiana, Arkansas, and part of Missouri to indicate that federal spending has become equal to the total incomes of the people of all those states. The deception lies in shading states having large areas but, because of sparse populations, relatively small incomes. With equal honesty (and equal dishonesty), the mapmaker might have started shading New York, the New England states, and Pennsylvania and arrive at the same conclusion.

OVERLAYS

A recent method of presenting statistical information is the use of transparent overlays. All the other visual methods of presentation can be used this way. A base chart gives the scale, grid, title, and so on, and comparatively simple data are superimposed through the use of different transparent overlays made with different-colored transparencies. This combination could be used as a line drawing, a bar chart, or even a statistical map.

Obviously, all the rules of constructing charts apply to this way of presenting data. It is an extremely effective method of presentation in that a specific comparison can be made and then removed. That is, on a chart of a single dimension once all the information is on the chart, it is difficult for the reader to eliminate some of the information; but when overlays are used, the reader can pick only those overlays that he/she is particularly interested in. Also, overlays permit the report writer to show the cumulative effect of different numerical data. One significant limitation of the use of overlays is in the reproduction of the report. However, this procedure is extremely effective when an oral presentation is made and only one set of visual aids is desired. The oral report will be covered in the following section.

Technical Assistance

The report writer or researcher may not always need to prepare his/her own illustrations. Many corporations furnish their report writers with technical assistance. Some corporations have full-fledged research departments that can gather the needed statistical data, so that the report writer needs merely to outline the problem to the research department, which will have staff members available to do actual field work. Often a company librarian can gather necessary secondary data and statisticians can help in compiling and interpreting the data. The same is true of the illustrations. Some larger companies have art staffs that will be glad to prepare charts, graphs, and other illustrations if the artists are furnished with proper information and sound direction.

Another possibility, where money is not a limitation, is the farming out of this type of work to independent artists. At first this practice might seem to be wasteful and expensive, but if you figure costs on an hourly basis and compare the report writer's time with that of a full-time professional artist, you may find it cheaper to have the illustrations prepared by the professional.

Some companies find it economical to make use of aids already prepared. There are vast numbers of charts, graphs, and the like, prepared by government departments, which a report writer may use at will; should the writer wish to publish the material, permission is easy to obtain. With this type of technical assistance available, report writers should think twice before limiting themselves to those illustrations which they must of necessity prepare for themselves.

METHODS OF PRESENTATION

To this point in this text one may have been led to believe that all reports, after careful preparation, are processed through the proper channels and finally reach the decision-making level of management in their pristine form. This is far from the way reports are employed in the business world. There are three possibilities through which the report may lead to decision-making activity. These are:

1. The report may be sent through channels to be read, digested, and used for further action.
2. The report, after preparation, may be orally presented to the proper committee or management team by the one who has taken the responsibility for the preparation or by his or her superior.
3. The two methods may be combined in that the report may go through channels and then at a later date a meeting may be held in which important aspects of the report may be orally analyzed and the supporting materials questioned and investigated.

In actual practice, the last two methods, both involving oral reporting, are the most commonly employed for following through on the problems of the business which have generated the need for a report. The most effective reporting is that in which the report writer, at a designated meeting, distributes to his or her colleagues the final form of the report and then proceeds to explain the various elements embodied in the study. At this type of meeting, the writer will find questions being raised as to the various concepts being worked with and also as to the nature and meaning of the materials being presented.

In this section we will be discussing much of the same information we discussed earlier in the sections on oral communication in Chapters 3 and 4. We do, however, believe it is important enough to bear repeating here, from this somewhat different writing perspective.

The Oral Report and Visual Presentation

In making the oral report one may employ a variety of devices. The most common of these devices are:

1. Straight presentation with no props or any distribution of supporting aids.
2. Distribution of the report accompanied by an oral presentation. The report itself is used as the text material. The main points are emphasized.
3. The oral report is presented and supported by effective visual aids.

It is the last method with which we are particularly interested in this chapter, since it is one of the most effective devices for presenting a particular set of facts to communicate research findings or, perhaps, to influence action in one direction or another.

As we have mentioned previously, some of the *advantages of an oral report* of this type are as follows:

First, you can communicate to a large number of people at the same time. In the routine presentation of a written management report, only a limited number of persons can be reached because some people are frequently out of the office, some are unavailable, some don't read their mail as often as others, and some may not be predisposed to wade through a good-sized document. It is unlikely that your report can reach your entire audience simultaneously when it is sent through regular channels.

Second, you can be certain that you have communicated at least to the point of having the contents of your report strike the perceptual mechanisms of the intended communicatee. You can never be sure of this with a written report. For example:

JONES: "Oh, I say, Mr. Bigdome. What did you think of my report on widgets?"
MR. B: "Great report, Jones! Wish I could have done that myself."
(To himself, "Gotta find that thing and read it one of these days.")

Third, when you employ the oral report, you are utilizing the advantages inherent in communicating with more than one sense organ. A well-conceived oral report uses both an audible and a visual presentation, and it is possible in an oral report to use other sense organs, like smell, feeling, and taste. It is a psychological fact that the more sense organs that are involved in the acquisition of an idea, the more readily is this idea accepted and the longer is it remembered. It is also true that the experienced management man or woman can observe reactions in an oral presentation. The speaker is in a position to work with the feeling-tone of the audience.

Fourth, an oral presentation is more likely to influence subsequent behavior than is a written report. It is possible to get group approval at the time of presentation. This is not always true, but in the usual management report it is much more likely that immediate action will be taken on the basis of an effective oral presentation rather than on the basis of a written report. It is a known marketing fact that the most effective selling is accomplished through face-to-face sales presentations. For instance, the most difficult products to sell are intangibles such as life insurance. To date, the only effective way of marketing life insurance is with the use of a salesperson who makes an oral presentation of his or her wares. It is obvious that although this may be a more expensive method than merely mailing letters, it is employed because of its effectiveness.

Another advantage of oral reports is that they are more dramatic, have more impact, and make a better impression on management personnel. With the plethora of written material that passes across management people's desks these days, they are much more likely to be impressed by and to note the impact of a report which gets to them through committee meeting channels where, away from their desk, in a modern conference room, they share and participate in decision making with their peers and actually become a part of the report deliberations. They have, in fact, through this device participated in the report recommendations.

This participation serves as a fifth advantage of the oral report. Only in an oral report can you get an immediate reaction to the ideas and information presented. In this fashion, if it can be determined from the participation that the presentation was unclear or that the level of communication desired was not achieved, the report can be modified, ideas can be worded in more concrete or different ways, and so on. It is also true that if a management person has a trivial or irrelevant objection to some aspect of the report being presented, it can be discovered and corrected in the oral reporting situation. An irrelevant objection to a specific point in a written report usually would go undetected because the reader would not be in the position to communicate with the writer. Any aspect of a report which is not accepted by the reader does, however, influence the reader's attitude toward the entire report.

One final advantage that some companies find in making use solely of oral presentations in certain instances is that material and concepts can be presented and discussed with no fear on the part of management that this material will fall inadvertently into unauthorized hands or that it will be published.

Some common *disadvantages of the oral report* are: First, people tend to have differential perception and memories. That is to say, people see and hear what they want to see and hear. They remember what they want to remember. This is not to say that any particular set of management people is biased, but rather that all people are biased in their perception of things around them. Therefore, some points in the presentation may be missed by part of the audience or may be misinterpreted in accord with their particular perceptions and backgrounds.

Second, in an oral presentation there is nothing to refer to once the presentation is finished (unless, of course, the oral presentation is accompanied by a written report which includes the pertinent items presented). Finally, an oral report, presented without an accompanying written one, does not give an opportunity for the audience or participants to make a thoughtful and thorough analysis of the contents. If an important management decision is to be made on the basis of an oral report, it must be made on the spot or management risks the possibility of failing to achieve its objective because of incomplete understanding of the contents of the report.

Increasing the Receiver's Interest and Attention

The presentation should be formal. The person who is making the presentation should know exactly what he or she is going to say and say it well. One must have the capacity to expand upon, explain in greater detail, or defend the thesis of one's report. All of the rules for effective public speaking would apply here. The speaker

must get and hold the attention of the audience, must not talk over their head
beneath their educational level, and must enunciate clearly, use gestures w
appropriate, and so on. As many visual presentations as are appropriate can be
in the oral report. These "visual aids" are extremely important in presenting rese
results or detailed information.

Naturally, all of the various visual presentations mentioned in the prece
sections on statistics as a means of presentation can be used. Charts, line graphs,
bar graphs are usually more effective than tabular information in a visual prese
tion, although simple tables that can be clearly read can be effective.

One of the chief objectives of the report writer is to get the report accepted. T
are many devices which one may use in order to assure a high level of interest. C
the devices, however, that can be put into play to assist the report writer, the u
illustrations is still the most effective. The use of illustrations does two thing
relieves monotony and it heightens the listeners' interest because it enables the
grasp the total situation in a quick pictorial summary and then have their impress
reinforced through the explanation as the ideas are presented in the spoken v
The use of illustrations to relieve monotony is amply demonstrated by mo
textbooks.

In selecting the most effective illustrations, the considerations which mus
examined are:

1. Your reader audience
2. The nature of your materials
3. The effect which you wish to achieve
4. The technical assistance you have at your disposal

1. In considering the nature of your audience, it is obvious that if you we
use an illustration for junior high school students it would have to be of a type
have a mode of presentation different from one explaining the internal workings o
explosive force of an atomic warhead to a group of M.I.T. scientists who
attempting to change the relationships which occur within our body politic. Man
ment, if it were attempting to illustrate to a broad group of its employees the effe
the increase of wages or the effect of the increase in the price of a product upo
total earnings of the company, would use a type of explanation which woul
readily grasped by all levels of its employees. If it were attempting to ex
something of this nature to the finance committee, it probably could use a
involved set of relationships, since the experience, background, and level o
ceptance of these people are different.

2. The nature of your materials. It is obvious that accounting material
opposed to areas of science such as chemistry and physics, would require a diffe
type of presentation. Most of you are familiar with the kinds of presenta
illustrating chemical formulas. There are also illustrations showing how raw mate
go through various stages, for example, in a gasoline cracking plant. There
involved and complex concepts which can more readily be described to ord
people through pictorial presentation than through the use of words. There
number of other areas which call for a particular kind of presentation dictated b
very nature of the subject matter. Good report writers know what type of aid will a
them in the presentation of the report and assist the reader in grasping the esser
of what they are attempting to explain.

3. The effect you wish to achieve is governed by the nature of your repor
the action pattern you desire. It may be that you are gearing your recommenda
for acceptance—or it may be that you wish to have your information studied b

management team and digested in order for it to govern their future actions. In any event, it is true that the types of responses desired will govern the nature of the presentation.

4. If you must rely upon your own devices to turn out a graph or a visual presentation, you may hesitate to prepare various types of visual aids. On the other hand, you may be in a position to make use of professional artists. In the latter instance, you would be remiss not to make the most effective usage of the talent available to you. It is axiomatic that a good presentation is half of the battle, and if you employ all positive means of getting your story across, then you have increased your chances for positive acceptance of the facts which your report delineates.

The Use of Slide Projector and Screen

One way of presenting charts and other statistical information is with a slide projector and screen. Although there are many different sizes of projectors, the cheapest way of developing this information is to construct the chart or graph on plain white paper (with colors if possible) and photograph it with 35 mm color film. Color slides used in this manner are relatively inexpensive and very effective. One advantage of inexpensive slides is that if the presentation is to be made more than once (as frequently happens in a large corporation), new data can be substituted simply by changing one slide. With modern 35 mm slide projectors, it is possible to store the slides in a magazine so that they are ready at a moment's notice.

Another advantage of slide projection is the fact that the entire attention of the audience must be focused upon the one point that the speaker is making, namely, the information presented on the slide. This is true because all visual detractors in the room are eliminated when the lights are turned off and the slide is displayed on the screen.

When making an oral presentation, you should observe this primary rule concerning the effective use of visual aids: *never* distribute charts or tables to each individual in the audience. If this is done, each member of the audience looks at a different part of the table and it is extremely difficult to hold the attention of the group on the specific thing that you are trying to emphasize. If it is desired to distribute the information to the management people attending the report, this can be done when the meeting is over rather than during the time that it is in session.

Another type of visual aid besides the 35 mm slide is the rear-screen projector or over-the-shoulder projector. This type of projector can generally be used without turning off the lights and is very adaptable for showing practically any kind of written material. Letters or any sort of handwritten or typewritten material can be placed on the projector and shown on the screen magnified many times. One corporation, the Technifax Company, Holyoke, Massachusetts, has produced diazotype equipment for making these kinds of presentations and frequently conducts a three-day seminar workshop in visual communications at their factory. Any interested party can attend the workshop at no cost other than the personal expenses incurred in attending.

The diazotype method lends itself very well to the presentation of material in overlays. Through this type of photographic process, different-colored transparent overlays can be made very quickly and for a reasonable price if the equipment is available.

Other visual aids in the oral report are charts and graphs made specifically for an easel presentation. There are also a number of ways of using flip charts to tell an effective story in an oral presentation. A number of companies have devised filmstrip presentations for training sessions and for use at the point of sale. Filmstrips and machines to project them can also be used very effectively in a visual presentation. Obviously, moving pictures and tape recordings can also be used in this regard.

Although the traditional chalk board can be used in oral presentations, a more effective way of accomplishing the same purpose is the use of an easel with large pads of newspaper stock and a felt pen. This type of writing on this material is easier to read than chalk on a dark background and it lends itself to better visual presentation. Naturally, recourse to any sort of visual aid during the course of the presentation should be well planned in advance and rehearsed before the formal presentation is made.

The Effect Which You Wish to Achieve

Very often one illustration will be more successful in making a point clear to your reader than any of the others you can select. There is a danger here of using your illustrations to achieve a preconceived purpose or to justify an opinion. Newspapers of conflicting political views can color the facts by the use of cartoons seemingly on the same subject, and it is not this type of illustration to which we refer when we talk about using visual aids to secure an effect which we wish to achieve.

For example, it is possible to prepare a graph showing a rise in the price of a security. In a time when the stock market is rising, a simple graph of the increase in price might be quite spectacular. If, however, you wish to make a comparison between the price of stock A and the general performance of the market, you would need to show market performance reduced to the same scale for comparison. Even better would be a graph in which the performance of the market was reduced to a straight horizontal line and the performance of the stock or group of stocks which you are discussing is shown as variations from the straight line. There is even a set of charts prepared on some securities showing their performance on both the upswing and the downswing of the market. It is possible through the choice of an illustration which is suitable to present your point fairly yet clearly to your reader.

Again, it should be emphasized that in the oral report, as well as in the written report, the language used should be understandable, precise, and to the point. It is true that a little humor is more appropriate in an oral presentation than in a written one. While it would be unlikely that in a written presentation one would take up the necessary space to present a joke, an oral presentation can serve to heighten communication as well as to keep the atmosphere informal.

EXERCISES

1. Attempt to reword the following statistics so that if offered in an oral report they would be more comprehensible.

    We found that 51 ³/₄ percent of the students . . .
    In 18.7 percent of the situations . . .
    There were 2,349,612 citizens who responded . . .
    The result was that 14 out of 21 responded to our survey . . .

2. Write a report on the most crucial problem facing businesspeople today. First use a problem-development organization pattern, offering several aspects of the

problem. Next, write on the same topic using a problem-solution pattern. This time, define the problem, suggest alternate solutions, and recommend one of them.

3. Prepare an oral report for presentation to your class. Develop an audiovisual aid to highlight your information. Make a transparency of this information and use it on the overhead projector during your address.

4. Write a report comparing and contrasting the advantages and disadvantages of oral reports with those of written reports.

5. Write a press release about a new course being offered in your school.

6. Visit the audiovisual department in your school. Learn how to operate videotape equipment, tape recorders, overhead projectors, and carousel projectors. Watch a transparency being made, and note how material can be blown up or reduced on a flat bed and see how charts are prepared.

FOOTNOTES

1. Stuart Chase, *Power of Words*, (New York: Harcourt, Brace & World, 1954; *Guides to Straight Thinking* (New York: Harper & Brothers, 1956).

2. Rudolf Flesch, *The Art of Plain Talk* (New York: Harper & Brothers, 1946).

3. *Adult Leadership*, vol. 4, no. 7 (January 1956), p. 1.

4. Sir Josiah Stamp, *Some Economic Factors of Modern Life* (London: P. S. King and Son, 1929), pp. 258–259.

5. John McElroy, "Is Business Language Fuzzy?" *Dun's Review and Modern Management* (July 1951), pp. 21–22, 39–49.

6. Frederick Croxton and Dudley Cowden, *Applied General Statistics*, 2d ed. (New York: Prentice-Hall, Inc., 1955).

7. Darrell Huff, *How to Lie with Statistics* (New York: W. W. Norton & Co., Inc., 1954).

8. Rudolph Modley and Dino Lowenstein, *Pictographs and Graphs* (New York: Harper & Brothers, 1952), pp. 25–26.

9. Huff, op. cit.

CHAPTER 11

THE IMPORTANCE OF LETTER WRITING

A talent for writing letters, like all developed talents, requires practice and a sense of style. One must commit time to the endeavor and concentration; one's skills must be brought to bear upon the creation of a studied effect.[1]

One of the important tools that a manager, and particularly one who is in public life, must possess is an effective skill of putting ideas into words. What the communicator is doing through the written word is getting across thoughts and making sure the recipient understands the message and accepts the intent of the message. The great difference between oral communication and the written letter is that there is no opportunity for the receiver of the letter to immediately ask questions, to look at the communicator, or to have the writer give an explanation of the meaning of the words in the letter. The recipient of the letter has only a one-dimensional medium. There is no support in facial cues or verbal statements such as, "Well, what I meant was . . . " The recipient of the letter, if not sure, must read and reread and mull over what was written and guess at the intent of the writer. For this reason, as can readily be seen, a letter writer must bring to the task many skills. The following are essential:

1. A clear understanding of the intent of the letter
2. The vocabulary that permits the writer to express ideas in shades of meaning
3. An empathic stance which will permit the writer to understand the position of the recipient
4. A thorough knowledge of the subject matter or the incident which is being related
5. The capacity to couch the message in accurate and precise terms

6. Awareness of the tone to be communicated in the message and the ability to communicate it
7. An ability to express clearly, explicitly, and succinctly all the concepts employed
8. The ability to write so that the reader will not misconstrue any of the letter's meaning
9. The ability to direct the action or reaction of the reader in a predictable manner
10. Finally, the skill and knowledge to appropriately package the letter

From a financial viewpoint, literally millions of dollars are spent annually in every type of organization, whether it be business, social, or political, in the act of writing—that is, in putting thoughts and messages onto paper. Of all the managerial activities, business letter writing ranks as the number 1 "putting it in writing" activity. Recent cost studies have reported projected figures in the range of $2.50 to $10 per letter, depending upon the salary of the dictator, the salary of the secretary, office overhead, etc. It is obvious that this is not only an important business activity, but one which bears a high cost tag. Because of the cost and importance of communication, most of the major business concerns specifically state that management trainees must possess communication skills, both oral and written. These skills are particularly necessary if a trainee has any hope of being promoted within the framework of the organization.

Because of the frequency with which the business practitioner must write letters and other documents, surveys were made of graduates of colleges of business. When these graduates were asked what subject they felt was the most beneficial to them while they were in school, they very frequently stated that they needed more training and education in the art of letter writing.

There is a high correlation between level of responsibility and the need for effective letter-writing skills. Managers in corporations and administrators in government, education, hospitals, and other service activities do spend significant amounts of time writing letters. For example, a first-line foreman may devote a relatively small amount of time to writing notes and letters; however, a second-level or middle-management foreman may spend as much as 20 percent of his/her time writing letters. As we move up from these levels, and particularly as we move over into staff activities, the letter-writing responsibilities escalate sharply. When we reach the top level of management, not only does the amount of letter writing rise, but the "effect curve" is in an even sharper dimension. One does not need an oracle to tell one that a letter from the president's office carries a great deal of weight and is analyzed, studied, and referred to over and over again as to its true intent and meaning. It follows that letters from individuals who are in critical decision-making positions in organizations must be very carefully composed—that the meaning of every word, every sentence, and every paragraph must be thoroughly analyzed and studied before any letter is permitted to go out over the sender's signature.

There are as many demands for letter writing in business as there are situations to be covered by letters. For example, letter-writing activities are sometimes broken down according to formalized areas, such as sales letters, collection letters, goodwill letters, letters to reactivate old accounts, opportunity letters, technical letters, letters of apology, letters that handle complaints, letters that answer inquiries, letters to turn down requests, complimentary letters, and condolence letters. This breakdown, however, only delineates certain categories. From the manager's viewpoint, letter-writing capabilities must necessarily be generalized rather than specific.

Those responsible for the activities in business organizations have long realized that letter writing is an important function of the organization. They are aware that the good letter gets the job done, that the poor letter causes friction, more trouble, more work, and more expense until problems are finally resolved. For this reason, business firms send many of their people to the several hundred letter-writing seminars that are held throughout the United States every year. In fact, one such seminar for practicing letter writers draws over four thousand participants each year. Figure 11-1 is a brochure of a letter-writing seminar held at one of the major universities in the United States.

At the outset it can be stated that of the many functions and usages of letters in business, the following are their general purposes and characteristics:

1. Put in writing verbal agreements and conversation.
2. Formalize concepts.
3. Direct a course of action.
4. Obtain information for clarification of a policy.
5. Document actions which have been taken.
6. Inform individuals of new plans, goals, and directions.
7. Obtain information.
8. Complain, censure, or commend.

The above list represents only a relative slice of the many ways in which the letter serves as a basic tool in business.

As a guide to the information which is presented in this chapter, one can summarize the functions and characteristics of a good business letter as follows:

1. A good business letter is clear in its purpose.
2. A good business letter is psychologically empathic—it makes the reader want to respond the way the letter writer intends.
3. A good business letter is aesthetically attractive.
4. A good business letter provides accurate, easily understood information.
5. A good business letter has tone—it is as informal or formal as the nature of the business discussed demands.
6. A good business letter is brief and concise.
7. A good business letter contains information in an organized, cogent format.
8. A good business letter always uses appropriate English and correct grammar.
9. A good business letter gets the job done, thereby cutting down on costs of doing business.
10. A good business letter leaves the reader with a pleasant psychological disposition toward the letter writer and the organization.

A PLAN FOR WRITING THE BUSINESS LETTER

Most letter writers approach their task in a relatively disorganized fashion. This is due many times to a lack of time or to conflicting pressures. They may need to meet a deadline or may have other interfering responsibilities. Be that as it may, this approach to letter writing takes much longer (and the results are much poorer) than when the letter writer begins with a rational, planned approach.

Those of you who may have observed letter writers will have noticed how often they back up, repeat, review, strike out, or sit for long periods in meditative silence. In order to avoid this kind of wasteful activity, letter writers should:

Two panels forming a seminar brochure.

Top panel:

Seminar No. 595
March 3-4-5, 1971

B R

LETTER AND REPORT WRITING WORKSHOP

(How to Modernize Your Business Writing)

Campus Inn
Ann Arbor, Mich.

Seminar Leader:
DR. DUGAN LAIRD
Training Consultant
Chicago, Illinois

DESCRIPTIVE OUTLINE

1. **Current Trends in Business Writing**
   a. The informality syndrome
   b. Usage or grammar?
   c. Should you write the way you talk?
   d. Contemporary formats
      1) To improve your image
      2) To cut your costs

2. **How to Organize Your Ideas**
   a. A logical plan
   b. A psychological plan

3. **Reorganizing Participant Letters**
   a. Consultation with seminar leaders

4. **How to Be Understood**
   a. Clarity
      1) Writing the thought unit
      2) The vocabulary of writing
      3) Handling technical jargon
   b. Conciseness
      1) How important is it?
      2) How do I achieve it?

5. **How to Create Readable Writing**
   a. The friendly approach
   b. Selling through style
   c. The positive approach
   d. Beginnings and endings
   e. Escaping cliches

6. **Communicating Unpopular Messages**
   a. Special considerations
   b. The employment turndown
   c. The disciplinary letter

7. **The Mastery of Rhetoric (Self-Help)**

8. **How to Draw Up a Report**
   a. Establishing objectives
   b. Aiding the decision-maker
   c. The four-part process

9. **Applying Principles and Techniques**

10. **Advanced Writing Clinics**
    a. Case histories dramatized
    b. Evaluations
    c. Summary and conclusions

11. **How to Edit**
    a. The editorial function
    b. Writing for the boss's signature
    c. Skill practice

12. **Summary Panel and Critique**

PARTICIPANTS ARE REQUESTED TO BRING
   a. Some letters or reports they have written
   b. Letters they must answer soon after the seminar
   c. A report on which they are currently working

Detach and mail to: **SEMINAR REGISTRAR, BUREAU OF INDUSTRIAL RELATIONS, THE UNIVERSITY OF MICHIGAN, 508 E. LIBERTY STREET, ANN ARBOR, MICHIGAN 48108, TELEPHONE (313) 763-0110.**

SEMINAR REGISTRATION FORM

Please register the following persons for the LETTER AND RE-PORT WRITING WORKSHOP SEMINAR No. 595 to be held in Ann Arbor on March 3-4-5, 1971.

Name _____
Title _____
Name _____
Title _____
Company _____
Address _____
Zip Code _____ Company Phone No. _____

☐ Check enclosed (Make checks payable to The University of Michigan)
☐ Bill my company (Billing information enclosed)
I will travel by ☐ Auto ☐ Plane ☐ Not certain
☐ Please send me a room reservation card

NOTE ABOVE—"Participants are Requested to Bring"

Registrations cancelled less than one week prior to the Seminar date are subject to a $50.00 charge.

Registration Fee: **$200** per individual (includes tuition, course materials, luncheons and one-year subscription to Management of Personnel Quarterly and Personnel Management Abstracts.) Sleeping accommodations, breakfasts and dinners are not included

FOR FURTHER INFORMATION CONTACT MISS JOAN D. WARREN, Program Director or Seminar Registrar, Tel. (313) 763-0110.

Bottom panel:

UMBIR

LETTER AND REPORT
WRITING WORKSHOP

DR. DUGAN LAIRD
Training Consultant

We at the Bureau of Industrial Relations believe that letters and reports are written to be read. We also want our readers to understand them. Having understood them we want them to take action as a result.

Evidence leads us to suspect that this might not always be so. Here's what some recipients of letters and reports tell us:

"I constantly receive written materials that are five—fifteen pages long. I set them aside to be read when I have time."

"The letters I get are so fogged by big words and long sentences that I have a hard time understanding them."

"The report I received last Friday had too much detail. It used highly technical language I couldn't understand."

"Fred's an awfully nice guy. It's too bad he's illiterate. His memos constantly refer to 'they,' 'he' or 'it' and I'm not sure who or what he means."

Our point is this. If you want someone to read, understand and act upon your writing, make your letters short and clear. This sounds very simple, but most of us make mistakes which cause our readers to tune out.

If you want your letters and reports to be read and understood, we suggest you attend the Bureau of Industrial Relations' "Letter and Report Writing Workshop" on March 3-4-5, 1971. Here's what you'll get at the Seminar:

- A hard look at your own writing skills with suggestions for improvement.
- Current trends in business writing.
- Critique of your own letters, reports and memos by the seminar staff.
- Solutions to such special problems as organizing your ideas, writing unpopular messages, handling technical jargon and writing in an informal style.

Because enrollment is limited and the seminar fills to capacity rapidly, we suggest you enroll soon. Read the descriptive outline then enroll by returning the attached registration form. Or call the Seminar Registrar, or me, Joan Warren at (313) 763-0110.

Figure 11-1

1. Thoroughly review the problem. Get all the facts.
2. Read the letter being answered carefully. Underline those points which are particularly important. Get your emotions under control. One cannot write effectively in anger of when one's attitude is biased.
3. Know what action or reaction you are striving for. Are you attempting to:

    a. Placate?
    b. Gain understanding?
    c. Motivate?
    d. Gain sympathy?
    e. Deny a request?

4. Preplan as to whether you are going to prepare a draft or are going to attempt to write the finished missive at the first sitting. Important documents, i.e., letters which set policy, should be prepared in rough draft and be carefully edited before the final draft.
5. Letters which are very important to the organization frequently are required to be read by several staff members or responsible individuals before being distributed to make sure that the message conveyed is correct in every respect.

    Frequently letter writers have found that in important situations it is necessary to write the letter and (if time permits) to wait a day before rereading the letter to make sure their intent and meaning are what they wished them to be.

Many letter writers find that, to raise their effectiveness in the art, they must set aside a period of time when interruptions, such as phone calls and visitors, are not allowed, so that concentration on the task is possible.

The following checklist designed by the authors may be helpful to embryo letter writers:

1. Do I understand the problem thoroughly?
2. Do I have all the facts?
3. Have I read the letter I am answering thoroughly?
4. Have I remained dispassionate?
5. Is the proper tone employed?
6. Is the word usage correct?
7. Are all possible meanings clear?
8. Is the letter concise or am I guilty of overexplaining?
9. Have I maintained an awareness of the reader's viewpoint?
10. Is there a clear indication as to what outcomes are desired?

In situations where letters or messages are not planned, strange outcomes may occur. As an example, the authors of this chapter were informed about a junior bank officer who wrote an explanatory letter to a senior executive to inform him that the scheduled meeting planned earlier in the year would not meet at the originally scheduled time. Since the earlier plan provided for the meeting to be held from 7:00 A.M. to 10:00 A.M., she therefore informed the executive, in her letter, that the meeting would henceforth last only two hours. The senior officer arrived for the meeting at 7:00 A.M. The junior executive arrived for the meeting at 8:00 A.M. Since the senior executive spent an hour waiting for his appointment, unnecessarily, he was indeed angry at the loss of otherwise profitable time. Careless ambiguity, a result of ineffective planning, irritates the receiver, slows down decision making, costs money, and destroys the worth of the letter.

STRATEGIC AWARENESS IN LETTER WRITING

In the world of sports and politics, one of the most common terms used is *game plan*. The letter writer must establish a game plan as well. We would call a letter-writing game plan "formulating your strategy for achieving your purpose." We have touched upon it in the preceding paragraph by establishing a primary strategy, *preparing* to write letters.

Several guidelines to keep in mind when devising a strategy for writing letters are presented here. The first is considering how to order the information to be discussed. If the letter writer wants the reader to be moved to a particular viewpoint, should that request be located at the beginning or the end of the message? A cameo example of the problem of order of presentation of material is best illustrated by the letter in Example 1.

The plant manager put this letter on his plant bulletin board after Charlie Smith, one of his employees, had broken his ankle as a result of slipping on spilled oil from a broken glass bottle. A few weeks later, after posting this letter, he checked with his secretary and learned that only four of the approximately seventy-five bottles in the plant had been brought in to be exchanged for plastic bottles. In the meantime, another accident had occurred. A worker, when sweeping up another broken bottle, had gashed his hand with a piece of cut glass—a gash requiring nine stitches and paid for through company workmen's compensation insurance. When the general manager asked why several such accidents now had occurred, and moreover, why the glass bottles had not been exchanged for plastic bottles, the plant manager was at a loss for a reply. He began to inquire informally among his foremen whether they had seen his letter requesting the glass bottle replacement. All remembered seeing a letter about how poor Charlie had broken his ankle, but few recalled the information about getting plastic bottle replacements. The plant manager went back to the bulletin board to reread his own letter. As can readily be ascertained, of the three paragraphs, the first two discussed Charlie's ankle. The third paragraph, which was also the longest one, requested the bottle exchange. The plant manager realized that after people had read the first two short paragraphs, they had not bothered to read the last long paragraph.

As this plant manager realized, it is better to explain first in the letter *what it is* that is being discussed, and then *why* it is being discussed. In the letter the plant manager wrote, the plant manager knew the *what* was to exchange glass bottles for plastic ones, and the reason was to prevent any more workers from getting into accidents like the one that happened to Charlie. In the reader's mind, however, the *what* of the letter was that poor Charlie had broken his leg, and the *why* was that he had slipped. Had the plant manager reversed the order of his material and used an anticlimactic approach, the readers would have more likely learned that the purpose of the letter was to exchange glass bottles for plastic ones.

The anticlimactic approach of first telling the reader *what* you want him to do and then why increases the probability that the reader will get the same message the writer sent. In fact, communication research suggests that in written messages, it is   **277**

. . . .

MEMORANDUM

TO: All Employees   DATE: 12/18/7-

FROM: Oscar Osterhout, Plant Manager

SUBJ.:   Broken Ankle--Charlie Smith, Unit Assembly Line

Most of you, who have been around here for a long time, know Charlie
Smith. He is one of our most valued employees, with 23 years' seniority.
Some of you remember that at our last awards banquet, Charlie Smith
received the accident-free award for our plant. I am quite sure you
remember Charlie bouncing across the stage and shaking hands with
Mr. Cartwright, our general manager.

Charlie Smith wouldn't be bouncing across the stage today, because two
things have happened: (1) His accident-free record has been shot to
pieces, and (2) Charlie is laid up in Memorial Hospital with a broken
ankle. It all happened because Charlie accidentally stepped on a machine
oil bottle which somebody carelessly placed in front of a milling machine.
We all feel sorry for Charlie and we are sorry that he lost the longest
accident-free record in the plant.

Directive #9934 which was sent out of my office on February 3, 1959,
explicitly stated that machine oil containers should not be placed on the
floor or in any position where a passerby could accidentally step on them.
This order was again brought to the attention of all employees in Directive #9937 from my office on July 8, 1969, after Herman Weaver had
accidentally kicked over a bottle and caused some material damage to
the shop. Evidently, this problem has got to be solved in some other
way, and, in going over with the plant safety committee, we have
come up with a solution. It is their recommendation that we go from a
glass container, which we have used these many years, to a plastic-type
container. Fortunately, we have been able to get four dozen plastic
containers, which I feel will serve the purpose very well. For this
reason, I am asking each machine operator to bring his glass container to
the tool crib and turn it in and get a plastic container as a replacement.
I am sure you all know how important this is. As soon as possible see to
it that you have replaced your glass container with a plastic container.
In this way we are all in high hopes that we will not have any more
accidents like the one which crippled Charlie Smith.

. . . .

Example 1

safest to place the purpose of the message both in the beginning and at the end of the letter.[2]

Tone

In reviewing letter-writing problems with executives, we found that a *paper barrier* develops when managers start to put their thoughts on paper. People who are fluent conversationalists and exchange verbal remarks with ease suddenly freeze and drop into stilted phrases and formal words and sentences when they are faced with the task of writing. The *why* of this is quite obscure, but that it does exist is readily apparent. It seems as though "Write like you would talk" is easy to say but in fact is hard to do.

The most frequent complaint that managers of managers make about junior executives' letters is that these letters are unnecessarily formal. The letters sound stilted and artificial. Don Michalak, a partner in Consulting Associates, Inc., Southfield, Michigan, says that his recommendation for people who have to write many business letters and need to informalize their tone is to pretend that the individual being written to just stepped into the office for a chat. Whatever words would be used in conversation to explain the point should be used in the letter.

Example 2 is an actual case where tone was not considered an essential part of a written message.

When Mr. Hoppe received this letter, he reacted: he immediately dashed over to Whalehammer's office and aggressively demanded of the boss's secretary an appointment. Whalehammer had to be hauled out of a conference he was having with someone else because Hoppe was so distraught and insistent. The secretary thought she had better get Mr. Whalehammer to immediately confer with Mr. Hoppe. Whalehammer was startled at Mr. Hoppe's reactions. He said, "I only wanted to go over a report we have due in a few months. There was no rush." The boss then added, "Why did you get so excited?" The boss had forgotten that to his subordinate a vague directive had looked like an urgent command. Had the boss indicated (1) what the problem was about, and (2) when the appointment should be made, the subordinate would have reacted with behavior appropriate to the writer's intent.

Length

A famous writer once was reported to have written a friend as follows: "I have written you a three-page letter because I did not have time to write you a one-page letter."

To write succinctly is a facet of planning. Most lengthy-letter writers are really explaining the situation to themselves. They are, in reality, arguing or convincing themselves. They do not remove extraneous material.

One popular business speaker stated that the writer should always employ the K.I.S.S. principle. When asked what this meant, he stated, "Keep It Simple, Stupid."

Another well-known lecturer in the field of business letter writing stated that the letter, like a girl's dress, should be short enough to be interesting but long enough to cover the subject.

Managerial assessors, who evaluate the letter-writing ability of businesspeople, report that unnecessarily lengthy letters are a frequent habit of letter writers. There is agreement among assessors that the best business letter is the succinct one.

. . . .

December 3, 19--

Darryl Hoppe
Quality Control

Dear Mr. Hoppe:

Please see me about a serious problem. I want to give
this immediate attention.

Sincerely,

Ralph Whalehammer
Unit Control Supervisor

. . . .

Example 2

Style

The elements of style for letter writing are grammar, word usage, punctuation, spelling, and title usage.

Punctuation may frequently determine the meaning of the words used. For example, without appropriate punctuation most men will look at the following sentence:

> Woman without her man is nothing.

and punctuate it to mean:

> Woman, without her man, is nothing.

while most women will punctuate the sentence to read:

> Woman! Without her, man is nothing.

Moreover, inadequate attention to spelling can place a negative impression in the reader's mind. One employee at a heavy-manufacturing facility repeatedly turned in a suggestion that went ignored for months. Then, the same suggestion was turned in by a coworker of the employee and awarded a prize. The worker who had initially turned in the suggestion approached his supervisor to find out why his suggestion had never been acted upon. He found out that his superiors had not bothered to read his proposal when they noticed he had misspelled "temperature" (as "tempratuture") three times in the first paragraph. The managers were convinced that if the employee could not spell "temperature," he could not know very much about it.

Often, words with quite different meanings but which sound alike easily become confused and by mistake are used interchangeably. Below are word pairs that are easily mistaken for each other although the members are quite distinct in meaning.

forceful — forcible
infer — imply
discreet — discrete
e.g. — i.e.
adverse — averse
policy — polity
luxuriant — luxurious

A quick dictionary check can alleviate an embarrassing misuse of words that could easily distort the meaning of the message.

Current title usage dictates that it is appropriate to use "Mr." or "Ms." only when you are not provided with the job title of the individual to whom you are writing. It is never necessary to distinguish the marital status of a woman in the title of a letter.

RIGHT	WRONG
James Anthony Wright	Mr. James Anthony Wright
Sales Manager	Sales Manager
The Humbug Company	The Humbug Company
12 N. Ellis	12 N. Ellis
Queen's City, NH 00202	Queen's City, NH 00202
Susan Smith	Miss Susan Smith
Project Director	Project Director
Bureau of Industrial Relations	Bureau of Industrial Relations
1215 Washtenaw	1215 Washtenaw
Ann Arbor, MI 48104	Ann Arbor, MI 48104

If the job title is not known when addressing a letter, it is acceptable to use the title "Mr." or "Ms." However, if the sex of the addressee is unknown, it is acceptable to simply use "M." The only exception to this current usage is the necessity of addressing judges and government officials as "The Honorable."

RIGHT	WRONG
The Honorable Charles Levin	Charles Levin
Supreme Court of Michigan	Supreme Court of Michigan

Attorneys typically address other attorneys by their name followed by the word "esquire."

RIGHT	WRONG
W. A. Newman, Esquire	Mr. William A. Newman
Attorney at Law	Attorney at Law

If the sex of the person or the people to whom the letter is being sent is not known, it is best to salute the level of office rather than to attempt to identify the sex of the people holding the office.

RIGHT	WRONG
Dear Chairperson(s):	Dear Chairman:
Gentlepeople:	Gentlemen:
Dear President:	Dear Sirs:
Dear Vice-President:	To Whom It May Concern:
Dear Officer:	Dear Mr. Judge:
Dear Judge:	

A signature on a letter does not require a "Mr." for men or a "Miss," "Mrs.," or "Ms." for women. It is current format to simply sign a name and repeat the same words in the signature identification below, and to provide a job title (if there is one) afterward:

RIGHT	WRONG
Jamey Smith	*(Mrs.) Jamey Smith*
Jamey Smith	(Mrs.) Jamey Smith
Personnel Officer	Personnel Officer

When in doubt one can find correct current title usage information in almost any secretarial handbook.

PACKAGING THE LETTER

The appearance of the letter is a part of the total impact. If the letter is not "packaged" appropriately, it may not have the acceptance it deserves. Items which go to make up the overall appearance include appropriate paper, appropriate letterheads, correct and easily readable type face, and, finally, a modern format.

The Stationery

The paper that businesses prefer to use for office stationery is rag paper. Typically, offices purchase a paper that has "25 percent" rag content, that is, 25 percent cloth fiber along with 75 percent wood pulp. This paper, which is costly as paper goes, is preferred to bond (all wood) paper because it is less smooth and shiny than bond paper, and consequently easier to type on, easier to read from, and easier to correct errors on. Typically, top-level executives prefer to use 100 percent rag paper, which is the most expensive paper but which has an exclusive feel and appearance.

While most offices order the less expensive plain white paper, colored stationery may be used, as it offers immediate recognition and identity. Typically, organizations which are seeking to vitalize their identity will select a distinctively hued stationery. The most practical colors are pastel shades, which allow for easy reading and fairly easy type correction.

The Letterhead

When choosing a printed letterhead for stationery, the most important consideration is to place the letterhead so that it allows for enough space on the page to get the body of the letter attractively positioned. Most organizations prefer to use black ink for letterheads. Others turn to identifiable shades of navy, green, or red. The *logos,* the identifying sign of the organization, should comfortably be placed near the address information. A letterhead includes the logos, name, address, zip code, telephone area code, and telephone number of the organization. Figure 11-2 shows some examples of letterheads.

Type Face Selection

Type selection for business writing is typically limited to two type faces. Elite type is generally used when there is a great deal of material in the letter. Elite type takes up less room, as it allows twelve characters (letters) to appear per inch. Pica type, at ten characters per inch, is used for shorter letters and/or when the letter writer wishes to increase the ease of reading of the document. Legal offices, accounting firms, and consulting firms generally prefer the variable-pitch type because it makes formidable documents easier to read. Pica type is easier to use when letters are mass-produced because it makes it easier to more exactly insert individualized information.

Format

Currently, and therefore the recommended choice of the authors, the most used format for business letters is a block style which places all the information flush with the left-hand margin. The date, inside address, salutation, body, complimentary close, signature, and signature identification are all flush with the left margin. The body of the letter does not require that any paragraph be indented, but instead two lines are skipped between paragraphs. While other formats are completely acceptable and often more acceptable because of space limitation, stationery typically looks best with this format. The block format is considered the easiest to read, as the eye simply scans one margin for the necessary information. An example of the block-format style is shown in Example 3.

Figure 11-2 **Letterhead Examples**

USEFUL
LETTER-WRITING
EXAMPLES

In order that this chapter may be of particular benefit to the college student, we are including three examples of letter-writing situations which students have a current need to meet. These are (1) the résumé and the cover letter for the résumé, (2) the information-seeking letter, and (3) the complaint letter.

Résumé

The résumé is a word picture of an individual's background for the use of a prospective employer. The résumé should be just that—a comprehensive summary,

284

October 10, 1973

Mr. John C. Tincu
Manager, Open Line Program
The J. L. Hudson Company
1206 Woodward Avenue
Detroit, Michigan 48226

Dear Mr. Tincu:

Thank you for your inquiry to Andrew Nelson (who is no longer with Wards) about our employee question/answer program.

About a year and a half ago, Wards initiated a program called "Let's hear it!" and we are pleased to be able to say the program has been enormously successful. It has the full support of top management and has proven highly effective as a problem-solver as well as a means of achieving communication with employees on a one-to-one basis.

Last December, we published in Forward an article on the program which explains in some detail its operation. I enclose a copy of that article and the last few issues of Forward. As we are still processing some 200 queries a month, the portion of the program appearing in print is just the tip of the iceberg. Every query - whether we print it or not - is answered by mail directly to the employee's home.

We feel that the success of such a program depends on firm adherence to two basics: the anonymity of the employee is guaranteed if they request anonymity - we will only reveal their name with a signed authorization - and every question will be answered - no query is swept under the rug, no matter how "sticky."

We appreciate your interest in our program. If you have any further questions, please feel free to write.

Cordially,

Charles H. Thorne

Charles H. Thorne

Employee Communications Manager

Example 3

not a comprehensive autobiography. To assure that this is the case, it is best to remember two rules: (1) keep the résumé down to one or two pages, never more than three, and (2) allow for a great deal of attractive spacing to allow the reader to grasp the details easily.

While there are many theories about how résumés should be done, the recommended résumé for the student seeking employment is one that is as simple as possible. Unless a creative position with an advertising agency is being sought, it is wise to avoid using brochures, glossy paper, or unusual formats. The best recommendation is to use classic simplicity: simplicity in format, information, and appearance.

The top of the page tells whose résumé it is. Under appropriate headings, personal information is presented, including the address and phone number where correspondence should take place, age, marital status, military status, height, and weight. Many objections have been raised recently about indicating marital status, height, and weight, so that if it is preferred not to indicate this information, one may justifiably omit it. However, not divulging particular information—for example, age— allows questions to be raised.

The next section, under "Education," lists educational history, starting with the most recent experience and working backward. If your current schooling is not quite finished, indicate the expected degree to be received and the pending date when you expect to complete the degree. It is not necessary to list where or when high school was completed unless this is your highest academic achievement. The name of the college, its location, and your major and minor fields of study should all be indicated. Personal preference may determine whether cumulative grade point is to be listed. However, job choice also affects this decision. While most businesses do not expect managerial applicants to indicate this information, engineering departments and accounting departments, among other specialized fields, do pay particular attention to grade-point information.

Any academic honors or awards received in college or in the community should be listed next in a separate category. Here, again, it is not necessary to go into high school activities. Moreover, if no particular honors or awards have been received, merely omit this category.

The following category will indicate job experience. A general rule is to list the last three jobs held, giving the most recently held job first. For each position, indicate the job title held and a brief description of the work done. It is essential to indicate the name of the company and its location, and the month and year that employment began and the month and year of your departure. If the job you held was a part-time one, indicate this. If two different jobs with the same firm were held, list these as separate entries. It is not advisable to list any more than the last three jobs held.

An optional entry to add includes a *job objective* statement which describes career goals. However, this may be explained in the cover letter attached to the résumé.

References are generally appreciated by the prospective job employer. It is advisable to list no more than three and no less than two references, preferably people who can easily discuss your employment record or academic record. (Individuals selected as references should be informed of your use of their name.) List the reference's name, job title, company, address of the company (including the zip code), and its area code and phone number. It is quite acceptable to also indicate that references will be furnished upon request or to leave this category off the résumé entirely.

A matter of crucial importance in the résumé is to have it checked to make sure there are no misspellings or typographical errors. Such errors immediately detract from the impression the résumé offers.

Omit: the spouse's name and education; the father's job; religion; names and ages of children; college fraternity or sorority; and hobbies or extracurricular activities. Also, omit any references to personality, such as, "I am considered an extrovert by my coworkers." The most important don't is: *Do not list any information that is not absolutely true.*

There are many professional résumé-writing services available. However, it is important to avoid getting into an obviously expensive, glossy, professional appearing résumé, as it can have a negative impact on the prospective employer. However, it is probably wise to invest the money required to have the résumé professionally typed and laid out, unless you can do it well yourself. A résumé that is typed on a *composer*, a machine that justifies the space between letters so all the information is equidistant, is more expensive than one typed on a typewriter, but it may well be worth the added cost. The cost for having the résumé duplicated depends on the method used. Photocopying tends to give a less clean copy on an inexpensive paper but is less expensive than the multilith process, which gives a perfect copy.

Once a résumé is completed on $8^1/_2$- by 11-inch paper, it may simply be mailed in a standard-size envelope along with an attached cover letter. Examples of résumés follow.

Résumé Cover Letter

A résumé covering letter makes use of standard letter-writing format, discussed earlier in this chapter. The objective of the letter is to indicate what type of position is desired. An indication as to why you are leaving the position you currently hold is desirable, along with a statement as to what special qualifications you have for this position. Also, note your willingness to relocate and that a résumé is enclosed with this letter. Make sure that the covering letter includes a current mailing address. Salary expectation may or may not be stated. Example 6 is a sample covering letter for a résumé.

Often students are not yet ready to apply for a position at a particular company but would like to have more information about potential job opportunities that the company affords. In this case one would write a letter of information.

Letter of Information

It is probably a good idea to start collecting information about various companies, agencies, and government offices during your junior and senior years of college so that by the time of matriculation valuable information about each type of firm will have been obtained. Some companies prefer to allow only M.B.A.s into their management training programs initially, while others pay for advanced education for the employee while working for them. Special certification or testing is sometimes required. Some companies put all new employees through an assessment center to measure their personal qualities, interpersonal skills, administrative skills, and general ability to communicate orally and in writing.

In writing a letter for information, whether it is job-related or not, be sure to state why information is being requested. Explain specifically what kind of information and materials are needed. Avoid asking for information that is easily obtainable. For

Personal Résumé

JOHN S. WHOLEHOUSE

Home Address: Telephone:
  324 Newton Street   617-333-2232
  Boston, Mass. 90054

PERSONAL DATA

Appearance: 5 feet 9 inches tall,   Marital Status: Single, free
          170 lbs.   to travel

Date and Place of Birth: Born
        January 1948, Framing-
        ham, Mass. 90681

Military Status: Member, Massachusetts
        National Guard

EDUCATION

Bachelor of Arts, Northeastern University, Boston, Massachusetts 90054.
  To be granted in June 1971. Major in Marketing (B average), minor
  in Journalism (B average). Emphasis on courses in salesmanship,
  advertising, product management, and communication.

CAREER OBJECTIVES

Hope to obtain position with direct customer contact which will lead to
  position in sales management. Prefer working with people and in an
  organization emphasizing customer service concept.

WORK EXPERIENCE

Salesman (Summer 1970)
  Brigham's Storm Door Company, 751 Rochester Street, Boston, MA 90054
  Sold storm doors and windows to local home owners. Earned over $1,000
  in commissions under supervision of the sales manager.

Sales Clerk (During 1969-1970 and 1968-1969 school years)
  Campus Men's Shop, 910 University Avenue, Boston, MA 90054
  Employed part-time (20 hours per week) as salesman of men's furnish-
  ings and sports clothes under supervision of the store owner.

REFERENCES

Dr. George L. Jones   Mr. Marin Edwards
  Professor of Marketing   Sales Manager
  Boston University   Bingham's Storm Door Co.
  Boston, MA 90054   751 Rochester Street
  (617)639-8342   Boston, MA 90054
                                    (617)617-4442

Example 4

Résumé of

MICHAEL P. HOGAN

H-107 Cornell Courts
Ypsilanti, MI 48197
Phone: (313)484-0697

PERSONAL DATA

Age: 26   Marital Status: Married
Height: 5'6"   Military Status: Honorable Dis-
Weight: 135   charge from U.S.N. with rank
Health: Excellent   of E-5

EDUCATION

B. S. expected August 1973 from Eastern Michigan University.
    Major: Industrial Technology--concentration in electronics.
    Minor: Science, and extensive business courses.

Aviation Electronics Technician School
    Naval Air Technical Training Command
    Memphis, Tennessee

Honors: Board of Regents Scholarship and MHRAA Scholarship
         Dean's List

ACTIVITIES

Young Republicans--University of Detroit

WORK EXPERIENCE

September 1971 to September 1972
    Employer: EASTERN MICHIGAN UNIVERSITY, Ypsilanti, MI
    Duties: Bus Driver, garage work

April 1971 to September 1971
    Employer: GAMBLES DEPARTMENT STORE, Belleville, MI
    Duties: General Sales, stock work, and repair work

April 1970 to March 1971
    Employer: MINNEAPOLIS HONEYWELL, Detroit, MI
               Technical Representative
               --supervising installation of Honeywell Control Systems
               --troubleshooting previously installed systems
               --negotiating subcontracts for installation of equipment

MILITARY INFORMATION

Four years' active duty in U. S. Navy, achieved the rank of second class
petty officer. Held several security clearances, including a secret
clearance with a krypto access.
    Duties: Troubleshooting and repair of aircraft radio and radar, and
             associated electronic systems. Quality Control Inspector
             for EA-3B and EC-121 aircraft.

Example 5

Résumé
Michael P. Hogan
Page 2

REFERENCES

Robert C. Walker
Minneapolis Honeywell
13631 Plymouth Road
Detroit, MI 48227
(313) TE 4-6020

Bill Wilson
Physical Plant Garage
Eastern Michigan University
Ypsilanti, MI 48197
(313) 487-1849

John Weeks, Assistant Professor
Industrial Education Department
Eastern Michigan University
Ypsilanti, MI 48197
(313) 487-1849

Example 5 (Continued)

<u>Résumé Covering Letter</u>

October 8, 19--

Daniel L. Smart
Vice President of Sales
The Texean Corporation
123 Sundale
Fort Worth, Texas 02343

Dear Mr. Smart:

You will observe from my enclosed résumé that I have extensive
experience selling oil-related products.

I am interested in applying for the sales management position
advertised by your firm in the October 4, 197-, <u>Wall Street Journal.</u>
I believe my background qualifies me for such a <u>career advancement.</u>

If additional information is needed, I will be happy to provide it.
I am looking forward to receive your response.

Sincerely,

David L. Hathburn

Mailing Address:
    1033 Morningside
    Ann Arbor, MI 48104
    (313) 627-7341

Enclosure

Example 6

example, annual reports of most large firms are probably easily accessible in the campus library.

Letter of Complaint

A frequent occurrence in this computerized age is the necessity of writing a company in regard to an incorrect billing. An effectively composed letter is likely to generate a favorable, positive response. When making a credit or billing complaint, be sure to refer to the account number in the letter, the item in question, where and when the item was purchased, and how much it cost. Make sure to indicate the specific grievance. Being billed twice for the same item? Billed for an item never received? Billed for an item never purchased? If an item was paid for by check, send a photocopy (*not the original*) of the check (both front and back) along with the letter. Make sure to indicate that the matter should be cleared up immediately and that correspondence indicating that it has been amended would be appreciated. Often, credit mistakes that go unchecked can later affect personal credit ratings.

STANDARDIZING THE LETTER-WRITING PLANNING APPROACH

From the material presented to this point, a formula for business letter writing evolves. This formula is much like the checklist every pilot uses whenever he/she taxis down the runway for takeoff. The experts say no matter how trained the pilot is, the pilot will always go through the steps listed on the cockpit visor for takeoff. In parallel fashion, every individual who writes business letters, no matter how many or how often he or she writes them, should abide by a formula that provides for a programmed follow-through.

LETTER-WRITING PLANNING PROGRAM
1. Determine the purpose.
2. Determine the strategy to be used.
3. Organize the information available about the situation being discussed in the letter. Gather the historical documents, including letters sent and received previously, telephone notes, recommendations of coworkers, and the opinion of higher management.
4. Outline the material. After the material is outlined, review the order in which it should be presented.
5. Draft the letter. Oftentimes, managers like to draft their letters on scratch paper and then ask their secretary to type the final copy. Other individuals prefer to dictate a draft to their secretary, who types it for editing purposes. Often, business letter writers complain that when they start to write, mental blocking occurs. This is usually because Steps 3 and 4 have not been executed.
6. Allow some time to elapse between writing the draft and the editing of the final copy in order to increase your critical ability. Editing the draft often takes as long as the writing did, if a thorough job is done.
7. Proofread the letter.
8. Mail the letter promptly. An excellent letter which arrives after the receiver has made another decision is a worthless letter. An invitation to attend a

meeting which arrives on the day of the meeting is generally worthless. Often, the difference between making a decision to send mail air mail or simply first class can mean the difference between getting a contract, a sale, or a job.

9. Make a note in a calendar as to when a reply to the letter is expected or needed. If one is not received, a follow-up letter or phone call may be initiated.

NEW HORIZONS

Students of letter writing should also be aware that there are a number of technological adaptations now being employed. The purposes of these new technologies is to help keep up with the volume of information that has to be transmitted.

Already in existence is the *magnetic tape selectric typewriter,* which allows an individual to write the same letter with individual differences to several thousands of people in a matter of hours. This is called *word processing.* For example, each letter can be individually typed, with each letter having a different inside address and salutation. Less sophisticated and less expensive than the MT/ST machine is the *multilith* process, which allows for the reproduction of unlimited amounts of letters, each with the same intensity of print.

Some offices are now using *telecopiers,* which allow the office owning one telecopier to send printed information instantly to another office which has a telecopier (see Figure 11-3).

In the far future the prediction is that secretaries may be replaced with a dictating machine which types from the verbal input received. While this audio-reception unit will not be available in our lifetime, it will eventually alter letter-writing techniques.

Letter writing is a major activity of every manager. The higher in the organization the manager is, the more responsible are his or her letter-writing activities. Letters also serve as historical documents. They serve as references for agreements, policy statements, etc., not only among employees within the organization, but between the organization and other companies. Letter writing is one of the important endeavors of the business manager. It necessitates serious study and a constant upgrading to cultivate the skill commensurate to the task.

EXERCISES

1. Find out from a dictionary the difference in meaning of the following often confused word pairs:

   forceful — forcible
   infer — imply
   discreet — discrete
   e.g. — i.e.
   adverse — averse
   policy — polity
   luxuriant — luxurious

   Write a sentence using each word appropriately.

2. Decide what the correct salutations would be if you had to write letters to people who sent you letters signed as follows:

Xerox introduces the insomniac.

Thought you locked up your office for the night and everyone went home?

Then how come information is coming in, right now, at one in the morning?

Because you were smart enough to get yourself a new Xerox Telecopier 410 transceiver. The machine that never sleeps.

Just like the original Telecopier, it lets you send copies from one place to another in minutes. With one big difference: It does the job by itself.

To send, a person simply dials the number, places as many as 75 documents in the automatic feeder, and the Telecopier 410 does the rest.

XEROX®, TELECOPIER® and 410 are trademarks of XEROX CORPORATION.

Figure 11-3

Meanwhile, the automatic answering device on your machine answers the phone, and the 410 takes everything down exactly as it was sent. Even when there's no one in the office.

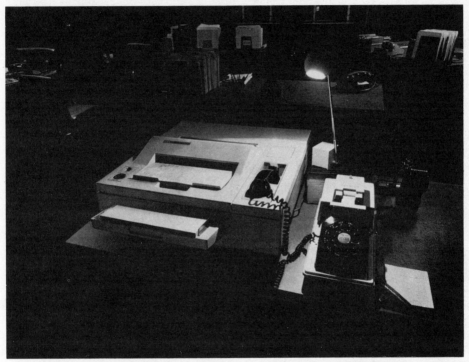

For more information, call our toll-free number (800) 255-4180.

The new Telecopier 410 transceiver. After putting in a hard day, it puts in a hard night.

XEROX

Roger Hawkins, Ph.D.
Head, Department of General Business

L. E. Shawser
Director, Minority Affairs

David Weber
Chief District Judge

Susan Alexander
Manager, Corporate Communications

3. Design a letterhead and logo which is attractive and economical and incorporates the following information:

Weathervane Products, Inc.
2341 Kellogg Road
Kalamazoo, MI 49008
(616) 346-2641
President: Mr. Guy Carlson
Established 1893

4. Write a business letter to remedy an overbilling of $6.49 on your October, 197 - bill from Saks Fifth Avenue, Second at Lothrop, Detroit, MI 48221.
5. Develop a résumé describing personal data, education background, job experience, awards and honors, and references about yourself. Attempt to limit your résumé to one attractively typewritten page.
6. Develop a checklist of your personal writing weaknesses. Note any words you typically misspell, punctuation problems, organization difficulties, use of inappropriate jargon, sentence construction, choppiness, and tone problems you encounter when you write. Use this checklist for all letters and reports you are required to write.
7. Select an ad from the Classified Mart Section of any *Wall Street Journal* when an employment opportunity is described. Write a letter to the company advertising the position, indicating your interest in the position, your desire to interview for the job, and that your résumé is enclosed.

FOOTNOTES

1. Peter S. Prescott, "From a Privileged Lunatic," criticism appearing in *Newsweek*, (October 2, 1972), p. 92.

2. Erwin Bettinghaus reports in *Persuasive Communication* (New York: Holt, Rinehart and Winston, Inc., 1968), p. 153, that placing an important piece of material in the middle of a message is not as effective as placing it either first or last. He reports some empirical research concludes that an anticlimactic order is more powerful than a climactic order, while the results of other research maintain the opposite.

APPENDIX A

A Case Study of the
Initiation and Success
of "Open Line"
at the Bank of America

Regional Administration #3540
Oakland

March 28, 1972

MEMORANDUM TO: Branch Manager

FROM: Harold Furst
                 Regional Vice President

SUBJECT: Open Line

On Monday, April 10, the pilot phase of an upward communications program
called "Open Line" will be initiated in our Region as well as Administrative Departments and Centralized Services, North and South. As a function
of the Communications Department, Open Line will provide employes with a
direct, confidential line of communication to management.

The success of this program will be measured by how well and how quickly
the questions which are received by the Open Line Coordinator are answered.
In some cases questions or commentary may concern policies, procedures,
or practices related to your branch. Although the program Coordinator will
supply editorial assistance, he will request you to answer the question.
As his experience level increases, however, the Coordinator will prepare
draft answers to similar questions for your approval and attribution.

You can further contribute to the success of Open Line by encouraging
your staff to use it. The program is not intended to interfere with relationships between supervisors and employes or supplant face-to-face communications. Rather, it provides a formal, complementary channel through
which employes can ask questions going beyond their daily jobs and from
which management can keep better informed about employe viewpoints.
And through Open Line we hope to take one more step towards achieving a
free-flowing communication climate which will benefit us all.

On April 5 you will receive copies of a letter explaining Open Line from
President Tom Clausen to the staff. Please distribute one copy to each
person in your branch. Shortly thereafter you will receive program material
for use at a staff meeting.

With your support and cooperation I am sure that Open Line will be a success.

Harold Furst

r

March 28, 1972

TO: Administrative Department Heads

On Monday, April 10, the pilot phase of an upward communications program
called "Open Line" will be initiated in Administrative Departments and
Centralized Services, North and South, as well as the Oakland-Alameda
Region. As a function of the Communications Department, Open Line will
provide employes with a direct, confidential line of communication to
management. Through this program we in management can take one more step
towards achieving a free-flowing communication climate which will benefit
us all.

The success of this program will be measured by how well and how quickly
we respond to the questions which are received by the Open Line Coordinator. In some cases questions or commentary may concern policies, procedures, or practices related to your area of responsibility. Although the
program Coordinator will supply editorial assistance, he will request
you to answer the question. As his experience level increases, however,
the Coordinator will prepare draft answers to similar questions for your
approval and attribution.

You can further contribute to the success of Open Line by encouraging your
staff to use it. The program is not intended to interfere with relationships between supervisors and employes or supplant face-to-face communications. Rather, it provides a formal, complementary channel through
which employes can ask questions going beyond their daily jobs and from
which management can keep better informed about employe viewpoints.

On April 5 you will receive copies of a letter explaining Open Line from
President Tom Clausen to the staff. Please distribute one copy to each
person in your department. Shortly thereafter you will receive program
material for use at a staff meeting.

Thank you for your assistance and cooperation in initiating Open Line.

Jerry G. South
Vice President - Communications

Circular L-4299

April 3, 1972

SUBJECT: OPEN LINE, New Communication Channel

TO BRANCH MANAGERS AND ADMINISTRATION

DEPARTMENT HEADS ADDRESSED:

Information	Open Line is a new two-way confidential communication channel between employes and Management.
	Through Open Line, all employes will be able to make comments, ask questions, or register complaints, directly to Management. The program will complement, rather than replace, existing employe-supervisor relationships and the "Let's Talk It Over" program.
	A pilot program will begin April 10, under direction of the Communications Department, in Region #3540, Headquarters Administration (North and South), Centralized Services (North and South), and International Banking (California Staff). Later, Open Line will be expanded throughout the State.
Material	You will receive the following materials by April 6.

Poster(s)
Forms
Pamphlets
Meeting Guide

Action	1. Review immediately upon receipt. 2. Hold staff meeting April 10. Include all prime-time and part-time employes. Discuss program as outlined in meeting guide. 3. Give one pamphlet to each employe during meeting. Also give one to each employe hired thereafter. 4. Place poster(s) and forms permanently in a location which is private but easily accessible to all your employees.
Questions and Additional Materials	Mr. Paul Allen Open Line Coordinator Communications Department #3400 (SF Ext. 8366)

C. H. Baumhefner
Vice Chairman of the Board and Cashier

April 4, 1972

Dear Fellow BankAmerican:

I am pleased to announce that we are taking steps to improve the upward flow of communications in the Bank. Through a new program called "Open Line" you will be able to advance your comments, questions, or complaints to management--and receive an authoritative, confidential and timely reply at your home. The confidential nature of this program cannot be overemphasized. Your name, if you choose to use it, will be known only by the Open Line Coordinator who is a member of our Communications Department. He will not reveal your identity to anyone without your permission.

Our success in working together as BankAmericans clearly depends upon effective two-way communications. While Open Line is not intended to replace face-to-face communications between employes and their superiors, it will give you an opportunity to comment on matters that may go beyond the scope of your daily supervisory relationships.

You are among those in Administration, Centralized Services, and the Oakland-Alameda Region, who will participate in the pilot phase of Open Line. Later in the year the program will be extended throughout the state. You will receive more details about how you can use Open Line at a staff meeting within the next few days.

Effective communication benefits each of us as individuals as well as the entire organization. I hope that you will find Open Line a positive and beneficial vehicle to make your voice heard in our Bank.

Sincerely,

A. W. Clausen
President

June 26, 1972

TO: Administrative Department Heads

The Bank's new upward communications program, called Open Line, will
be extended statewide on Wednesday, July 12. It has been operating as a
pilot program in Administration, Centralized Services (North and South),
and the Oakland-Alameda-Contra Costa Region. As a function of the
Communications Department, Open Line provides employes with a direct,
confidential line of communication to Management. Through this program
we in management can take one more step towards achieving a free-flowing
communications climate which will benefit us all.

The program is not intended to interfere with relationships between supervisors and employes or supplant face-to-face communications. Rather, it
provides a formal, supplementary channel through which employes can ask
questions going beyond their daily jobs and from which management can
keep better informed about employe viewpoints.

Open Line also enables employes to communicate personal problems, and
to this extent "Let's Talk It Over" and Open Line complement each other;
they provide an additional means of upward communications when direct
channels break down. You can personally contribute to the success of Open
Line by encouraging your staff to use it.

On July 5 you will receive copies of a letter from President Tom Clausen
to the staff explaining Open Line. Please distribute one copy to each
person in your department. Shortly thereafter you will receive program
material for use at a staff meeting.

Thank you for your assistance and cooperation in expanding Open Line.
With your support, I am sure that it will continue to be a success.

Jerry G. South
Vice President--Communications

```
                                        Circular C-1523
                                        July 5, 1972
```

SUBJECT: OPEN LINE

TO BRANCH MANAGERS AND ADMINISTRATION

DEPARTMENT HEADS:

Information Open Line, a two-way confidential channel of communication,
began on a pilot basis April 10 in Region #3540, Administration (North and South), and Centralized Services (North and
South). Initial response has been enthusiastic and the
program will be expanded statewide on July 12.

Action The following instructions are for branches and departments
which did not participate in the pilot program.

1. About July 7, you will receive an envelope containing
the following material concerning the Open Line program.
Review it immediately.

   Poster(s)
   Forms
   Pamphlets
   Meeting Guide

2. Hold a staff meeting on July 12. Discuss the program
as outlined in the meeting guide. Be sure to include all
prime-time and part-time employes, or hold a separate
meeting for them, if necessary.

3. Give one question-and-answer pamphlet to each employe
during the meeting.

4. Place the posters and forms in an area accessible to all
employes in your branch or department, such as your
staff room.

Questions   Mr. Paul Allen
and Addi-   Open Line Coordinator
tional   Communications Department #3400
Materials   (SF Ext. 8366)

                     C. H. Baumhefner
                     Vice Chairman of the Board

July 5, 1972

Dear Fellow BankAmerican:

In my recent letter to you summarizing the results of the Employee Opinion Survey I mentioned that a new program called Open Line was being tested as a positive step toward improving upward communications. The seven hundred items received to date indicate the enthusiastic staff response to our pilot program. I am pleased to announce that Open Line will be extended statewide on July 12.

Through Open Line you will be able to forward your comments, questions, or complaints directly to management--and receive a responsive, confidential, and timely reply at your home. I cannot emphasize too strongly the confidential nature of the program. Your name will be known only to the Open Line Coordinator and he will not reveal your identity to anyone without your permission.

While Open Line is not intended to replace face-to-face communications between you and your supervisor, it will give you an opportunity to comment on or question matters that may go beyond the scope of your daily supervisory relationship. Open Line will also supplement the "Let's Talk It Over" program which many BankAmericans, through the Employe Opinion Survey, said needs strengthening. You will receive more details about Open Line at a staff meeting next week.

I cannot speak often enough about our objectives to open channels of communications throughout the Bank, because expressing viewpoints and reaching understandings benefits each of us as individuals as well as the entire organization.

·I hope that you will find Open Line a positive and beneficial way to make your voice heard in the bank.

Sincerely,

A. W. Clausen

President

ARTICLE FROM
Management Newsletter,
VOL. 2/NO. 15, MARCH 30, 1972

PILOT TEST OF NEW "OPEN LINE" PROGRAM BEGINS APRIL 10

A new two-way confidential channel of communications between employes and management, under the direction of the Communications Department, will begin on a pilot basis on April 10. The program, called "Open Line," will operate initially in Oakland, Alameda, and Contra Costa Region #3540; Administrative Departments (North & South); and Centralized Services (North & South). After evaluation and refinement of the pilot program, it will be expanded statewide.

Through Open Line, all officers and non-officers will have a new opportunity to communicate with management. The program will not interfere with the existing supervisor-employe relationship or replace the "Let's Talk It Over" program. However, it will complement them and provide an additional means of upward communication when direct channels break down. (Suggestions which employes believe to be eligible for cash awards will be handled through the Suggestion Program.)

For the employe, Open Line provides an opportunity to express opinions, make comments, ask questions, and register complaints. The program provides the means for a direct, prompt, and confidential reply from management. For management, Open Line provides a more informed view of employe attitudes and concerns, and provides a forum to explain its programs.

To create a willingness to use the program freely and to ensure confidentiality, only the Open Line Coordinator will know the identity of each writer who chooses to use his or her name. For those people who sign the form and want a reply, answers will be mailed directly to their homes. A limited number of questions and answers of Bankwide interest will be printed in the *Bankamerican* each month.

ARTICLE FROM
Management Newsletter,
VOL. 2/NO. 30, JULY 6, 1972

OPEN LINE PILOT TEST A SUCCESS: PROGRAM GOES STATEWIDE JULY 12

Open Line, our confidential upward communications program, will be extended statewide on July 12. It has been operating as a pilot program since April 10 in Administration, Centralized Services and Region #3540.

The response to the program has been enthusiastic both from employes, who submitted 650 Open Lines in the first eleven weeks of the program, and from management, which has sought to provide informative and candid answers. Open Line enables employes to question or comment on management policies and to communicate personal problems. To this extent "Let's Talk It over" and Open Line complement each other and provide an additional avenue of communications when direct channels break down.

The program does not promise that all problems will be solved to the employee's satisfaction or that management policies will change overnight. But change can come about only if employe viewpoints are expressed and conveyed to those who formulate policy. Open Line provides this channel and gives all employes a chance to be heard.

ARTICLE BY VICKI ESLER IN *BANKAMERICAN*

WILL ANYONE LISTEN? B OF A'S OPEN LINE MAKES SURE SOMEONE WILL Will Anybody Listen? Why do we have to keep having those incentive contests? I'd like to know how the Bank selects people to fill open positions. What should I do if I want to get ahead in the Bank? Why did the rates for medical insurance go up more for single people than for married employes?

You probably can think of a few beefs of your own—questions, comments, complaints you may have kept to yourself or only told your husband or wife. Now you'll be able to let management know about them and still keep your anonymity. Somebody *is* listening. A new program started on a pilot basis in April offers a two-way completely confidential channel of communication between employes and management. The program will be extended statewide in the near future.

Open Line lets you voice your views directly to management and assures you of a personal reply. The only one who will know your identity is the Open Line coordinator, Paul Allen.

You may say, "Any problem I have I take to my supervisor or manager." Fine. Open Line is not intended to replace face-to-face communications, or the "Let's Talk It Over" Program, but to complement them by providing an additional means of upward communication when direct channels break down. You now have an option—you can speak up and still remain anonymous. Management at the same time is gathering invaluable information on what employes are thinking, what they like and don't like about working at the Bank, what they think of Bank policies. But, again, they only learn employe opinions, not names.

As Coordinator Paul Allen put it, "I see myself as trying to do a positive thing for everyone in the Bank. The program offers something to each person—either as a user or from the standpoint of gaining an idea of what people are thinking."

Paul went on to define his functions: to preserve the anonymity of the author; to get the question to and answer from the subject matter expert; and to provide the author of the letter an honest answer or solution.

To take advantage of this new opportunity to sound off, all you'll have to do is take a form from the poster in your administrative area or branch, then write in your comment. You may choose to discuss the matter with a qualified person in the Bank instead of receiving a mailed reply. The form also asks your permission to print the letter in the *Bankamerican* if it's of general interest—without your name, of course. You need not sign the form, but only those with a name and address can receive a personal reply. "There are some problems which we could help alleviate, but if there's no name, there's no opportunity to do that," said Paul. "'It's very frustrating—we really want to be able to do something for the individual."

Only the program coordinator will know your identity if you sign the form. You can send it by interbranch mail or stick it in a mailbox (postage is prepaid). That portion of the form with your name on it is detached from your letter when it is received at the 11th floor office of Open Line in World Headquarters and placed in a locked box. Your letter is retyped on plain paper identified only by a code number that also appears on your name stub. The reply will be sent directly to your home. Stubs will be kept for 30 days in case a follow-up letter is necessary, then will be destroyed.

Some natural questions that might occur to you are: What happens if the person who answers the letter insists on knowing who wrote it? How can I be sure no one will see the stubs?

Paul assured me he would refuse to divulge the name of any person. Even though you hadn't specifically requested an interview, if it looks as if the solution to your problem might involve one, he will personally contact you for your permission before proceeding. If you decide to discuss your question personally with someone, the coordinator will make the arrangements and then contact you to let you know whom he has selected as best qualified to help you. Only if you agree will he go ahead. Only the officer you see and the coordinator will know your identity.

As for the stubs, Paul grinned and said, "I have a little box and I swallow the key to it every night before I go home." In a more serious vein, he informed me that the box will be locked except when he is depositing or removing a stub.

When Paul goes through the forms that arrive in his mail (currently about 20 to 25 a day), he selects the person in the Bank he thinks is the best one to answer. "We'll go to the highest level it takes to get the right answer," he said.

Asked his opinion of the program, Ted Wootton, VP of Headquarters Administration—South, who has answered a number of employee questions, replied, "I think it has tremendous potential. It lets us know how employes feel, and helps us resolve misunderstandings. This will have a fairly significant impact on changes we will make. I strongly urge employes to raise questions even though they may not see immediate results. Changes can't be made overnight—some involve a fair amount of study. But employe inquiries and comments are being considered carefully. My only concern is that people won't use it enough."

Questions concerning branches would probably be answered by district administrators. Bill Manis of Region #40, which is part of the initial pilot program, is also enthusiastic about the program's potential. "I think it can be very beneficial to all concerned—particularly managers and operations officers. They don't always get the true feelings of their employes."

Paul and his assistant Pam Smith review each answer and, if they feel it is vague or doesn't clearly deal with the problem, suggest it be revised. If your letter raises questions on several different topics, each would be answered, if necessary by several individuals. But you can get a quicker answer if you put each question on a separate form.

"We're going to attempt to stay within a ten-day turn-around time," he said. "If the question is so complicated we can't make the deadline, I'll write and tell the author when he can expect an answer. If the question's on his mind, he wants an answer while it's still on his mind, not two months later when it may no longer be a matter of concern to him."

If the comment is in the nature of a suggestion to be considered for a cash award, Paul will forward those comments to the Bank's suggestion program.

The pilot program is being conducted in administrative departments and Centralized Services, North and South, as well as in the Oakland Alameda-Contra Costa Region—15,000 people in all. The first week of its operation saw about 150 orange forms arrive on Paul's desk. Questions about salaries, benefits, supervisory problems, tuition assistance, working conditions, social responsibility, even cafeteria prices are among the subjects on people's minds.

What's on *your* mind? Perhaps giving the Open Line program a chance to hear about it may solve your problem, answer your question, or convince you someone is at least listening.

**ARTICLE BY BOB
WENDLINGER FROM**
Management Magazine,
VOL. 3/NO. 4, APRIL 1973

OPEN LINE ONE YEAR OLD

In 1971, Bank of American completed an unusually comprehensive one-year study of our internal communications needs. It all began when a task force of senior officers, appointed by President Tom Clausen, set out to investigate upward, downward, and horizontal communications at all levels of the Bank. Special studies were undertaken, personal interviews were conducted throughout the state, and a written communications survey was distributed to all employes.

One of the major findings of the Task Force was that many employes felt that there was no way to confidentially express an opinion or solve a problem when normal channels had broken down. Some employes feared the possibility of reprisals as a result of by-passing their supervisors with such ideas or proposals, and others were concerned that management—seemingly remote in a rapidly growing organization—was not really interested in their attitudes and opinions.

This feeling was evident in comments such as these:

"There is little means to determine if our communications go upstream, especially more than one level or two."

"I think the establishment of a 'gripe' or 'complaint' department would result in some surprising and profitable suggestions."

"A lot is said about expressing your opinion and voicing complaints, but when it actually comes down to the time when an employe desires to complain, his complaint is passed over with nothing being done about it."

"It would be nice and more comfortable to have a department or person outside of one's own branch to write to . . . "

A solution to these upward communications problems was contained in the more than 20 major recommendations of the Task Force. And as a result, the Open Line program was born in early 1972.

First, it offers a confidential channel to any officer or non-officer who wants to submit a problem, complaint, or opinion to management. The writer's identity is known only to the Open Line Coordinator in the Communications Department.

Secondly, it guarantees a candid written reply from management (sent to the employe's home) or, with the employe's permission, an interview with an Employe Relations Officer or District Administrator.

Confidentiality and Candor

The two keys to a successful Open Line program are confidentiality and candor. The employe's identity must be protected and the answers generated must be honest.

How does one go about establishing an Open Line program? Fortunately, several Open Line-type programs around the country could be used as models (particularly those of Sun Oil and IBM), and the machinery for such a program was pretty much available to adapt to our own needs.

One initial problem was the identification of subject-matter experts at management levels who would answer the questions. While putting together lists of those officers, the Open Line Coordinator and the head of the Communications Department visited numerous administration departments and regional vice presidents. They explained how the program would work, meanwhile exploring how certain unusual types of questions might be answered.

For example, who should answer a question regarding vacations that was written by an employe in the California Division? Someone in Personnel with policy responsibilities or someone in California Division with line responsibilities? The rule of thumb was to send policy questions to Compensation and Benefits in Personnel Administration, and to forward questions on implementation—such as the scheduling of vacations—to California Division.

This early decision evolved to a standard procedure for most policy-versus-implementation questions. Anything regarding how a policy is implemented generally goes to the responsible line or operating unit. And some letters—as say, on dress code—go to both types of officers. On a dress code question, for example, Personnel may explain the overall policy while California Division or an administration department head may explain the implementation within a particular work unit.

Setting Up the Program

To make certain that the program would not suffer from the administrative failures sometimes caused by enthusiastic haste, Open Line was tested with the 15,000 people who work in three representative Bank areas: the Oakland-Alameda-Contra Costa Region; San Francisco World Headquarters; and Centralized Services in San Francisco and Los Angeles.

The objective was to give the Coordinator and his staff a chance to debug the system and gradually build up developed administrative procedures that could handle the expected volume of a statewide program. (We were told by other companies to expect about six questions per 100 employes a month; this would mean about 250 questions a month for the Bank.) Our concern was to keep within the ten-day turnaround time we had promised in the initial stages of the program.

Employes believed in Open Line and they used it. During the first week of the pilot program, 150 letters crossed the Coordinator's desk and were referred out for answers. The volume settled at from 20 to 25 letters daily during the three months of the pilot program. On Open Line's first birthday, the statewide response was 15 letters, and that's about average now.

Why do employes use Open Line? Informal surveys have shown that employes use Open Line for one major reason: they have something important on their minds and need someone to listen to it—confidentially. Recently, employes have added another reason for using the program—the candor and responsiveness of the answers from management they have personally received or read about in the *Bankamerican.*

Employe letters have ranged from dress codes to drug abuse; retirement benefits to rest rooms; mileage allowance to Mary Marvelous; parking to performance reviews.

When questions arrive at the Coordinator's desk, they are classified so that employe concerns and trends can be analyzed from time to time. What kinds of subjects are posed in Open Lines? As one might expect, the various categories of compensation and benefits together add up to nearly a quarter of the nearly 3,000 Open Lines received during the first year. The next most frequently received Open Lines deal with job opportunities and promotions. Over 100 employes have sought **309** advice about promotions and about getting information concerning jobs in other departments and community offices. And questions about supervisory policies and practices form a large share of the total number.

Who Turned Down the Heat?

Many questions deal with everyday human problems and interests. One employe wanted help in getting her unemployed father a job (he got it). Twelve employes complained about the "freezing" temperature in their office and thought the platform officers were responsible since they controlled the thermostat (the problem was traced to a faulty heating unit). One former employe thought he had been dismissed unfairly (he had been treated fairly).

During the first year of operation, more than 200 employes have complained about the alleged unfairness, inconsistency, or misdoings of their supervisors.

Questions such as these need to be investigated thoroughly to see both sides of the issue. Before any steps are taken, the employe is contacted and asked whether his or her identity might be revealed. If the employe does not give permission, the subject is dropped and the letter is considered answered. If permission is granted, the Open Line Coordinator will coordinate the information gathered and may also help to bring together the employe and the responsible officer.

Very often, problems have resulted from misinterpretations of Bank policy either by the employe or the supervisor. Sometimes, for example, an employe complains of receiving a smaller salary increase than he or she felt was deserved. When the employe turns out to be justified in the request, he or she can get the raise through the cooperation of a district administrator or administration officer. But the employe's supervisor could have gotten the same action by checking with the appropriate administrative unit or Salary Administration. And the employe can always go directly to his or her district administrator or administration department head.

Measuring Open Line's Success

How do we gauge the success of the Open Line program? One indicator of success is, of course, the number of letters received. Another is the frequency of *signed* letters. While the average for other programs is between 80 and 90 percent, Bank of America's average has remained at 93 percent since the program began, suggesting a faith in the confidentiality of the program and in management's assurance that the identity of writers will not be revealed without their specific permission.

To preserve confidentiality, Open Line includes a security program that, in the words of the present Open Line Coordinator, "combines elements of James Bond and the Strategic Air Command."

First, the Coordinator opens all the incoming mail behind closed doors. He assigns a number to the name stub at the bottom of the form and puts a corresponding number at the top. He then separates the two and places the name stub in a locked box to which he has the only key. The stub remains in the locked box until it is time to mail a reply. Meanwhile, the Open Line writer is known only by number.

To be certain that no one can identify the writer's handwriting, the letter (now with the identifying number) is retyped on white paper before being circulated for a response. Included on the form are codes which indicate whether the letter was signed, whether or not the publication of the letter is restricted, and whether or not the employe wants a personal interview.

After the letter has been retyped, the Coordinator reads it and decides where to send it for an answer. Sometimes the question has been answered in an earlier Open Line; if this is so, the Coordinator or his assistant will check with the person who answered the first question to make certain the answer is still current.

What happens when the writer names specific offices, officers, or statistics which are important but would probably reveal the identity of the employe? The employe is telephoned and asked whether his or her name may be revealed. If the employe agrees, further contacts are made until the question is answered. If the employe objects, the name is not revealed and the Coordinator gets the question answered as best he can—but possibly less satisfactorily.

Evaluating the Response

When the response is returned to the Coordinator's office—normal turnaround time is ten working days, although answers involving several departments may take longer—the Coordinator reviews it from the employee's point of view. Will it be perceived as candid? Does it really answer the question? In cases where management policy does not permit comment (revealing the nature of our business relationship with a major borrower, for example), the Coordinator makes certain that the letter explains why the information can't be disclosed.

If the answer is considered as complete, it is retyped on Open Line letterhead stationery and given to the Coordinator—still without the employe's name—at four o'clock every afternoon. Once again behind closed doors, the Coordinator removes the name stub from the locked box and matches the numbers with corresponding numbers on the letters. Then—providing the ultimate security—the Coordinator hand-addresses and stamps the 15 or so Open Lines that go out each day, and personally drops the letters in a U.S. mail box outside the bank on his way home.

Most answers are handled by mail, but if a telephone call should be necessary, the Coordinator will not leave a message if the employe is out or busy. As a result, it may take several days to catch someone by phone. But what could be more damaging to the success of the program than for an employe to return from lunch and find a note that read, "Call the Open Line Coordinator about your problem!"

What Have We Learned?

What has been learned after a year of Open Line? Employes have learned, certainly, that there are logical explanations for our policies and procedures; that supervisors are human and can make mistakes and correct them (and be corrected); and that Bank management is willing to respond reasonably to reasonable questions and criticisms offered with good will.

What has management learned? For one thing, one knows that many policies traditionally unquestioned because of a lack of feedback are now being more closely scrutinized and evaluated. For another, it is hoped that Open Line will give management continuous information on current employe attitudes. Although Open Line questions are insufficient in number to provide statistical validity, we won't have to wait for monthly, quarterly, or annual meetings with employes to learn what and where our problems are. Open Line will tell us quickly, and a series of reports has been prepared that will enable management at senior levels to decide what problems require action at any particular moment.

In short, Open Line reflects the commitment of Mr. Clausen "to the proposition that communication is a two-way street."

And what of Open Line in the future? Each Open Line Coordinator is given one charge—"work yourself out of a job." Which means that we're working toward the day when free and open communication at Bank of America precludes the need for Open Line. As mutual trust and understanding develop, this goal draws nearer.

Anyone who is seriously interested in beginning a program such as Open Line is asked to contact Bank of America for more detailed information. You may write directly to:

> Mr. Robert M. Wendlinger
> Assistant Vice President
> Communications Department
> Bank of America
> P.O. Box 37000
> San Francisco, California 94137

APPENDIX
B

The Actual Reports
Presented by
Dr. Arnold E. Schneider
upon Completion of Consulting Visits
to
Various National
Decentralized Companies

I arrived at the office early on the 14th. Mr. A was very cordial and very receptive. He stated that he had arranged his schedule during my visit to accommodate whatever time I would need with him. We had a very informal discussion about his staff. I outlined to him that I had no preconceived concepts as to the direction we ought to move in terms of management growth and development and the direction in which we should move. I stated that I was in hopes of getting a better handle on the problem and a more in-depth analysis by visiting with the staff people who were present and also by visiting with him and later with some of his management group. He seemed to be agreeable to this. We then reviewed the members of his staff who were in the city. He stated that his staff meetings were held on every other Friday and that unfortunately at this time there were a number of people who were out of the office, and although they generally sent a representative, nevertheless I would not gain a great deal by my sitting in at the staff meeting on Friday, April 16th. I left this open and tried to encourage him to review this, but I sensed that he preferred at this time that I did not sit in on this particular staff meeting. It may be that I am wrong, and it also may be due to the fact that he felt that he didn't have enough of the staff people there to give him an opportunity to show the staff in its best light.

He offered to revise his schedule for the evening of Wednesday, the 14th, so that we could go out to dinner, but I told him that if he had previous arrangements to honor those. He also stated that he would then make himself available for the evening of the 15th and I stated that, if he had other plans and if he would prefer that we delay this to a future date, I would be willing to go along, and he seemed to want to put this off until my next trip.

For my own personal assessment, and in order to establish bench marks to guide me in my attempt to recognize the nature and dimensions of the problems that might exist, I raised the following mental questions:

1. Was there strong leadership capable of producing a team effort?
2. Does he establish realistic goals, not only for himself, but for all of his people, which they accept, which they understand, and which they translate into their own working capability and working plans?
3. Is he unconsciously or nonconsciously authoritarian?
4. Is he too structured?
5. Is he very competent technically, yet lacking the overall conceptual grasp, the charisma, which would make him a positive force in the zone?
6. Does he make decisions or does he only execute the decisions?
7. Does he have the unique capacity to recognize a problem before it escalates to the point where his management must call it to his attention and then have him move upon it? In other words, is he problem-sensitized?
8. Is he supportive of his people rather than critical, and does he guide, counsel, work with, and develop them?
9. Does he seek the opinion of his subordinates and does he take the time to get them to see the rationale of his decisions?
10. Does he have a strong or weak staff? In other words, some people to me seem to have the penchant for picking weak people who are members of their staff rather than strong people. This may be an accident; on the other hand, it may be an unconscious security motivation.
11. How does he see his problems and what plans, strategies, and techniques does he hope to bring to bear on the resolution of his problems, agency-wise, management-wise, in order to get the best resolution?

12. Are there any loyalty problems involved?
13. How do his subordinates view him? Given a free atmosphere in order to express themselves, how would they relate to him and how would they view him as their leader?

I am not sure whether he has a zone organizational manual with the appropriate job descriptions; I did not ask him for it, although I was on the verge of so doing in our conversations and meant to. I did ask him for his organization chart and he did not bring out an organization chart, but rather I scribbled an organization chart in front of him in order to get a basic impression of the various staff people and the areas of their responsibility. I will want to check on this again, and if we do not have an organization chart and the job write-ups for the zone which I believe are in existence, perhaps we will also move in this direction and we will have a review with the various staff people as to the meaning of their job descriptions and how their job descriptions serve as a basis for their relationship with the manager and their colleagues. Shown below is the organization chart as Mr. A, in talking with me, explained it to me as I sketched it.

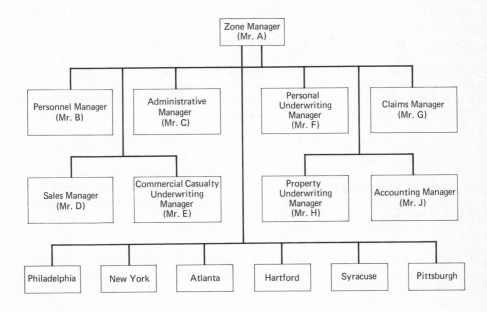

SUMMARY OF MAJOR STATEMENTS FROM INTERVIEWEES

1. Mr. G

He stated that he felt morale was improving because they were looking forward to having the best quarter in 1971 that they have ever had for a long time previously. He felt that the reason for this was that the agency force had been cleaned up and, of course, there was far better claims handling. He stated that he thought the Ohio business had put them back into the hole for a little while.

He stated that they had staff meetings every two weeks, and upon being questioned on his assessment of the value of these meetings, he stated that some good came out of these meetings. As questions were raised, he stated that in his opinion they were open meetings and that people could discuss things. In this connection, other interviewees felt that the meetings were very structured and that there was very little discussion but merely a framework for reporting and reporting within the area of each one's specific area of responsibility. He stated that he felt that Mr. A is "open" in his communications with the staff members and that he saw him as an open individual. He stated that he feels that Mr. A wants him to "tell him what he should know." He stated that Mr. A thinks that certain facets of the business are "none of his business," and he will tell me so. He felt that there was a very good working relationship between him and Mr. A. He talked about the fact that perhaps we need a human resource audit. He stated that frequently, in claims in particular, they took a top technical claims adjuster and they made a manager out of him without any previous training, direction, and help, and that, in his opinion, the man is not a manager. He stated that after they take the new manager and put him into his new area of responsibility, the company abandons him as far as management development and management assistance are concerned. We talked about the organizational relationships and the lines of responsibility. He said that in his opinion Claims is responsible to Mr. A, although there is a great deal of staff authority from the service offices through the branches to the zone. He said, "Although I try to keep everyone informed, I go to Mr. A, and then Mr. A will go directly to the home office. This in a way leaves others out in the cold. I try my best to keep my lines of communication open. When I was with 'Y' Company, the problem was entirely different. I worked in the zone and our contact with the home office was nil. In fact, we had no contact with the home office, and all evaluation was done on the zone level."

He said, "What we do need is a lot of exposure to management philosophy and management principles, both in relationship to claims and the claims management group and in our relationship to Mr. A and the home office. I think that we have a lot of strength in this zone and that we have a strong management team. We did have some lectures on some management techniques, but I think we ought to set up some claims and staff meetings in various areas and start building our claim management team."

At this point I suggested to him that he might get some problems from his claim management personnel in relationship to the people that they were supervising. It was my thinking that if we could get various managers to write down some problems in management which they have faced, then the case studies would be very realistic and they could be used as a basis for discussion and leading to a better understanding at our meetings of what the various avenues of solution might be. This would be a better vehicle than pure theory.

2. Mr. F

"I think we have more of a problem here in relationship to our underwriters and the agency group. At 'Z' Company, we had many agency meetings in which support was given to underwriters and claims.

"I would say that we need a lot of development in this zone. We all stay in our own bailiwicks.

"As far as zone staff meetings are concerned, we don't seem to stick to the schedule as we should. We have skipped too many meetings. However, I keep in close contact with Mr. D and Mr. A.

"One area that we need the most help in is in training our people who are moving into a management position for the first time. It seems to me that we just move a technician over into being a manager. He does not know how to interact as a manager. He might have too much introversion. One of the things we have to do, we have to get the sales force more underwriting-minded, and at the same time we've got to get the underwriters more sales-minded.

"I would say that we are tradition-bound; what we have to have is more rapport between all of the segments of the zone. Also, each branch doesn't want to be compared with the other branches in the zone. Each manager of a branch feels like his branch is something special. We need more agency meetings to work toward a good book of business. Another thing that I would say is that our agency plan lacks the disciplines of the Midwest. In my opinion the agent takes a line of least resistance and the easiest way. We controlled this in Chicago, for example, having regular meetings. However, I would say that the branches are holding more meetings and their staff meetings are very informative. The branches are doing a good job on their meetings."

In answer to the question, "What would you like in terms of management development?" he said, (1) management techniques—"how to get people to do what you want them to do," (2) more communications, and (3) better work flow, better planning.

3. Mr. H

I knew Mr. H from the time that he was in the Chicago office and during the period of time when he was in the Midwest zone. Therefore, he spoke very freely. This was also the case of Mr. F.

Mr. H said: (1) We have good technicians. (2) We have a strong team. (3) The company is strong.

I talked about the fact that he had worked for different people and asked whether he saw any differences in style. He said that he would have to be perfectly honest and that, of course, he hated to be negative, but he would be critical. He said that Mr. A is a one-man manager. He said we run our own little area, but *we are not part of a management team.* He went on to say that we have gone through harsh times. However, in his opinion, most of the decisions in the zone seem to be unilateral decisions. There is no communication. There is no looking for other ideas. There is only "This is the way I see it and this is the direction we've got to move in."

"I would say that the staff meetings are not really staff meetings. There is no encouragement of discussion. There is no asking for any ideas. There is no feeling for an opportunity to talk things out or bat things around. I would like to see a three-way move to some counseling, some review, and some guidance. I would say in this zone that the biggest lack is the lack of training. We are always putting in new people in various spots, but perhaps part of that is due to the folding together of the various companies." He went on to say, "What we need here is leadership." He talked about the fact that (1) the leadership could be negative, (2) it could be average, (3) it could be dynamic, (4) it could be driving, and (5) it could be neutral. In his opinion, A had a tremendous devotion to his job, and he had a good deal of personal drive, but, he said, "I wouldn't call it leadership by leadership, but by the way the person himself works in his job." He said, "A is strong in his devotion and determination to try to get the job done." He said he is "solid and quiet."

He said, "You don't get close to him, he has a different style."

He then moved over to the state of the level of profit. He said, "I have hopes of turning profits." He said, "We are better off in commercial property than before," and, "As far as his underwriters are concerned, he has a well-experienced team, and they are handling themselves well." He went on to say that the men that he likes best in underwriting branches are those who are willing to call him and who are willing to talk about a risk, and who are willing to review and analyze facts. "People in the business have to have a humility about their decisions and a willingness to review them with their superiors without acting like they didn't know their own jobs." He said, "Sometimes you could call underwriters the merchants of declination."

He further pointed out that Mr. A isn't one to walk out of his office and visit with his senior staff people. He said, "I have yet to go out and have lunch with that man." He suggested that maybe Mr. A is too close to all of the problems in that maybe he loses his objectivity. He said there may be something in there being a clique. He said that what he likes in a senior manager is warmth, accessibility, physical opportunity to visit with him. He further pointed out that all the management meetings he attended were formal, and that they were very much only reporting meetings, that there was no communication or growth going on at the meetings. He said, "There should be more discussion at the team level." He said they used to have luncheon meetings where they kicked around their common problems. This must have been in another zone.

I asked Mr. H the question, "Do you think that he is or isn't authoritarian in his leadership style?" He replied, "I think he is." He said he thinks this stems from the stresses or his fearfulness. He went on to say that he thought that A maintained control of all decision making. He said that Mr. A says, "This is what we are going to do," and the rest of the staff doesn't get involved in the overall thinking and analysis of the outcome of the decision. He said that in this kind of climate the weak men are supported and are comfortable and that a number of the men, he felt, were blunted in their growth in a climate where all the decisions were made for them and they did not participate in the decision making (this is a pretty good insight). Furthermore, he said that people tend to withdraw themselves from involving themselves in the decision making and taking responsibility for their part in the final decision. He talked about Mr. E, who is the casualty underwriting manager, and talked about the fact that he is new in management.

4. Mr. C

Mr. C and I left the office and had breakfast together. It was difficult to get Mr. C to commit himself, and his lack of communication, although he apparently seemed open, led me to make a summary decision that he was relatively weak. He stated that he maintains an open door with Mr. A, and Mr. A keeps him fully informed. He pointed out that Mr. A makes the major decisions, but he also pointed out that he makes decisions in certain areas, but he keeps him informed while he makes the decision. He says there are times when there is joint decision making between himself and Mr. A. He went on to say that from his viewpoint Mr. A. was easy to work with and that he was very easy to talk to, but he said that, in his opinion, Mr. A was very much a listener, and he felt that in his opinion this was a primary requirement of a manager. He said that he felt very comfortable when he went in and talked with Mr. A. He felt also that branch managers were very cooperative with him, and that he felt free to talk with Mr. A at any time about any problems.

5. Mr. B

In my initial talks with Mr. A, he pointed out that Mr. B was "leaving" and from the general tenor of conversation, I assumed that he had been fired. I bumped into Mr. B near the men's washroom and he began to talk to me, so I visited with him and I made up my mind that, although he was *persona non grata,* nevertheless, I was going to learn what I could from him, because I know when a man is on his way out at least he'll talk and tell you the truth, and the truth even from an average person can be enlightening.

And so, on my own, I set up a time and slid into his office unobtrusively and visited with him. Mr. B stated that he felt he got along with Mr. A. He said, "I don't feel I failed." He said that he felt that he never had the opportunity in his own line of work with the company. He did state that he never had any criticisms along the way and perhaps he didn't have any direction. From time to time he said he raised questions about different facets of what he was told to do and he was told, "Don't raise any questions, just do it." Other than that, he felt that the relationship was fine. He stated that, as for the opportunity for him to contribute to the organization, "It did not exist." He said, "Everybody should have the opportunity to contribute, and whether the contribution (verbal, I presume) is right or wrong, nevertheless, they ought to have the opportunity to contribute." He didn't think, for example, in underwriting, that sometimes the people have the opportunity to use their mind, and he said, "Many companies lose people because they don't give people the opportunity to think." He said that, in trying to get his job done, he didn't get any feedback—any constructive feedback. He said this is possibly also true in relationship to middle management, in that "what a person spends his time at is second-guessing what top management wants to hear." He said, "Everybody ought to have the opportunity to ask questions and not be afraid of asking that question."

I asked him, "Did you have any counseling sessions or at least any sessions with management in relationship to what they wanted you to do and how they wanted you to do it, and what their philosophy was, and how you were to fit into that philosophy?" And he said, "No." He said that communication was through staff meetings once a month, and he said these meetings were skipped and would be missed for a period of a month or two. The meetings were formal—"You would make your reports"—and that was the end of it. He wondered if this was a total management concept of "X" Company. He also said that he thought the philosophy of the organization—zone organization, at least—was that there are certain things we better do in a specific way, that it was a conform-or-else kind of situation, and "there was an edict" from the front office. He felt that he had been in an authoritarian situation, but he didn't know whether it was Mr. A's fault or whether it was a total organizational structure.

6. Mr. J

Mr. J seemed to have a feel for what one might call "the people-oriented or Theory Y" style of management. He said he talks over many of his problems with the people in the department. He pointed out that they were mostly girls (so I noticed!). He said that they worked together and established objectives, and because of the composition of his staff, he spends a lot of time in guidance and counseling with his people. He feels that they have developed a good management team in the accounting area and that it functions well without his being there. He says that he has a lot of people trained who can handle their jobs. He stated that he reports to Mr. C through to Mr. A. On the other hand, he reports to Mr. A on many problems.

I asked him what he felt about the staff meetings. He said that, as far as he was concerned, "they get into too much technical detail at them." He said, "Many of the people like to show off, and they have a great deal of knowledge in their own area and they get too technical and they talk on too much detail." However, he said that the meetings were informative, and, "You get a better insight into the other fellows' problems." However, he felt that, as far as he was concerned, the meetings were too long, and he said, "Although they are booked to start at 8:30 in the morning and quit at 10:15, they usually run through 12:15 to 12:30." He said that that was too much time, and that "you really didn't need to get in that much depth." He pointed out that Mr. A alternates the chairman and that the chairmen have a natural tendency to show off when they are running the meetings, particularly as it relates to their area of expertise. However, he said these management meetings in his opinion are tremendous morale builders.

SOME GENERAL QUESTIONS, A.E.S.

1. Does Mr. A have the capacity to make tough decisions, or are these decisions made after the fact or when he is faced with the necessity of meeting a standard which has been established by the home office?
2. Is his style such that it is work-oriented rather than people-oriented?
3. Does his style elicit warmth and a willingness of people to commit themselves to the team goals?
4. Does he have charisma, or that ability to make people want to participate in arduous tasks to get the job done?
5. Is he a very strong technician, but poor in the human qualities that make for commitment to goals?
6. Is he insecure and defensive about people, particularly the people whom he has recommended and worked with over a long period of time?
7. Is he realistic? Does he lead from strength or does he lead from weakness?
8. Is he sufficiently flexible that he can read what the changing times call for, and can he, through his zone team, develop a program or plan of input that will change the need of the zones to meet the needs of the home office and the realities of doing business in the present? I guess what I'm saying is, is he a captive of his past?
9. In terms of his managerial style, how do we go about bringing him support and bringing him assistance so that he can work effectively?

There are some problems in relationship to the long-time manpower planning and whether there is a second man in relationship to the key people we have in the zone. There are some problems in relationship to delegation and decision making. There are some problems in relation to the authority structure. There are problems in relation to whether the people on the way up are getting the kind of training, managerial and other—guidance and counseling—they are entitled to in order to make them succeed. There are problems as to whether the managerial styles are too authoritarian or whether the senior man is an "edict" manager who states, "You support company policy or else!" There are some problems as to making a determination as to whether the style is out of his insecurity or out of the fact that the dimensions of the job may be larger than he is accustomed to, or whether his managerial role is being incorrectly expressed. We could ask questions: Are the messages he is giving received correctly? What image is he portraying? and, What differences are there between his communications and the receiving of that communication?

APPENDIX C

Two Actual Interviews
Conducted
in the Field
by
Dr. Arnold E. Schneider

(All names have been changed except that of Dr. Schneider)

REPORT TO: Tom Mills

FROM: Dr. A. E. Schneider

INTERVIEW WITH WILLIAM CONRAD

Mr. Mills called and asked if I could see him. I made an appointment with him for the following day and we met at approximately 10:00 A.M. Mr. Mills and I visited about various aspects of management and then he brought up the problem of Mr. Conrad, whom he said he brought into his department some time ago when he was being released by the File Company. He told me some of his background—to the effect that he had been a Six at one time and, subsequently, he had taken employment with the Statistical Department as a Four. He told me that he had been on the verge of moving Mr. Conrad up to a Five and that Mr. Conrad seemed to get along fine for a period of time, and then suddenly he seemed to develop aggressive and hostile tendencies toward his supervisors and other people with whom he worked. He pointed out that what precipitated this incident was the fact that Mr. Conrad had been asked to do a report, and that when he turned it in, the supervisor stated that the report was wrong. Thereupon, Mr. Conrad invited the supervisor out into the alley to settle it on a man-to-man basis, or something of this nature.

Mr. Mills stated that this man was capable of doing excellent work as a technician and that he seemed at all times more than willing to do his share of the work, but that he fell into these periods of stress and emotional strain and particularly aggressiveness.

It was suggested that I undertake a nondirective counseling program with him, and what follows represents our first interview, which took approximately an hour and a half. I feel that we could have spent even more time on our first interview, but this would not have been wise.

We arranged for the interview in Mr. Broom's office. Mr. Conrad came into the room and I introduced myself.

DR. S.   "Do you know why we are going to have this interview?"

W. C.   "Yes, I do."

DR. S.   "Do you know who I am?"

W. C.   "Yes, in general, I do."

DR. S.   "Are you nervous?"

W. C.   "Not any more than usual."

DR. S.   "How long have you been with the company?"

W. C.   "Since December 6, 1940—that is when I first came to work for them, although I haven't worked here all of the time."

DR. S.   "Where is your home?"

W. C.   "I am a native of Chicago."

DR. S.   "Are you the only one in your family?"

W. C.   "No, I have a brother who is younger."

DR. S.   "Tell me more about yourself."

W. C.   "I am a graduate of a Chicago High School and then I went to State University for a semester. I had more schooling because at the age of 38, I went to Northwestern University for two years at nights. I took accounting courses there and I also took some of those ICS courses there."

(At this point, it was noted that the subject talked very rapidly. He didn't say "ICS"; he said, "ISC." When I asked him if he meant International Correspondence Schools he stated, "Yes." He also had the habit of not completing sentences. He would think in one direction and speak in another from time to time.)

DR. S. "Would you say that you are relaxed or under tension right now?"

W. C. "This is rather new for me."

DR. S. "What do you mean by that?"

W. C. "The last time I talked to a man of your caliber, it was for the draft."

DR. S. "Were you drafted?"

W. C. "No, sir, I had a hernia. When I got it fixed up, it was too late."

DR. S. "What did you do during the war?"

W. C. "I worked in the Tab Room of the 'X' Corporation and then I went to Miami, Florida. I worked for the State Ice and Fuel Company there as assistant purchasing agent. Nights while I was there, I worked at the 'Y' Airlines."

DR. S. "Did you like being assistant purchasing agent?"

W. C. "It was different. I like being around people. I like to work. I like to talk to them, believe that or not, but I liked it."

DR. S. "Do you like what you are doing now better than being a purchasing agent?"

W. C. "I have given that a lot of thought. This kind of a job is more or less kind of like being an introvert. When I was in purchasing, I had the chance to meet new people and I liked that. On the other hand, I enjoy this work too."

DR. S. "If you had a chance to change jobs with us, what would you take?"
(He thought a long time. He did not answer rapidly for the first time since we began our conversation. He turned in his chair, looked out the window, and smiling finally said to me:)

W. C. "That is a tough question. My education has been along this line. You see, I was with the File Company for ten years. I kept books for a contractor on the side at that time because I kind of like to do that and also because I like to earn a little spare change. I don't know. Maybe I shouldn't even do that kind of work. Maybe I am not that kind of temperament."

DR. S. "How did you happen to get into that field of work?"

W. C. "I went to work for 'X' Corporation when I got back from Florida."

DR. S. "Why did you go to Florida?"

W. C. "I had just gotten married and it sounded quite interesting. We did it for the adventure and because my wife and I had never been anywhere before anyway."

DR. S. "Well, then, why did you leave Florida?"

W. C. "I came home to help my brother through school. My father had died while I was in Florida."

DR. S. "Oh!"

W. C. "My brother is connected with the Volkswagen. He has been in Germany. Both of us are mechanically inclined, but he followed it up. Both of us worked in a garage at one time."

DR. S. "You have been with the Company eleven to twelve years?"

W. C. "That is right."
(At this point he suddenly stopped talking and it was very quiet. I looked at him and he looked at me. Then, in order to get the counseling situation in a direction which I hoped it would proceed, I asked the following question:)

DR. S. "Would you say you are happy or unhappy?"

W. C. (After some hesitation) "That is a state of mind. You make your own happiness like you make your own breaks. Some days you are way behind, and some days you are on top of things."
(He then giggled quite uncontrollably and then he went on without any further encouragement.)
"Maybe it is the definition of happiness. When I face a problem which is

323

difficult, I will sometimes start something to do with my hands. If I do that, either the problem gets worse or it may disappear. You see, I kind of think that a person makes his own happiness. Someone, for example, said I went around scowling in the office. Well, if that is so, I didn't know that I was scowling. But your question of whether I am happy or unhappy—well, I don't know. I guess we would have to narrow it down."

DR. S. "Well, let's narrow it down. Would you say that you are happy with your home life?"

W. C. "Well, I have a daughter twelve years old. My wife is very nice. She puts up with me. She is very decent. I would say that we have the average number of spats. She knows how to handle me—after all, we have been married sixteen years. Our biggest enjoyment is making and remodeling the house. Even right now I am in the middle of re-wiring my basement. I enjoy doing something I have not done before. My wife likes to check on what I am doing, and if she doesn't like the way I am doing it, she lets me know."

DR. S. "Do you think you are better or smarter than your wife?" (At this point it was quiet, and then I said:) "Do you know what I mean?"

W. C. "I know what you mean. She will say yes, but you can't answer that just on one plane. That question was on two different planes. She is a lot smarter on some things. She sets me back when I smart-off, for example. No, I can't say that she is smarter than I am. I would say that she has a better background than I do."

DR. S. "Why do you say that—a better background than you do?"

W. C. "Let's put it this way—she comes from a larger family. I am a second-generation American. On the other hand, her people have been here for years. Her outlook is different. I have the Old-Country outlook on life. It makes us different in our type of personality or our temperament."

DR. S. "How old were you when your dad died?"

W. C. "Twenty or twenty-one."

DR. S. "Would you say you knew him well?"

W. C. "No, sir. He worked nights seven days a week and he was pretty active in labor politics."

DR. S. "What did he do?"

W. C. "He was a bus or streetcar driver. He was a typical labor man. I would say he was very pro-labor."

DR. S. "How old was he when he died?"

W. C. "He died at fifty-two."

DR. S. "What from?"

W. C. "Heart trouble."

DR. S. "Did you like him?"

W. C. "We got along very well."

DR. S. "Did he have a temper?"

W. C. "Definitely."

DR. S. "Did you ever see any of his outbursts?"

W. C. "Yes, I lived at the YMCA for a week or two because of it."

DR. S. "Tell me about it."

W. C. "He had been imbibing just a bit and he was after my younger brother and I decided to take it off his shoulders —that is, my younger brother. Well, now my dad, he wasn't an alcoholic or drunkard. Once in a while he liked a drink or two. I guess I was thirteen at the time."

324 DR. S. "Would you say you are like your dad or different from him?"

W. C. "It is about split. I am something like an uncle in some respects, and my mother can see traits similar to my dad in me."

DR. S. "Is this good or bad?"

W. C. "I don't know."

DR. S. "Do you have any idea why I am asking you questions like I am at the present time?"

W. C. "I am an amateur psychologist in a way myself. I would say it has something to do with correlation of ideas. You see so much material on tests which will make a person this way or that way that some of this stuff is too difficult to understand."

(Again here, although I didn't get everything that W. C. was talking about, he would from time to time ramble at a very rapid rate and it was difficult to follow. He has an idea but then there is no rationality or logic to the execution of his ideas. He has hold of a lot of concepts but he doesn't understand their true meaning. Again, in my own terminology, it is the old story of an individual being rational in many different directions except for one wire being loose, and this wire sparking like mad whenever a current operates, which makes it impossible for a complete connection to be made.)

DR. S. "Do you think you know yourself?"

W. C. "Sometimes I do and sometimes I don't. They tell me I can be the best fellow in the world at times, and at other times I ought to be taken out and shot."

DR. S. "Yes."

W. C. "Why I get on a streak once in a while, I don't know. I am not feeling sorry for myself, but on the other hand I think I get into a mood and then I do certain things that I shouldn't do when I get like that."

DR. S. "Do you understand these actions?"

W. C. "That is rather a hard question. If you mean do I know what I am doing and do I know whether it is wrong or not, yes, I think so. You see, whether something is wrong or right is pretty hard to explain here because this means that you believe that you can tell the difference, and in my opinion there is no such thing as black and white. I would say I know when I am happy and also I know when I have my streaks of orneryness, and I have a good idea what is causing it."

DR. S. "Then what causes them?"

(He didn't answer at this point and we both laughed. He was quiet for a while and then he said:)

W. C. "Impatience!"

DR. S. "Yes."

W. C. "I have got lots of patience like I have got patience for the job. Sometimes some of the people I am working with think they know a lot and I don't think I know so much, but lots of times I know as much about what I am doing as they do, and when some problem comes up, I just lose patience and I let fly. Now maybe losing my patience isn't good, but lots of people get ulcers, and anyhow, I don't get ulcers."

DR. S. "What do you mean by that?"

W. C. "Well, on this line of thought, I read a great deal. You know, I like to read a lot, and I read all kinds of books about the business world. For example, I read *The Organization Man*. I guess I am baring my soul now. You see, I am not a believer in a social ethic, but on the other hand, I don't believe the business world ought to operate to the point where it is a question of dog-eat-dog."

DR. S. "Yes."

W. C. "Now, for example, this is an insurance office. Insurance is our business, not progress, and it is a profit-making organization. This isn't one of those places where you can mix business and pleasure too much. Also, the idea of calling everybody by their first name is O.K."

(At this point he talked so very rapidly and the words gushed out so fast and the thoughts were so highly unrelated that I could not follow. He went along with several concepts which were drawn from some of the current novels in the field of business, but he had not thought them through or grasped their basic significance. He had latched onto an idea, a concept, and these were like isolated statements having no central tendency at all. At this point he certainly seemed to be "disjointed.")

DR. S. "Well, what you say is interesting, but we were talking about the problems you sometimes have."

W. C. "You mean, what causes the clash? You mean what I think is causing the trouble? Well, you don't need a dozen supervisors. I don't believe in decentralization, because that boosts costs. Insurance is going up in its price. It is getting itself priced out of the market."

(At this point the preceding was fairly accurately stated and what will follow is a fairly accurate recording of what was stated. He spoke again and again in abstractions and highly disjointed ideas.)

W. C. "I read a lot. Now insurance is getting competitive. I have been competitive when I was a younger man. When I work, I am competitive. I remember when I got my first job I told my first boss that I would handle the work or he wouldn't have to pay me after two or three weeks. Some of the people working today don't understand that everything is competitive and they have to be able to carry their load."

(There seems to be an underlying feeling in the man which is expressed by his words that he is more competent and able to do more with the time involved as far as his aspect of machine operation is concerned than those who are working around him. Although he has not verbalized this, it is showing through the aggressiveness of his statements in regard to others.)

W. C. "I was told by one person that you were expendable as an employee. That wasn't here, but that was at another place I worked. I don't mean that as harshness, but what I mean is that if you don't toe the mark, particularly in the old days, it was goodbye. In my other jobs I had a complete outline— that is, I knew what it was that I was doing. This was the way the work was supposed to get done, and this is the way I believe in getting the work done. Sometimes I don't talk in the morning, for example. Sometimes I can whoop it up with the boys, but that isn't very smart."

(Again note, at this particular time he began trying to analyze his working philosophy and his difficulty. Again, he did not track too accurately.)

W. C. "Now, if a fellow is a supervisor, you have got to set an example. You can't drive them. I don't think I own the place like some of the fellows do. As far as I am concerned, it is far from it. What a lot of people don't understand is that you don't own the company. You are just working."

(At this point he had been moving along so rapidly and had been jumping through so many ideas I just sat still and looked at him. He laughed in his own way and said, "Have you found a category for me yet?" This was so unrehearsed that I laughed and then he laughed.)

DR. S. "I don't know. Have you decided that there ought to be a category? You see, in the things that we do, there are no answers." (It was quiet for a few minutes.) "How old are you anyhow?"

W. C. "Forty-four years old."

DR. S. "Do you think you look forty-four?"

W. C. "I was told that I didn't. At twenty-one they took me for sixteen. It seems when you look young like I do, that that comes under some kind of a classification."

DR. S. "How do you get along with people?"

W. C. "I don't have a chip on my shoulder. I don't think the world owes me a living. In fact, I am indebted to people. On the other hand, I know you can't stop for every dog that barks; otherwise you will not get to the other side of the road. It doesn't make any difference to me, for example, whether someone says hello or not."

(At this point I believe he is showing some resentment to the interview which he has had on some of the so-called employee evaluation interviews. In other words, he is resisting any comments as to the personal aspects of how he gets his job done in relationship to his own self-confidence in the technical aspects of how he gets his job done. He has not analyzed it yet, but he feels he should be rated on his technical competence and that all these other matters do not really count. He feels put out that he has been rated on them. In other words, he feels that he has failed, if he has failed, on the basis of these personality factors, and he resents it.)

DR. S. "Would you say that at your age you are successful or failing?"

W. C. (A long period of thought ensued at this point.) "I would say that I am successful. I will never reach the top of the heap, nor do I care. My job is a job to accept and to do the best that I can at it. I spent a number of years at this business. I don't expect to get to the top nor do I think that I am great or that I need to be a vice president. I have a compelling drive to accomplish something. I am interested in doing a good job right where I am now. In other words, success doesn't come overnight and I know that. Even though I am my age, I think I am just getting started. The biggest mistakes that they make is making vice presidents of guys who are just thirty-five. Those young fellows really don't know anything about life yet. What are these young fellows going to do when they get my age? I think we are going to have more maladjusted men than what we even have today. We are going to have more maladjusted people when they get my age. After all, I have always lived conservatively and I have lived within the financial framework of what I was earning. I am not a status seeker. I don't go for cliché rule. I don't have resentment against the other people. For example, some of these young fellows who make more money, they get themselves in debt and then when they get some pressure on them, they can't take the pressure. No money or other economic theories come into my way of doing things."

(You will notice the underlying aggression which was voiced as to young men being promoted to vice president level, which really means his immediate supervision. Although the resentment is not out in the open, it is so hidden that he is not aware that it exists as of yet. He has masked it in his thinking in different directions. He is dissatisfied with the "organization" and the way it has treated him, but he is not aware of the hostile forces which reside in him which bring him to this particular mixed-up state.)

DR. S. "Are your immediate supervisors younger or older than you?"

W. C. (He laughed.) "Van is the only one older. No, I don't have any resentment towards them. I don't resent them. Their ego is such that they have to have the title that they do, such as supervisor. Now, I don't believe in things like that—I believe in production. For example, if there is a machine that we are paying $1,000-a-month rent on, I would like to see them utilize it to the utmost—at least 7³/₄ hours a day."

DR. S. "What do you dislike the most about any one of your supervisors?"

W. C. (He thought for a long time.) "Well, I would say I hate to be flubbed off, that is, by no one in particular. I am not talking about anyone in particular right now. I would give you an example. You see, I asked about another classification not too long ago and I was told that someone else had it and that nothing was available for me. That was perfectly all right with me. It was an insult to my intelligence, though, because if the supervisor wants to do it, it is his to do and it is in his power to do it; and if he doesn't want to do it, he should tell me what it is that he wants me to do, such as work harder. But when he tells me what he did, I don't want my intelligence insulted. You see, if the supervisor got his job by playing it rough, then he has to expect it back. It is just like I say, if you live by the sword, then you have to expect the sword to be turned against you. There is one other thing—I won't stand being cussed at, and I will fight that whether I am right or wrong. I don't think it is right for a supervisor to cuss you at any time."

DR. S. "You said before you were with the File Company. When was that?"

W. C. "From 1940 to 1944. I would say that it lacks six months of being ten years."

DR. S. "Who was your immediate supervisor in the File Company?"

W. C. "I would rather not talk about that."

DR. S. "Would you have liked to stay in the File Company?"

W. C. "Well, I don't know. The File Company has experienced all of these financial storms. You see, the auto insurance is getting jittery. The fellows are getting jittery. That is so since this business has a lot of problems, and the fellows can sense this jitteriness from the higher-ups. Now, take that 650 program and bringing in those machines. The fellows who owe money are getting jittery because they worry about the jobs."

(At this point he went on here for a number of minutes in this same vein and it was impossible to follow or to make sense out of what he was trying to say. He just rattled on in that same vein. When he hit a break point, I said:)

DR. S. "Did you enjoy working with the File Company?"

W. C. "I enjoyed the File Company very much."

DR. S. "Why did you leave the File Company then?"

W. C. "I felt that I was getting a pretty rough deal there. I felt that I wasn't getting a good shake, and they felt that I wasn't taking it properly, and so I wrote a memo requesting a transfer, and when I went over to the Auto Company I was told that it was to be forgotten. I told the supervisors to forget it, and they don't forget it lots of the time. I tell them they ought to be big enough to forget it, and he doesn't forget it and brings it up every once in a while."

DR. S. "Who is 'he'?"

W. C. (Laughing) "Oh, no, not on paper. No names. You are writing some of these things down, and so I am not going to say anything about anybody. Anyhow it is not side-by-side." (Dr. S.—I don't know what this means.)

"Anyhow, he hasn't forgotten, and I am talking this way because I know I am here to unburden myself and so I might as well do it."

DR. S. "Well, then, your leaving the File Company was voluntary on your part?"

W. C. "Yes, sir, definitely. What do you know about it?"

DR. S. "All I know about you is that you were a Six in the File Company and that now you are a Four."

W. C. "Well, I took this gracefully and I never really complained, and my production is the best."

DR. S. "Do you want to talk some more later?"

W. C. "This is up to you. After all, your time is a lot more valuable than mine."

DR. S. "Do you want to say anything else?"

W. C. "Yes, there is one more thing right now. I do not quite go along with this appraisal system because it doesn't tell all about my work. You see, my personal life is up to us. I refuse to sign an appraisal. When you sign it, it means you have agreed with the person. Do you think you ought to sign something without knowing what you are going to sign? Some of the things that they have in that appraisal form, from my viewpoint, have to do with my personal life and the things in my personal life—this is an opinion. Somehow when they put them in those appraisals, an opinion has a way of becoming a fact."

DR. S. "I think we ought to talk some more at a later date."

W. C. "I am perfectly willing to cooperate."

DR. S. "In your opinion or in your own words, what good did this do?"

W. C. (A long thought period.) "It is rather early to comment on this, but I said what I thought, and that is one of my bad faults or one of the bad features about me. It is too early to judge some of the things that I have been doing or saying. I haven't said them to be spiteful, and I am really not resentful of anything."

DR. S. "How do you view me?"

W. C. "You, sir, you are doing a job—that is your job. It is a professional job. All I know about you is they say that you are one of the top men in this business in this part of the country, and I accept you as another person who is doing their job in this company."

DR. S. "Do you think you and I could get along?"

W. C. "No." (Then he laughed.) "Don't take that as I said it. That was just a joke."

DR. S. "Is there anything else you want to say?"

W. C. "Well, I have been doing all of the talking. I want to hear what you believe. After all, it takes two to get together."

DR. S. "Whose ideas do you think are more important to you—yours or mine?"

W. C. "Well, there has to be a meeting of the minds, or agreements. I have to know how you think, because a lot of these things are sort of like a give-and-take situation."

DR. S. "Would you say that you agree with yourself?"

W. C. "Well, I would say it is about fifty-fifty. I would say I have become more in agreement with myself as I get older. I wonder if this is a step in the right direction. As I get older I like to read more. In fact, in my reading I go from the sublime to the ridiculous."

DR. S. "Well, our time for this meeting is up and I will just get in touch with you directly and will continue with our conversation. I will not talk with anyone in your department, but I will just tell you to meet me in a conference room."

W. C.   "I have enjoyed it very much because the interesting thing is that I don't think we have any more time just to visit and talk about things like we used to. It relieves you to talk and to unburden yourself. It seems that we have lost this just visiting and having a bull session with one another, and this seems to be going out of our way of life nowadays."

REPORT TO: Mr. Bill Tucker
FROM: Dr. A. E. Schneider

INTERVIEW WITH ROBERT WILSON

This conference was based on a letter from John Anderson and a face-to-face interview with Bill Tucker.

The interview took place in Mr. Tucker's office during a period of time when Mr. Tucker was gone and there were no interruptions or phone calls. This permitted a good background and a good foundation of rapport and mutual understanding to exist. It should be noted here that Dr. Schneider and Mr. Wilson had had previous conversations and interviews so that there was a background of communication established prior to this particular meeting.

After a few generalities had been exchanged, Dr. Schneider asked the following question:

DR. S.   "What would you say that your job consists of, Bob?"
ANS.   "I have a job which, I feel, if it becomes anything other than assistance to the line operation of the company, it loses its significance."
DR. S.   "What would you say your function is?"
ANS.   "Our function is service."
DR. S.   "Well, then, what would you say bothers you the most in relationship to your function within the total framework of the department?"
ANS.   "What do you mean?"
DR. S.   "Well, would you say that you get bothered by certain occurrences or in the attempt to get your job done?"
ANS.   "I would say so. I think that I get bothered frequently and very much from time to time."
DR. S.   "Well, then, what bothers you?"
ANS.   "I can sum it up in this way: (1) the principal object of my function, as I see it, is to provide consistent service and technical service to all segments of the organization so that no one segment of the organization profits or loses at the expense of any other segment."
DR. S.   "Well, now, let's put that in simple words so that we will both know what we are talking about."
ANS.   "Okay!"
DR. S.   "Well, let's put it this way. (1) There are X number of dollars available for salary; (2) there is X amount of work that has to get done in the company; (3) management is not in a position to evaluate all of the people throughout the whole organization at any one time because they can only evaluate those that are in front of them at that time. Do you agree to that, Bob?"
ANS.   "Well, I would agree that we spent on our payroll approximately $30 million which was spread out over 8,400 employees on about 850 specific jobs on which we had job descriptions. Our problem is internal consistency and geographical variations."

DR. S. "Part of the problem, then, is that all the people must be rewarded in an appropriate manner, but yet, all of them must be rewarded individually."

ANS. "Well, it is difficult because diversity cannot be administrated."

Dr. Schneider and Mr. Wilson then discussed some general concepts of what some of the basic problems were for managers evaluating and managing the people in front of them. The conversation got around to an article that recently appeared in the *Harvard Business Review* which had to do with the problems inherent in management evaluation. Three points were made at this particular junction of the conversation. They were: 1) a management person has to learn to think about his job objectively so that he understands what it is that he is doing in relationship to the rest of the organization; (2) he must make a careful assessment of his own strengths and weaknesses; (3) he must formulate some specific plan in order to accomplish his goals.

DR. S. "In terms of the main points that appear in the *Harvard Business Review* article, Bob, what would you say your weaknesses are?"

ANS. "(1) Inability to express my thoughts and ideas to sell them; (2) lack of my aggressive action (I think that I would relate this second point as a failure of the first point which I stated); and (3) I would say, which is a part of 1 and 2, I'm inherently afraid to be aggressive because I can't sell my ideas or the things I believe in."

There was a pause at this point, and Dr. Schneider said, "Well, keep going, Bob."

ANS. "Well, I would say under (4) it is difficult for me to accept the lack of aggressiveness on the part of someone else on the basis of the fact that if something is right, that individual ought to state that it is right and go on record. Under the circumstances, it should be such that the final answer might not be just that nothing can be done, but in the last analysis, it should be that the person has gone on record expressing the right thought and the right action and that it should be the right principle so that they do the right thing."

DR. S. "Okay! Let's put these thoughts that you have been expressing down in simple terms. Let's put it this way. Would you say that you do or do not get emotionally upset when you present something or you want to attain a goal and you get blocked?"

ANS. "I do."

DR. S. "Would you say that you do or do not lose easily?"

ANS. "I lose easily—in other words, if my superior says one thing and I say another thing, I accept this as far as what my superior has said from an authoritative viewpoint."

DR. S. "Well, would you say that you fight back?"

ANS. "Well, that is hard for me to say. I'd say, not always."

DR. S. "Would you say that you are flexible, Bob? Do you know what I mean by being flexible?"

ANS. "I think I understand what you mean, and I would say that I think I am reasonably flexible."

DR. S. "Would you say that you have conceptual knowledge?"

ANS. "Well, my answer would be that I think I'm able to rationalize a point on the basis of the surrounding circumstances to a problem."

DR. S. "Well, Bob, how about a statement like this: If I were an executive in the

331

organization, and I would look upon you and your work, Bob, that you are a controlled symbol in the expense division; and that you furnish me with sound logic in my decision-making process insofar as salary determinations are concerned."

ANS. "Well, I don't know whether I would go along with that."

DR. S. "Well, then, let's put it this way: Would you say that you tell me or I tell you insofar as management is concerned in relationship to salary administration?"

ANS. "I tell you."

DR. S. "You tell me when?"

ANS. "I tell you constantly, either that you are doing right or wrong."

DR. S. "Do I have to listen to you?"

ANS. "Yes!"

DR. S. "Why?"

ANS. "Because you have said that it is part of my responsibility to report to you on these matters, particularly where salary variations exist or that certain salaries are out of line, or where you are paying salaries which are not consistent with the overall structure."

DR. S. "But supposing you do report to me about some things where it looks as though I am out of line, but I am still the manager and still want to do it my way. How about that?"

ANS. "Then, that is your privilege."

DR. S. "What do you mean by that?"

ANS. "Well, that is your privilege because I have no authority in the matter from an overall viewpoint."

DR. S. "Has there been a case like this that you want to talk about that has bothered you?"

ANS. "Yes, there was one involving Jones, Butler, and Wagner."

DR. S. "What's this all about?"

ANS. "They wanted to change the classification on three jobs and establish three new jobs. One was to be a 3-C and the other two were to be C-5's. All they knew about it is that they knew what grades they wanted the jobs to fall into, but they don't know what the jobs are going to consist of and what the jobs involved in order to justify this classification for the jobs. What bothered me is that here are three men on the management level who have been associated with our salary evaluation systems since 1950 and, here, they want to establish three jobs that I cannot, in my mind, justify the classifications for these jobs on the basis of my knowledge as to what the jobs would entail. Yet, all three of these men have agreed that it would be all right to set up those three jobs, disregarding what they should be according to the job classification processes and procedures in accordance with the way we classify jobs in this organization. In other words, if I accepted these three classifications which these management men set up, this would mean that I would be dishonest to the other 847 job classifications in our organization, and it would be essentially violating, in my opinion, my responsibility for applying relativity among these various jobs. Now, what I have been doing is merely talking about my own philosophy insofar as job evaluation is concerned."

DR. S. "Well, Bob, let me ask you several questions. Question number one. Would you say that these management men are sincere men in their objectives insofar as the company is concerned?"

ANS. "Yes."

DR. S. "Question number two. Would you say these men are honest?"

ANS. "I don't know. I presume so, from their viewpoint."

DR. S. "Question number three. Do they have the good of the company at heart?"

ANS. "I think so."

DR. S. "Question number four. Would you say that they are uninformed men insofar as the company's procedures and processes are concerned?"

ANS. "In some matters I suppose they are less uninformed men than in others. In matters of job classification, I would say they are uninformed."

DR. S. "Question number 5. Can you guess why they did what they did in regard to the three classifications about which you are talking?"

ANS. "Well, I would hazard to guess."

DR. S. "Well, what is your guess?"

ANS. "They were unaware of what they were doing."

DR. S. "Go ahead and tell me about what your problem was in relationship to this occurrence as you see it."

ANS. "There was a memo which was written by Clayton Wagner which was sent to me and the other men involved in covering these jobs."

DR. S. "Did you blow your top when you read it?"

ANS. "Yes, essentially it did make me blow my top. I guess the amount of steam that I blew off was considerable, and that is what troubled me."

DR. S. "Was this the only area in which you ever had problems in relationship to line management and wage and salary evaluation?"

ANS. "No, there was a fire company problem in regard to classification. The fire company changed certain classifications, and this involved Mr. Smith and Mr. Woods in the fire company."

DR. S. "Were there any other areas that you can recall?"

ANS. "Well, I was also involved with some work that Mr. White was doing that was in violation of our principles of job and salary evaluation. As I saw it, he created some jobs, then classified the jobs, and then he published these jobs before I even knew about it. I had a mild explosion over that, and right after that, this deal with Wagner, Jones, and Butler came up from the auto company, and it seems to be the *capper* to it all."

DR. S. "Well, were there some other incidents?"

ANS. "Well, I could go back further and relate some other incidents that were similar. For example, there was one where Al changed the class on a job and I objected to it. Bill Tucker and Mr. Chase got together and Bill let me down terribly in this case. He agreed with Mr. Chase and he let them have the change, and then he directed me to back away from the thing, which, as far as I am concerned, let me down considerably. I walked out of that one a very unhappy man. There was another case also where Mr. Fuller, Bill, and myself and two or three of Mr. Fuller's cohorts had it out in regard to certain job classifications that they wanted for their people which wasn't in line with the classifications as I saw them."

DR. S. "Well, how do you see this now in relationship to yourself and the personnel function at large?"

ANS. "I was taking my responsibilities pretty seriously, and I tried to work the thing out on the basis that we were not violating the trust and responsibility to the other segments of the organization. It's pretty hard for me when I have to deal with men on their level. You see, they are up here and they exercise line privilege in these matters because of their rank. They exercise rank privileges, and because they are uninformed on these procedures in job and salary evaluation, sometimes they need help. I think that part of my problem when I need help in working with these people, there just isn't any help for me and there isn't anyone whom I can turn to to help me— someone who is reasonably dedicated to job evaluation like I am."

DR. S. "Is that all you want to say?"

ANS. "I want to restate the fact that I am extremely loyal and sympathetic to Bill Tucker and with Bill on all of his problems, but it puts me in a very uncomfortable position to try to have to promote this dedication to job evaluation alone, since it is my idea altogether. This thing has been set up by fire management, and according to my understanding of it, I have been given the responsibility. I am to perpetuate it and activate it, and also to provide a technical understanding and concept in the organization, not only to the people within our company, but also to provide an awareness to them of what others in the industry are doing, so that they will understand their actions and whether or not they are appropriate or unappropriate."

DR. S. "I think, Bob, that we have been hitting at the key or central problem that has been bothering you."

ANS. "Basically, I think part of my problem is I am inherently too damn honest, and anything that reflects itself against that grain of fiber, I sort of rebel against it. I object against being dishonest in any way, whether it be mental or whether it has to do with what it is I am supposed to be getting done. You see, I think that if you have to reach your objective on the basis of being dishonest, this strains me too much."

DR. S. "Would you say that reasonable men have the right to disagree reason- ably? Well, let's get back to some of the things that you have been talking about. Bob, would you say that Al was dishonest?"

ANS. "Not intentionally."

DR. S. "Would you say that Chase was dishonest?"

ANS. "Not intentionally."

DR. S. "Would you say that the other men were dishonest?"

ANS. "Not intentionally."

DR. S. "Well, would you say that people are black or white, honest or dishonest?"

ANS. "I think that everyone has a slight streak of dishonesty in him."

DR. S. "Well, if you found a hundred dollars on the street, do you think you'd tell someone about it or wouldn't you tell them about it?"

ANS. Bob laughed and said, "I don't know. Maybe I wouldn't tell anyone about it."

DR. S. "Have you ever read a book by a Dr. Johnson from the University of Iowa called *People in Quandaries*?"

ANS. "No."

DR. S. "You had better get that book and read it, because it shows one how you can get into trouble mentally when you have certain word symbols that you associate with certain things."

The rest of the conference then took the direction of a discussion of semantics, and there were some diagrams drawn as to the nature of the task which Jones, Chase, Wagner, Butler, and White were attempting to achieve and how the intermediaries were the personnel staff that we made up of Mr. Tucker as the leader and the rest of the staff implementing the concepts for the line group, and how there were objectives for each on part of the goal. Certain statements were made, such as (1) the management men are concerned with line people; (2) they have to get things done; (3)

they know how they want to get the job done; and (4) they gave part of their responsibility away to major staff areas, such as personnel, in order to help them achieve their goals, but from a line viewpoint, these men still had the basic responsibility for seeing to it that the ultimate job was performed. When a certain problem was reached, management frequently has to say, "Now, even though all these staff requirements are in existence, nevertheless, I have to get a job done, and this is how I propose to get the job done."

DR. S.   "Bob, what management is saying is that they want to get the job done from their understanding and knowledge of what it is that they are administering; they also say they want it done the way they see it best because they understand what their goals are."

A great deal of discussion went on in this area, and I gave him several illustrations on how this operates, even in educational administration as well as in business administration. I also talked to him about line and staff, and I also pointed out that at times there may be a difference in thinking between line type of action and thinking and staff type of action and thinking because line has the responsibility in the last analysis for seeing to it that the elements are put together and that the job gets done. I also pointed out that what he didn't seem to understand is that Jack, who to him seemed to represent a senior staff capacity, was in functional viewpoint one-half a staff man and one-half a line man, because, as the senior leader of the personnel department, he functioned as the senior staff man. However, when he was working with the other senior elements of both line and staff and assisting them in getting their job done, and particularly through the operating committee, he was a line man, since he had to work with all the other elements to get the total job done. We talked about the fact that this job to him was an end in and of itself, and to line, his job was only a means to an end. We talked about the danger sometimes in management of becoming too much of a perfectionist, and about the high desirability of retaining one's flexibility.

I talked to him of Mr. Hawkins, who is on my staff, and I pointed out to him that Mr. Hawkins, who has a very high I.Q. and is a very intelligent man, was the kind of individual who always wanted everything to add up numerically to a given and foreseeable total. I further pointed out to him that in management not all things can necessarily add up to a total. I pointed out to him that the field of management is political in nature, and that it has to do with getting different groups of people to work together for common goals. He answered at this point that job and salary evaluation is the only thing that crosses all political and organizational boundaries within the framework of the company, and that is what created his basic problem. He further stated that he felt very strongly that there should be a great deal of consistency within the organization in the administration of salaries.

In closing, I said to him:

DR. S.   "What would you say your future is in relationship to this organization?"
ANS.   "Operating the job evaluation organization."
DR. S.   "Well, let's talk about that."
ANS.   "Well, I mean bringing a direct salary structure to every job in every segment of the organization. Secondly, to serve line management, and third, bringing understanding and reasonable meaning governing the thinking in regard to salary evaluation."

In closing, Dr. Schneider said to him that it seemed to him that Bob's job is to learn how to communicate to all people so that he could sell his ideas to all areas of management in order that they would accept him. He could not hope to get other people to take his word from an authoritative viewpoint unless he sold them on the idea that he was helping them. That it was his function to help line management make sense out of the administration of the salary dollars that they had in front of them to the end that these salary dollars would be used most effectively in getting the job done with the people at hand. It was also pointed out to him that a saying could well express that part of his philosophy: "Your persuasion will force me to do what your force cannot persuade me to do."

There seemed to be a great deal of understanding at the end of the conference, and it is hoped that this was noticed in the past two weeks, or during the period between our conference and the present reading of this report. He seemed to be a very cooperative man and understands that he has problems, but certainly he is worthy of development. He is a competent man who is somewhat emotionalized and does not have the capacity to live up to the inherent ability that resides within him. From an educational viewpoint, this is one of the great problems that we have. For someone who seems to have separately all of the various capabilities which should make him a top man, yet they are put together in just somewhat a little bit of an erratic manner, and we have someone who does not live up to the potential that resides within him.

APPENDIX
D

Four Short
Communication Case Study Situations

PERSONALITY PROBLEM

Sally has been with the company approximately five years and has a responsible position. She is a very intelligent, efficient, and capable employee in handling the details of her work. However, there is one trait which mars an otherwise excellent work performance.

Basically, the problem is that now and then she will do something to antagonize her fellow workers, which results in bad feelings. She knows at the time when she has gotten out of line in this respect.

These incidents sometimes arise because she gives the impression that she feels she is better than some of the other employees. Then when she does something which would ordinarily be overlooked, it causes "ruffled feathers." An example of this is that when she delivered work to others, she tossed it on the desk as she went by—not in a manner that would ordinarily cause any comment, but still it was not as it should be. In answering questions or in returning errors, the impression was left that the person should know the answer to the question or that the error should not have been made.

These things were not done all the time, but occasionally, and then not always to the same people: one time here, next time some place else—but just enough to cause a dislike for her that has become fairly general.

I don't want to leave the impression that she has no friends. She can be and is very nice to her friends and others when she wants to be. In her home, when she entertains, she is a very gracious hostess.

None of these things occur so I can observe them. I get them from others. She is married and works only because she wants to.

I have talked with her about these occurrences and have been told each time that she didn't intend to offend the person. I have pointed out to her that in all her work contacts she represents me and the unit. Therefore, when she does something wrong, it reflects on all of us. In addition, I have told her that I would consider her an outstanding employee if she would correct this.

These discussions did not solve the problem.

MAL-ATTITUDES IN WORK GROUP

Selma had been working with the company almost fourteen years and was in her early thirties. She knew her job well but, so far as I could determine, had been no more than adequate in the performance of her duties. She was the sort of employee who does a reasonable amount of work day in and day out but who never shows much improvement. She exerted considerable influence over some of the younger girls— largely, I think, because she was a better talker and because she obviously knew the company better than most. I would not say that the influence she exerted was a good one; the younger girls did not seem to be her true friends but rather were inclined to accept Selma's word on how to act and what to think.

All went along reasonably well until Nona appeared. Nona was young, quite good-looking, and inclined to be rather quiet, though friendly enough when one got to know her. She turned out to be a whiz at production and soon was outdoing almost everyone in the section—especially the older hand, Selma.

Selma appeared to take an instant dislike to Nona, and as the latter improved, Selma's dislike became more obvious. Selma's following—especially Marie, Pearl, and Marilyn—followed Selma's lead and shared her prejudices against the new girl and closed ranks against her, refusing to go to coffee with her or even to speak unless the work made this necessary. I heard mutterings on their part against Nona, but there was nothing I could really put my finger on. I talked with the dissident clique and also with Nona. For a while the situation became less tense, but I had the feeling that the improvement was not going to be permanent.

One day, to my surprise, Selma and her two most loyal followers, Marie and Pearl, turned in their resignations, to be effective in one month. They declared they could no longer work around Nona, but that they did not wish to leave me stranded. I put in a requisition for three employees to substitute for them, and the new girls turned out to be very promising. Selma, however, refused to have anything to do with training them, saying she did not like them. Marie followed suit. I consulted with my superintendent, and he counseled me to have another talk with them but to take no direct action beyond this, in the hope that the situation would clear up in time. It got worse, however; now Pearl joined her friends and refused to train the new girls. Marilyn hung back and neither refused to train nor took an active part in doing so. Nona came to my rescue and helped with the new girls, who soon grew to like her.

I saw that one girl could not adequately train three others and still do her own work, especially if she were relatively new herself, so again I turned to Selma, Marie, Pearl, and Marilyn, and asked their cooperation in training the replacements. Once again they flatly refused to have anything to do with the new girls.

What would be your next course of action with this situation?

HOME PROBLEM

This is a study of a personality and its effect upon the individual's work habits and performance. Here is the general background of this person, whom we shall call Joan.

Joan presents a neat appearance and her personal habits are not to be criticized. She is a high school graduate and has attended modeling school at night while with her present employer. She lives in a middle-class neighborhood environment which externally appears to be pleasant. However, Joan's family is not typical. From childhood to her present age of twenty-two she has been guided by her widowed mother and directly obedient to her brother. He has taken the place of her father as dominating head of the household. Joan's brother is educated but stubborn and domineering, the family being of Old World culture. Joan follows her brother's commands, loving him deeply but being hurt severely, especially when he forbids her to go out with men of other than her own national background.

This emotional conflict is readily apparent in her job attitude. It causes moodiness and fluctuations from a pleasant, effective job well done one day to depression, disagreeableness, and short temper resulting in a poor job the next day. Unexplained tardiness also is a result. Attempts to make Joan feel a responsibility toward lateness often met with failure. Absenteeism also has stemmed directly from this brother's influence.

On one occasion, for example, Joan told her supervisor that she wanted to take time off from work to take an automobile driver's test. She was told that permission for a few hours off would be granted. Later in the week she was absent and had not called into the office. Upon contacting her home, it was found that her brother had decided that she should spend some additional time practicing driving that morning before taking her test in the afternoon. This was contrary to Joan's wishes, as she did not want to miss a whole day's work. However, she had again let her brother make the decision.

Joan, although initially slower to learn her job than some others, is considered of better-than-average intelligence, and her overall job performance is satisfactory. What should be the supervisor's course of action?

FACT OR FICTION?

John Jones, B.A. degree, master's degree, some work toward a doctorate, married, two children, former experience as a schoolteacher and principal. Applied for employment in order to get into a field where advancement and opportunity could develop. Interviewed extremely well and was impressive to several interviewers. Hired into a trainee position.

Personality good, but John did possess some feminine characteristics. Soon after employment, there were several girls within the units where John was training who felt as though there might be something wrong with him. He would continually join in girl-type talk (this report not confirmed), and became very chummy with some, repulsive with others.

From this point, rumor developed that John was a homosexual. This again was strictly an opinion expressed by one girl, but the overall effect did greatly hamper the effectiveness of the training program. (It should be noted here that John was an exceptional individual in learning ability. All training he received was quickly grasped, and his application of the knowledge excellent. At one period it appeared as though our trainers would not be able to hold his interest, in that he was able to comprehend in the minimum of time.)

At this point, John, still not aware of the problem, began offering rides to and from work to one of the girls in the unit. This information was relayed to the supervisory force, who in turn worked diligently to put some teeth into the accusations, either true or false.

Finally, the problem was relayed to the Personnel Department to see if through our employment investigation any basis for the rumors existed. The files were thoroughly reviewed. Nothing that would point up the rumor was found; however, it was noted that the interviewer had noted the feminine characteristics. From this point additional reports were ordered to see if anything could be turned up.

Again no information came to light that gave any indication as to abnormalities in John, but the feeling did exist within the unit among a few of the employees.

He is an outstanding employee with exceptional capabilities who, because of actions or pure gossip, was damaging the unit, and he himself was being damaged.

How do you as his supervisor handle this situation?

APPENDIX E

Feedback on a
Management/Communication Seminar
at West Coast Life Insurance Company

TO: Operations Staff and Management Development Seminar
           Participants

FROM: Sherrod E. Turner

SUBJ: Feedback Information on the Management Seminar

DATE: May 2, 197-

        Attached is a recap and summary of the feedback
information from the Management Development Seminar
held the week of April 23-27. This data, as well as a
proposed total two-way communication structure, was
presented to the top operations staff. The staff agreed
to implement the communication structure, with the first
Operations Staff Meeting being held Tuesday, May 8.
Other meeting schedules will be announced thereafter.

SET:kls

Attachments

TO: Operations Staff   April, 1973

As you are all aware, we have been in the planning phase for the presentation of a supervisory and management development program for a considerable period of time. Due to internal shifts and demands made upon the organization, we have delayed undertaking this until the present.

The formal thrust of this program was in the areas of:

1. Leadership
2. Communication and the Business Organization
3. Understanding the Aims of Management
4. The Supervisor as a Teacher
5. The Place of a Supervisor in a Management Organization

The plan of the program was to:

1. Use Dr. Schneider's text
2. Employ appropriate visual aids which were obtained from the Training Department of the "X" Bank
3. Develop a feedback from the participants so that the presentation could be built on their demand schedules as they viewed them

It was felt that an overview of the needs and demand schedule of the participants would be an effective device at the very outset of the sessions. This supposition proved to be a very strong reality, as the written unsigned statements submitted on the following pages will testify.

You will find the results of this feedback mechanism in the following pages. This report is divided into areas as listed below:

1. Feedback from participants on their views of Problems Encountered.
2. Feedback from participants on their views of "What do you want to get out of these sessions?"
3. Recommendations based on the feedback generated by these sessions.
4. Feedback "bench marks."
5. Suggested structure and system for an ongoing organizational communication activity.

PROBLEMS ENCOUNTERED

Group One

	Agree	Disagree
1. I feel that I receive personal job satisfaction—more so than not.	1	7
2. Management passes responsibility but doesn't pass along the authority to act.	3	7
3. Direction is undefined, except in the broadest terms.	7	2
4. A lack of feeling of "belonging" together among the employees within a department.	1	7
5. There are too many people who are waiting around for the mythical "they" to provide the answer or the authority for making a decision.	4	5

343

		Agree	Disagree
6.	Determining the style preferred by the management.	6	1
7.	People are too status conscious. Below middle management, there exists a fear of communicating with the management.	3	5
8.	Lack of "full" communication from superiors.	7	1
9.	Corporate objectives are not clearly understood.	5	4
10.	Authority is neither clearly defined nor delegated.	6	2
11.	Know what the Company's policy or approach is to a problem.	3	4
12.	Department heads and supervisors need to manage their departments more on their own.	7	0
13.	Employees do not realize how important their jobs are as a piece of the whole.	9	0
14.	Supervisors need to know the abilities of their people.	7	1
15.	Lack of a clearly-defined salary administration policy.	8	1
16.	Too many managers, and not enough workers.	4	3
17.	Inter-departmental problems and goals are not discussed enough.	7	1
18.	Lack of understanding from superiors regarding the details of changes due to computerization.	3	2
19.	Important projects are interrupted for less important activities.	7	3
20.	Some relationships are too formal.	0	11
21.	Education, as to the overall workflow, should be initiated so that each employee knows and fully understands the impact of his or her duties.	9	1
22.	There does not seem to be an evident scheme of major objectives that relate to intermediate objectives.	4	5
23.	There is an uncertainty as to who is responsible for what within the Company.	9	1
24.	Finding many tasks meaningless or unimportant.	5	4
25.	Things seem to happen on a "put out the fire" mode, instead of a planned approach to problem solving.	9	1
26.	There is no program for productivity incentives—i.e., stock purchase or profit sharing.	10	0
27.	A general air of lack of confidence among the management.	4	5
28.	The purse strings are drawn too tight to replace equipment or personnel adequately.	3	3
29.	I do not feel that the junior members of my staff receive very much job satisfaction.	2	8
30.	Many job frustrations come from outside my department, and I have no control over them.	7	2

	Agree	Disagree
31. Enrichment goals appear to be contradictory to profit ability.	2	3
32. In many instances, endurance is equated with experience.	7	1
33. My boss doesn't really seem interested in the problems I have—therefore, I tend not to discuss anything with him.	1	8
34. Objectives are not spelled out to the clerical level.	9	2
35. Communication of problems on an exception basis, but also have an available means for realizing that problems exist if the exception basis of reporting is not adhered to.	3	1

Group Two

	Agree	Disagree
1. Poor relationships between various departments. My work is often delayed by other departments being behind schedule.	10	4
2. It appears that the boss does not realize how long the work actually takes, nor is he aware of all of the problems in the department.	11	3
3. Quick decisions are made in the top level management, without regard or research in the effects on the employees of a department.	11	3
4. There is too much work to be done.	4	10
5. The high rate of personnel turnover.	7	5
6. Lack of communications when doing new procedures.	12	3
7. Not being allowed sufficient time to complete a job correctly the first time.	8	5
8. Absenteeism and tardiness.	4	10
9. Negative attitude on the part of young employees towards supervision.	2	13
10. Constant interruptions which prevent me from quickly completing any job.	11	3
11. How can upper management be encouraged to communicate to those under them the various "secret" plans and the changes in the organizational structure?	8	5
12. Who to promote, and on what merit.	5	9
13. The showing of favoritism from top level management.	4	9
14. Where am I going and what am I doing this job for?	4	8
15. The Company needs to better define their policies to employees, e.g., vacation, hours, sick leave, etc.	9	5
16. Why can I make decisions involving thousands of dollars, and yet not be able to spend some money for equipment which is badly needed?	10	4

345

		Agree	Disagree
17.	Why are "inefficient" employees retained?	11	3
18.	My department is not sufficiently staffed to do cross-training. Turnover can only be solved by up grading our salaries.	7	8
19.	I am not certain of my authority as a supervisor.	5	8
20.	The Company has a very slow and irregular promotion scale.	8	7
21.	Some of the work is repetitious and nonchalleng-ing.	4	10
22.	Many employees feel that they should be able to do whatever the bosses do.	7	6
23.	Many employees do not respect their supervisors.	5	8
24.	I feel that I do not have direct communication upward, except through my immediate supervisor.	7	6
25.	Centralizing work from other departments.	10	4
26.	Getting departments to act as a whole and not autonomously.	11	2
27.	There is not enough time in the day to accomplish everything that needs to be done.	9	5
28.	Not familiar with who handles what problems and what areas within the other departments.	5	8
29.	No opportunity to discuss common problems.	10	4
30.	Not enough instructional material.	7	5
31.	How do I know when I am effective?	6	6
32.	Where can I go in this Company?	8	4

Group Three

		Agree	Disagree
1.	Better communications within the organization.	8	1
2.	We need a set of priorities.	7	1
3.	We need more long range planning.	4	3
4.	We need to have fewer crash projects.	2	3
5.	High rate of turnover within the Company.	6	1
6.	Lower level employees do not identify with the Company. "What is good for the Company, is good for the employee," does not necessarily follow here.	4	3
7.	Standardization of job descriptions throughout the Company.	3	2
8.	Competent employees are blocked in their advancement potential within the Company by their supervisors.	4	4
9.	There is no feeling of "teamwork" among the employees.	5	4
10.	Workflow is not followed on a regular basis.	4	4
11.	I do not have enough authority to complete all the responsibilities that are expected of me.	3	5

WHAT DO YOU WANT TO GET OUT OF THESE SESSIONS?

Group One

1. The qualities necessary in an effective leader.
2. Consistency among the members of the management as to method, style, approach, and goals.
3. Methods of communications between upper and lower management.
4. Closer understanding between the managers for each others' problems and responsibilities.
5. Realizing that people work "with" me, and not "for" me.
6. Ability to analyze my own capabilities objectively.
7. Develop a better ability for problem solving.
8. Develop a better understanding of employee objectives, and the methods that can be used to help them attain their goals.
9. What style of management does this Company advocate?
10. Improve my ability to manage my employees.
11. How to grow in my job, and not stagnate.
12. How to train employees.
13. Applications for inter-company communications.
14. How to reward my personnel.
15. How to communicate my requirements to others.
16. How to better understand what exactly my responsibility to the Company is.
17. How to evaluate the way others look at problems.
18. I wish to be able to gain some management techniques that I can *readily apply* in the management of my department.
19. Examine case studies on some managers with problems similar to ours.

Group Two

1. Social and cultural differences among people. How to compromise or should we completely ignore it?
2. How to communicate to your coworkers that their tasks are just a part of the whole.
3. The alienation that seems to frequently occur between lower and upper management. Also, how can lower management learn to "manage" upper management.
4. How to apportion the workload.
5. How to interview personnel for a job opening.
6. Proper way to criticize without creating hard feelings.
7. How to best bring to the attention of line authority problems involving another department.
8. How to cope with family problems of employees.
9. How to better communicate with the people whom I work with.
10. Discuss methods of improving cooperation between fellow employees.
11. Training of employees.
12. What to do with a "problem" employee.
13. Ways of making yourself understood.

14. How to make the job more interesting.
15. How to assert authority.
16. The psychological traits that a supervisor should possess.
17. How to handle the "problem" boss.
18. The "tools" that are used to develop employees where promotion and raises are obviously unusable.
19. What incentives can the Company offer as inducements for a better job consciousness?
20. How to make employees realize that no matter how menial the job is, it is still important to the whole finished product.
21. How much of a task oriented workload should a supervisor be expected to carry?
22. What methods could be used to introduce the team concept?
23. How honest can a supervisor afford to be with his people regarding management policies, salary scale, etc., especially when you disagree with them?
24. An examination and discussion of some experiments in the work day, e.g., a flexible day schedule, four-day week, beginning anytime between 6:30-8:30, etc.
25. Business, society, and the individual—how do these things interact in a work situation?

Group Three

1. I would like to gain a better understanding of management ideas and concepts.
2. New ideas in the daily approach to work.
3. Managing time more effectively.
4. How to gain more self-confidence in working with people.
5. How to handle employees under your supervision.
6. How to encourage and improve rapport with employees.
7. How are other insurance companies meeting the same problems that we face at West Coast Life?
8. How to "manage" management.
9. Techniques used in people optimization.
10. How to determine the productiveness of a given employee, and how to discuss it with them.
11. Daily organization on the job.
12. How to determine goals and priorities.
13. What are the employees expected to do in helping a company reach its goals?
14. I need a stronger business management background in order to be able to use what knowledge I have of social behavior in the business setting.
15. The ability to relate my ideas to others and vice versa.
16. Setting an example for other employees to want to emulate.
17. How can I present work assignments so that they do not seem like "assignments," but merely a function of a team?
18. How to develop leadership abilities.

BENCH MARKS
ABSTRACTED FROM
PREVIOUS FEEDBACK

1. The need for ongoing communication at all levels was dramatically portrayed by all of the participants.
2. Communication blocks exist within some departments.
3. Communication blocks between departments is a prevalent phenomenon and makes it difficult for cooperation and teamwork to be employed.
4. Lack of communications heightens problems which cause dissatisfaction at all levels of activity.
5. The "grapevine" may be a more actively used communication media than normal channels.
6. The communication stratification seems to have existed for a long time and may be the outcome of what is perceived to be a rapid managerial turnover.
7. Items 3, 4, 5, 7, 8, 9, 11, 13, 15, 17, 18, 22, 23, 27, 34, and 35 from Group One are directly attributable to communication problems.
8. Items 1, 2, 3, 6, 11, 15, 17, 19, 24, 26, 28, 29, 31, and 32 from Group Two are directly attributable to communication problems.
9. Items 1, 3, 6, 9, and 11 from Group Three are directly attributable to communication problems.
10. It is felt that an all-out effort to build a total communication system within the organization, and to create an awareness of the need to maintain a consistent and on-going delivery and interaction system of communication will serve to resolve many of the problems which were expressed by the participants of the Management Development Seminar.
11. Too many top management persons do not seem to be aware of the effect of frequent interruptions of private office or conference room meetings.

On the following pages is a suggested structure and system within the structure for making it possible for communication efforts to be implemented and maintained.

The essence of making the structure and system effective lies in the cooperation of all of the people related to the communication structure and system to commit themselves to making it so. There must be more than lip service—there must be an instinctive understanding of the total results of this type of effort. This may be expected when all of the people in the organization see their roles, understand their roles, and their loyalties are with the organization and with those people working in the organization. The daily attitude should be that West Coast Life is a good place to work.

Upward communications within the organization seem to have been consistently blocked. This may be due, in part, to the belief of the first line supervisors and middle management that there is no real value to attempting to communicate upwards, for receptivity is at the "zero" level.

COMMUNICATION STRUCTURE AT WEST COAST LIFE

A. Operations Staff Meeting
    Frequency: Monthly
    Conductor: Rotating
    Agenda:

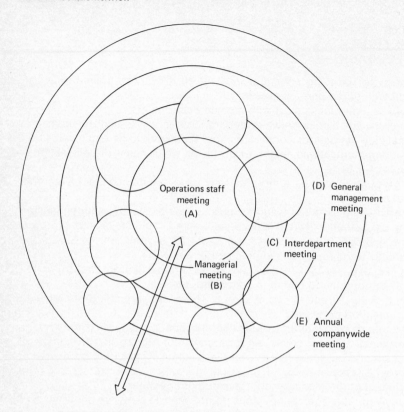

Operations staff
meeting
(A)

(D) General
management
meeting

(C) Interdepartment
meeting

Managerial
meeting
(B)

(E) Annual
companywide
meeting

(See attached outline for details of various levels of meetings.)

     1.   Long range objectives
     2.   Short range objectives
     3.   General problems
     4.   General information
     5.   Personnel changes
     6.   Special situations
     7.   Report back from Managerial Meeting
Format: Person conducting asks for agenda items one week in advance and limits the meeting to 2–3 hours. Minutes of the meeting are to be taken by a secretary.

B.   Managerial Meeting
     Frequency: Monthly
     Conductor: Operations staff member
     Agenda:
     1.   Long range objectives
     2.   Short range objectives
     3.   General problems
     4.   General information
     5.   Special situations

6. Report back from Operations Staff Meeting
7. Report back from Departmental Meeting
Format: Developed internally

C. Interdepartmental Meetings
    Frequency: Bi-monthly
    Conductor: Rotate among Managers
    Agenda:
    1. Workflow problems
    2. Personnel problems (not specifically individual)
    3. New systems requirements
    4. General education
    Format: The person conducting asks for agenda items one week in advance.
    Meeting limited to 2–3 hours, with minutes taken by a secretary. Conductor is
    responsible for extracting pertinent information and getting it on the agenda of
    the next Operations Staff Meeting.

D. General Management Meeting
    Frequency: Semi-annually
    Conductor: Rotating
    Agenda: (any of the following)
    1. Report on departmental objectives, status, and expectations
    2. General announcements on new programs or development
    3. Management training and education (special speakers, films, etc.)
    Format: Attended by operations staff, managers, supervisors, and high level
    technical personnel (about 60 persons). A breakfast meeting starting at 8:00
    A.M. and lasting 3 hours.

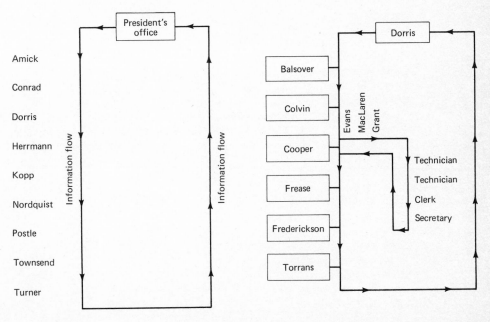

E.   Annual Company Meeting
    Frequency: Annual
    Conductor: By appointment
    Agenda:
       1.   Service awards
       2.   Educational achievement awards
       3.   Attendance awards
       4.   Annual summary by President and a preview of the coming year
    Format: Christmas luncheon on last working day before Christmas, starting at 12:30 and no returning to work afterwards.

APPENDIX F

Report of a Task Force
on Cooperation and Teamwork
in a Corporate Group

TO: Home Office   DATE: Aug. 20, 19--

ATTN: T. C. Hilton

FROM: Task Force IV - Eastern Zone

SUBJ: Cooperation and Teamwork

During our many brain-storming meetings much time was devoted to an
analysis of this category as it pertains to Eastern Zone. Fundamental
questions to be resolved were:

(a)   Is there a significant lack of cooperation and teamwork in
      our Zone in any area?

(b)   If so, what factors create the problem, and is it part of a
      larger problem?

In discussing the subject in all its aspects, we were forced to conclude
that we are by no means immune from cooperation and teamwork problems
in the East - even though the tabulated results of the opinion poll would
seem to place Eastern Zone above the countrywide level and in an acceptable rank in several categories. In this connection note particularly the
answers to questions 3 and 7 ("Feeling a part of the T/A team" and
"Cooperation between Departments") where our scores were "outstanding"
and "good." In contrast, we scored well below the Nationwide percentage
on question 34 ("The ability of the manager to whom you report to get
along with people"). Here the percentile rating of "very much" was only
4.3% - well below the nationwide average of 4.9%.

Regardless of the questionnaire indicia, however, our committee determined
that a potentially serious problem does exist in our Zone. So many specific instances were cited in the area of cooperation and teamwork breakdown that it would be dishonest to conclude that the problem could not
become a serious one - one that should be corrected before it assumes
greater proportions.

We explored in some depth the reasons creating the problem, and arrived at some tentative conclusions:

(1) Where the problem exists, it is often the direct result of poor communication or absence of communication. In this context it would seem that whatever recommendations are put forth by the Communications Task Force should, if implemented, go a long way to solve the subsidiary problem of Communications and Teamwork. In this connection we noted that poor communications (particularly lateral and downward communications) not only created difficulties in our area of study, but often served to create inefficiency ("Why wasn't I told - I'll have to do it over again") and, as a corollary created resentments with an attendant effect on morale.

(2) Of perhaps lesser importance than poor communications in creating cooperation and teamwork breakdowns, but still in our view signi- ficant factors bearing on our problem, were the following:

   (a) Attitude of the Boss - We concluded that a poor attitude on his part must inevitably be transmitted to his subordinates, thereby creating attitudes in them which in all probability would inhibit cooperation. To restate, we feel that the "Boss" - at whatever level - sets the tone for his people by his attitude. A poor attitude begets a similar attitude in sub- ordinates, to the detriment of cooperation. Here again we find a close relationship between our subject and that of the Task Force involved with "supervision."

   (b) Absence in the Boss of the ability to instruct subordinates, and particularly to orient them as to their role in the entire Company framework creates a situation where cooperative in- stincts are stifled. We felt it to be self-evident that if the employee is uncertain as to his role and responsibility, and cannot because of poor training visualize the relationship of his department with other departments in the company, there is little likelihood that he will reflect a spirit of cooperation.

Insularity - ignorance of what the other fellow is doing and why he is doing it - does not foster a teamwork approach.

We are proposing several recommendations which we feel will help to solve the problem besetting us. Because of our strong conviction that many of our problems are so closely interrelated with or caused by communications failures, it will be noted that several of our suggestions of necessity have a communications aspect and could be grouped under a communications heading. We are hopeful that the Communications Task Force in its recommendations will provide further solutions to our common problem.

RECOMMENDATIONS

1. Reestablishment of a Training and Education program geared particularly to the indoctrination of new employees.

2. Revival of training courses in management techniques. Our concept is that this program would emphasize the practical aspects of the concepts and principles studied in the Management Development Program to which the Company committed itself several years ago.

3. The release of up-to-date organization charts embracing all functions - Home Office, Zone and Branch. We feel that because of the dynamic changes in our organization existing material of this nature is out of date, if available at all. We firmly believe that many misunderstandings arise - with attendant deterioration of cooperation and teamwork - because of ignorance of company organization and lines of authority. A detailed organization chart would also be useful in demonstrating a fundamental principle, the violation of which has apparently caused occasional confusion and conflict of orders in our Zone - the principle that instructions and directives to employees should emanate from their immediate superior. In other words, communication up and down should follow the direct chain of command.

4. Greater emphasis on the Staff Meeting as as important forum for
    planning, decision-making and communication. It is the recommenda-
    tion of the Committee that an inflexible schedule be adhered to for
    Zone or Branch Staff Meetings. Regularity we feel, would ensure
    adequate preparation by the participants and more fruitful results.
    It is our further recommendation that all non-confidential matters
    discussed at the meeting and action initiated should be imparted to
    all employees by each department head immediately following the
    meeting. Such action we believe would serve to foster a sense of
    identity on the part of the employee, would dispel rumors and specu-
    lation and in general would enhance a cooperative attitude.

    We also feel that consideration might be given to enlarging partici-
    pation in the staff meeting on a periodic basis to include supervisory
    employees below the rank of Manager.

5. Somewhat in the same vein as recommendation #3 above, we feel that
    it would be helpful if the internal telephone directories showed
    not only the name, but also the departmental association of the
    listed individuals. Such action in our opinion would serve to more
    fully acquaint Zone personnel with the roles and duties of their
    fellow employees.

Minutes - Task Force #4

On June 13, 1969 the initial meeting was held and the selection of the chairman and secretary was agreed upon by the following group.

    M. B-----

    D. C-----, Secretary

    D. H-----

    R. J-----, Chairman

    R. W-----

    J. U-----

Our topic of discussion was Cooperation and Teamwork.

What is Cooperation? According to Webster, "To act or operate jointly with another or others." The term is easy to define but difficult to put into practical application. It was agreed that Communication and Cooperation go hand in hand, and with both factors functioning the result is teamwork.

Cooperation should be stressed at the very beginning in the indoctrination of new employees. Supervisors and Managers should communicate during the educational process and particularly demonstrate the role of the individual and his job in the total Company picture. In this way the employee is made aware of the importance of his role in the whole scheme of things and will be receptive and interested in cooperating with and giving cooperation to others in and outside of his department.

The attitude of the "Boss" (whatever his level) is a prime factor in instilling a cooperative (or non-cooperative) attitude in his subordinates. The "Prima Donna" rarely gives or gets cooperation. A word of caution - don't be hasty to condemn an individual for non-cooperation. Perhaps he is too busy at the moment on some matter of greater importance, or with a greater time priority. Perhaps it should not be part of his job - you should be talking to someone else.

Don't be too critical of new employees - it takes time. Examine your own attitudes. Are you really communicating in giving the novice a proper job orientation? The job is not merely "A to C" - it may also go to "Z". Good communication lays the foundation for good cooperation.

The meeting adjourned on this final note. Next meeting June 23.

Minutes - Task Force #4 - Meetings 6/23/69 and 6/26/69

Discussion at these two meetings centered on Question #34 - "The ability of the Manager to whom you report to get along with people." In this area the Eastern Zone Questionnaire results point to a serious problem in that the average "very much" current rating of 4.3 is well below the company total average of 4.9.

There was considerable speculation as to what factors would engender a feeling in subordinates that their Manager/Supervisor can't get along with people.

Our findings suggest that the attitude of the Boss is of paramount importance in getting the tone and establishing the attitudes of his subordinates. Under the pressures of day-to-day operations, the Manager who lets himself be abrupt and short-tempered with colleagues in other departments creates the image of not "getting along." Conversations and tone of voice are often overheard, and sometimes a Manager may work off his frustrations by consciously or unconsciously communicating his impatience with others to his subordinates.

The Boss's attitude towards others is inevitably reflected by his staff, and if the attitude is a poor one, Teamwork and Cooperation suffer. The fault described often results from a lack of self-discipline on the part of the Manager.

<u>Recommended Solution:</u>

<u>Short Term</u> - Don't talk too much to subordinates; don't let off steam by damning another department or individual in front of your staff or in conversation with your key people. Don't color their thinking by voicing your prejudice (and it may be just that). Remember that you are creating attitudes.

<u>Long Term</u> - Implementation of a training and education program on a Managerial/Supervisory level. Many managers and supervisors were appointed for merit, but not guided or instructed in management techniques. Training and education courses instituted some years ago should be reutilized.

It was noted that resulting from the pressures in our business, many managers do not take the time to really get to know their counterparts or the problems of other departments. Acquaintanceship and knowledge of the other fellow's problem goes a long way in avoiding friction and creating a cooperative atmosphere.

As a partial answer to this problem, it was suggested:

1. That supervisory personnel be invited to attend an informal managers meeting (after bi-weekly staff meeting?) to describe their jobs and problems.

2. Establishment of an informal regularly scheduled breakfast or luncheon get-together to become further acquainted with supervisory individuals as people.

3. Expansion of the Zone and Branch telephone charts to include the departmental association of the listed individuals.

Next meeting - July 8, 9:00 a.m.

Minutes - Task Force #4 - Meeting 7/8/69

The suggestion was made that because it is evident that the problems
under study by each task force interrelate in many areas, it might be
helpful for the chairman of all task forces to get together for an exchange of ideas. After discussion the consensus seemed to be that we
should defer such a meeting until we have come closer to a finalization
of our own conclusions and recommendations, although we might consider
exchanging minutes with the other committees.

It was felt that the comments expressed by Zone and Branch personnel in
the opinion poll shed a great deal of light on specific problem areas.
Mrs. Galligan is to isolate those comments which relate to Cooperation
and Teamwork and have them ready for discussion at our next meeting.

Cooperation was defined and distinguished from mere compliance - the
former implying interest and willingness as opposed to blind acceptance.
It was generally felt that one problem confronting us which adversely
affects cooperation is the frequent lack of communication and proper
dissemination of information to all levels. Everyone cited examples
where information relating to changes in procedures and people were not
made available to individuals, some of whom were directly involved. This
lack of communication we felt often creates resentments which adversely
affect working relationships and does not foster a spirit of cooperation.
People like to be told what is going on. The absence of information
tends to create an atmosphere which breeds uncertainty and fosters
rumor circulation.

It was felt that the proper forum for exchange of information is the Staff
Meeting (Zone and Branch). When properly conducted the formal staff
meeting should serve as an arena for the free expression of ideas and
communication of information relating to all departments. Specific
recommendations were made that:

(a)   Staff meeting should be held on a rigid schedule, not subject to
        alteration because of absences. Adherence to an inflexible
        schedule would give the participants adequate time for prepara-
        tion.

(b)   After each staff meeting, the participants should hold a short
        meeting with their staff to convey to all the problems, changes,
        and policies discussed at the staff meeting (obviously not touch-
        ing on confidential material). In this way planning and decisions
        would be fed back to all employees.

Next meeting - July 17, 9:00 a.m.

Minutes - Task Force #4 - Meeting July 17

The committee isolated from the written comments expressed in the
Branch and Zone opinion polls those relating to the subject matter of
this Task Force. Of these critical comments (15 in the Branch poll,
10 in the Zone) many were parallel. We concluded, therefore, that
the problems when they exist are widespread and not confined to Zone
or Branch.

Those criticisms which relate to "contradictory or conflicting orders;"
"...information withheld from lower levels"; "not being consulted on
changes in my department" and many more of this nature suggest the
existence of two possible problem areas:

(1)   The chain of responsibility is not clearly understood.

(2)   Employees in some cases appear to receive instructions from
        two or more individuals.

As a partial solution of these difficulties, the following recommendations
are offered:

(1)   The organization flow should be clearly defined by write-up
        and charts and made available to all employees to the end
        that misunderstandings are resolved as to conflicting or
        overlapping areas of authority.

(2)   Instructions and directives to employees (at whatever level)
        should emanate from their immediate supervisor. In other
        words, communication up and down should follow the direct
        chain of command.

Once again, these concepts merely reflect what we believe to be good
management principles.

INDEX